THE CIVIL
RIGHTS
MOVEMENT
IN AMERICAN
MEMORY

EDITED BY RENEE C. ROMANO
AND LEIGH RAIFORD

THE CIVIL RIGHTS MOVEMENT IN AMERICAN MEMORY

THE UNIVERSITY OF GEORGIA PRESS   ATHENS AND LONDON

Set in New Caledonia by BookComp
Printed and bound by Maple-Vail
The paper in this book meets the guidelines for
permanence and durability of the Committee on
Production Guidelines for Book Longevity of the
Council on Library Resources.
Printed in the United States of America

10   09   08   P   5   4   3

Library of Congress Cataloging-in-Publication Data
The Civil Rights movement in American memory /
edited by Renee C. Romano and Leigh Raiford.
    p. cm.
    Includes bibliographical references (p.) and index.
    ISBN-13: 978-0-8203-2538-5 (hardcover : alk. paper)
    ISBN-10: 0-8203-2538-4 (hardcover : alk. paper)
    ISBN-13: 978-0-8203-2814-0 (pbk. : alk. paper)
    ISBN-10: 0-8203-2814-6 (pbk. : alk. paper)
    1. African Americans in popular culture.   2. African
Americans—Civil rights—History—20th century.
3. Civil rights movements—United States—History—
20th century.   4. Racism in popular culture—United
States.   5. United States—Race relations.   6. Popular
culture—United States.   I. Romano, Renee Christine.
II. Raiford, Leigh.
    E185.615.C587 2006
    323.17309'045—dc22   2005028940

British Library Cataloging-in-Publication Data available

This book is dedicated to the life and legacy of Rosa Parks

CONTENTS

ACKNOWLEDGMENTS

Putting together an anthology requires a level of cooperation and coordination often hard to find in the academic world. We would like to thank all of the contributors to this volume for their fine work and for their patience with our seemingly endless requests for further revisions. They have made this a joyful learning process, and we are grateful for their collegiality. We'd also like to acknowledge the scholarship of those who responded to our call for papers, fascinating work all.

The University of Georgia Press has provided us enthusiastic support in all stages of putting this book together. Derek Krissoff, who is no longer with the press, deserves thanks for approaching Renee about doing this volume and for serving as an advocate for it. Nancy Grayson has done a wonderful job of stewarding the volume through the final publication process. We'd also like to thank all of the readers of the volume, and especially Fitzhugh Brundage, for their excellent critiques and suggestions. Thanks also to other supporters of the project, including Jacqueline Dowd Hall and Tim Tyson.

Leigh wishes to thank Renee for bringing her on board, and for picking up the slack throughout the course of this project through three moves, two new jobs, and one new child. Renee would like to thank Leigh for making this entire process enjoyable. Both of us would like to thank our families. And both of us share a debt of gratitude to those former and present activists who continue the struggle for justice and equality.

LEIGH RAIFORD AND RENEE C. ROMANO

Introduction

The Struggle over Memory

"Rosa Parks ain't do nothin' but sit her black ass down," contends the can-
tankerous character Eddie in what became one of the most controversial
scenes from any film in 2002. The hit movie *Barbershop*, produced by a
largely African American crew and starring Ice Cube leading an almost
entirely black cast, depicted for mainstream audiences the freewheeling
yet significant conversations that take place in black barbershops across
the United States. Cedric the Entertainer played Eddie, the gruff, iras-
cible older barber who tells it like he sees it, offering alternative if ribald
opinions to the African American "mainstream": O.J. was guilty, Rodney
King deserved to get beat down, and Rosa Parks didn't do anything special. In fact, as Eddie expounds to his incredulous and irritated barbershop audience, Parks was not the first person to refuse to give up her
seat on the Jim Crow buses of the mid-twentieth-century South; she received public attention only because she was a member of the NAACP.
Martin Luther King Jr., as Eddie continues, was a "ho," widely known for
his extramarital affairs. On Martin Luther King's birthday, he says, people
should celebrate King's life not by going to a memorial service or a speech:
"I want everybody to take the day off and get your freak on."[1]

    Barbershop generated uproar among many well-known civil rights
leaders. Jesse Jackson, himself a target of Eddie's humor in the film, insisted that joking about Parks and King signaled only disrespect and could
adversely influence young African Americans' views of these "heroic" figures. "The filmmakers crossed the line between what's sacred and what's

serious," Jackson charged.[2] New York civil rights activist and 2004 presidential candidate the Reverend Al Sharpton maintained that the scene degraded and belittled the memory and legacy of King and Parks. Sharpton threatened to lead a boycott of the movie if MGM, the film's distributor, refused to edit out the offending scene.[3] In newspapers around the country, columnists and academics debated whether joking about figures like King and Parks was hurtful to African American history and the legacies of King, Parks, and the civil rights movement, or whether it proved more harmful for African Americans to call for self-censorship. Those involved in the making of the film, including star Ice Cube and director Tim Story, both African American, counterattacked critics for being overly sensitive and making too much of Eddie's comments.[4]

Fifty years after Rosa Parks refused to give up her seat on a bus in Montgomery, Alabama, and forty years after mass demonstrations and protests forced the federal government to pass the 1964 Civil Rights Act and the 1965 Voting Rights Act, some of the most heated battles in the arena of the black freedom struggle are not about resources or laws. Rather, many of today's conflicts revolve around *how* the civil rights movement should be remembered.[5] The debate in and around *Barbershop* was fundamentally about memory: how should civil rights figures, events, and accomplishments be memorialized in contemporary American life and what is at stake in how they are portrayed in the arena of popular culture?

In the past twenty years, the civil rights movement of the 1950s and 1960s has assumed a central place in American historical memory. Today memories of the movement are being created and maintained in a wide variety of sites, from memorials to art exhibits, advertisements, community celebrations, legislative battles, and even street names. Films and television shows, including *Mississippi Burning* (1988), *The Long Walk Home* (1990), Spike Lee's documentary *Four Little Girls* (1998), and *I'll Fly Away* (1991–93) have dramatized movement events for national audiences, while an increasing number of movement veterans are publishing memoirs about their experiences.[6] At least fifteen museums dedicated to remembering and honoring the civil rights movement have opened since 1990, including the Birmingham Civil Rights Institute in Birmingham,

Alabama, a multimillion dollar museum located directly across the street from Kelly Ingram Park, where police trained fire hoses and turned attack dogs loose on protestors in 1963, and the National Civil Rights Museum in Memphis, Tennessee, located in the motel where Martin Luther King was assassinated in 1968. There is a Voting Rights Museum in Selma, Alabama, a Rosa Parks Museum in Montgomery, and a Martin Luther King Jr. historic site run by the National Park Service in Atlanta, Georgia. Every year, scholars and local activists recreate major movement events, such as the Freedom Rides of 1961 and the 1965 Selma-to-Montgomery march. Corporations such as McDonald's, Alcatel, and Apple employ movement images to sell their products and their own image, while politicians engage in advertising of their own by invoking movement rhetoric and events to push their own platforms to the widest possible audience. In very recent politics, President George W. Bush appealed to Martin Luther King's spirit on the 2004 King holiday to sell his "compassionate conservatism" agenda, while former President Bill Clinton spoke of the movement as an "American crossroads" at the 2004 Democratic National Convention in his effort to build support for Democratic presidential candidate John Kerry. Each of these spaces, whether film or television, museum or tourist destination, advertisement or political speech, is engaged in the process of memorializing the movement, albeit in divergent and often contradictory ways.

The essays in this volume explore the many facets of the memory of the modern black freedom struggle of the 1950s and 1960s. By "memory," we refer to the process by which people recall, lay claim to, understand, and represent the past. These memories may be personal and individual; they might be collective and widely shared. Frequently they are public as well, manifested in official monuments and documents of a state. But whether individual, collective, or official, memories of the past are not static. As French historian Pierre Nora avers, "Memory is life. . . . It remains in permanent evolution." Individuals and collectives are constantly reshaping memory, renewing and retying, and sometimes undoing, in Nora's words, our "bond to the eternal present."[7]

Historical memory is distinct from, though not necessarily in opposition to, what is usually described more formally as history. Reductively, history can be described as the objective narrative of the past produced by professionally trained and politically dispassionate scholars who base their arguments on the available historical evidence. Conversely, and only slightly less reductively, memory consists of the subjective, selective, and potentially unreliable accounts of the past told by those outside of the academy and circulated in the media and popular culture. Popular memory of a historical event, such as the Battle of the Alamo, may bear little resemblance to the event as recounted by historians.[8]

Indeed, some scholars have viewed memory and history as being totally at odds, suggesting either that memory is nothing more than an "antihistorical discourse" bent on "softening" history or, as Nora contends, that history's "true mission is to suppress and destroy" individuals' memories of the past.[9] But this is a narrow and limited division. Academic histories necessarily rely on memory (through personal papers, oral interviews), and our memories of the past are frequently informed by and elaborate on codified history. As many good works on memory have shown, history and memory necessarily challenge and blur each other's boundaries.[10] The essays assembled here illustrate memory as the *use* of history by a wide range of constituencies primarily outside of the academy. In other words, they explore the historical memory of the movement as revealed in popular culture, political arenas, and sites like museums rather than the history of the movement as described in scholarly works. These essays thus examine the stories various groups choose to tell about the movement and the past in order to make sense of and mobilize in the present.

While there are many constituencies that lay claim to being bearers of the "true" memory of the civil rights movement, there exists today what we might call a consensus memory, a dominant narrative of the movement's goals, practices, victories, and, of course, its most lasting legacies. This consensus memory offers that *the* "Civil Rights Movement" began in 1954 with the Supreme Court's *Brown v. Board of Education* decision to desegregate southern schools "with all deliberate speed" and ended in 1968 with the death of Martin Luther King Jr. and the rise of Black Power in the country's northern and western cities. Charismatic and eloquent leaders led a nonviolent movement of African Americans and supportive whites in a struggle that sought to change legal and social, rather than economic, barriers to equality. Of course there are many powerful scholarly histories that reveal the breadth and depth of the civil rights movement and challenge this consensus history.[11] However, in the realm of memory, such a narrative of the movement persists, though alternative memory traditions are coming to the foreground by way of memoirs, films, and the like. And in the dialectic between remembering and forgetting that is a central component of memory, such narratives beg us to ask what is at stake in these dominant representations of the past. What kind of civil rights movement is produced through this consensus memory and what vision of the present does it help legitimate, valorize, or condemn? The essays collected here address these questions by identifying and describing the production and shape of civil rights movement consensus memory, how this memory is challenged or perpetuated, and by whom.

The articles here range widely in subject, covering everything from the contested process of naming streets after Martin Luther King Jr. to the use of Black Panther icons to sell clothes to films like *Sunshine State* and *Boycott*. This volume is divided into four parts. The first section, "Institutionalizing Memory," seeks to understand how civil rights memories become "official" through such sites as museums, city streets, and courtrooms. The second part of the volume, "Visualizing Memory," interrogates the role visual culture plays in transmitting memory, exploring how the visual media has been central to the production, circulation, elaboration, and, in many cases, the containment and sanitizing of the movement's memory in subsequent years. The essays in the third section of the anthology, "Diverging Memory," focus on the processes by which certain elements of civil rights history have come to be ignored in contemporary historical memory or the "official" narrative of the movement. The last section, "Deploying Memory," explores the different ways in which the memory of the civil rights movement has been put to use in other political struggles.

The essays in this volume seek to understand the significance of particular memories of the movement for contemporary politics and culture. They urge us to consider why the civil rights movement is so ripe for appropriation. They explore how different memories of the movement have been mobilized to serve various and sometimes competing agendas. The articles interrogate the ways in which the "official" narratives of the movement constructed by political elites may differ from the ways in which everyday people invoke movement histories. They focus our attention on not only the kinds of memory the civil rights movement invokes but also what kinds of civil rights movement(s) are produced through these various memories. They ask how memory sites from civil rights museums to legal trials are serving as "institutions of cultural memory, selecting, legitimating and interpreting the past."[12] Some essays here examine the process by which certain movement figures have emerged as national heroes and icons, while others ask when and why the movement is invoked in contemporary political discourse about affirmative action, racism, and poverty. Although the authors in this volume write about many different subjects, they all agree that those interested in the struggles of the civil rights era need to be aware of how similar battles continue today in arguments about how the movement should be represented, about what its goals were, and about who has the right to draw on the movement's legacy. Freedom, in the words of the classic movement song, truly is a constant struggle.

Understanding the nature and significance of the historical memory of the civil rights movement is especially crucial at this particular moment in U.S. history. In the contemporary United States, arguments rage about whether racism is still a force in political and cultural life. Pundits and politicians disagree vehemently about why racial inequalities seem to persist between blacks and whites. Current debates about the Confederate flag and the issue of reparations for slavery demonstrate the vital role that understandings of the past play in contemporary politics. As historian Michael Kammen notes, "What people believe to be true about their past is usually more important in determining their behavior and responses than truth itself."[13] Contemporary representations of the movement can have a powerful influence on how people understand not only the past but the present as well. Those who believe the movement was successful in incorporating America's black minority into the mainstream may see little role for the state in ameliorating current racial inequalities, for example. How people represent and remember the movement can thus have great political, ethical, and cultural consequences. Remembering the movement, then, is an ongoing—and frequently contested—political project, as well as a historical one.

The fact that many representations of the historical memory of the civil rights movement are officially sanctioned by the state in some way makes it even more vital to explore the nature of that memory. State actors seek, with varied success, to shape historical memories to suit their perceived political and ideological agendas. Especially in the case of the civil rights movement, which can be held up as a shining example of the success of American democracy, the state has a strong interest in using the memory of the movement as a tool of nation-building and of fostering and fomenting hegemony through consensus. The movement in this way can become proof of the vitality of America's legal and political institutions, and evidence of the nation's ongoing quest to live up to its founding ideals of egalitarianism and justice. Politicians and educators have sanctified King, currently the only American memorialized with his own national holiday, in ways reminiscent of the Founding Fathers. This was made starkly clear when one of our daughters came home from her public school kindergarten singing the version of "Rudolph the Red-Nosed Reindeer" taught to her in music class. The song ended with the lines: "Rudolph, the red-nosed reindeer, you'll go down in history—like George Washington, Abraham Lincoln, and Martin Luther King Jr."

Many groups besides the state have a vested interest in civil rights memory, as the debate over whether one can make jokes about civil rights icons raised in *Barbershop* reveals. What does it mean to canonize civil rights icons like Martin Luther King Jr. or Rosa Parks, both of whom have been made into larger-than-life figures in the past forty years? Both King and Parks have museums dedicated to them, and Parks's refusal to give up her seat on a bus in 1955 has become a legendary act of social defiance and civil disobedience. Indeed, Parks has become something of a symbol for any sort of defiance against the established order, as Sarah Vowell's satirical yet sobering contribution to this collection points out.[14] Thus members of the rap group OutKast claimed recently that by taking "a stand" with their music, "We gonna be like Rosa Parks in the civil rights movement. We ain't gonna do what everybody's doing. We gonna sit up front like she did and cause a ruckus." Rosa Parks, however, was not pleased to see rappers comparing their own efforts to dominate the music field to hers to challenge segregation. She sued the rap group over its song

"Rosa Parks," in which OutKast tells other rappers, "Ah ha, hush that fuss / Everybody move to the back of the bus." In a settlement, OutKast and its record companies agreed to help develop educational programs "to enlighten today's youth about the significant role Rosa Parks played in making America a better place for all races."[15]

Jesse Jackson and other critics of *Barbershop* feared that the jokes about Rosa Parks and Martin Luther King might lead young people to discount the accomplishments and sacrifices of civil rights leaders. This reflects the concern on the part of many of those involved in the movement that the post–civil rights generation is increasingly ignorant of the fight that was required for blacks to achieve legal and political rights in the South. Former activists have responded by writing their memoirs, touring on the lecture circuit, and advocating for the creation of civil rights museums in the hope that fixing—both in the sense of repairing and adhering—the memory of the movement in memorials, museums, and memoirs will ensure that young people today have a proper understanding of the civil rights struggle.

Yet what is considered the appropriate civil rights story to tell is hotly contested. For example, many argue that the image of Martin Luther King Jr. perpetuated in collective public memory has been effectively sterilized, made nonthreatening and harmless by ignoring King's struggles against poverty, his critique of capitalism, and his attack of American foreign policy. King is instead revered publicly for his nonviolent, integrationist rhetoric, especially for the "I Have a Dream" speech, with its hope that one day little white children and little black children would hold hands and be judged on the basis of their character rather than their skin color. The process of turning Martin Luther King into a national icon, historian Vincent Harding has argued, has required a massive case of national amnesia about what King really stood for.[16] As Edward P. Morgan's article in this volume highlights, the media has played a crucial role in propagating a vision of King as a "good" civil rights leader as opposed to supposedly more threatening figures like Malcolm X. School curricula and political figures have played their part as well in grooming King into an acceptable national hero.

While Jesse Jackson might fear that comedy about civil rights leaders lessens their influence on younger generations, others worry that the canonization of King and other civil rights icons has the potential to impede future struggle. Current representations of King and, to a lesser extent, Rosa Parks put forward what historian Clay Carson has termed a "Great Man" myth about history.[17] The dominant narratives about King and Parks do not focus on how people worked together to achieve social change; they tell the story of singular, extraordinary individuals who made history by acting in ways that are consistent with longstanding American values. Lost in the process are the organizations that stood behind the individuals (the NAACP, which Eddie the barber noted in Parks's case), the many individuals who acted but who are not famous (all those others who refused to give up their seats on the bus before Parks), and most significantly, the sense that ordinary people cannot change their lives unless they have a great, almost superhuman, leader to guide them. The *Barbershop* debate became so heated because memories have power, not only to educate people about the past but also to dissuade or propel action. How we remember the movement, in other words, can discourage us from or encourage us toward future activism.

Our memories of the movement can also play a critical role in shaping our personal, group, and political identities. As historian John Gillis has noted, identity and memory depend on each other; the core meaning of any individual or group is sustained in large part by remembering a particular past, which helps us both locate ourselves and make sense of the world in which we live.[18] As essays in this volume by Owen J. Dwyer and Glenn Eskew suggest, new forms of heritage tourism commemorating sites of civil rights activism are helping the South construct a new regional identity for itself. Individuals, too, may turn to memories of the movement to shape their identity, as Leigh Raiford's exploration of the commodification of Black Panther symbols demonstrates.

Memories of the past, and especially of an event like the civil rights movement, can also provide, in the apt phrase of historian Emily Rosenberg, "rhetorical resources" to support a variety of different political agendas.[19] In the last few years, many different groups, with widely varied political interests, have tried to associate themselves with the movement in order to propel their own political agendas. As essays by David John

Marley and R. A. R. Edwards in this volume explore, many groups, from Christian conservatives to the disabled, have sought to portray themselves as carrying on the legacy of the civil rights movement. Even opponents of government programs like affirmative action have wrapped themselves in Martin Luther King's mantle and claimed to be the true inheritors of his legacy. In California, in 1996, proponents of Proposition 209, the referendum aimed at ending affirmative action in that state, sought to appropriate the memory of the civil rights movement in their campaign. Proponents titled the proposed constitutional amendment the California Civil Rights Initiative, and its supporters frequently asserted that they were seeking to fulfill Martin Luther King's dream of living in a colorblind society. Ward Connerly, the chairman of the campaign for Proposition 209, proudly quoted King's speeches about how people should be judged by the content of their character rather than the color of their skin. He attacked civil rights leaders who charged that he was misusing King's legacy: "I think it is outrageous for Jesse Jackson and all of those from the past, from the 1960s, to somehow suggest that it is inappropriate for any of us to use Dr. King's memory. . . . He belongs to all of us."[20] The success of Prop 209 indicates that the movement and its memory are available for multiple interpretations. Such interpretations have the power not only to shape understandings of what the movement was, but also to effect political change in the present.

The battle of who can use King's and the movement's legacies to further their own political fortunes has real import in contemporary politics, as the recent debate over gay marriage makes clear. Some gay marriage advocates have compared their fight to that of black civil rights activists, painting themselves as the torchbearers of the civil rights standard and those opposed to gay marriage as the segregationists of the new era. Civil rights lawyer Evan Wolfson thus contended that gay couples heading to the courthouse for a marriage license were akin to those who sat-in at segregated lunch counters in the 1960s: "An act as unremarkable as getting a wedding license has been transformed by the people embracing it, much as the unremarkable act of sitting at a Formica lunch counter was transformed by an act of civil disobedience at a Woolworth's in North Carolina 44 years ago this month." A *New York Times* columnist meanwhile described those fighting to ban gay marriage as "donning the roles" played by arch-segregationists Lester Maddox and George Wallace during the civil rights era. While some 1960s civil rights activists, including John Lewis, Julian Bond, and Coretta Scott King, have called gay marriage a civil rights issue and denounced calls for a constitutional amendment to ban the practice as a form of bigotry, other black leaders, especially some ministers, have balked at the comparison, insisting that gay marriage is not about civil rights, but "special rights." Reverend Eugene Rivers, the head of the National Ten Point Leadership Foundation, declared in March 2004, "Just as Jews would not tolerate the exploitation of the Holocaust, black people must not tolerate the exploitation of the civil rights movement."[21] Which comparisons to the past are legitimate and which represent a form of "exploitation"? And who is the legitimate judge of how the past should be used?

This volume insists that representations of the past matter. Representations of the past can be mobilized to serve partisan purposes; they can be commercialized for the sake of tourism; they can shape a nation's sense of identity, build hegemony, or serve to shore up the political interests of the state; and they can certainly influence the ways in which people understand their world. The past, as George Orwell noted in his political novel *1984*, can be a site for struggles over power and dominance. "Who controls the past controls the future," Orwell argued. "Who controls the present controls the past."[22] The effort to determine what is known and remembered about the past, then, is an effort to claim and exert power.[23]

As the essays in this collection demonstrate, the struggles over the memory of the civil rights movement are not a diversion from the real political work of fighting for racial equality and equal rights in the United States; they are key sites of that struggle. The contests over the meanings of the movement must be understood as a crucial part of the continuing fight against racism and inequality. The civil rights movement didn't end in 1965, with the passage of the Voting Rights Act; in 1968, with Martin Luther King's death; or even in the 1970s, with the splintering of civil rights organizations amid the rise of Black Power. The movement was, and remains, an ongoing process with meanings that remain contested, a fact underscored by the centrality of the memory of the movement in American culture and politics. The work of remembering the movement has been undertaken not just by individual or isolated communities, but by multiple, far-reaching, and interrelated constituencies as well. The pervasiveness and significance of the 1960s African American freedom struggle in current historical memory may highlight a desire to celebrate the power of the American political tradition. Or it might demonstrate a political desire to put the larger question of civil rights and the struggle for racial justice in a simplified past, even as new communities of black and brown peoples find their rights infringed on in this post–civil rights, post-9/11 era. Ultimately, our hope is that this nation will not be lulled by the memory of an activist past into slumbering during a present and future that needs our activism now more than ever.

Notes

1. *Barbershop*, directed by Tim Story (2002: Metro-Goldwyn-Mayer).

2. "Commentary: Film Criticized for Jabs at Black Icons," *Atlanta Journal-Constitution*, September 20, 2002, sec. E, 1.

3. "MGM Stands by Beleaguered *Barbershop*," *Washington Post*, September 26, 2002, sec. C, 1.

4. See for example Mary Mitchell, "*Barbershop* Shows Blacks—Warts and All," *Chicago Sun-Times*, September 17, 2002, 14; Michael Eric Dyson, "Speaking Freely in the Barbershop," *New York Times*, September 27, 2002, 31.

5. The civil rights movement here refers to the specific 1954–68 social revolution that sought primarily to grant African Americans full and true equality under the law. The way in which people choose to set the parameters of the modern civil rights movement—1954–68 or 1945–70, to consider the longer history of the African American freedom struggle for example—indicates another site through which historical memory of the movement is constructed. See especially Jacquelyn Dowd Hall, "The Long Civil Rights Movement and the Political Uses of the Past," *Journal of American History* 91, no. 4 (March 2005): 1233–63.

6. Examples include John Lewis's *Walking with the Wind* (New York: Harvest Books, 1998), Andrew Young's *An Easy Burden: The Civil Rights Movement and the Transformation of America* (New York: Harper Collins, 1996), and the anthology by white women involved in the movement, *Deep in Our Hearts: Nine White Women in the Freedom Movement*, by Constance Curry et al. (Athens: University of Georgia Press, 2002).

7. Pierre Nora, "Between Memory and History: *Les Lieux de Mémoire*," in

History and Memory in African-American Culture, ed. Geneviève Fabre and Robert O'Meally (New York: Oxford University Press, 1994), 285.

8. See for example, Richard Flores, *Remembering the Alamo: Memory, Modernity, and the Master Symbol* (Austin: University of Texas Press, 2002).

9. For examples of arguments that memory is simply "antihistorical discourse," see the articles assembled in "Grounds for Remembering," special issue, *Representations* 69 (Winter 2000), especially Kerwin Lee Klein, "On the Emergence of *Memory* in Historical Discourse." The Nora quote is from "Between Memory and History," 286. We disagree with Nora's distinction, particularly that history is nothing more than a static representation of the past, always incomplete. As representations themselves are always incomplete and always negotiated, we believe that memory too can be "representations of the past."

10. See especially Michel-Rolph Trouillot, *Silencing the Past: Power and the Production of History* (Boston, Mass.: Beacon Press, 1997); David Blight, *Race and Reunion: The Civil War in American Memory* (Cambridge, Mass.: Harvard University Press, 2001).

11. See groundbreaking contributions by Aldon D. Morris, *The Origins of the Civil Rights Movement: Black Communities Organizing for Change* (New York: Free Press, 1984); John Dittmer, *Local People: The Struggle for Civil Rights in Mississippi* (Urbana: University of Illinois Press, 1994); Charles Payne, *I've Got the Light of Freedom: The Organizing Tradition of the Mississippi Freedom Struggle* (Berkeley: University of California Press, 1995); Barbara Ransby, *Ella Baker and the Black Freedom Movement: A Radical Democratic Vision* (Chapel Hill: University of North Carolina Press, 2003); Tim Tyson, *Radio Free Dixie: Robert F. Williams and the Roots of Black Power* (Chapel Hill: University of North Carolina Press, 1999), and *Blood Done Sign My Name* (New York: Crown, 2004).

12. Alan Radley, "Boredom, Fascination and Mortality: Reflections upon the Experience of Museum Visiting," quoted in Bernard Armada, "Memorial Agon: An Interpretive Tour of the National Civil Rights Museum," *Southern Communication Journal* 63 (1998): 235.

13. Michael Kammen, *Mystic Chords of Memory* (New York: Knopf, 1991), 39.

14. See the essay by Sarah Vowell in this volume for more on how everyone—from Ted Nugent to topless dancers—is comparing his or her own acts of social defiance to Rosa Parks's.

15. "Sense of Humor Lands Musicians in Court," *New Orleans Times-Picayune*, December 19, 2003, 7; Associated Press, "Settlement Announced in Rosa Parks–OutKast Case," April 14, 2005, http://www.detnews.com/2005/metro/0504/14/parks-150870.htm (accessed September 20, 2005).

16. Vincent Harding, "Beyond Amnesia: Martin Luther King, Jr., and the Future of America," *Journal of American History* 74 (September 1987): 468–76.

17. Clayborne Carson, "Martin Luther King, Jr.: Charismatic Leadership in a Mass Struggle," *Journal of American History* 74 (September 1987): 448–54.

18. John Gillis, "Memory and Identity: The History of a Relationship," in *Commemorations*, ed. John Gillis (Princeton, N.J.: Princeton University Press, 1994), 3–24.

19. See Emily Rosenberg, *A Day Which Will Live: Pearl Harbor in American Memory* (Durham, N.C.: Duke University, 2003), 2.

20. Connerly quoted in George Derek Musgrove, "Good at the Game of Tricknology: Proposition 209 and the Struggle for the Historical Memory of the Civil Rights Movement," *Souls* 1 (Summer 1999): 14.

21. Frank Rich, "The Joy of Gay Marriage," *New York Times*, February 29, 2004, sec. 2, 1; Elisabeth Beardsley, "Gay/Civil Rights Debate Splits Black Leaders," *Boston Herald*, March 10, 2004, 6.

22. George Orwell, *1984* (New York: Harcourt Brace, 1949), 37.

23. W. Fitzhugh Brundage, "No Deed But Memory," in *Where These Memories Grow: History, Memory, and Southern Identity*, ed. W. Fitzhugh Brundage (Chapel Hill: University of North Carolina Press, 2000), 11.

PART ONE

INSTITUTIONALIZING MEMORY

How has the memory of the civil rights movement become part of the nation's public landscape and what memory of the movement is expressed and legitimized through public sites? The four essays in this section explore the ways in which historical memory of the movement is being translated into public memory in sites such as museums, memorials, and courtrooms. If civil rights memory is indeed a process of negotiation, one in which meaning of the movement is constantly remade, the essays by Owen J. Dwyer, Glenn Eskew, Derek H. Alderman, and Renee C. Romano reveal how these processes manifest and are institutionalized in public spaces and public records. But as Dwyer reminds us, these sites do not so much seal and settle the movement as "open a new chapter . . . intimately associated with the mechanisms of memory—place, narrative, and interpretation." The struggle to name a boulevard after Martin Luther King Jr. or to bring the Birmingham bombers to justice or to build the Birmingham Civil Rights Institute remains, as Alderman, Eskew, and Romano demonstrate, a fraught, though enormously generative, process.

Dwyer's essay focuses on the various memorial landscapes dedicated to civil rights memory and the competing memories they attempt to incorporate but cannot always contain. While contemporary civil rights movement memorialization espouses a necessarily antiracist perspective, such monuments, museums, streets, and the like both tend to adhere to grand historical narratives of the movement and eschew much discussion of contemporary racial issues. Nevertheless, Dwyer argues that civil rights memorials do less to "authoritatively pronounce" the legacy of the move-

1

ment than to open up new spaces for a continuing dialogue about what the meanings and the legacies of the movement are.

The remaining essays in the section explore individual sites in more depth. Eskew's article takes as its subject the thirteen-year process "to memorialize 'the epic Birmingham civil rights movement'" in the Birmingham Civil Rights Institute. Eskew describes in fascinating detail the many constituencies and fluctuating interests that competed over the mission and purpose of the museum from its inception in 1979 until its opening in 1992. Corporate interests, civic groups, political machines, and grassroots organizations at turns heralded the institute as a road to urban renewal, touted it as a means to racial reconciliation, used it to mobilize the black electorate amid political scandal, and even at times abandoned the project. What ultimately emerged was an institution broad enough to encompass and contain these various contending interests. Eskew demonstrates that while memorialization of the movement often presents a singular narrative—in this case one of the "triumph of toleration"—the unified message obfuscates the fraught process that brought it into being.

Moving from the museum to the street, Alderman explores street names as specific kinds of memorial arenas, public spaces for representing the images of historical figures and debating the meaning and relative importance of these figures to contemporary society. Focusing on two failed attempts to name a major thoroughfare for Martin Luther King Jr. in Bulloch County, Georgia, not far from Savannah, Alderman observes what he calls "reputational politics" at work in the effort to commemorate King and institutionalize civil rights memory in the shared public space of the street. The reputational politics debate the "worthiness" of one subject to be memorialized over another, and the meaning and meaningfulness of the subjects to various communities. Perhaps most significantly, Alderman describes how the debates in Bulloch County exposed African Americans' multiple allegiances: not all black residents supported naming the street for a civil rights leader, some preferring instead to commemorate military veterans. Alderman's essay reveals that divergent memory of the civil rights movement cannot merely be categorized as "black versus white" but rather speaks to the multiple meanings the movement holds and places it occupies among racial communities.

Romano's article concludes the first part with an interrogation of the ways in which the civil rights movement has been institutionalized through the highly publicized 1977, 2001, and 2002 trials of Robert Chambliss, Thomas Edwin Blanton, and Bobby Frank Cherry, respectively, for their roles in the September 15, 1963, bombing of the Sixteenth Street Baptist Church in Birmingham. Though not a memorial arena in the same way as streets, parks, and museums, the reopened trials of civil rights–era crimes institutionalizes movement memory by entering evidence and testimony into the public record. Moreover, as Romano points out, these trials, especially the most recent two, received extensive media coverage, which brought the movement and its history into people's homes and everyday lives, thus fostering a form of engagement with civil rights memory in ways distinct from museums and monuments. She further argues that these three trials relied on a specific narrative of the movement, a "familiar storyline" that excised African Americans from their own struggle, isolated the crime as that of a small group of brash, ignorant white men, and effectively froze the events and actors in a forty-year-old past. Romano illuminates the conflict in the effort to redress past wrongs while acquitting the survivors and legatees of the movement of any responsibility for or to the past. The result of such institutionalized narratives of redemption, she warns us, is incomplete justice.

OWEN J. DWYER

Interpreting the Civil Rights Movement

Contradiction, Confirmation, and the

Cultural Landscape

The 1990s witnessed a remarkable profusion of efforts to commemorate
the American civil rights movement. Beginning with Maya Lin's 1990
Civil Rights Monument in Montgomery, Alabama, no fewer than a dozen
museums and monuments associated with the movement were produced
over the course of the decade. Clustered in the South, the most extensive memorials span a broad arc that traces the history of the movement
from the site of lunch counter sit-in protests in Greensboro, North Carolina, to the motel in Memphis where Martin Luther King Jr. was assassinated. Memorials have been erected in towns and cities whose names are
synonymous with the struggle against white supremacy: Topeka, Kansas;
Little Rock, Arkansas; Oxford, Mississippi; Montgomery, Alabama; Albany, Georgia; and Orangeburg, South Carolina.[1] In addition to this self-
consciously monumental infrastructure of memory are the more mundane trappings of civic commemoration: streets, schools, and health
clinics named in honor of civil rights leaders.[2] The result is a rich, multi-
layered environment that through its symbolic power and the large number of visitors who seek it out serves as a forum in the continuing struggle
to define the contemporary significance of America's civil rights revolution.[3] Ironically, while the manifest purpose of a memorial is to summa-
rize and synthesize the past into a coherent narrative, memorials often

open new chapters of struggle associated with the meaning and significance of the past.

The arrival of the movement's memorial legacy on the "cultural landscape"—the term used to describe the reciprocal influence of people and the places around them—offers insight into that legacy's victories and shortcomings, especially since memorials are elements of the built environment that help (un)fix and represent social identities.[4] Studying memorials in their spatial context is important because a memorial's "place" goes beyond mere geographic coordinates to simultaneously reflect and influence society. Students of the cultural landscape pay special attention to a memorial's visibility, accessibility, and symbolic elements. They also examine a memorial's location vis-à-vis the area's mosaic of social and economic groups; its proximity to symbolic places such as the central business district or other memorials; and the flow pattern of tourists who visit, and, just as important, those who do not. This emphasis on studying memorials as elements in a broader cultural landscape is particularly important in the context of civil rights memorials. Movement activists challenged the legitimacy of racial boundaries, many of which were inscribed in laws and habits that admonished individuals to "know" their place. For latter-day civil rights activists, establishing memorials that transcend these boundaries—boundaries related to whose history belongs where—provides a litmus test of how far society has progressed toward the goal of racial equity and justice.

In the course of producing civil rights memorials, the public portrayal of American history has been profoundly affected.[5] Unlike the majority of representations of American history in public space, civil rights memorials present an explicitly antiracist rendering of the past. These sites reflect an insurgent ethos among some public historians to shift the field away from the celebration and commemoration of elite individuals and their homes and toward the remembrance of more socially representative lives and landscapes. More specifically, civil rights memorials reflect a turning of the tide away from a version of history that underwrote white supremacy toward one that celebrates its downfall. In this sense, civil rights memorials offer a stunning rebuke to centuries of American public history.

Nevertheless, there are significant elisions and exclusions in the cultural landscape's treatment of the civil rights era. The museums and monuments associated with this landscape are major heritage attractions, and the tourism industry is responsible in part for their development and promotion; this influence on memory's landscape requires careful consideration. Additionally, at the nation's largest civil rights memorials, there is a growing consensus as to what the movement stood for and who the protagonists were. This mainstream narrative is forcing women's, working-class, and local histories to the margins in order to focus on charismatic leaders and dramatic events—public history's customary leitmotif. Further, in its treatment of racism, civil rights memorials focus on its most violent, brutish expressions. While this approach offers a bracing challenge to the sort of polite, casual fare that all too often typifies public history, it nevertheless overlooks the more insidious and pervasive elements that constitute contemporary white privilege and patriarchy.

This chapter examines the version of the past presented at the country's leading civil rights memorials. Taken as a whole, these powerfully evocative sites are places at which the meaning of "civil rights"—how they are achieved, their current status, and future promise—is currently undergoing active negotiation. In complex ways, civil rights memorials simultaneously contradict and confirm the conventions that characterize American commemoration: while they *contradict* longstanding practices that naturalized and excused racism, they simultaneously *confirm* customary occlusions and assumptions about how history is made. The result, to follow the cultural geographer Stephen Daniels, is a thoroughly "duplicitous" landscape, one whose ultimate allegiances are ambiguous and incapable of definitively being known.

Birmingham's Kelly Ingram Park, named after the first American casualty of World War I, is a one-block area of civic green space closely associated with the civil rights movement. At one time a segregated park for whites only, Kelly Ingram Park was inscribed in the country's collective memory in 1963 by Bull Connor's police dogs and fire hoses. The park was redesigned in 1992 as "A Place of Revolution and Reconciliation" to commemorate the protests that led to the desegregation of the city that activists referred to as "*Bomb*ingham" and "America's Johannesburg." Its location augments the park's gravity inasmuch as it sits astride the relict border between the white and black business districts, while across the street is the historic Sixteenth Street Baptist Church and the city's Civil Rights Institute.

The "Freedom Walk," a broad, slate stone walkway along which large, forebodingly dark sculptures of iconic figures from the protests have been installed, circumscribes the park. The installations straddle the pathway and confront visitors with a gauntlet of snarling police dogs, jailed protesters, and enormous water cannons. The sculptures' visceral presence has the effect of offering a spatial primer in the tactics of provocation and confrontation used by protesters to secure their rights. The inscription on the base of one of the installations, showing two black children behind a jail cell's bars, reads: "We ain't afraid of your jail." From the pedestrian walkway, which goes between the statue of the children and that of the jail bars, the visitor can look toward the cell and read along the top of the sculpture: "Segregation is a sin." In the process of scrutinizing police violence and valorizing the resistance of the marchers, the subject-object relation of racism is upended and elements of the white power establishment are called out in a very public manner.[6]

In addition to the park's compelling name and confrontational bearing, the fact that the endeavor was funded by local government and corporations, overcoming significant opposition in the process, testifies to the remarkable changes in public history that have occurred in the movement's wake. Of course, there has long been a tradition of using place and memory to confront racism. Antiracist communities have long remembered their own insurgent history of oppression, transgression, and resistance. These alternative memories contested racist conceptualizations of the past, especially those that sought to naturalize its historical origins. To paraphrase antiapartheid activists in the context of South Africa: "Ours is the struggle of remembering against forgetting."[7]

Before emancipation the primary conduit of African American memory work was oral practice, especially stories, songs, and sermons that contrasted the worlds of slavery and freedom, recalled slave uprisings and defiant "bad men," and celebrated festivals, weddings, and communal processions.[8] In those instances where blacks had a significant degree

The statues of ferocious police dogs and of children behind jail bars that line the "Freedom Walk" at Birmingham's Kelly Ingram Park reclaim and give new meanings to images that will always be associated with the 1963 civil rights protests in that city. The bronzed snarling dogs and jail bars place spectators in the position of civil rights demonstrators, who here are valorized by a city that once viciously opposed them. (Photographs by Owen Dwyer)

of control over their own communal institutions, especially in the segregated cities of the late nineteenth and early twentieth centuries, alternative "monuments" included the (re)naming of schools, churches, libraries, and parks to create a landscape of memory.

While vibrant and of central importance to the communities from which they emerged, these older forms of commemoration were nevertheless largely confined to the private and semipublic spaces associated with African American communities. Whereas African Americans employed the tactical politics of transgression and resistance, white supremacist imagery enjoyed official endorsement and scientific legitimacy.[9] On the whole, African Americans were ignored or marginalized on—and partly through—the cultural landscape.[10] For instance, the memorial statuary that commemorates the loss and sacrifice of the Civil War is almost exclusively dedicated to whites.[11] In the few public monuments to the role played by African Americans, either as soldiers or to emancipation more generally, they are portrayed following their white officers or crouching before Abraham Lincoln in return for their freedom. There are even a few isolated memorials in the South to "loyal" slaves who served the South during the war. Cast as such, the relative absence and marginalized presence of African Americans on the cultural landscape has served to conflate white history with public history.

In contrast, civil rights memorials like Kelly Ingram Park—built largely by the city of Birmingham for the purpose of commemorating the black freedom struggle—offer a vigorously public and authoritative challenge to racism. The significance of this challenge can be gauged in part by recalling that monuments and museums differ from other memorial media such as books, documentaries, or photos inasmuch as they must pass a higher threshold of public scrutiny and capital investment. The formal and public situation of these monuments confirms the status of their narratives as "real" history and provides an influential basis for identity formation.[12] As a result, they are among the preeminent places at which the dynamic relationships between that which is forgotten and remembered, between history and identity, are simultaneously confirmed and contested. Thus, the arrival of civil rights memorials on the cultural landscape represents a major departure from the tradition of alternative commemorations imposed on African Americans in the past.

In the wake of the past decade, the public portrayal of history in the United States has never been more inclusive of such a distinctly antiracist perspective. There are, however, notable exclusions in the movement's portrayal. As is the case at the preponderance of American memorials, the "Great Man" paradigm of history dominates the retelling of the civil rights movement. This version of the past focuses on leaders rather than on organizers or participants and valorizes the national at the expense of the local. The "Great Man" paradigm obscures the role of women, most of whom were local, working-class activists. Indicative of this situation is the manner in which the life and career of Martin Luther King Jr. has assumed a prominent place on the cultural landscape: in Atlanta with his birthplace, church, and crypt; in Birmingham, the site of his 1963 campaign against segregation; in Selma with his leadership of the Voting Rights March of 1965; the site of his assassination in Memphis in 1968;

and, finally, in the form of a national holiday and the naming of civic infrastructure in his honor across the country. While this attention to King is in keeping with the tenets of mainstream public history, which tend to stress the primacy of the individual leader, it plays out on the cultural landscape in a particularly gendered manner. Museums in Atlanta, Birmingham, and Memphis picture alongside King his male lieutenants, Ralph Abernathy, Andrew Young, or Jesse Jackson, while little or no mention is made of King's female advisors. For instance, Ella Baker, who for over fifty years was active in antiracist politics and was a moving force in the development of the Student Nonviolent Coordinating Committee, is generally ignored.[13] Likewise, the significant role played by Septima Clark, a pioneer in the creation of the movement's Freedom Schools, which emphasized participatory democracy and critical literacy and organized local communities for voting rights, is neglected.[14]

This relative absence of women at civil rights memorials stands in contrast to recent scholarship demonstrating the predominance of women in organizing and staffing the movement. Further, it was local organizers who made it possible for someone like King to be effective at using his international status in order to transform what had been considered to be "merely" a local issue into a national crisis that merited international attention.[15] Jo Ann Robinson's relative anonymity is illustrative of this ironic marginalization: she was one of the local activists in Montgomery who organized the bus boycott and who in turn invited a young, previously unknown minister—Martin Luther King Jr.—to act as its spokesperson, the position that brought him national and international fame.[16]

When individual women are commemorated, they are usually celebrated for their personal courage rather than for their organizing within broader social networks. Thus civil rights museums across the South—in Atlanta, Birmingham, and Memphis—prominently display iconic images of Rosa Parks sitting on a city bus, an image that testifies to her determination and courage. Few museums, however, follow the lead of Troy State University's Rosa Parks Library and Museum in Montgomery and present Parks in a more nuanced fashion. In addition to being a seamstress who had the courage to refuse segregation, Parks, as the Troy State exhibit makes clear, was an activist organizer who existed within the framework of a larger community.[17] For instance, she participated in activist training at the Highlander Folk School and was the local secretary and youth leader of the Montgomery branch of the NAACP at a time when it was dangerous to belong to that organization. So on the day of her fateful bus ride, in addition to being a tired seamstress, Rosa Parks was an activist organizer within the broader struggle against segregation.

In fact, the most prominent role allocated to women at civil rights memorials, or for that matter the role accorded to the vast majority of movement participants, is that of allegory. This echoes the longstanding tradition within Western art of employing the female form not to commemorate individual women but rather to embody some feminized virtue or vice, in the process confirming an individual's masculinized character and destiny.[18] On and through the cultural landscape the leadership of individual men is allegorically confirmed via the feminized mass—so-called due to the manner in which throngs of unnamed, enthusiastic protestors are pictured sitting in the pews vis-à-vis the pulpit or as marching in the ranks vis-à-vis the head of the march. These gendered representations—in photos, displays, and dioramas—play out on the cultural landscape in a number of ways. While the formal leadership of the movement may have come from businesses, churches, and national organizations, it was often private citizens who served as catalysts and made efforts to organize for change.[19] Yet within the major museums, the movement is represented as having been won on the streets, from the pulpit, and in the courtroom, places intimately associated with masculinized leadership in the movement's iconic legacy. Rarely mentioned are the private and semipublic spaces of citizenship schools, neighborhoods, and homes where activists found food, shelter, and community. In this sense, there is a distinct privileging of the public over the private as the spaces generative of civil rights—a situation that maps closely onto the traditionally gendered division between public and private space.

Likewise, there appears to be a gendered scaling of participation: women are cast as local—working in the home, meeting at church—whereas men are national and international actors—speaking in Washington, meeting with officials, arguing court cases. The conflation of space, scale, and identity yield the notion that an elite, male leadership won civil rights at a national scale, transcending distance to move between various corridors of power, shuttling between pulpit and street, courtroom and legislative chamber. For their part, a feminized body of participants, while not invisible, is thoroughly local and led.

As these observations attest, civil rights memorials do not simply present an already available history of the movement. Rather, the narratives they *re-present* are themselves choices, ones that in contemporary America are highly politicized. The politics associated with representing the modern freedom struggle mirror positions that divided the movement itself over the proper balance between leaders and participants, concentration and diffusion. In response to those in the movement who called for a more central role for King, Baker expressed a primary difference: "My theory is, strong people don't need strong leaders."[20] Both Baker and Septima Clark wanted to establish vibrant local organizations capable of responding to local conditions. To this end, they encouraged King to lead fewer marches and focus more on developing local leaders and organizations. While they did not deny the utility of leadership and politics at the national scale, Baker and Clark also felt that its influence tended to inhibit the leadership capabilities and participation of nonelites and render the movement susceptible to fickle public approval.

In a similar vein, two historiographical perspectives are in tension at civil rights memorials. These paradigms differ markedly in their representation of agency and leadership in pursuit of civil rights.[21] The first perspective, reflecting the "Great Man" school of historiography, emphasizes elite-led institutions, such as the NAACP and the Southern Christian Leadership Conference, and their leaders. This interpretive paradigm portrays the movement as a series of key moments (the Montgomery bus boycott, the march on Washington) that, under the orchestration of charismatic leaders, served to shift the balance of power between a vanguard African American community and those seeking to maintain white supremacy. This narrative is characterized by an overarching, if unstated, sense of inevitability of a regional transformation undertaken at seemingly preordained locales.

In contrast, a second perspective on civil rights history shifts attention away from the "Great Man" in order to stress difference and agency within African American communities, noting that the grassroots struggle for civil rights was an *everyday* activity.[22] What has been conceived of as a single, unified movement in pursuit of integration and voting rights is reconceptualized as multiple freedom movements striving to create and sustain antiracist activism. This perspective is manifested in memorial elements that narrate the tension between national and local aspects of the movement. Accordingly, the representational focus shifts from the documentation of national legislative and judicial campaigns and toward the activities of grassroots organizations. This version of civil rights history examines social networks within black communities, class and gender differences among African Americans, color consciousness, and the role of local black churches in resisting racism. What emerges is a sense of the ways in which local conditions motivated organizers, as well as the deeply ambiguous connections between local activists and national leaders and their institutions.[23]

No single memorial site is wholly given over to one perspective or the other; rather, a dynamic tension exists between the two as memorials respond to tensions that characterized the movement itself. A case in point is the Birmingham Civil Rights Institute's treatment of the tension pervading the relationship between Fred Shuttlesworth, the leader of a local civil rights organization, and Martin Luther King Jr. In particular, Shuttlesworth clashed with King over the aims of the demonstrations, yet relied on King's "star power" to attract national and international attention. The institute's portrayal of this episode has drawn criticism from local activists and churches for focusing too much on the leadership of the Birmingham campaign, to the exclusion of the "foot soldiers" of the movement.[24] Partially in response to these critics, the institute has designed a new exhibition gallery that makes available interviews with local activists via interactive workstations in order to include more information from the "regular" people who staffed the movement.

Nevertheless, these two perspectives, by turn sweeping and fabulous or contextual and mundane, attract considerable controversy as to which is more accurate and compelling. Proponents of the former believe that attracting visitors in an entertainment market saturated with the spectacular and hyperreal requires an emphasis on individual greatness and dramatic events. Ironically, tourism professionals confide that it is the widespread desire for authenticity that motivates many visitors to seek out civil rights memorials. This desire for authenticity prompts visitors to look for sites with relics that promote a tangible, unmediated encounter with the past—however untenable such an experience may be. Taken to extremes, some civil rights tourists discount popular sites, deeming them to be excessively hyped and simplified. In response they seek out rare, marginalized experiences—the personal effects of protestors and forgotten sites being especially popular—that they believe have not yet been "soiled" by the heavy hand of public history. While some tourists will find these pilgrimages deeply rewarding, others will despair that despite their best efforts the "real" past remains out of reach, its meaning endlessly deferred to related narratives.[25]

Further, critics of the "Great Man" approach charge that it undercuts the potential for future activism because it presents the movement as the result of the combined forces of history and individual greatness. Alternatively, these critics champion an approach that strives to initiate a dialogue with and among visitors as to the mundane, socially embedded condition of social change. The self-guided cyber tour through the Birmingham Civil Rights Institute's archives is illustrative of this concern to undermine the sweeping narrative of traditional public history. Likewise, a focus on the dynamics of the local political scene characterizes the National Voting Rights Museum in Selma, Alabama. Disturbed by the manner in which the local school district and history museum ignored the 1965 voting rights campaign, a group of activists came together to show the voting rights struggle in a way that reflected more of the experiences of the local women who organized it. One exhibit, "The I Was There Wall," consists of a mirror covered with Post-it notes on which the memories of participants have been written. "Living history" exhibits celebrate the role played by local activists, while other exhibits preserve the material effects of activists who marched on Montgomery. The emphasis here is definitively on everyday heroics.

The antimonumental impulse finds its most robust expression in the protests of Jacqueline Smith, a lone poverty rights activist in Memphis, Tennessee, at the National Civil Rights Museum. In a daily protest that has lasted over ten years, she argues that the most fitting memorial to the movement would be the creation of institutions that promote democratic rights and economic goods and services, such as schools, emergency shelters, and organizations that focus on continued activism.[26] The presence of Selma's National Voting Rights Museum and Jacqueline Smith testify to the foment that characterizes efforts to commemorate the movement.

The commemoration of the movement in the memorial landscape is also influenced by the political-economic context of heritage tourism. The development of civil rights memorials coincides with, and is in part a result of, a phenomenal rise in heritage tourism among African Americans, which contrasts sharply with the previous absence of attention paid to blacks by the tourism and museum industry.[27] The changes wrought by the movement and the public commemoration of its memory have opened the doors of museums and monuments to blacks, inviting them into places that heretofore were the domain of white elites. Memorials to the civil rights movement offer African Americans and antiracists more generally an opportunity to take part in a tourism that recognizes their impact on American history. Further, African Americans often visit civil rights memorials as part of a family reunion, highlighting the welcome afforded them and suggestive of the sites' relative importance among cultural attractions.

The amount of money involved in this sort of tourism is considerable; a tour bus of twenty-eight to thirty-two people spends approximately $5,000–$7,000 per day on travel-related goods and services.[28] Interviews with state tourism officials and the widespread presence of state-produced promotional literature testify to the desire on the part of local and state governments to rectify their public image and attract tourist dollars at the same time.[29] These twin motivations suggest why states like Alabama and its neighbors promote an unabashedly heroic recounting of the movement a generation after issuing pledges of massive resistance to integration.

Heritage tourism's representation of history has been widely assailed as compromised by this political and financial expediency, and indeed, at many of the largest civil rights museums, treatment of *contemporary*

Many southern states are seeking to capitalize on heritage tourism by producing brochures documenting civil rights sites. In 2004, state officials in Arkansas unveiled their new civil rights tourism brochure at the visitors' center of the Little Rock Central High School National Historic Site. (AP/Wide World Photos)

racism and racial politics is conspicuously absent.[30] Portrayals of racism at these sites focus on white supremacy's most violent and widely scorned expressions: segregation, lynching, and the Ku Klux Klan. Absent is a sustained treatment of the more mundane and insidious forms of racism that valorize whiteness over other social identities and reinforce it as a way of knowing and negotiating difference.[31] In fact, most of the memorials and museums fail to make convincing connections to the present condition of racism in the United States. At these sites, there is scant, if any, mention of debates about affirmative action, discriminatory loan policies, or current economic inequalities between blacks and whites.[32]

This absence of a sustained treatment of contemporary racism's institutional or ideological manifestations is particularly discordant relative to the rich historical treatment the movement's origins receive at the major museums. At these sites, resistance to slavery, Reconstruction-era politics, and the reign of Jim Crow are variously cited as antecedents of the movement and are depicted in considerable detail. Similarly expansive are the strong connections drawn between the movement and a worldwide struggle for "human rights." In Birmingham and Memphis, the movement is cited as a precursor to transnational efforts to increase access to free speech, freedom of religion, and the end of political violence and torture; references to Amnesty International and the United Nations abound. This expansive vision of both the past and future stands in marked contrast to the scanty treatment of contemporary racism in the United States. In fact, the connections drawn to the worldwide struggle for human rights shifts attention away from the contemporary and local toward the spectacular and global.

Interviews and fieldwork conducted over the summers of 1998 and 1999 with curators and historians at memorials in Atlanta, Birmingham, Memphis, and Selma suggest that the financial dependency of these institutions on governmental, corporate, and philanthropic donors limits the degree to which they can engage in a thorough appraisal of contemporary racism.[33] While these sites attract accolades from national and international commentators, their funding situation is tied to local interests and is thus threatened by local controversy. This situation suggests that a focus on the national, general, and otherwise distant past is "safe," whereas sustained treatment of the local, specific, and contemporary is not. Thus, in a complex and ambiguous manner, these museums obscure as much about contemporary, local racism as they portray about its national past and the future of international human rights.

This situation renders civil rights memorials vulnerable to becoming mere repositories of a history that, while powerfully decrying the racism of the past, does not always make clear its connections to a local present.[34] The issue of police brutality and repression is a case in point. Given its ongoing significance, this is a particularly difficult issue for sites to address. An early edition of the official Illinois African American heritage guide noted the site at which Fred Hampton and Mark Clark, members of the Black Panther Party, were assassinated by the Chicago police and FBI in 1969. Upon review, however, reference to the site was omitted from the guide because it was deemed "too controversial" from the perspective of those who would not admit the role the state played in upholding white supremacy.[35]

It would be inappropriate, however, to dismiss civil rights memorials as corrupt, prima facie, due to the influence of state and corporate promotion. In the case of the well-capitalized sites in Birmingham and Memphis, interviews indicate that the promise of increased tourism revenue helped secure the necessary financial and political support in the face of protests against their "controversial" subject matter.[36] In the case of the King National Historic Site in Atlanta's Sweet Auburn District, the confluence of local, national, and international politics were responsible for establishing the site. Initiated by Coretta Scott King in 1971 and managed by the National Park Service since 1980, the site has been strapped by budgetary constraints and, until recently, consisted of little more than a small visitor's kiosk on an empty lot adjacent to King's grave and birthplace. Nevertheless, it attracted over one million visitors annually. With Atlanta's successful bid to host the 1996 Summer Olympics and the threat of international scrutiny, previously uncooperative authorities at the federal, state, and local levels appropriated funds for the construction of a multimillion-dollar visitor center and the restoration of King's childhood neighborhood. Just as during the 1950s and 1960s, when the threat of embarrassment before an international audience over the condition of civil rights in the United States was in part responsible for the federal government's grudging support for the movement, the specter of international visitors arriving in Atlanta to seek out the legacy of the Nobel Peace Prize winner and finding only a small kiosk motivated otherwise indifferent politicians to take action.[37]

Further, heritage tourism can serve as an entry point for a more nuanced understanding of ourselves insofar as memorials can situate persons, materials, and events in the context of their time and place, with all of its messy complexity. Civil rights museums in Atlanta, Birmingham, Savannah, and Memphis have installed scale reproductions of the landscape of segregation. Visitors are invited to walk among and across the boundaries characterizing white supremacy in replica schoolhouses, kitchens, and theaters. These reproductions strive to create emotional connections to the present by recreating the spatial milieu of the past.

Perhaps the most fitting endorsement of the relevance of these sites comes from the activists who make them the scene of their protests. The number and variety of groups protesting at these sites suggest their political relevance as well as the contested nature of the movement's contemporary meaning. The King National Historic Site is a case in point.[38] In 1985, the Ku Klux Klan staged a rally at the King National Historic Site to protest what they described as the "corruption" of King's message of equality by the "antiwhite" policy of affirmative action. In another instance, African Americans living in the vicinity of King's birth home in Atlanta protested the proposed renaming of a street in honor of Mahatma Gandhi, claiming that it would detract attention away from King and the historic Auburn Avenue neighborhood in which they resided. In a related incident, expatriate Pakistanis protested the installation of a statue of Mahatma Gandhi at the site, claiming that Gandhi, as a young officer in the British army, was responsible for atrocities in Africa and was thereby an inappropriate figure to commemorate at the King National Historic Site. As these examples demonstrate, memorials cannot fix the movement's meaning once and for all; rather, they open a new chapter of struggle intimately associated with the mechanisms of memory—place, narrative, and interpretation. Memorials, as sites of historic memory, are constitutive of contemporary politics.

The civil rights movement derived its political energy in part from the manner in which its participants transgressed and violated the norms of white supremacy. They shattered its boundaries, both literally and figuratively. These actions served to articulate new boundaries and new discourses regarding what was to be considered "just," "moral," "racist," and "revolutionary." Set in place at civil rights memorials, these new discourses are now the object and medium of contemporary politics such that the "past" and the "future" are implicated in one another's production. Civil rights memorials do not—indeed, cannot—authoritatively pronounce the movement's legacy. Rather, they instigate a new dialogue about the movement's history, meanings, and legacies. Like the contentious debates over the place of the Confederate battle flag, congressional redistricting, and the struggle to rename streets in honor of Martin Luther King Jr., the study of memorials dedicated to the civil rights movement offers a spatial perspective on the confluence of memory, identity, and political action. In writing the past in such a rich, provocative fashion, civil rights memorials are sites at which the agenda for the *next* civil rights movement is presently undergoing negotiation.

Notes

I am indebted to numerous friends and colleagues for their thoughtful comments and generous support, among them: Derek H. Alderman, John Paul Jones III, Paul Kingsbury, Karl Raitz, Rich Schein, Dell Upton, Camille Wells, Dana White, and the ever-patient editors of this volume. This chapter is a revised version of "Interpreting the Civil Rights Movement: Place, Memory, and Conflict," which first appeared in *Professional Geographer* 52, no. 4 (2000): 660–71. The original research for this chapter was made possible by a Doctoral Dissertation Improvement grant, SBR-9811145, from the National Science Foundation and a Dissertation Research Grant from the Otis Paul Starkey Fund of the Association of American Geographers; subsequent research on this topic was generously supported by Indiana University's Center on Philanthropy and the Indiana University Fund for the Humanities.

1. For a broad overview of the various sites see Jim Auchmutey, "Tributes to a Cause: A Roundup of the Museums and Monuments Commemorating the Movement That Changed the South—and the Nation," *Atlanta Journal-Constitution*, August 24, 1997, sec. R, 2; Jim Carrier, *A Traveler's Guide to the Civil Rights Movement* (Orlando, Fla.: Harcourt Books, 2004); Townsend Davis, *Weary Feet, Rested Souls: A Guided History of the Civil Rights Movement* (New York: W. W. Norton, 1998); Gary Lee, "Freedom's Path: A Journey on the Road to Civil Rights," *Washington Post*, January 15, 1998, sec. E, 1; Kevin Sack, "Museums of a Movement," *New York Times*, June 28, 1998, sec. 12 (Travel), 22.

2. For the memorial significance of municipal infrastructure see Derek H. Alderman, "A Street Fit for a King: Naming Places and Commemoration in the American South," *Professional Geographer* 52 (Fall 2000): 672–84.

3. The literature on race, memory, and place is rich and growing. A good point of entry includes the following: Dolores Hayden, *The Power of Place: Urban Landscapes as Public History* (Boston, Mass.: MIT Press, 1995); John Paul Jones III, "The Street Politics of Jackie Smith," in *The Blackwell Companion to the City*, ed. Gary Bridge and Sophie Watson (Oxford: Blackwell, 2000), 448–59; Scott A. Sandage, "A Marble House Divided: The Lincoln Memorial, the Civil Rights Movement, and the Politics of Memory, 1939–1963," *Journal of American History* 80 (1993): 135–67; Kirk Savage, *Standing Soldiers, Kneeling Slaves: Race, War and Monument in Nineteenth-Century America* (Princeton, N.J.: Princeton University Press, 1997).

4. Regarding the reciprocal condition of landscape and culture see James S.

Duncan and Nancy Duncan, "(Re)Reading the Landscape," *Environment and Planning D: Society and Space* 6 (1988): 117–26; Denis Cosgrove and Stephen Daniels, eds., *The Iconography of Landscape* (Cambridge: University of Cambridge Press, 1988); Stephen Daniels, "Marxism, Culture, and the Duplicity of Landscape," in *New Models in Geography: The Political-Economy Perspective*, ed. Richard Peet and Nigel Thrift (London: Unwin Hyman, 1989), 196–220; James S. Duncan, *The City as Text: The Politics of Landscape Interpretation in the Kandyan Kingdom* (Cambridge: Cambridge University Press, 1990); Sanford Levinson, *Written in Stone: Public Monuments in Changing Societies* (Durham, N.C.: Duke University Press, 1998); David Loewenthal, *The Past Is a Foreign Country* (Cambridge: Cambridge University Press, 1985); Simon Schama, *Landscape and Memory* (New York: Vintage Books, 1995); Richard H. Schein, "The Place of Landscape: A Conceptual Framework for Interpreting an American Scene," *Annals of the Association of American Geographers* 87 (Fall 1997): 660–80; James E. Young, *The Texture of Memory* (New Haven, Conn.: Yale University Press, 1995).

5. Fath Davis Ruffins, "Mythos, Memory, and History: African American Preservation Efforts, 1820–1990," in *Museums and Communities: The Politics of Public Culture*, ed. Ivan Karp, Christine M. Kreamer, and Stephen D. Lavine (Washington, D.C.: Smithsonian Institution Press, 1992), 506–611; Robert. R. Weyeneth, "Historic Preservation and the Civil Rights Movement," *CRM Bulletin* 18 (Fall 1995): 6–8.

6. For a fuller interpretation of the park and its inception see Thomas Hughes Cox, *Reflections on a Place of Revolution and Reconciliation: A Brief History of Kelly Ingram Park and the Birmingham Civil Rights District* (Birmingham, Ala.: Birmingham Civil Rights Institute, 1995); Catherine Howett, "Kelly Ingram Park: A Place of Revolution and Reconciliation," *Landscape Architecture* 83 (March 1993): 34–35; Dell Upton, "Commemorating the Civil Rights Movement," *Design Book Review* 40 (Fall 1999): 22–33.

7. John Western, *Outcast Cape Town* (Berkeley: University of California Press, 1997).

8. Herbert Aptheker, *American Negro Slave Revolts* (New York: International Publishers, 1939); Eugene D. Genovese, *Roll, Jordan, Roll: The World the Slaves Made* (New York: Vintage Books, 1976); Darlene Clark Hine, "Lifting the Veil, Shattering the Silence: Black Women's History in Slavery and Freedom," in *The State of Afro-American History: Past, Present, Future*, ed. Darlene Clark Hine (Baton Rouge: Louisiana State University, 1986), 223–49; Earl Lewis, "Connecting Memory, Self, and the Power of Place in African American Urban History," *Journal of Urban History* 21 (Summer 1995): 247–71; Earl Lewis, *In Their Own Interests: Race, Class, and Power in Twentieth-Century Norfolk, Virginia*

(Berkeley: University of California Press, 1991); Fath Davis Ruffins, "'Lifting as We Climb': Black Women and the Preservation of African American History and Culture," *Gender and History* 6 (Spring 1994): 376–96; Jeffrey C. Stewart and Fath Davis Ruffins, "'A Faithful Witness': Afro-American Public History in Historical Perspective, 1828–1984," in *Presenting the Past: Essays on History and the Public*, ed. Susan Porter Benson, Steven Brier, and Roy Rosenzweig (Philadelphia, Pa.: Temple University Press, 1986), 307–38; Dell Upton, "White and Black Landscapes in Eighteenth-Century Virginia," *Places* 2 (1985): 59–72; John Michael Vlach, *Back of the Big House: The Architecture of Plantation Slavery* (Chapel Hill: University of North Carolina Press, 1993).

9. Regarding the politics of transgression and resistance see Michel de Certeau, *The Practice of Everyday Life* (Berkeley: University of California Press, 1984); Tim Cresswell, *In Place / out of Place: Geography, Ideology, and Transgression* (Minneapolis: University of Minnesota Press, 1996); J. C. Scott, *Domination and the Arts of Resistance: Hidden Transcripts* (New Haven, Conn.: Yale University Press, 1990). For the ubiquity of white supremacist imagery and its reliance on a debased black other see, James Boskin, *Sambo: The Rise and Demise of an American Jester* (New York: Oxford University Press, 1986); Toni Morrison, *Playing in the Dark: Whiteness and the Literary Imagination* (Cambridge, Mass.: Harvard University Press, 1992); Patricia Morton, *Disfigured Images: The Historical Assault on Afro-American Women* (Westport, Conn.: Praeger, 1991); William Van Deburg, *Slavery and Race in American Popular Culture* (Madison: University of Wisconsin Press, 1984).

10. John Bodnar, "Public Memory in an American City: Commemoration in Cleveland," in *Commemorations: The Politics of National Identity*, ed. John R. Gillis (Princeton, N.J.: Princeton University Press, 1994), 74–89; John Bodnar, *Remaking America: Public Memory, Commemoration, and Patriotism in the Twentieth Century* (Princeton, N.J.: Princeton University Press, 1992); David Burnham, *How the Other Half Lived: A Peoples' Guide to American Historic Sites* (New York: Faber and Faber, 1995); John P. Radford, "Identity and Tradition in the Post–Civil War South," *Journal of Historical Geography* 18 (1992): 91–103.

11. Savage, *Standing Soldiers, Kneeling Slaves*; John J. Winberry, "Lest We Forget: The Confederate Monument and the Southern Townscape," *Southeastern Geographer* 23 (1983): 107–21.

12. Maurice Halbwachs, *The Collective Memory*, trans. F. J. Ditter and V. Y. Ditter (New York: Harper Colophon, 1980); Claudia Koonz, "Between Memory and Oblivion: Concentration Camps in German Memory," in *Commemorations*, ed. Gillis, 258–80; Pierre Nora, "Between Memory and History: Les Lieux De Memoire," *Representations* 26 (Spring 1989): 7–25; Young, *The Texture of Memory*.

13. Baker's legacy is lauded at her alma mater, Shaw University, in Raleigh, North Carolina. For more on Baker's role in the movement see Carol Mueller, "Ella Baker and the Origins of 'Participatory Democracy'," in *Women in the Civil Rights Movement: Trailblazers and Torchbearers, 1941–1965*, ed. Vicki L. Crawford, Jacqueline A. Rouse, and Barbara Woods (Brooklyn, N.Y.: Carlson, 1990), 51–70; Charles Payne, "Ella Baker and Models of Social Change," *Signs: Journal of Women in Culture and Society* 14, no. 4 (1989): 885–99; Charles Payne, "Men Led, But Women Organized: Movement Participation of Women in the Mississippi Delta," in *Women in the Civil Rights Movement*, ed. Crawford, Rouse, and Woods, 1–12.

14. Clark's contributions as an educator were recently commemorated along Charleston's waterfront; see the entry "Septima Clark Memorial," in Carrier, *A Traveler's Guide to the Civil Rights Movement*, 120–21. More generally, see: Cynthia S. Brown, ed., *Ready from Within: Septima Clark and the Civil Rights Movement* (Trenton, N.J.: Africa World Press, 1990); Peter Ling, "Local Leadership in the Early Civil Rights Movement: The South Carolina Citizenship Education Program of the Highlander Folk School," *Journal of American Studies* 29 (1995): 399–422; Grace Jordan McFadden, "Septima P. Clark and the Struggle for Human Rights," in *Women in the Civil Rights Movement*, 85–98.

15. Susan Ruddick, "Constructing Difference in Public Spaces: Race, Class, and Gender as Interlocking Systems," *Urban Geography* 17, no. 2 (1996): 132–51; Neil Smith, "Homeless/Global: Scaling Places," in *Mapping the Futures: Local Cultures, Global Change*, ed. Jon Bird, et al. (New York: Routledge, 1993), 87–119.

16. Stewart Burns, ed., *Daybreak of Freedom: The Montgomery Bus Boycott* (Chapel Hill: University of North Carolina Press, 1997).

17. Douglas Brinkley, *Rosa Parks* (New York: Penguin, 2000); Brown, ed., *Ready from Within*; Mary Fair Burks, "Trailblazers: Women in the Montgomery Bus Boycott," in *Women in the Civil Rights Movement*, ed. Crawford, Rouse, and Woods, 71–84; Burns, ed., *Daybreak of Freedom*.

18. Janice Monk, "Gender in the Landscape: Expressions of Power and Meaning," in *Inventing Places: Studies in Cultural Geography*, ed. Kay Anderson and Fay Gale (Melbourne: Longman Cheshire, 1992), 123–38; Mariana Warner, *Monuments and Maidens: The Allegory of the Female Form* (London: Weidenfield and Nicolson, 1985).

19. Aldon D. Morris, *The Origins of the Civil Rights Movement: Black Communities Organizing for Change* (New York: The Free Press, 1984); Mueller, "Ella Baker and the Origins of 'Participatory Democracy'."

20. Mueller, "Ella Baker and the Origins of 'Participatory Democracy,'" 51.

21. John E. Fleming, "African-American Museums, History, and the Amer-

ican Ideal," *Journal of American History* 81 (1994): 1020–26; William H. Harris, "Trends and Needs in Afro-American History," in *The State of Afro-American History: Past, Present, and Future*, ed. Hine, 139–53; Stephen F. Lawson, "Freedom Then, Freedom Now: The Historiography of the Civil Rights Movement," *American Historical Review* 96 (1991), 456–71; Weyeneth, "Historic Preservation and the Civil Rights Movement."

22. Clayborne Carson, "Civil Rights Reform and the Black Freedom Struggle," in *The Civil Rights Movement in America*, ed. Charles W. Eagles (Jackson: University of Mississippi Press, 1986), 19–32; Hine, "Lifting the Veil, Shattering the Silence"; Morris, *The Origins of the Civil Rights Movement*.

23. Joan T. Beifus, *At the River I Stand* (Memphis, Tenn.: St. Luke's Press, 1990); William H. Chafe, *Civilities and Civil Rights: Greensboro, North Carolina, and the Black Struggle for Freedom* (New York: Oxford University Press, 1980); Glenn Eskew, *But for Birmingham: The Local and the National Movement in the Civil Rights Struggle* (Chapel Hill: University of North Carolina Press, 1997); Richard J. Norrell, *Reaping the Whirlwind: The Civil Rights Movement in Tuskegee* (New York: Vintage Books, 1986).

24. "St. Paul Played Significant Part, Wants History Told," *Birmingham News*, November 15, 1992, sec. P, 37; Marcel Hopson, "The Unfinished Agenda Must Now Include Roll Call of Unnamed 'Footsoldiers,'" *Birmingham World*, December 9, 1992, n.p.; Nick Patterson, "Civil Rights Activists Want Stories Told," *Birmingham Post-Herald*, February 16, 1993, n.p.

25. David Lowenthal, *The Past Is a Foreign Country* (Cambridge: Cambridge University Press, 1985); Schama, *Landscape and Memory*; Young, *The Texture of Memory*.

26. Bernard J. Armada, "Memorial Agon: An Interpretive Tour of the National Civil Rights Museum," *Southern Communication Journal* 63 (1998), 235–43; Jones, "The Street Politics of Jackie Smith"; Eileen Loh-Harrist, "Vigil of a Lifetime: Jacqueline Smith's Views Are as Concrete as the Sidewalk before the Civil Rights Museum," *Memphis Flyer*, November 19–25, 1998, 14–17.

27. Susan La Tempa, "Rediscovering Black America," *Chicago Tribune*, February 14, 1993, sec. 12, 1; Charles Leerhsen and Vern E. Smith, "An American Mecca," *Newsweek*, October 14, 1991, 58; Pat Mines, "Travel in the Black," *Atlanta Tribune*, May 15–31, 1998, 14–16; Dinah Spritzer, "Exploring African-American History," *Travel Weekly*, October 14, 1993, sec. G, 3; Jim Yardley, "Black History, Civil Rights Luring Tourists to the South," *Atlanta Journal-Constitution*, November 13, 1992, sec. A, 1.

28. Frances Smiley, interview by author, July 20, 1998; Travel Industry Association of America, "The Minority Traveler: Travelscope Survey," (Washington, D.C.: Travel Industry Association of America, 1996).

29. Sarah Fuller, interview by author, June 22, 1999; Joe Nabbefeld, "Institute Should Have Strong Impact on City Economy," *Birmingham News*, November 15, 1992, sec. P, 14; "Case Study No. 2333: Intensive Media Campaign Fuels Support for Civil Rights Facility," *PR News*, January 25, 1993, 4–5.

30. For instance see Burnham, *How the Other Half Lived*; James W. Loewen, *Lies Across America: What Our Historic Sites Get Wrong* (New York: The New Press, 1999); Robert Lumley, ed., *The Museum Time Machine: Putting Cultures on Display* (London: Routledge, 1988).

31. Owen J. Dwyer and John Paul Jones III, "White Socio-spatial Epistemology," *Social and Cultural Geography* 1 (2000): 209–22.

32. Armada, "Memorial Agon."

33. Horace Huntley, interview by author, July 7, 1998; Dean Rowley, interview by author, July 16, 1998.

34. For a broader discussion of this point see Michel-Rolph Trouillot, *Silencing the Past: Power and the Production of History* (Boston, Mass.: Beacon Press, 1995).

35. Robert R. Weyeneth, "Historic Preservation and the Civil Rights Movement of the 1950s and 1960s: Identifying, Preserving, and Interpreting the Architecture of Liberation: A Report to Preservation Agencies," http://crm.cr.nps.gov/archive/19-2/19-2-12.pdf (accessed September 26, 2005).

36. Jerry Huston, "Site of Shame Now Glows as Beacon for Civil Rights," *Commercial Appeal*, July 17, 1994, 10; Nabbefeld, "Institute Should Have Strong Impact on City Economy"; Nick Patterson, "Institute May Both Hurt and Heal," *Birmingham News-Post-Herald*, December 26, 1992, sec. C, 1; Mary B. W. Tabor, "King's Dream Lives Again at the Site of His Death," *New York Times*, July 1, 1991, sec. A, 1.

37. After initially supporting the expansion of the National Historic Site, the King family opposed it when they learned the visitor center would include an exhibit on Martin Luther King Jr.'s life and career. In place of the National Park Service plan, the King family proposed building an interactive, "edu-tainment" center called King Dream, to be modeled after the Universal/MGM Studios venue in Orlando, Florida. The family argued that the park service was stealing their intellectual property and as a federal agency was not in a position to interpret "people's history." Nonetheless, African American community leaders, local residents and business owners, city council representatives, the mayor, and state and federal representatives continued to back the park service's plan. A series of editorials and opinion columns lambasting the family as greedy appeared in newspapers and magazines across the country; in addition, an *Atlanta Journal-Constitution* investigation into King Center finances revealed an institution beset by disorganization and improprieties. In the face of the criticism and lacking any outside

source of funding for their proposed facility, the King family withdrew its protest of the visitor center. The much publicized affair is described in Charles Rutheiser, *Imagineering Atlanta: The Politics of Place in the City of Dreams* (London: Verso, 1996).

38. Troy Lissimore, interview by author, September 18, 1997; Richard Mc-Collough, interview by author, September 18, 1997.

GLENN ESKEW

The Birmingham Civil Rights Institute and the New Ideology of Tolerance

In 1963, Birmingham, Alabama, gained worldwide notoriety when police used high-powered fire hoses and snarling dogs against peaceful civil rights protesters, many of them children and teenagers. Almost thirty years later, in 1992, the city again gained worldwide attention when the Birmingham Civil Rights Institute (BCRI), commemorating the struggle in Birmingham and the quest for human rights worldwide, opened its doors. Confederates and their loved ones a century before created an ideology of the Lost Cause as a civic religion that privileged the intolerance of white supremacy, erecting courthouse statues of soldiers and monuments to Confederate leaders as a way to celebrate the South's fruitless struggle during the Civil War. But in the Birmingham Civil Rights Institute, and a host of other civil rights memorials and museums that have spread throughout the South in the last twenty years, a new civic religion that celebrates the triumph of racial tolerance and the assimilation of blacks into the existing political and capitalist world system has begun to displace the old racist symbols of the Lost Cause.[1]

How is it that the city that was widely regarded as the most segregated in America in the 1960s now hosts one of the premier sites celebrating the civil rights movement? This chapter examines both the complicated history behind the creation of the Birmingham Civil Rights Institute and the dissemination and acceptance of the message of tolerance and worldwide universal human rights that the institute preaches. Building a multimillion dollar museum to the movement in a city like Birmingham depended on a confluence of interests between former activists and scholars who wanted to memorialize the movement and political and corporate interests who saw in the museum the possibility of redeeming the city's racist reputation and of attracting tourist dollars. As David Vann, a former mayor of Birmingham, understood, "the best way to put your bad images to rest is to declare them history and put them in a museum."[2] Others saw a potential to use Alabama's racial history for economic gain. In 1983, the administration of Alabama Governor George Wallace, famously known for promising to defend segregation forever in the 1960s, compiled a state Bureau of Tourism and Travel booklet detailing the state's many black heritage sites. The Wallace administration understood the financial potential of black heritage tourism and aggressively marketed Alabama's civil rights sites. Aubrey Miller, the black director of the state's Bureau of Tourism in the late 1980s explained that "inviting travelers to see firsthand the darker side of Alabama's past" gives them "the kind of travel experience they can find nowhere else."[3] Hence city, state, and federal governments were willing to subsidize civil rights heritage tourism not only in Birmingham but also in Selma, Montgomery, Atlanta, and Memphis.

For Birmingham, as for a host of other southern cities that have transformed old sites of civil rights protests into tourist attractions, memorialization of the movement has become a way to turn a stigmatized past into a commercial asset. The rationale of African American heritage tourism proved too great for politicians to resist, and weak opposition from reactionary whites and construction scandals involving political corruption could not stop the project's momentum. Yet to be palatable, a constructive message had to accompany the negative racial history. Thus the story line of the movement at the BCRI resolved into the Whiggish progressivism of the American master narrative, with a message that celebrates the moral righteousness of nonviolent protest, the potential of interracial unity, and the success of qualified integration. With exhibitory that takes local history and casts it in an international context, the institute champions multiculturalism and universal human rights. Since its opening in 1992, the BCRI—pitched as a place of revolution that has given way to reconciliation—has become Alabama's most visited historic site and an important symbol for the new, racially tolerant Birmingham. To outsiders like Susan Crystal, the editor of *Meetings and Conventions* magazine, the Birmingham Civil Rights Institute "looks really positive to me, like the city is doing a lot."[4]

A detailed history of the effort to construct a civil rights museum in Birmingham illustrates the acceptance and dissemination of this new ideology of tolerance in relation to a keen interest in using black history to encourage tourism. Local racial liberals, activists, and scholars conceptualized the message of the Birmingham Civil Rights Institute. A core group of six individuals deserve credit for seeing the project through to completion, from the initial idea to memorialize "the epic Birmingham civil rights movement" in 1979 to the grand opening of the Birmingham Civil Rights Institute in 1992.[5] Throughout the process, these same six people—joined by others—met, discussed ideas, and determined the content of the message to be delivered by the museum exhibits and institute activities. Four of the six were trained as historians and earned doctoral degrees. The other two worked as public servants. Four were white men, David Vann, Marvin Whiting, Robert Corley, and Edward LaMonte, while the other two were African Americans, Horace Huntley and Odessa Woolfolk. Over the course of thirteen years these individuals clarified the mission and message of the institute.

Perhaps Woolfolk more than anyone else deserves credit for overseeing important committee meetings, organizing the efforts of others, and making sure the project moved forward. A native of Birmingham, Odessa Woolfolk graduated from Ullman High School, which during segregation served the black community on the south side of the city. After attending Talladega College, she returned to Ullman to teach. A member of the black middle class, Woolfolk shared its parochial values but felt the sting of segregation and wanted access to the white world. She did not join the civil rights movement but did watch students leave Ullman during the Children's Crusade of May 1963. By the time the University of Alabama at Birmingham had renovated the old black school into new offices for its history faculty, Woolfolk had taken a job with the college's Center for Urban Affairs. She represented UAB in numerous capacities

from chairing the biracial initiative Operation New Birmingham to leading the state's chapter of the National Conference of Christians and Jews.
While working as a special assistant to UAB's president, Woolfolk volunteered to direct the various committees, task forces, and boards set up
over the thirteen-year period it took to make the idea of the Birmingham Civil Rights Institute a reality. Once it was completed she served the
memorial as president. "We took our charge seriously," she said of the
volunteers who conceptualized the commemoration, and the outstanding
facility shows their dedication.[6]

The idea for the Birmingham Civil Rights Institute originated with
David Vann, a white racial liberal who played a central role in the spring
demonstrations of 1963 and later won election as mayor of Birmingham.
A native of rural Randolph County, Vann had attended law school at
the University of Alabama and clerked for Supreme Court Justice Hugo
Black, a job that enabled Vann to hear Chief Justice Earl Warren read
the landmark *Brown v. Board of Education* decision in 1954. Return-
ing to Alabama to practice law in Birmingham, Vann joined other white
racial liberals in efforts to reapportion the state legislature and change
the form of city government so racist politicians could be removed from
office. When the Alabama Christian Movement for Human Rights and
the Southern Christian Leadership Conference launched a boycott of
downtown stores in 1962, merchants hired Vann to represent them in
negotiations with the civil rights activists and the federal government.
Vann became—in the words of Assistant U.S. Attorney General for Civil
Rights Burke Marshall—the only white man in Birmingham willing to
talk with the Reverend Dr. Martin Luther King Jr. After the spring 1963
civil rights demonstrations, Vann won election to the city council in 1971
by attracting widespread black support. A fragile coalition of black and
white voters elected him mayor of Birmingham in 1975. Vann's fortunes
changed in 1979 when an incident of police brutality fractured his biracial
coalition and defeated his re-election bid.[7]

As the incident polarized the city and Vann's black political support
eroded, his African American colleague on the city council, Richard Arrington, decided to run for mayor on the platform of police brutality. Although born in the Alabama black belt town of Livingston, Dick Arrington

grew up in Birmingham's industrial suburb of Fairfield, where he received his education in the secondary schools and graduated in 1955 from Miles College, a private institution supported by black Methodists. After earning a master's degree in zoology from the University of Detroit, Arrington returned to teach at Miles. The professor lived in Birmingham during the civil rights upheavals of the 1960s and watched his students participate but did not personally get involved. In September 1963, he began doctoral work in zoology at the University of Oklahoma, and after completing his Ph.D. in 1966 he returned to Birmingham and joined the administration at Miles. From there Arrington entered politics, winning election to the city council in 1971. When he ran for mayor in 1979, a demographic shift in Birmingham's population gave Arrington the edge, since white flight had left the city with a black majority.[8]

With polls showing Arrington and a white conservative in the lead, Vann proposed as his swan song the building of a museum to memorialize the civil rights movement and to highlight the biracial cooperation that had ended the demonstrations in 1963. During a trip to the Holy Land he had visited Israel's memorial to the Holocaust Yad Vashem and concluded that such a site in Birmingham could institutionalize the past and promote racial healing. Although he lost his re-election bid, Vann championed the museum idea in the waning weeks of his administration, convincing the city council to adopt a resolution of support on November 10, 1979, that created a study committee to determine the feasibility of a civil rights museum.

Vann's advocacy continued into Arrington's administration, although it took the new mayor eighteen months to respond. The concept received an important endorsement when the civic and biracial Operation New Birmingham recognized the proposed museum as a contributing factor to the urban renewal efforts outlined in the 1980 *Master Plan for Downtown Birmingham*. The city council applied pressure when it adopted a second resolution six months later that again called on Arrington to appoint the Study Committee. Yet the mayor seemed unwilling to tackle the issue. Woolfolk later explained, "I certainly remember a time when very few people were enthusiastic about the idea," adding, "they were tired of the movement era image of Birmingham and thought a museum would only serve to open up old wounds." Wanting to overcome its negative reputation, people in Birmingham thought the committee "should do something more positive." They could not conceive how the ugly images of racial hatred could be packaged for heritage tourism.[9]

Nearly two years passed before Arrington appointed the Birmingham Civil Rights Museum Study Committee that began its work on June 19, 1981. The mayor and the city council asked it to determine the "specific nature" of the museum and the "tasks and procedural steps" necessary to implement the idea. The Study Committee could recommend the composition of a formal board of directors, the structure of a permanent staff, and the potential sources of funding. Of the ten members of the committee, four had directly participated in the 1963 demonstrations: Vann, the Reverend Abraham Woods, the Reverend N. H. Smith Jr., and Councilman Arthur Shores. Henceforth, Woods represented the interests of movement veterans. Other members of the Study Committee included Whiting, Huntley, Savannah Jones, a member of the Birmingham Board of Education who later served the initiative as secretary, Councilwoman Bessie Estell, Winnie Mae Schaffner, and Rabbi Melvin Roseman. The Study Committee and its successor group, the Task Force, helped conceptualize the exhibits and the message of the institute.[10]

The Study Committee selected Huntley as chairman, and his interests, like those of several others, drove the final report's recommendations. As a native of Birmingham, a history professor at UAB, and an authority on African American studies, Huntley brought years of experience and local understanding to the project. He had completed his dissertation at the University of Pittsburgh in 1977 on the "Iron Ore Miners and Mine Mill in Alabama, 1933–1952." His work evaluated the interracial unionism of the radical Congress of Industrial Organizations affiliate and its successful effort to gain recognition from the Tennessee Coal and Iron Company of U.S. Steel. As Huntley recounted the postwar red-baiting and race-baiting that ultimately destroyed the union on Red Mountain, he charted the growth of black consciousness among the miners. Oral history provided an invaluable resource for his dissertation, and Huntley saw oral history as central to the work of the new museum.[11]

As the progenitor of the idea, Vann drafted a memorandum to the

Study Committee that outlined his "concepts for consideration." He recommended the incorporation of a nonprofit agency governed by a board of directors appointed by the mayor and city council, with the corporation then contracting with the city to run the museum. He encouraged the creation of a national advisory committee made up of individuals who had participated in the movement such as civil rights leaders and representatives from business, labor, and government. Vann identified the corner of Sixteenth Street and Sixth Avenue North opposite from Sixteenth Street Baptist Church and Kelly Ingram Park as the proper site of the museum. He outlined the use of photographs, film footage, and audiotapes to tell the story of the freedom struggle within an international framework. Vann saw the museum collecting oral interviews of "people who were involved in any way in the Birmingham experience." And, in what has remained a bone of contention, Vann saw the museum as a repository of archival material "relating to the civil rights movement and the history of racial discrimination." He believed the collection could be managed in conjunction with the archive's staff of the Birmingham Public Library.[12]

When the Study Committee filed its report on October 7, 1981, it proposed that, rather than a museum, the city create "an educational and research center," hence the new name for the facility, the Birmingham Civil Rights Institute. To fulfill its purpose, the committee recommended the institute focus on three areas: exhibitions, education, and archives. The Study Committee saw the institute developing a fixed exhibit using multimedia and sculpture, rotating exhibits featuring changing themes and topics, and a "cycloramic presentation" of film, photography, and sound that chronicled the history of the Birmingham movement. The Study Committee envisioned educational programs for students and community groups to accompany the exhibits, although this was left unexplained. Finally, they wanted the institute to become a "major depository" of civil rights materials and a research center for scholars.[13]

To assist in fundraising, the Study Committee endorsed Vann's proposal that two advisory boards be created: one composed of prominent local citizens such as Judge Oscar Adams Jr., Bishop Furman C. Stough, and community activist Adine Drew; the other with national figures such as Coretta Scott King, black historian John Hope Franklin, and *New York*

Times editor Howell Raines. In a departure from Vann's vision, the Study Committee selected the lot on Fifth Avenue North and Seventeenth Street catercorner to Kelly Ingram Park as the site of the institute, with the goal of linking the facility to urban renewal efforts in the historically significant black business district along Fourth Avenue North. In the end, however, the city bought Vann's recommended site.[14]

On most points the Study Committee had quickly reached consensus but members disagreed over the issue of an archive. Vann insisted that the institute become a depository for civil rights materials, but Whiting, the archivist at the Birmingham Public Library, argued that creating a competing facility wasted resources. He had reason to be concerned, for since coming to Birmingham in 1975 Whiting had amassed for the city library one of the most significant collections of civil rights documents in the country. Whiting became committed to civil rights causes when he found himself on the faculty of the prestigious Lovett School in Atlanta when it was picketed for failing to admit the children of the King and Abernathy families. A son of Fort Valley, Georgia, Whiting had first attended Emory University, where he earned undergraduate, master's, theological, and library science degrees, and then trained in intellectual history at Columbia University, earning a doctorate there in 1970. He arrived in Birmingham at just the right moment to preserve irreplaceable municipal documents detailing postwar civil rights protests, unique photographs, recordings, film footage from area media outlets, and materials released from the FBI under the Freedom of Information Act. As an archivist, Whiting was reluctant to see the papers he had processed split apart and housed in a separate civil rights facility, but Vann recognized that significant collections held by African Americans were not being offered to the library because of perceived racism on the part of staff. The financial records of the Alabama Christian Movement for Human Rights, for example, were in the attic of an abandoned funeral home, and the widow of the group's treasurer refused to share them with scholars or donate them to the Birmingham Public Library. An independent institute seemed the best way to secure these important documents before they fell victim to time. The disagreement between two of the Study Committee's leading members over archives came out in debates about where materials should be stored, for both Vann and Whiting wanted the institute to be active in collecting new materials.[15]

City council members also expressed concern that a civil rights institute would erode the city's limited budget for smaller museums, and that the institute would compete with the Birmingham Museum of Art. Picking up on the Study Committee's subtext regarding the archives, city councilwoman Nina Miglionico noted that building the institute around a nonexistent collection "would be like starting a museum with one painting." Referring to the Reagan recession that hit Birmingham hard, Miglionico explained, "As I see the problem, the Birmingham Museum of Art has been the recipient of some $25 million of monies, grants and collectibles, and there is no way that the public in this time of inflation and lowered expectation could meet the needs of another museum of the same quality. I would be opposed to any museum of inferior status or quality." Councilman Pete Clifford cited a report by the Birmingham Arts Commission asking that "no more struggling museums be added to the list." In addition to the art museum, the city funded three smaller museums, and all of them saw the proposed BCRI as encroaching on their already tight budgets. At first the director of the art museum, Richard Murray, offered lukewarm support for the initiative, but once he left the city to head the Smithsonian Institution's archives, Murray strongly endorsed the concept. "It may be a controversial idea in Birmingham. But I tell you, outside of Birmingham, people would come to a civil rights museum there."[16]

In making its report to the mayor and city council, the Study Committee completed its work on behalf of the Birmingham Civil Rights Institute and left the next move to others. The Study Committee had outlined the purpose of the institute and its organizational structure and had even attached a draft copy of articles of incorporation for Arrington and Miglionico to sign in order to make the idea a reality. Seven months passed before the city council adopted an ordinance empowering a Civil Rights Museum Board to create the institute. All that remained was for Mayor Arrington and the city council to approve the nominations of nine members to the board of directors. Again Arrington failed to act. Neither he nor the council appointed the members or appropriated money to fund the initiative.[17]

Although municipal elections were a year and a half away, politics apparently stymied efforts to establish the institute. In his mayoral campaign of 1979, Arrington had easily defeated Vann in the primary but had faced stiff competition in the runoff from Frank Parsons, a white conservative whom Arrington beat by a margin of only 2 percent. Arrington and his staff saw the institute project as potentially alienating already weak white political support. Vann recalled that "it was sort of dropped for the election and then it was never started up again." Even after Arrington won re-election to a second term in 1983 by pulling 60 percent of the vote to defeat white city councilman John Katopodis, the mayor did not return to the issue of a civil rights institute. Instead others picked up the cause.[18]

In 1984 the Alabama legislature took the lead in promoting the civil rights museum. The initiative fit in with fourth-term Governor George C. Wallace's strategy to use black and white heritage tourism for economic development. State Senator Earl Hilliard of Birmingham proposed two bills that would create two agencies, the Alabama Institute of Civil Rights History and the Alabama Institute of Civil War History. If passed, the bills would finance the building of two separate museums and research facilities, both located in Birmingham. As Hilliard explained, "I recognize the diversity of opinions of people in Birmingham and I'm ready to deal with that, and that's why we have two different bills." The House of Representatives approved the measure even though Birmingham had played no role in the Civil War and lacked an antebellum past, but both bills failed in the state senate. Nevertheless, local advocates for the Birmingham Civil Rights Institute took heart from the action.[19]

The senator's proposed legislation redoubled efforts to preserve civil rights materials. Birmingham Public Library Director George R. Stewart believed state funding would make the difference. In a March 1984 letter to Edward S. LaMonte, Mayor Arrington's executive secretary, Stewart outlined his and Whiting's concerns, demonstrating that two interests had coalesced around the institute: "those who have proposed a civil rights museum, and those who are concerned that important records may soon be lost." Stewart spoke for the second interest, explaining that although some people "have felt that the Public Library was in competition with the proposed Civil Rights Museum . . . that has never been the case" because "the Public Library is not, and has not been, interested in operating a museum." However, Stewart emphatically noted,

> The Birmingham Public Library, like its counterparts in other cities, has often seen important records and memorabilia vanish while everyone waited for someone to save it. In the twenty years since the Civil Rights Movement in Birmingham, much materials, and many memories, have already been lost. Records have been allowed to decay due to poor storage. Individuals have died and the remaining family members have not realized the importance of certain records. Where these records are ultimately housed and serviced is not of immediate importance. Locating, obtaining, and preserving these records is of immediate importance. If the records are not saved now, there will be little need for a Civil Rights Institute later.

To LaMonte, Stewart implored, "In obtaining this important material we need the assistance of all who are interested in its preservation. We seek the assistance of the Mayor, the Council, and particularly members of the Black Community in this matter."[20]

In his letter Stewart ranked the loss of memory as important as the loss of material, underscoring the immediate need to conduct oral interviews, a conclusion simultaneously reached by others. Professor Tennant S. McWilliams, then chairman of the history department at the University of Alabama at Birmingham, volunteered his resources for an oral history project on the civil rights movement. In a letter to Dr. Robert Corley, the director of the National Conference of Christians and Jews, McWilliams outlined his endorsement of Senator Hilliard's bill and expressed concern that the oral history effort be coordinated with the Birmingham Public Library Archives. McWilliams believed "that specialists in oral history and museum experts [should] be consulted on the development of the project and that someone with major civil rights research experience and contacts—perhaps Howell Raines—[should] be involved in these discussions." Stewart seconded this view in an estimate he prepared for Ed LaMonte and the mayor's office. He noted that an oral history project of the Birmingham movement would require $75,000, with the hiring of an "interviewer . . . well trained in the practical aspects of oral history and respected by those being interviewed" as the major expense. Stewart matched the $10,000 promised by LaMonte as start-up money.[21]

LaMonte made another suggestion that revealed the forces that ultimately got behind the institute. He advocated a civil rights pageant held under a tent in Kelly Ingram Park in the summer of 1984 that would dramatize "the significant events which took place in Birmingham." The model would be the "Trail of Tears" pageant in the Smoky Mountains, and the audience would be tourists en route to the New Orleans World Fair. LaMonte envisioned Birmingham black civil rights re-enactors confronting white policemen and firemen. He couched the pageant in the context of the downtown master plan of 1980 and identified Operation New Birmingham as endorsing the proposal. Although the pageant never took place, the rationale of heritage tourism proved successful in lining up corporate support for the institute.[22]

When the spring 1963 demonstrations left Birmingham with a negative international reputation, one segment of the city's white power structure transformed the Downtown Improvement Association into Operation New Birmingham, a biracial consortium of merchants, realtors, and attorneys representing the city's emerging service economy. Although reflecting private interests, Operation New Birmingham determined public policy in a fashion not unlike the Big Mules earlier in the century, for both groups translated economic power into political power. Downtown revitalization became the central theme of Operation New Birmingham, which drafted a "Design for Progress" in 1965 that made a treescape out of Twentieth Street and built the Jefferson County Civic Center to host conventions. When Arrington and other black leaders complained of persistent racism, Operation New Birmingham appointed twenty-seven leading black and white citizens to a newly created Community Affairs Committee and empowered it to find solutions to racial problems in the community. Although private in nature, the Community Affairs Committee consisted of public officials, black leaders, and white businessmen, and it actively engaged in public policy. In 1984, Ed LaMonte turned to Operation New Birmingham and its Community Affairs Committee to pursue the BCRI proposal.[23]

Birmingham first crossed the consciousness of Edward Shannon LaMonte as he was completing his undergraduate degree at Harvard College in 1964. LaMonte's dean, John U. Monro, had resigned his position at Harvard and accepted a job at Miles College. Monro encouraged LaMonte to follow him to the South. At Miles in 1965–66, LaMonte worked with Richard Arrington, the academic dean of the college. After his year in Birmingham, LaMonte began graduate work at the University of Chicago, where he studied urban history under Richard Wade. Birmingham provided the scholar with both rich sources for research and a job at UAB's Center for Urban Studies, where he worked with Woolfolk. In his 1976 dissertation, "Politics and Welfare in Birmingham, Alabama, 1900–1975," LaMonte argued that through privatism, Birmingham's businessmen maintained a pared-down municipal government that enacted public policies favorable to their interests. While welfare concerned LaMonte the most, the issue of race relations remained a subtheme throughout the study. During Arrington's first mayoral campaign, LaMonte hosted a party for the candidate to meet white racial liberals on UAB's faculty. After his election, Arrington turned to LaMonte for advice, asking him to join his staff as chief administrative assistant and then as executive secretary. LaMonte accepted the job, recognizing an opportunity to fulfill Richard Wade's challenge to his students "to play significant roles in public affairs." His research on Birmingham had introduced him to civic leaders such as bankers Mervyn H. Sterne, Charles Zukoski, and especially George Ward, who as Birmingham's mayor in the progressive era had risen "above a preoccupation with the daily affairs of municipal government, holding a vision of what his city ought to be like." LaMonte wanted Arrington to be like Ward, "Birmingham's Urban Statesman."[24]

On November 5, 1984—five years after Vann's initial idea—the Community Affairs Committee of Operation New Birmingham convened a meeting "to assess the present status of the museum proposal." Ed LaMonte, David Vann, Odessa Woolfolk, and Marvin Whiting joined State Senator Earl Hilliard, committee members, and others in discussing the various proposals for a civil rights institute. The group decided to appoint two committees, one chaired by Vann and designed to arrange with the Birmingham Public Library Board a policy whereby the department of archives could function as "a temporary repository for civil rights documentation gathered in the name of the museum," and the other, cochaired by Vann and Woolfolk, to investigate the feasibility of a museum. LaMonte volunteered to ask the mayor and city council to pass a resolution establishing a civil rights museum steering committee. But again the mayor and council neglected to act. Another year passed before the city took any concrete steps forward.[25]

In November 1985, LaMonte announced the $500,000 purchase of the half-block west of Kelly Ingram Park along Sixth Avenue North as the site of the future civil rights institute. The mayor's executive secretary described the "multimillion dollar museum" as one of several projects underway that made this "one of the most positive periods in the city['s]" history. LaMonte acknowledged that not everyone agreed. "I've been surprised by the vehemence of some whites in saying 'Don't bring that up,' " referring to the demonstrations of 1963. Also LaMonte suggested the city still had to figure out "how to serve both tourists and historians at the center." In reality, the city had yet to appoint a board of directors, incorporate the institute, or fund the initiative.[26] Still the purchase of land signaled a change in Arrington administration policy.[27]

The city council responded to Arrington's move by appropriating money for the project. On April 15, 1986, the city council allocated just over $900,000 and budgeted an additional $1.5 million taken from federal revenue sharing funds. With the previous $500,000 lot, the city's investment in the institute now reached nearly $3 million. White councilwoman Bettye Fine Collins protested the expense, but her colleague Linda Coleman defended the act, arguing that the institute was "as important as [the] 'Bear' Bryant Museum" in Tuscaloosa that the council had given $100,000 to help build. The promotion of African American heritage tourism by the Wallace administration with its aggressive marketing of the state's racist past through its publication of *Alabama Black Heritage* promised great returns on investments in black history sites.[28]

In May 1986, Mayor Arrington finally appointed the Civil Rights Museum Task Force and authorized it to work with the architects he had hired to design the institute. In his letter asking people to serve on the Task Force, Arrington explained, "I believe that the Civil Rights Museum has great potential for our community in establishing Birmingham as a tourist attraction." No doubt the initiatives in Atlanta and Memphis and the endorsement of the state encouraged his change of heart. Picking up on the *Master Plan for Downtown Birmingham*, the mayor described the institute as anchoring a civil rights district created to revitalize the Kelly Ingram Park area. Arrington named seventeen people to the Task Force including Corley, Huntley, LaMonte, Vann, Whiting, and as chairwoman, Woolfolk. He also appointed Councilman William Bell, city urban planner Mike Dobbins, and community activist the Reverend Abraham Woods.[29]

To design the facility, Arrington hired Bond, Ryder, James, and Associates, a minority architectural firm out of New York City that had designed the King Center in Atlanta. J. Max Bond headed the New York firm's efforts while Birmingham architect David Jones worked out local details. On June 16, 1986, Bond, Ryder, James made an initial presentation of preliminary findings regarding the building of the civil rights museum. Drawing on previous jobs, such as the renovations to Harlem's Schomburg Library, Bond, Ryder, James proposed a standard institutional format that allocated space for the lobby, gift shop, auditorium, museum exhibits, workshops, library, archive, classrooms, and administrative offices. Given the chance, the architects proposed to conceptualize, design, and build the entire facility including the exhibits with little input from the local community. Bond, Ryder, James hired as subcontractors Marjorie Peters of MP Enterprises and Tarlee Brown of Milkey and Brown, individuals affiliated with Mayor Arrington's administration through other minority contracts.[30]

The architects and subcontractors scheduled a "New York Workshop" on June 21, 1986, to introduce LaMonte, Whiting, and Woolfolk to museum consultants previously used by the firm. The experts from the Schomburg Center, the Studio Museum in Harlem, and the Cleveland Museum of Art assisted the New York architects in letting the locals from Alabama know just what kind of museum they needed. They entertained the visitors and subcontractors with lunch at the Barking Fish—an upscale Manhattan restaurant—and tickets to Broadway shows. The experience proved an eye-opener for the three members of the Task Force, for not only did the extravagant spending of Marjorie Peters and Tarlee

Brown surprise the public servants, but the aggressive planning of Bond, Ryder, James made their heads spin.[31]

During the workshop, several of the museum consultants offered advice that the Task Force members followed when conceptualizing the Birmingham Civil Rights Institute. Foremost was the recommendation that the museum's mission be clearly stated. All other concerns centered on this essential issue that had yet to be determined. Suggestions for the creation of a " 'living' institution" that "should take an active role in documenting the on-going history of Civil Rights" for "all minorities" received special notice. While Woolfolk described to the consultants the composition of the Task Force, LaMonte admitted that "many individuals in Birmingham would like to head or be involved in the museum." Voicing the mayor's perspective, Marjorie Peters announced that "tourism is a major concern of the city and should be considered in relation to the museum's development," and she outlined a proposed civil rights district.[32]

The mayor's initial decision to turn the entire BCRI project over to the architects disturbed members of the Task Force who wanted to control the process independently. Having worked so hard and waited so long to get the mayor behind the initiative, the Task Force members were frustrated by having to slow developments, but they did so to control the outcome of the institute. They received help from others in Birmingham. Following the Bond, Ryder, James presentation, City Attorney James K. Baker wrote Ed LaMonte of his concerns, describing the architects' presentation as "troubling." Acknowledging that Bond, Ryder, James would design "a fine structure," Baker noted that "we diminish rather than enhance their potential by looking to them to determine (albeit in consultation with others) the material the city wants in the museum, and the focus or concepts those materials will illuminate." Baker insisted nationally prominent African American scholars be recruited to conceptualize the museum; otherwise, technicians hired by the architects would determine the content. As he explained to LaMonte, it would be like "taking a telescopic view of the desired completed product" and beginning "from the wrong end of the instrument." After the New York experience LaMonte felt likewise, desiring "to clarify the sequencing of events" and to slow "down the development of a specific building."[33]

Back in Birmingham, Arrington responded to the reports from the Task Force members and the questionable activities of Peters by reevaluating the city's relationship with Bond, Ryder, James. In a June 25, 1986, letter to architect J. Max Bond, the mayor specified, "In the future, I would like Ed LaMonte to review with you and Odessa Woolfolk proposed expenditures from the reimbursable line item. I think it important that all of the participants in this project carry their work forward in a coordinated fashion and would like to be certain that we get our greatest return possible on expenditures from the reimbursable funds." As if answering complaints made by LaMonte and Woolfolk regarding Peters, Arrington flatly stated to Bond, "I am particularly interested in getting maximum benefit from the use of any consultants by coordinating their work with the ongoing work of the Task Force." He then sent copies of the letter to Peters, Woolfolk, and LaMonte.[34]

Answering LaMonte's particular concerns, Arrington slowed the development of institute plans. He delayed the next meeting with the architects to give the Task Force time "to define the mission" of the institute, for he agreed with LaMonte and the museum consultants on "the importance of having a clear mission statement before proceeding into the design of the building." Empowered by the mayor, LaMonte, Woolfolk, Whiting, and the other members of the Task Force exerted a controlling influence over the design of the institute by exercising a veto power regarding the allocation of space in the building, the parameters of museum themes, and the content of the exhibits. While internationally recognized architectural firms and museum experts participated in the process, local people determined what actually went into the Birmingham Civil Rights Institute.[35]

Yet the broader community of local people in Birmingham had yet to be convinced that funding the museum, which Bond, Ryder, James estimated would cost up to $12 million to build, was a good idea. Mayor Arrington proposed a bond issue to pay for the institute, asking voters to approve a $5 million tax increase to raise $65 million in bonds to be used for schools, museums, parks, sidewalks, and sewers, with $10 million earmarked for the BCRI. Frank Young III, the president of the Birmingham Chamber of Commerce and a Task Force member, advocated the tax hike as a way to "draw more tourists and conventions to the city." But voters defeated the bond issue on July 8, 1986, by a vote of 13,638 to 23,381. Resistance surfaced from both an antitax group headquartered in mostly white east Birmingham and from blacks, who, Woolfolk explained, "don't want to remember what's traumatic in their history."[36] Despite the defeat, Councilman William Bell assured the Task Force that "the commitment of the Mayor and City Council is firm." Finding the money would remain a problem, but as Whiting later recalled, the Task Force "assumed all along—and it was not an assurance that we dealt with but an assumption—that, if we moved to produce with the architects and the exhibitory people a concept, the funding would be found."[37]

The Task Force met with the mayor on July 11, 1986, and reviewed the previous seven-year effort to build a civil rights museum in Birmingham and drafted a mission statement. Horace Huntley distributed the Study Committee's original report and Odessa Woolfolk led the discussion. A general consensus emerged regarding the basic themes of the mission statement. Everyone believed that the institute should celebrate "the success of Birmingham in dealing with civil rights" through "the resolution of conflict and struggle." The museum would be "a reflection of the past and hope for the future," with exhibits and activities designed to turn the city's image "from a negative to a positive symbol." The preamble placed the movement in the national and international context of the freedom struggle and identified "educational, cultural, and research" efforts as key to developing a "living institution" that looked at historical events in realistic and creative ways. The concluding slogan of the Birmingham story, "from revolution to reconciliation," underscored the ideological dogma of nonviolent resistance to oppression and support for human rights.[38]

In emphasizing tolerance, the mission statement reflected the life work of Task Force member Bob Corley. Through his position as regional executive director of the National Conference of Christians and Jews, Robert G. Corley promoted harmonious relations among diverse people, an interest that had initially led him to study history. After graduating from Birmingham Southern College in 1970, Corley attended the University of Virginia, completing a dissertation there in 1979 under the direction of Edward Younger. The title of the study, "The Quest for Racial Harmony: Race Relations in Birmingham, Alabama, 1947–1963," explored the efforts at biracial cooperation in the years before the civil rights demonstrations. Corley found that although black and white businessmen promoted interracial cooperation within a segregated framework, the rise of massive resistance severed the lines of communication and led to the events of 1963. The intolerance of white supremacy had trumped the tolerance of biracial communication. Corley later described that legacy as setting "Birmingham on the road toward a more open and just community" because the resolution of the civil rights crisis allowed for the potential of racial reconciliation. The closing paragraph of the institute's mission statement echoed this belief. The Task Force wanted to show "the success in race relations and the progress that has been made through interracial cooperation since then." In reference to Arrington's election, the statement read, "the 'new' Birmingham of the 1980s, which has emerged in a relatively short time, is the ongoing example of this progress." In practice the institute would fulfill the brotherhood week objectives of the National Conference of Christians and Jews by becoming "an important catalyst in Birmingham's continuing efforts to heal the wounds of the past and to become a truly biracial community." As chairman of the mission statement committee, Corley carefully selected a language of tolerance that the Task Force adopted on August 20, 1986. With LaMonte, Huntley, Vann, Whiting, and Woolfolk, Corley played a central role in the outcome of the institute and the expression of its ideological content.[39]

When the Task Force met with representatives from Bond, Ryder, James in September 1986, the architects presented five conceptual schemes for the group to consider. Describing the value of civil rights film footage, Huntley promoted the use of an IMAX-type theater as the focal point of the institute. Further analysis suggested the prohibitive cost of the theater, the lack of converted film footage, and the need for large audiences to be cost effective. While IMAX proved impractical, the Task Force retained Huntley's idea of a film to introduce Birmingham to the visitor. The building committee's progress report outlined two related questions regarding the design of the institute: how to achieve the proper mix between a tourist destination and a scholarly conference center, and how to define an institute as site specific while anchoring a larger heritage tourism district. Huntley wanted the visitor to leave the institute "knowing what the Civil Rights Movement was about," and he recognized "exhibitory . . . as the key to the success of this goal." Consequently the Task Force insisted that "the script for the exhibitory needs to be controlled locally."[40]

It certainly would have been possible to tell a more general, national story at the BCRI. In the same years that the Task Force was considering the museum's content, civil rights studies exploded as popular presses published new major interpretations of the movement and PBS broadcast the watershed documentary series *Eyes on the Prize*. Millions of Americans watched the six-part series, and thousands more bought the companion book, edited reader, and video set.[41] While the wealth of civil rights studies influenced the thinking of the Task Force, members sought to develop a chronology particular to Birmingham that nonetheless followed an increasingly standard Montgomery to Memphis trajectory of King's public life.[42]

To assist the Task Force in conceptualizing the exhibitory of the Birmingham Civil Rights Institute, Bond, Ryder, James solicited proposals from several design groups and then selected American History Workshop for the job. The New York firm headed by Richard Rabinowitz had planned more than 150 projects including the United States Holocaust Memorial, the Museum of American Constitutional Government at Federal Hall, and the Center for Southern Folklore in Memphis. With his undergraduate and doctoral degrees from Harvard, his hands-on museum work at Old Sturbridge Village, and his prior position at the National Endowment for the Humanities, Rabinowitz brought to the project invaluable contacts and experience. He also charged $750 a day for his time plus staff and travel costs.[43]

After weeks of consultation with Task Force members, American History Workshop submitted a preliminary exhibit plan for review, and the Task Force helped Rabinowitz revise the rough draft into a formal proposal that ultimately set the thematic program of the Birmingham Civil Rights Institute. Rabinowitz was expensive but in his rough draft he offered several satisfactory themes: Threshold, Background, Movement, Vision, Face to Face, Legacies, and The Struggle Continues. The Task Force kept the first six themes, which corresponded to traditional museum design, but for reasons of funding and practicality altered the last one, which emphasized experimental educational approaches to understanding civil rights. Phase 1 incorporated the first six themes in its exhibits, while phase 2 used computer-based educational tools to explore how "the struggle continues" for human rights around the globe. The final product, "Walking to Freedom: The Museum of America's Civil Rights Revolution," fit the story of the civil rights struggle into America's master narrative by using a progressive view of history that concludes with the triumph of tolerance.[44]

The dramatic entrance planned by American History Workshop and the Task Force immediately aligns the visitor with the civil rights revolution. Just as a believer enters church, so one walks under the entrance fronting Sixteenth Street and Kelly Ingram Park, passes through a courtyard, and climbs up steps to reach the sanctuary. Rabinowitz called this part of the Bond, Ryder, James design the "Threshold" to invoke "a recreation of one of the most important events in the history of human freedom." Like on nearby Sixteenth Street Baptist Church, a dome crowns the pinnacle of the institute. To cross the threshold and enter the lobby, one must pass through a series of arches intended to inspire both awe and anticipation. Bond, Ryder, James designed the multicolored brick structure to reflect the architecture and building materials of nearby black churches. The design makes one feel like a civil rights supporter going to a mass meeting.[45]

Just as the movement indoctrinated its followers, so the exhibits use artifacts, reader rails, images, and sound to explain racial intolerance. A brief film on the early history of Birmingham that suggests economic reasons for racial exploitation ends with images of segregated drinking fountains. Then a raised screen reveals reproductions of segregated fountains and admits the audience into the "Barriers" exhibit. The simple point is reinforced by displaying a proverbial sock hop lunch counter with apparently "white" monochromatic life-cast mannequins enjoying their order while "black" monochromatic life-cast mannequins wistfully peer in from outside. The design industry that serves museums coined "life cast" to describe the lifelike mannequin representations (often of real people) appliquéd with street clothes and covered in a protective coat of gray epoxy paint. All of the civil rights museums use them, often to display

Displays like this one at the Birmingham Civil Rights Institute try to impart the emotional pain caused by segregation. Here, a young black woman looks on forlornly as two white girls laugh and gossip at a segregated lunch counter. (Birmingham Civil Rights Institute)

segregation in action. Nearly one third of the museum displays regard the subject of segregation to emphasize the intolerance of white supremacy and to set the stage for the drama of the movement. Exhibits defined as "mini-environments" consider the ideology of segregation, the institutions within the black community, the inequalities of the system, and the confrontations with white people that kept segregation intact. Rabinowitz wanted to recreate "key spaces in the lives of black people" and to use materials without excessive detail so as to open up a dialogue and to offer "a multiplicity of levels of interpretation." The section has no "defined single pathway" so the visitor wanders through the exhibits sensing the limited opportunities, frustrations, and cramped living spaces of African Americans in Birmingham.

The "Barriers" section catalogs grievances while providing a barometer by which one could potentially measure the success of the movement. The displays analyze social and cultural segregation through a look at sep-

This display of typical "white" and "colored" water fountains in the Birmingham Civil Rights Institute's "Barriers" section highlights the inequalities of the separate but equal fiction of the segregated South. (Birmingham Civil Rights Institute)

Monochromatic life-cast statues are used at many civil rights heritage sites to represent civil rights demonstrators. This display of a civil rights march at the Birmingham Civil Rights Institute encourages visitors to join with civil rights demonstrators in their symbolic march toward freedom. (Birmingham Civil Rights Institute)

arate churches, businesses, theaters, and sporting teams. Racist stereo-types used commercially to sell products nationally are juxtaposed next to images of black popular culture that both races consumed. Other exhibits in the "Barriers" section look at economic inequalities in home life, schooling, healthcare, and the legal system, concluding that separate was grossly unequal. Sections on the black church, black businesses, and black neighborhoods showcase a vibrant segregated black community, while still emphasizing the goal of assimilation. The visitor follows a walkway that narrows out of black Birmingham as he confronts not only the white people who enforced segregation but also the black people challenging the system.[46]

Rabinowitz intended the next part of the museum—which tells the story of the civil rights struggle—to proceed like a theatrical production. A prologue introduces the movement in Montgomery with a monochromatic life-cast Rosa Parks sitting on the bus. Act 1 links the sit-ins with the Freedom Rides by emphasizing the student protests of the 1960s. Act 2 looks at community struggles in Albany and elsewhere over the right to vote. Act 3 features the Birmingham demonstrations as the climax of the civil rights movement with ample film footage to show "the world is watching" and to introduce the international context of the freedom struggle. An epilogue recapitulates the Birmingham success with the celebration at the March on Washington and the ratification of the 1964 Civil Rights Act.[47]

The recounting of the struggle culminates in the symbolic triumph of tolerance. Emerging from the civil rights timeline of events, the visitor—like the movement volunteer of the historical struggle—joins "The Processional" of monochromatic life-cast mannequins marching against the backdrop of the famous photograph by James H. Kraals used in the opening credits to *Eyes on the Prize*. This clear message of African American assimilation into the white mainstream underscores the history of racial progress expressed throughout the exhibits. Even the shock that the visitor confronts when looking out the picture window at the Sixteenth Street Baptist Church where four black girls were murdered by an early morning bomb in September 1963 is muted by a series of "Milestones" that chart the success of the struggle. The brief placards set up as "Legacies" to the movement identify African American firsts in Birmingham and elsewhere, most of which measure outcomes in political gains. A different type of assessment might have evaluated success in light of the economic, social, and cultural inequalities identified in the "Barriers" section, but the results would not have fit the progressive theme of tolerance. The final third of the exhibit, wary of addressing contemporary race issues in the United States, instead looks at how "the struggle continues" through a segment on worldwide "human rights." Using the standards of the United Nations, the institute emphasizes a growing global triumph of tolerance expressed through international human rights. At that point the visitor, as if leaving a nearby church, exits the building through the arched doors of the rotunda, down the steep steps, and empties into Sixteenth Street and Kelly Ingram Park in a symbolic re-enactment of the Children's Crusade.

The influence of the Task Force members can be seen in the thematic program designed by Rabinowitz. While internationally significant, the story told is a local one that features the indigenous movement rather than King and the SCLC. Reference is made to Montgomery, but the chronology is tightly focused on the early 1960s as the pivotal period in civil rights history. The role of biracial communications in the postwar period, during the 1963 demonstrations, and since then is analyzed according to an interpretation proposed by Corley and LaMonte. Black institutions appear as unequal byproducts of segregation as argued by Woolfolk. Rather than overemphasize the black bourgeoisie, the exhibit highlights the black working class, reflecting the interests of Huntley. Vann's opinion that the televised broadcasts of the fire hoses and police dogs marked the turning point in the movement is not only stressed in the exhibit but actually re-enacted through the Hunt-Brinkley Reports shown on period television sets. Finally, the flow of events emphasizes Whiting's contention that Birmingham marked a watershed celebrated at the March on Washington. The chronology presented in the museum charts a particularly narrow trajectory. It defines the early 1960s as the key years of the struggle and events in Birmingham with the subsequent adoption of the 1964 Civil Rights Act as the climax of the civil rights movement all framed within the standard Montgomery to Memphis refrain. The victory over white supremacy presupposes the triumph of tolerance and the fulfillment of King's dream of assimilation, goals married to a master narrative of America's history that charts an ever-expanding democracy.[48]

The planning for the institute completed in 1987 suggested that at last it would soon be built, but internal conflicts and funding problems stymied the project again. When Max Bond refused to pay a forged invoice to Peters, the city replaced Bond, Ryder, James as the principal contractor with Diversified Project Management (or DPM), a minority firm founded by contractor H. R. Russell of Atlanta. In place of Bond, Ryder, James, DPM used Birmingham architect David Jones and city urban planner Mike Dobbins to solve the problems that arose from the initial plans designed by Max Bond. The architects and their consultants had nearly depleted the $3 million allocated for the institute in 1986. The Task Force wanted American History Workshop to complete the design of phase 1 outlined in the thematic "Walking to Freedom," but Woolfolk sadly informed Rabinowitz of the city's inability "to offer a long term contract for exhibitory and programming" because of "limited up-front funding."[49]

Again Arrington turned to a bond issue. In what amounted to a referendum, city voters had a second opportunity to fund the civil rights institute on May 10, 1988. Although Birmingham's black population neared 65 percent, residents rejected the initiative a second time. With the failure of the 1988 bond issue, institute plans sat suspended for over a year.[50]

In the fall of 1989—a decade after Vann's initial idea—Arrington made the final push that resulted in the completion of the project. In August, Diversified Project Management under the leadership of William Gilchrist appointed a steering committee to oversee the construction of the institute. Architect David Jones and city planner Mike Dobbins joined Woolfolk, LaMonte, Whiting, Huntley, and later Corley and Vann, among others, on the committee. The mayor himself replaced Marjorie Peters as the advocate of black heritage tourism. He promoted a Jazz Hall of Fame fitted into the renovated Carver Theater and had this museum join the institute in a Civil Rights and Cultural District. Arrington accessed federal funds through the Street Improvements Warrant Program to fill historic Kelly Ingram Park with five sculptures depicting the spring 1963 demonstrations. Although there remained the question of money, the mayor's hands-on involvement signified that funds would be forthcoming.[51]

In November 1989, DPM hired Joseph A. Wetzel and Associates of Boston to implement the thematic program of American History Workshop. DPM budgeted $2 million for the exhibits, from the introductory film to the processional exit. Wetzel sent its building exhibitory consultant Howard Littman to work with Corley, Huntley, LaMonte, Whiting, Woolfolk, and movement veteran Abraham Woods. On February 2, 1990, Wetzel Associates presented a program outline to the Steering Committee that developed Rabinowitz's ideas in "Walking to Freedom." By finding suitable artifacts and graphic materials, local people determined the content included in the exhibits. To expedite the process, DPM divided American History Workshop's thematic program into two parts with phase 1 being the story of the movement and phase 2 being the exploratory features Rabinowitz called "The Struggle Continues," which allowed visitors to resolve civil rights conflicts and cast the Birmingham story in an international framework. This division enabled Wetzel to complete the design of phase 1 by 1990. Wetzel installed the ambiguous phase 2— "Birmingham, America, the World: Civil Rights and Human Rights"—in 1994.[52]

To make the initiative permanent, Mayor Arrington formalized the Steering Committee by incorporating it as the Birmingham Civil Rights Institute Board of Directors. The mayor had decided to sell the old city-owned Social Security Center and use the $7.2 million in proceeds to pay for the construction of the building. He then informed the board that it would have to raise the money for the exhibits. In July 1990, the city council passed a resolution authorizing Arrington to award the construction contracts. The board hired professionals to raise the now estimated $4 million required to fund the exhibits. Actual work on the institute was about to begin.[53]

The program outline developed by Wetzel with the assistance of the Steering Committee had been filled in with particular design components by the fall of 1990. Wetzel's exhibitory remained true to the thematic program of American History Workshop while reflecting the artifacts and film footage provided locally. Yet Steering Committee members complained that the design failed to emphasize the "Birmingham component to all events." Wetzel complied by revising the design accordingly and presenting the final exhibit program for approval on January 30, 1991.[54]

But just as the institute moved from the design phase to the construction phase, scandals began to erupt about the financing of the project as the U.S. Attorney's Office and the Internal Revenue Service began a federal investigation into the financial relationships between city hall and minority contractors. When a grand jury subpoenaed the records of a dozen companies, including DPM; Bond, Ryder, James; Milkey and Brown; and MP Enterprises, Arrington responded by obstructing the investigation and informing the Congressional Black Caucus that he, like other elected black officials, had been targeted for harassment by the Bush administration. After a year of testimony, the grand jury indicted Marjorie Peters in July 1991 for defrauding the city of monies earmarked for the BCRI. Arrington defended her saying, "To my knowledge, the services that we paid for were rendered." In September, federal prosecutors named Arrington as an "unindicted co-conspirator" while indicting Tarlee Brown, who then confessed his guilt in a plea bargain struck for the possibility of a lenient sentence. Using the testimony of Brown, investigators prepared their case against Peters.[55]

Denouncing the "unindicted co-conspirator" charge, Arrington claimed the justice department had timed the investigation to coincide with his re-election bid for a fourth term as mayor of Birmingham. Indeed, the Peters trial started nine days before the mayoral election on October 8, 1991. Arrington faced strong opposition from an African American contender, municipal judge Emory Anthony, but the incumbent shrewdly used the investigation as a political platform, suggesting the federal government had a "personal vendetta against him." The voters agreed and returned Arrington to office. Indeed, the mayor used the charges of corruption to unify the black community behind his administration.[56]

The scandal worried the board of directors, for it occurred at the moment the institute made appeals for contributions and preparations for ground breaking. Board members questioned Marjorie Peters's role in the project and asked the mayor to clarify the relationship by providing the "dates and nature of her work" and the "dollar amount of services rendered." They received their response in the pages of the newspapers that published the details of the fraudulent activity.[57]

While the scandal temporarily tainted the mayor's role in the institute, it was not enough to stop the project from moving forward. On February 22, 1991, ground-breaking ceremonies occurred in front of the weather-beaten plywood sign that for seven years had announced the future site of the Birmingham Civil Rights Institute. City Council President Eddie Blankenship called it "holy ground." Although Vann joined Woolfolk in the symbolic turning over of dirt, Corley, Huntley, LaMonte, and Whiting were excluded from the event. In their place stood Birmingham's black leadership and movement veteran the Reverend Fred L. Shuttlesworth. Also excluded was a black protest group headed by the Reverend Tony Cooper, who complained that the poor had been left out of the planning of the institute.[58]

The board of directors regularly met during the construction of the institute. LaMonte kept track of the building schedule and proudly informed the board that the principal contractor, Interstate-Harbert, reported a minority participation rate of 40 percent. Corley chaired the committee reviewing the exhibit copy prepared by Wetzel Associates. Huntley and Whiting helped in the search for an executive director. Woolfolk worked on collaborative ventures with area schools to conduct oral interviews of movement participants. The board prepared brochures and other public relations materials explaining the purpose of the institute. Nearing the completion of programmatic work involving museum content, the board expanded from fourteen to twenty-four members to generate support from prominent African Americans. Under the leadership of Herb Sklenar, the chairman of Vulcan Materials, the board raised a $2.5 million endowment from corporate sponsors.[59]

In January 1992 Arrington's alleged role in the corruption at city hall became the focus of prosecutors as U.S. Attorney Frank Donaldson subpoenaed the mayor's appointment calendar. Arrington refused to surrender the book that possibly could show the dates and times of meetings with the already convicted co-conspirators and corroborate the testimony of Tarlee Brown. The mayor attributed the case to "racism and politics" and accused Donaldson of "targeting him because he is black." Donaldson retorted that it was Arrington who was "stoking racial tensions." The judge charged Arrington with contempt of court for failing to release the appointment book and sentenced the mayor to spend every weekend in jail for eighteen months beginning on January 23, 1992. In an act that bordered on the bizarre, Arrington joined supporters at Sixteenth Street Baptist Church, handcuffed himself to the Reverend Woods and Atlanta's Hosea Williams, and marched the three blocks to the federal courthouse. There Birmingham's mayor surrendered himself to authorities, who whisked him off to his first night in the federal penitentiary at Talladega. Twenty-four hours later, Arrington released the records and emerged from prison. Having wrapped himself in chains and retraced the route King took on his march to the Birmingham jail, Arrington assumed the moral authority of the civil rights activist, but charges of petty corruption by an elected official paled in comparison with King's principled stand against unjust laws. The questionable comparison did not stop the hundreds of Arrington supporters from waving signs that read Racism Is Corruption and We Shall Overcome.[60]

As the U.S. Attorney's office determined whether to indict Arrington on charges of corruption, Birmingham's ministers stepped into the breach to heal the racial divide polarizing the city. This time the various bishops, rabbis, and heads of the state's white denominations were joined by their black counterparts in issuing a letter of concern. Rather than chastise Arrington for his actions, the appeal reflected the white man's guilt felt by many of the letter's signers, including Corley and LaMonte. As the white Methodist minister Mike Harper explained, "We pointed fingers at ourselves." Unlike King, Arrington offered no letter in response, and he remained an "unindicted co-conspirator."[61]

The mayor used his troubles to solidify his control over the black community while staging events around the completion of the civil rights institute to reflect his own trial by fire. In September 1992 at the dedication of a renovated Kelly Ingram Park, Abraham Woods declared, "We love our mayor," and threatened to lead a march of Arrington supporters back to the federal courthouse, but he refrained at the request of the mayor, who in the name of "reconciliation" asked them to "give justice one more chance." The day before in Boutwell Auditorium, the Reverend Joseph Lowery, the president of the SCLC, had criticized the "rampant racism in the criminal justice system." The institute's board had overseen the installation of the sculptures in the park that depicted the fire hoses and police dogs placed along the new Freedom Walk. Bronze figurines crouched down in anticipation of the imaginary water or peered out from behind symbolic prison bars. Across the park, Sixteenth Street Baptist Church experienced a renaissance under the dynamic leadership of its new pastor, the Reverend Christopher Hamlin, who by September 1992 had completed a million dollar makeover of the sanctuary. The pieces of Arrington's Civil Rights Cultural District fell into place with the mayor capitalizing on each one in a crescendo leading up to the dedication of the institute.[62]

On Sunday, November 15, 1992, the Birmingham Civil Rights Institute opened phase 1 to great acclaim. Fittingly Woolfolk and LaMonte presided at the dedication of the institute, which was followed by a week-long celebration featuring remembrances and symposia, choir concerts and theatrical performances, protest meetings and church services. Arrington described the institute as marking "a Place of Revolution that has given way to Reconciliation." Creating the institute had taken thirteen years and cost $12 million, but Woolfolk and LaMonte, along with Vann, Corley, Huntley, and Whiting—all still serving on the institute's board—could take pride in the final product. The exhibitory told the local story within a national and international framework while emphasizing the centrality of Birmingham to the civil rights struggle. It deftly linked the 1963 protests with the ratification of the 1964 Civil Rights Act, which launched what Hugh Davis Graham has called the "American Rights Revolution" and in time reinforced an international human rights movement. The positive reception of the institute by the media helped secure corporate funding that financed the final components originally planned to complete the tripartite mission of exhibits, education, and archives.

When phase 2 of the museum opened in 1994, the connections between the local movement in Birmingham and an international ideology of human rights were even more starkly presented. The exhibit, "Beyond Birmingham: Human Rights around the World," which opened in 1994, transitioned the earlier individualistic call for civil rights found in phase 1 into a universal demand for equality "under the law regardless of race, beliefs, or color," to which one might add gender or sexual preference, as the message of phase 2. The brochure quotes from King's "Letter from Birmingham Jail" as the basis of its reasoning: "Injustice anywhere is a threat to justice everywhere."[63] In the exhibit, a jumble of cement blocks cut from the Berlin Wall form the structure of an installation piece of art, which includes several television monitors inserted among the rubble and tied together by barbed wire. Continuously showing on the screens are cartoon interpretations of the United Nations Human Rights Declarations with the points illustrated by internationally famous artists. In the next room life-size photographs and audio recordings of people from South Africa, India, El Salvador, and the Ukraine tell their stories of suffering for being black, female, politically active, or Jewish. This personalized representation of international human rights abuses is brought home by reminding the visitor of the historic fight for civil rights and asking him to sign "The Birmingham Pledge." Similar to the commitment cards used during the actual struggle, the pledge provides a tangible link to the past nonviolent movement but also forces one to embrace an international call for human rights.[64]

In his essay in this volume, Owen J. Dwyer suggests that the focus on international rights at the BCRI is a way to avoid discussions of current racial inequalities in the United States. But the focus on international rights reflects too a call for the ideas expressed in the civil rights movement to be spread around the world in a quest for human freedom. These links are made concrete at the Richard Arrington Resource Gallery, where the visitor ends after finishing the exhibit. The gallery contains recordings of thousands of hours of interviews with local people done as part of its oral history project; there are also links to educational resources such as the United Nation's High Commissioner for Refugees CD-ROM RefWorld, Amnesty International, and other nongovernmental organizations. Publication of site-specific lesson plans to maximize the experience of visiting school groups documents the institute's human rights pedagogy similar to that found in the Southern Poverty Law Center's *Teaching Tolerance* magazine and online materials such as the National Park Service's Teaching with Historic Places Web site. And in 2004 the facility hosted more than two hundred primary and secondary school teachers over four weeks who took part in a National Endowment for the Humanities workshop on placing the Birmingham experience in the framework of an international freedom struggle.[65]

By fulfilling Vann's admonition to place its racist past on display in a museum, the city institutionalized and then put aside its difficult heritage. The international association of the city with the civil rights struggle created the name recognition necessary to attract people traveling through Birmingham who recalled the film footage that showed the use of fire hoses and police dogs against nonviolent protesters. The institute became an immediate tourist attraction with more than 25,000 people visiting the facility in the first two weeks and nearly 70,000 walking through the museum in its first five months. Within five years over 100,000 people annually toured the institute, many of them with school and church groups from the black community although white people visited too, often as college students or connected to convention travel. Having commodified the 1963 demonstrations as a product, the institute made accessible to the informed tourist the past while inculcating values of tolerance and offering a positive message on human rights.[66]

Today, the monochromatic life-cast mannequins marching to freedom, riding on the bus, or sitting in at the lunch counter in civil rights museums in Alabama, Georgia, and Tennessee have become as ubiquitous as the limestone sentinels standing watch over county courthouses across the country. Where once public displays of white supremacy at Civil War monuments took place on Confederate and Union Memorial Days, now civil rights sites host observances of King Day. Despite the ambiguous resolution of the struggle that paradoxically showcases equality in an age of growing economic inequality, the overwhelming message in the new civic religion is one of tolerance and support for universal human rights. Constructed by financial supporters who believed the commemoration would fuel heritage tourism, the process of memorializing the movement has created a tangible expression of a new international ideology that links the American story with the universal demand for human rights.

Notes

1. On the Lost Cause, see Charles Reagan Wilson, *Baptized in Blood: The Religion of the Lost Cause, 1865–1920* (Athens: University of Georgia Press, 1980); Gaines M. Foster, *Ghosts of the Confederacy: Defeat, the Lost Cause, and the Emergence of the New South* (New York: Oxford University Press, 1987); David W. Blight, *Race and Reunion: The Civil War in American Memory* (Cambridge, Mass.: Belknap Press of Harvard University, 2001); and Kirk Savage, *Standing Soldiers, Kneeling Slaves: Race, War, and Monument in Nineteenth-Century America* (Princeton, N.J.: Princeton University Press, 1997).

2. *Birmingham Post-Herald*, November 19, 1992.

3. See "Alabama Black Heritage," brochure published by the state of Alabama. Miller quoted in *Atlanta Journal-Constitution*, January 19, 1996.

4. Birmingham Civil Rights Institute attendance totals, November 1992–March 1993, in the Birmingham Civil Rights Institute Collection, Marvin Yeomans Whiting Papers, Birmingham Public Library, Department of Archives and History, Birmingham, Alabama (hereafter referred to as BCRI Collection); *Birmingham News*, November 14, 1992; in the Winter 1993 issue of *Southern Changes*, Julian Bond wrote a wonderful piece entitled "History, Hope and Heroes" that looks at the first visitors to the institute and what they wrote in a ledger used to record the comments of tourists. By the end of its first year over 200,000 people had toured the facility; *Atlanta Journal-Constitution*, June 29, 1996.

5. Quotation from the loan agreement between the city of Birmingham and the BCRI, March 25, 1991, BCRI Collection.

6. *Birmingham Post-Herald*, November 19, 1992.

7. David Vann, interview with author, December 20, 1994; Marshall quote in Henry Hampton and Steve Fayer, *Voices of Freedom: An Oral History of the Civil Rights Movement from the 1950s through the 1980s* (New York: Bantam, 1990), 135; the best account of the Bonita Carter killing is in Jimmie Lewis Franklin, *Back to Birmingham: Richard Arrington, Jr., and His Times* (Tuscaloosa: University of Alabama Press, 1989), 92–133.

8. Franklin, *Back to Birmingham*, 3, 42–43, 46, 54, 66.

9. *Birmingham Post-Herald*, November 19, 1992; second council resolution on July 29, 1980; City of Birmingham and Operation New Birmingham, *Master Plan for Downtown Birmingham, Alabama*, December 1980. Although Arrington suggested at the opening of the institute in 1992 that "when David Vann first mentioned the idea of a civil rights museum, I became sort of enslaved by that idea," his actions suggest otherwise. Arrington and Woolfolk quoted in *Birmingham Black and White*, February 19, 1998.

10. Richard Arrington, June 16, 1981, BCRI Collection.

11. Horace Huntley, "Iron Ore Miners and Mine Mill in Alabama, 1933–1952" (PhD diss., University of Pittsburgh, 1977); see also Horace Huntley, "The Rise and Fall of Mine Mill in Alabama: The Status Quo against Interracial Unionism, 1933–1949," *The Journal of the Birmingham Historical Society* 6 (January 1979): 4–13.

12. David Vann, "Memorandum to Civil Rights Museum Committee: Concepts for Consideration," n.d., attached to "Report of Civil Rights Museum Study Committee" October 7, 1981, BCRI Collection.

13. "Report of Civil Rights Museum Study Committee," October 7, 1981, BCRI Collection.

14. Ibid.

15. *Over the Mountain Journal*, November 6, 1992; Marvin Y. Whiting to George Stewart, July 25, 1986, BCRI Collection; *Birmingham Post-Herald*, February 14, 1984.

16. *Birmingham Post-Herald*, February 14, 1984. The Discovery Place, the Southern Museum of Flight, and the Red Mountain Museum were the three other museums.

17. Ibid.

18. Ibid.; Franklin, *Back to Birmingham*, 297–305.

19. *Birmingham Post-Herald*, February 23, 1984; Glenn Eskew, "From Civil War to Civil Rights: Selling Alabama as Heritage Tourism," *International Journal of Hospitality and Tourism Administration* 2, no 3/4 (2001), reprinted in *Slavery, Contested Heritage, and Thanatourism*, ed. Graham M. S. Dann and A. V. Seaton (New York: Haworth Press, 2001), 201–14.

20. George R. Stewart to Edward LaMonte, March 28, 1984, BCRI Collection.

21. Tennant S. McWilliams to Robert Corley, April 19, 1984, and Stewart to LaMonte, May 23, 1984, BCRI Collection.

22. Edward S. LaMonte, "Proposal for a Civil Rights Pageant," [1984], BCRI Collection; on the "Trail of Tears" pageant see Richard D. Starnes, "Creating a 'Variety Vacationland': Tourism Development in North Carolina, 1930–1990," in *Southern Journeys: Tourism, History, and Culture in the Modern South*, ed. Starnes (Tuscaloosa: University of Alabama Press, 2003).

23. Edward Shannon LaMonte, *Politics and Welfare in Birmingham, 1900–1975* (Tuscaloosa: University of Alabama Press, 1995), 34, 193–98.

24. Ibid., xv–xvii; Franklin, *Back to Birmingham*, 184–87; Edward S. LaMonte, *George B. Ward: Birmingham's Urban Statesman* [an essay in honor of Mervyn H. Sterne] (Birmingham, Ala.: Birmingham Public Library, 1974), 45.

25. Marvin Whiting to Mary Besws Paluzzi, November 5, 1984, BCRI Collection.

26. *Birmingham News*, November 17, 1985.

27. The city council informally approved funding in February 1986, enabling Arrington to anticipate the building of the institute. Tarlee Brown, an Atlanta architect who headed the company Milkey and Brown and partnered with Mayor Arrington in several consulting firms worked closely with Marjorie Peters of MP Enterprises. Arrington rewarded Brown with several lucrative city contracts including the work on the Birmingham Turf Club and Boutwell Auditorium while Peters received over a million dollars worth of city contracts including the renovation of Legion Field and the landscaping of Birmingham Green. Apparently Peters told Brown that he "needed to show" his "appreciation to the mayor," so in March 1986 Brown allegedly met with Arrington and agreed to kick back to the mayor a quarter of all profits his company received on city contracts. Shortly thereafter, the mayor selected an architectural firm to build the civil rights institute. The architects then hired as consultants Marjorie Peters and Tarlee Brown. See the *Birmingham Post-Herald*, April 16, 1986; *Birmingham News*, September 5, 6, 25, 1991. City law authorizes the mayor to hire architects and project managers without going through the normal bid procedure because this work is considered professional service.

28. *Birmingham Post-Herald*, April 16, 1986; Eskew, "From Civil War to Civil Rights," *Alabama Black Heritage: A Tour of Historic Sites* (Montgomery, Ala.: Bureau of Tourism, 1983).

29. Arrington to Whiting, May 6, 1986; Mayor's Office to Birmingham City Council, May 5, 1986; Arrington to Whiting, June 10, 1986, BCRI Collection.

30. J. Max Bond to LaMonte, June 12, 1986, BCRI Collection.

31. Marjorie Peters to Participants of Birmingham Civil Rights Museum Workshop, June 19, 1986, BCRI Collection.

32. Ibid.

33. James K. Baker to LaMonte June 17, 1986, Ann Kaufman, Minutes of Birmingham Civil Rights Museum Meeting, June 21, 1986, BCRI Collection.

34. Arrington to J. Max Bond Jr., June 25, 1986, BCRI Collection.

35. Ibid.

36. *Birmingham News*, July 6, 1986; Bond Issue of 1986 flier, Tutwiler Vertical File, Southern History Collection, Birmingham Public Library.

37. Odessa Woolfolk to Task Force, July 2, 1986, minutes of July 11, 1986, meeting, BCRI Collection; *Birmingham Post-Herald*, November 19, 1992.

38. Ibid.; draft of mission statement, August 20, 1986, BCRI Collection.

39. Robert Gaines Corley, "The Quest for Racial Harmony: Race Relations in Birmingham, Alabama, 1947–1963," (PhD diss., University of Virginia, 1979). See also Corley, "In Search of Racial Harmony: Birmingham Business Leaders and Desegregation, 1950–1963," in *Southern Businessmen and Desegregation*,

ed. Elizabeth Jacoway and David R. Colburn (Baton Rouge: Louisiana State University Press, 1982), 170–90; "Racial Harmony," *Birmingham* 28 (October 1988): 40; Vann and Woolfolk served on the board of the NCCJ; mission statement, BCRI Collection.

40. Minutes of Task Force Meeting, September 18, 1986; Warren L. Ansley, memo, September 30, 1986; Summary Report of the Building Committee to the Civil Rights Museum Task Force, October 13, 1986, BCRI Collection.

41. David J. Garrow, *Bearing the Cross: Martin Luther King, Jr., and the Southern Christian Leadership Conference* (New York: William Morrow, 1986); Taylor Branch, *Parting the Waters: America in the King Years, 1954–63* (New York: Simon and Schuster, 1988); Adam Fairclough, *To Redeem the Soul of America: The Southern Christian Leadership Conference and Martin Luther King, Jr.* (Athens: University of Georgia Press, 1987); Juan Williams, *Eyes on the Prize: America's Civil Rights Years, 1954–1965* (New York: Penguin Books, 1987); Hampton and Fayer, *Voices of Freedom.*

42. After the broadcast of episode 3, "No Easy Walk," Mayor Arrington wrote Henry Hampton, the president of Blackside Production Company, which produced *Eyes on the Prize*, to ask him to donate the series so that it could "make a significant contribution to the program of the institute." Much of the film footage and many still photographs used in *Eyes on the Prize* came from the Birmingham Public Library's archives. Whiting had spent several weeks assisting Blackside in the search for materials, but when it came to content in the institute, Whiting helped the Task Force develop its own interpretation. Arrington to Henry Hampton, January 22, 1987, BCRI Collection.

43. Richard Rabinowitz to Ann Kaufman, October 31, 1986, November 13, 1986; Rabinowitz estimated it would take him thirty-nine days, for a personal total of $29,250.

44. Rabinowitz to Woolfolk and Task Force, April 8, 1987, American History Workshop "Preliminary Exhibit Plan for the Birmingham Civil Rights Institute," April 1, 1987; American History Workshop, "Walking to Freedom: The Museum of America's Civil Rights Revolution," June 1987, BCRI Collection.

45. American History Workshop, "Walking to Freedom," BCRI Collection.

46. Ibid.

47. Ibid.

48. Diversified Project Management, meeting summary of April 3, 1990; BCRI exhibitory presentation, March 22, 1990, BCRI Collection; in some ways the *Eyes on the Prize* series fits a progressive theme of American history with the triumph of movement goals realized through the 1964 and 1965 congressional reforms.

49. Woolfolk to Rabinowitz, February 3, 1988, BCRI Collection; *Birmingham Post-Herald*, October 9, 1991; October 11, 1991. The dome provided one of the problems the architects worked on.

50. According to the 2000 United States Census, Birmingham's total population in 1990 was 265,968, with 168,277 or 63 percent African American.

51. Diversified Project Management BCRI memos dated August 25, 1989, September 19, 26, October 10, 17, 1989, BCRI Collection.

52. Diversified Project Management, November 21, 1989, minutes of Steering Committee meeting held on November 9, 1989; Brenda G. Burrell of DPM to Howard Litwak of Wetzel, January 9, 1990; Gail Ringel to Brenda Burrell, February 13, 1990; BCRI memo 1 from Woolfolk to Board of Directors, March 6, 1990; Gail Ringel to Brenda Burrell, March 27, 1990; DPM memo of February 28, 1991; minutes of BCRI exhibitory presentation dated February 7, 1990, BCRI Collection.

53. Woolfolk to BCRI Board of Directors, March 12, 1990; William Gilchrist to Woolfolk, February 28, 1990, BCRI Collection.

54. *Birmingham News*, July 4, 1990; DPM memo, June 27, 1990; DPM minutes of August 29, 1990, meeting dated September 25, 1990; Wetzel memo, September 7, 1990; BCRI notes on Wetzel design, September 19, 1990; Wetzel Exhibit Program of January 30, 1991; DPM minutes of January 30, 1991, meeting dated January 30, 1991, BCRI Collection.

55. *Birmingham News*, September 5, 1991; September 6, 1991. Peters was indicted on July 26, 1991, for stealing $220,000.

56. *Birmingham Post-Herald*, September 30 1991; October 9, 1991.

57. BCRI minutes, November 15, 1990, BCRI Collection; *Birmingham News*, September 5, 1991; the U.S. Attorney's Office subpoenaed the civil rights institute records on August 30, 1990.

58. BCRI memo on ground-breaking ceremonies, February 22, 1991, BCRI Collection; *Birmingham News*, February 23, 1991.

59. BCRI minutes of October 17, 1991, May 21, 1992, July 28, 1992; BCRI memo, March 26, 1992, BCRI Collection.

60. *Atlanta Journal-Constitution*, January 23, 1992; *Birmingham News*, January 22, 24, 25, 26, 1992; *Birmingham Post-Herald*, January 21, 1992; *Time*, February 3, 1992. As *Time* recognized: "But equating the mayor with King is as bogus as comparing Donaldson to Bull Connor. . . . The racial battleground is no longer black or white, but a murky gray, and Arrington's bizarre performance only adds to the confusion and frustration."

61. *Birmingham News*, January 30, February 5, 8, 1992.

62. On the sculptor James Drake and his art see *Birmingham News*, Septem-

ber 6, 15, 16, 1992; on Hamlin and the renaissance of Sixteenth Street Baptist Church, see the *Atlanta Journal-Constitution*, September 12, 1998. Reverend Hamlin left in 2000.

63. BCRI, brochure, "Beyond Birmingham: Human Rights around the World," n.d., BCRI Collection.

64. "The Birmingham Pledge" borrows from the demands of the United Nation's Universal Declaration of Human Rights; see Paul Gordon Lauren, *The Evolution of International Human Rights* (Philadelphia: University of Pennsylvania Press, 1998), especially 204–80.

65. BCRI, "Welcome to the Richard Arrington, Jr., Resource Gallery," n.d.; "CD-ROM Titles and Internet Access," 2000; "Oral History Interviews and Other Resources," 2000, BCRI Collection; for an exploration of public and private advocacy for human rights see William Korey, *NGOs and the Universal Declaration of Human Rights: "A Curious Grapevine"* (New York: St. Martin's Press, 1998); BCRI, *Making Connections: A Curriculum Guide for Grades K–12*, 2000, BCRI Collection; since the 1980s the anti–Ku Klux Klan crusading attorney Morris Dees has arranged for his Southern Poverty Law Center to publish the biannual *Teaching Tolerance* and send it to educators free of charge. It proselytizes the new ideology and casts it in an international framework; National Endowment for the Humanities, "We the People Summer Workshop: 'Stony the Road We Trod,'" Birmingham, Alabama, June and July 2004.

66. *Birmingham Post-Herald*, November 19, 1992; Hugh Davis Graham, "Legacies of the 1960s: The American 'Rights Revolution' in an Era of Divided Governance," *Journal of Policy History* 10, no. 3 (1998): 268.

DEREK H. ALDERMAN

Street Names as Memorial Arenas

The Reputational Politics of Commemorating

Martin Luther King Jr. in a Georgia County

In 1994, African Americans in Bulloch County, Georgia, sought to have a new perimeter highway named for Martin Luther King Jr. They struggled with some military veterans, who wanted the street naming to recognize their own sacrifices and achievements. Through newspaper editorials, speeches at local government meetings, and a name-suggestion campaign, outspoken veterans were successful in representing King's historical legacy as less important and less racially inclusive than their own commemorative cause. While the debate exposed traditional racial divisions within the county, it also displayed an interesting counterintuitive pattern—because of divided loyalties, many black men went on record in support of naming the perimeter highway for veterans rather than for the slain civil rights leader.

The street naming struggle in Bulloch County was not a single, isolated event, but indicative of a growing commemorative pattern in the United States.[1] Over 730 places in the country have named roads in honor of Martin Luther King Jr. These streets are found in thirty-nine states and the District of Columbia. Over 70 percent of places with a King street are located in seven southern states (Georgia, Mississippi, Texas, Florida, Louisiana, Alabama, and North Carolina).[2] This is not surprising, given that so many civil rights organizations, campaigns, and leaders—including

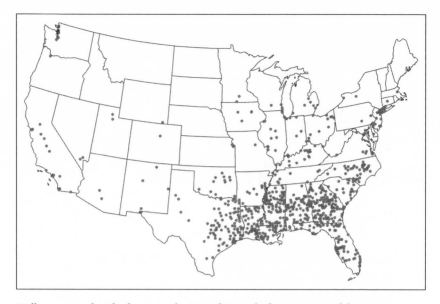

Well over seven hundred cities in the United States had a street named for Martin Luther King Jr. by 2003. Streets named for King are found everywhere from large cities such as New York, Los Angeles, and Chicago to some of the country's smallest places such as Cuba, Alabama (pop. 363), and Denton, Georgia (pop. 269). On average, African Americans constitute approximately 37 percent of the population in a location with a street named for King, and over 50 percent of Martin Luther King Jr. streets are in places with fewer than ten thousand residents. (Data compiled by Derek H. Alderman with the assistance of Matthew Mitchelson and Chris McPhilamy, August 2003)

King himself—originated in the region. Although a nationwide movement, street naming after King is proposed by local activists—usually African American—and decided by city and county leaders as they face the task of interpreting the meaning of the civil rights leader's legacy and selecting a road that is most fit or appropriate for remembering him. As Roger Stump observed in a seminal article, roads named for Martin Luther King Jr. are "public symbols of community values, attitudes, and beliefs, revealing the character of both the figure commemorated and the community that has honored him."[3]

King's commemoration is part of a larger movement on the part of black Americans to address the exclusion of their experiences from the national historical consciousness.[4] Although the past contributions of African Americans certainly do not begin or end with King, he has become the most widely identified symbol of the civil rights movement and black heritage in general. King's status rose when the federal government established a holiday to honor him in the early 1980s. In a 1999 Gallup public opinion poll, 34 percent of surveyed Americans named Martin Luther King Jr. as the most admired person of the century, placing him second only to Mother Teresa.[5] Yet just because King is a highly admired figure does not mean that his commemoration does not generate public debate. Indeed, the attaching of his name to streets and roads often evokes great controversy not only between blacks and whites but also within the African American community.[6] In part, this is because even those with great respect for the civil rights leader interpret and personally connect with his historical legacy in different and sometimes competing ways.

While street naming conflicts occur throughout the country, the debate in Bulloch County is especially instructive of how street names serve as key battlegrounds for representing King's historical image and debating his meaning and relative importance within contemporary society. Participants in Bulloch County faced three important issues as they engaged in the discussion of commemorating King. The first was the *legitimacy of commemoration*, or the politics of constructing the historical and political worth of remembering one figure or cause over another. The second was the *resonance of commemoration*, or the politics of making a commemorated figure universally relevant or resonant to the various social groups that constitute the public. The third dimension was the *hybridity of commemoration*, which refers to the political complications that can arise when social actors, specifically African American activists, have multiple and sometimes overlapping commemorative interests.

Street Names as Memorial Arenas

Street naming is an important and contentious commemorative practice that has been largely ignored until recently. Recent scholarship demonstrates that the naming of streets after historical figures and events is an important part of modern political culture; it not only provides spatial and semiotic orientation to the city, but it also serves to naturalize or legitimatize a selective vision of the past.[7] The seemingly ordinary and practical nature of street names makes the past "tangible and intimately familiar."[8] Named streets are powerful memorial spaces because they inscribe a commemorative message into many facets of daily urban life such as through road maps, phone book listings, the sending and receiving of mail, the giving of directions, advertising billboards, and of course, road signs themselves. These signs contribute significantly to the creation of a sense of place.[9]

Street names are unique and potentially politicized memorials because of their ability to touch diverse neighborhoods and social groups that may or may not identify with the person or event being memorialized.[10] Street naming is also controversial because when one version of the past is commemorated, another vision is often decommemorated. Named streets, like any place of memory, can become embroiled in the politics of defining what is historically significant or worthy of public remembrance. The naming of streets is an uneven, negotiated process open to a multiplicity of meanings and interests.[11] And while powerful elites often control the commemorative messages communicated through street names, the naming process can also serve as a form of resistance as marginalized groups seek to redefine how people interpret the past.[12] Street naming thus can become a contest about who has the power to determine how the landscape is represented and whose history will be told on that landscape.

America's street-name landscape has long served as a place for social groups, including minorities, to gain public recognition of their historical achievements.[13] Recently, however, the United States has witnessed a flurry of commemorative street-naming campaigns led by racial and ethnic groups.[14] Joseph Tilden Rhea suggested that the movement to recognize the role of minorities in American history is not simply "because of a general drift toward cultural pluralism." Rather, it is the result of direct political action by minority activists, who seek a greater identity within society by challenging white-dominated interpretations of American history and creating new representations of their past within cultural landscapes.[15]

Despite the ever-increasing importance of the street name as a platform for elevating minority heritages, little attention has been paid to the role of blacks in commemorative street naming and place naming in general. There is ample evidence that African Americans view the naming of streets as a means of asserting their historical value and legitimacy within the country. Although Martin Luther King Jr. is the figure most frequently commemorated, communities have identified streets with other notable black Americans such as Rosa Parks (Montgomery, Alabama, and Detroit, Michigan), Harriet Tubman (Columbia, Maryland; Winston-Salem, North Carolina; and Knoxville, Tennessee), Malcolm X (Brooklyn and Harlem, New York, and Dallas, Texas), and Thurgood Marshall (Kingstree, South Carolina). As Melvin Dixon so keenly observed: "Not only do these [street] names celebrate and commemorate great figures in black culture, they provoke our active participation in that history. What was important yesterday becomes a landmark today."[16]

Although street names are seemingly ordinary and mundane memorials, they represent important public spaces for remembering the civil rights movement and its heroes as well as establishing the importance of all African Americans. In recognizing their potential to provoke participation with the past, it is useful to conceptualize street names as "memorial arenas." In naming streets for King, people actively interpret his legacy and reputation and, in many instances, debate the social connotations and meaning of memorializing him.

On the Importance of Reputational Politics

A critical analysis of King's commemoration requires not only recognizing the cultural importance of street names but also understanding the politics that surround the remembrance of historical figures. Heroes and other notable historical figures play an important role in public remembrance of the past.[17] Gary Fine discussed this very point when he wrote: "By shaping images of their leaders, social groups create social mnemonics to help audiences define events within a moral context."[18] The historical image of a person—whether a hero such as Abraham Lincoln, a villain such as Benedict Arnold, or enigmatic personalities such as John Brown and Joseph McCarthy—is a social product open to multiple and competing constructions and interpretations.[19] There can be any number of different discourses or common ways of thinking and talking about a person and his or her contribution to society.

The struggle to define an individual's memorial legacy is what Fine has called "reputational politics." The historical reputation of a person is not simply made by the individual in question but also is used and controlled by social actors and groups who seek to advance their own commemorative agenda and derail the agendas of other parties.[20] Custodial agents or "reputational entrepreneurs" carry out the shaping and control of historical reputations. Fine also recognized that the "control of history may be contentious, and the claims of one group may be countered by another that wishes to interpret the same . . . person through a different lens."[21] In the politics of constructing and asserting the historical importance of commemorating one figure over another, reputational entrepreneurs engage in "discursive rivalries," the trading back and forth of statements and claims about the commemorative legitimacy and meaning of their respective heroes' reputations.[22] As this chapter illustrates, discursive rivalries over the meaning of historical figures such as King do not simply appear out of thin air, but often accompany, revolve around, and participate in the production of memorial spaces and places.

The commemoration of fallen heroes, martyrs, and great leaders has been the most common motive for designating a physical site as a "sacred" memorial space.[23] While memorial spaces affirm the importance of certain historical figures, they also offer insight into the social tensions that often underlie the remembrance of these legacies and reputations. Memorializing Martin Luther King Jr. began after his death in 1968, but he did not receive "widespread popular acclaim immediately." Indeed, it took over two decades to convert the Lorraine Motel, the site of his assassination, into a national civil rights center and museum.[24] It was not until 1976 that Atlanta, King's hometown, placed his name on a street. The majority of King streets have been named in the years following the passage of the Martin Luther King Jr. federal holiday, which brought official legitimacy to his historical reputation. The transformation of King into a national hero and the creation of memorial spaces in his honor have occurred only after many years of opposition and debate.

The Politics of Remembering King in America

As with other major figures in American history, public memory of King is the result of ongoing negotiation and debate within society. In King's case, many of these debates have revolved around the designation of his birthday as a holiday, both at the federal and state level.[25] Before being passed in 1983, the federal holiday was the center of heated discussion in the U.S. Senate, with opponents accusing King of being a communist and having extramarital affairs.[26] But even before the holiday proposal ever made it to the floor of the Senate it had traveled a long and arduous journey through a variety of political struggles. Passage of the holiday came fifteen years after Representative John Conyers (D-Mich.) first proposed the idea in legislation and thirteen years after Congress received an unprecedented six million signatures in support. Perhaps the most interesting of these commemorative struggles took place within the African American community between members of the Southern Christian Leadership Conference (SCLC) and the civil rights leader's wife, Coretta Scott King. While the SCLC sought to honor their recently fallen leader through increased social activism and protest, Mrs. King placed more emphasis on establishing the King Center in Atlanta, Georgia, and favoring calls to establish a holiday in her husband's memory. The two parties even differed on when best to commemorate the civil rights leader—while the SCLC focused on April 4, the date of King's death, the King family preferred January 15, the date of his birth.[27]

While King's annual commemoration is more accepted now than in the past, it remains a contested terrain in many communities. Ceasar McDowell has described the still controversial nature of the King holiday: Martin Luther King "may have spoken the common language of human dignity. But to many white people, he remains primarily a black man, and his birthday a black holiday, for black people."[28] African Americans in Memphis were outraged by a McDonald's restaurant calendar that labeled January 16, 1989, as "National Nothing Day."[29] In May 2000, Jesse Jackson visited Wallingford, Connecticut, to mark a new state law forcing the town to observe the King holiday. Wallingford had been the only town in the state that still kept its offices open on the holiday. During his visit,

Jackson confronted a group of white supremacists opposed to King's commemoration, citing the group as proof that there is "unfinished business" in the struggle for civil rights.[30] While more of the country's businesses are recognizing the holiday, only 26 percent give a paid day off to their employees.[31] Nor do African Americans all agree on how to observe King's birthday. For example, in 1998, a rift emerged in Houston's black community as two factions struggled over which one should organize and lead a parade to mark the Martin Luther King holiday. African American leaders also disagreed about the extent to which the civil rights leader's memory should be "commercialized."[32]

Controversy over the legacy of Martin Luther King Jr. has not been confined to the making and observing of holidays. In Memphis, Tennessee, black activist Jacqueline Smith has spent over a decade protesting the conversion of the Lorraine Motel into the National Civil Rights Museum. Her protest has been literally street politics in that she has lived, eaten, and slept on the sidewalk across the street from the museum.[33] She advertises the museum as the "National Civil Wrong Museum," distributes protest literature, and provides museum visitors with an alternative vision of how to commemorate King. According to Smith, "The best monument to Dr. Martin Luther King Jr. would be a center at the Lorraine offering housing, job training, free community college, health clinic or other services for the poor."[34] While Smith's protests take place outside the civil rights museum in Memphis, more subtle yet no less important struggles occur within civil rights museums and memorials. As Owen J. Dwyer notes elsewhere in this volume, there is frequently a tension in civil rights memorials between the commemoration of local, grassroots participants versus charismatic, national leaders such as King. While King's prominence in these memorial landscapes is consistent with the tendency of public historians to stress the importance of individual leaders, it has led to historical neglect of lesser-known civil rights activists, particularly women.[35] King is, of course, not always the focus of civil rights commemoration. At the civil rights museum in Savannah, Georgia, local mobilization efforts are given much greater attention than King and the larger national movement. Arguably, this reflects the fact that African Americans in Savannah were able to carry out several successful protests in the

Debates over how best to memorialize Martin Luther King Jr. occur not just between blacks and whites but also within the African American community. One of the most interesting examples of this is Jacqueline Smith's protest of the National Civil Rights Museum in Memphis, Tennessee, ongoing since 1988. Smith was the last resident of the Lorraine Motel—the site of King's assassination—before its conversion from low-income housing to the museum and tourist attraction. She argues that the museum does not embody or truly commemorate the ideals and beliefs of the slain civil rights leader, who would never have allowed the displacement of poor people for the purpose of establishing a memorial. (Photograph by Derek H. Alderman)

1960s without significant outside leadership. In some instances, they actually opposed King's direct involvement in these protests.[36] Black Americans connect with King's historical reputation in multiple and sometimes contradictory ways, particularly when it involves weighing his reputation against other commemorative interests that are of equal or greater importance.

Like holidays, museums, and other memorials dedicated to King's memory, street names serve as important arenas for debating how King is best remembered.[37] In Americus, Georgia, city officials did not rename a portion of U.S. Highway 19 until black community leaders planned a boycott of city businesses. The controversy in Americus was made worse by the comments of an assistant fire chief, who said that he did not oppose naming half of the street for King if the other half was named for James Earl Ray, the man convicted of assassinating the civil rights leader.[38] In Dade City, Florida, vandals painted the name "General Robert E. Lee" over nine Martin Luther King Jr. Boulevard signs, an incident symptomatic of the South's ongoing struggles over identity and memory. In a single year, almost one hundred street signs with King's name in Hillsborough County, Florida, were either spray painted, shot at, or pulled completely from their poles.[39] These controversies are not confined to the South. African Americans in Milwaukee protested and marched against the city's decision to restrict the naming of Martin Luther King Jr. Drive to the boundaries of the black community, a common complaint among black activists across the nation.[40] And in Portland, Oregon, in 1990, a debate erupted when the city council voted to rename Union Avenue after King. Over two dozen people picketed and heckled the street-naming ceremony and more than fifty thousand people signed a petition opposing the name change. Because of this backlash, Portland voters were to be given a chance to vote on an initiative in an upcoming primary election that would change the name of the street back to Union Avenue, but before the election was held, a county circuit judge ruled that placing such an initiative on the ballot was illegal.[41]

Despite the growing frequency and controversial nature of commemorating King, scant attention has been devoted to examining how individual communities debate and struggle over the street-naming issue. This case study of Bulloch County provides an opportunity to fill this void and analyze some of the issues that shape the "reputational politics" of defining the historical importance and social relevance of King's memory.

Commemorating King in Bulloch County, Georgia

Although the historical significance of King is certainly not limited to one state, Georgia serves as a useful context within which to study his commemoration. Georgia has the largest number of places with a street named after him.[42] Further, since King was born in Atlanta, which is now the location of a national historic site that recounts his life and work, he recently was recognized as "Georgian of the Century."[43] Despite these strong historical connections, African Americans across Georgia have faced significant controversy and opposition when attempting to attach King's name and memory to streets and roads.[44] Perhaps no location illustrates this fact better than Bulloch County, where black activists carried out two unsuccessful street-naming campaigns before finally succeeding in late 2002. The first of these two campaigns is the focus of this discussion. By examining where street naming has failed rather than succeeded, we can perhaps gain greater insight into the challenges that confront African Americans as they engage in the politics of redefining public representation of the past, particularly King's meaning and importance within contemporary society.

Bulloch County is located approximately seventy miles west of the Atlantic Ocean. It lies between the two population centers of Macon, in central Georgia, and Savannah, on the coast. Statesboro is the county seat, the location of Georgia Southern University, and the setting for many of the political struggles described in this chapter. According to 2000 U.S. Census data, Statesboro has a population of 22,698 while Bulloch County's population is 55,983. Although African Americans do not constitute a majority, they have a significant presence in both the city (with 41 percent of the population) and the county (29 percent). The Bulloch case also allows for an analysis of the "reputational politics" of commemorating Martin Luther King Jr. within a predominantly rural county. According to sociologists Bruce Williams and Bonnie Thornton Dill, persistent inequality characterizes African Americans in the rural South, and the exclusion of southern blacks is most pronounced at the county level, the scale of analysis of this study.[45] Journalistic reports, moreover, have tended to focus on urban areas where the naming of streets after King is perhaps best represented, although the practice is also common in nonmetropolitan areas.[46] At least in the case of Georgia, there is strong historical evidence that there are stark differences between black activism in rural and urban areas.[47]

On February 1, 1994, a special committee of the local chapter of the National Association for the Advancement of Colored People (NAACP) requested that the Bulloch County Board of Commissioners name the then-unfinished perimeter road after Martin Luther King Jr. Although some suggestions had been made in passing, this constituted the first formal request to name the highway. Because the road would run through both the city (Statesboro) and the county, a joint perimeter-naming committee was organized. Then, at a county commission meeting a month later, a representative of the local American Legion officially requested that the road be named "Veterans Memorial Parkway" in honor of area military veterans.[48] Recognizing the politically contested nature of naming the perimeter road, the joint city-county naming committee asked citizens to mail in name suggestions. From these suggestions, the committee would recommend two names (a primary and a secondary suggestion) to be considered by both the city and county governments. Yet, as the committee pointed out and as was eventually realized, a high number of suggestions would not guarantee that one particular road name would be favored over another.[49]

Bulloch County residents mailed in 2,196 suggestions, offering more than 100 different names. Of the suggestions submitted, 1,680 (or 77 percent) wanted the perimeter named "Veterans Memorial." Over 18 percent of submissions suggested naming the road after Paul Nessmith, a farmer and former state representative currently living in the county. (Nessmith would later be eliminated from consideration because he was not deceased.) Only 72 (or 3.3 percent) suggestions called for naming the perimeter for Martin Luther King Jr. Behind King in the number of suggestions was Bulloch Memorial Parkway with seven (or 0.32 percent) suggestions. There appeared to be concerted support for having the perimeter's name serve as a memorial in some way since the memorializing of veterans and King combined assumed almost 80 percent of submitted suggestions. An additional 12 suggestions requested that the word "Memorial" be included in the road's name more generally, as in the cases of Bulloch Memorial Parkway, Mémorial Scenic Parkway, and Memorial Parkway.[50]

At first glance, the low number of suggestions submitted for naming the perimeter for King would indicate indifference on the part of the African American community. Although blacks accounted for more than 25 percent of the county's population at this time, little more than 3 percent of submissions called for the perimeter to be identified with King.

But the low number may reflect, instead, the manner in which the suggestion campaign was advertised. From all indications, the call for road name suggestions was announced only a few times in the local newspaper. Rather than interpreting these mail-in results as showing weak support for King, it may be more useful to see them as showing very strong, mass-organized support for memorializing veterans. In fact, the vast majority of the suggestions for "Veterans Memorial" came in as form letters. As will be discussed later, King's weak following in the suggestion campaign may also be indicative of the extent to which African Americans battled a divided loyalty between commemorating King versus military veterans. Nevertheless, the low quantitative support for King should not divert our attention away from the qualitative value of analyzing the efforts and comments of individual "reputational entrepreneurs" and the "discursive rivalry" that took place between African Americans and veterans over defining King's historical legacy and the appropriateness of naming a road for him.

After the June 1, 1994, deadline for the submission of suggestions, the perimeter-naming committee members reduced the one hundred suggested road names down to five. These suggestions were placed on a line ballot and ranked one through five in order of committee members' preference. The committee then submitted the two highest-ranking names to the city and county governments for a vote. The committee preferences from highest to lowest were Bulloch Memorial Parkway, Veterans Memorial Parkway, University Parkway, Bulloch Heritage Parkway, and Martin Luther King Jr. Parkway. Preference for Memorial Parkway, University Parkway, and Bulloch Heritage Parkway perhaps reflected attempts to sidestep the controversial decision of choosing a memorial either to veterans or King. For example, County Commissioner Bird Hodges, a member of the perimeter-naming committee, supported the name "Bulloch Heritage Parkway" because this appellation would serve a "memorial umbrella" for all causes and heroes without elevating one over the other. Despite the numerical results of the original mail-in suggestion campaign, the naming committee chose to recommend the names Bulloch Memorial and Veterans Memorial Parkway to the Statesboro City Council and the Bulloch County Board of Commissioners.[51] Thus, despite a disagreement between city and county officials and last-minute lobbying on the part of African American leaders, the new perimeter highway was eventually designated Veterans Memorial Parkway.[52]

Newspaper and government archives, interviews with several participants in the struggle, and written suggestions submitted by citizens to the perimeter-naming committee provide a means of identifying multiple and competing discourses about King as a historical figure, his reputation or legacy, and the resonance of this legacy to contemporary social life.[53] Doing so exposes how common-sense beliefs about King's memory are represented and made socially important through the public dialogue about street naming. In Bulloch County debates, at least three factors shaped the "reputational politics" of commemorating Martin Luther King Jr. through street naming: the legitimacy of commemoration, the resonance of commemoration, and the hybridity of commemoration.

The Legitimacy of Commemoration

Dydia DeLyser has discussed how authenticity is not an inherent condition or quality but a notion that has different meanings to different people in various social and spatial contexts.[54] Historical legitimacy—while often represented as a universal and objective standard—is similarly open to competing constructions. In the case of naming a street for King in Bulloch County, the first and perhaps most obvious barrier was the belief held by opponents that memorializing Martin Luther King Jr. was less important or less legitimate than other competing historical figures or commemorative causes. Specifically, supporters of naming the perimeter for King found themselves in a struggle with the local chapter of the American Legion. While carried out on many fronts, local newspaper editorials and letters to the editor were a common platform for struggles to determine the primacy of commemorating King versus veterans.

After the initiation of the mail-in suggestion campaign, school board member Charles Bonds (an African American) attempted to establish the legitimacy of naming the perimeter after King. In a May 22, 1994, letter to the editor, he reminded readers that King had been awarded a Nobel Peace Prize in 1964 for his nonviolent campaign against racism. In building a reputational account of King's legacy of equality and justice, Bonds also pointed to the moral authority and public image that Bulloch County stood to gain (or lose) in deciding whether or not to commemorate the civil rights leader:

> Isn't it ironic that we, the citizens of Bulloch County, have minimized and viewed as mediocre what Dr. King has done for our country in fostering equality? His fight for equality and justice has not only led to racial equality but human equality. South Africans, blacks, coloreds, whites, Indians, and others have come to grips with the recognition of the importance of equality and justice. . . . Can't we dedicate a minuscule portion of our county's constructions in memory of Georgia's and the world's greatest citizen? . . . Name the new bypass "The Martin Luther King Jr. Boulevard" and let visitors and newcomers to our fine community know that we value equality and justice for all who may drive on the named highway.[55]

In a letter to the editor a week later, local veteran Edgar Godfrey reacted to Bonds's comments, calling into question the legitimacy of King's dedication to peace rather than equality: "If his [Bonds's] criteria is to honor this road with the name of someone who has been designated as a 'peacemaker,' let us honor the truly great peacemakers of our locality—the veterans who gave their lives or endured great physical hardship to preserve our continued peace and freedom. As a former combat infantryman, I salute the veterans of all races and propose that the new perimeter road be named 'Veterans Memorial Parkway' in their honor."[56]

What is perhaps most evident in Godfrey's statement is the implication that King is somehow not "truly great" or somehow less worthy of commemoration than war veterans. Ray Hendrix, leader of Bulloch County's American Legion chapter, articulated this belief much more firmly, when he lobbied the city council to name the perimeter for veterans. Hendrix proved to be an especially powerful "reputational entrepreneur" in not only legitimizing the cause of veterans but also delegitimizing King's commemoration. For example, Hendrix was quoted as saying: "I respect Dr. King's accomplishments but the soldiers and sailors who fought for America's freedom helped make it possible for Martin

Luther King to be a great man."[57] In Hendrix's statement is an attempt to represent the achievements of King as not only subordinate to, but also dependent on, the historical legacy of veterans.

In the reputational politics of representing King's commemoration as less important, Hendrix further connected the legitimacy of his memorial cause to the idea that area veterans had long been overlooked in terms of public recognition: "We've [veterans] supported everything in this county. Veterans of Bulloch County do volunteer work, support scouting, support other community programs and nothing has ever been dedicated on behalf of the veterans. Veterans of this county include all citizens, represent all people, and naming the road Veterans' Memorial Parkway is the least you can do."[58]

As seen here, the politics of memory engage not only marginalized social groups such as African Americans contesting the hegemonic order for power to reconstruct collective memories of the past. The politics of memory also involve competition with other groups, such as veterans, who also perceive themselves as "subordinate" to the prevailing commemorative powers. Indeed, several mail-in suggestions submitted to the perimeter-naming committee expressed the sentiment that honoring veterans represented a justifiable cause. Two supporters of "Veterans Memorial Parkway" wrote: "I am writing in support of this idea [naming the perimeter for veterans], as we know there are many veterans who served our country that have never gotten the recognition they deserve. This would certainly be a fitting tribute to everyone who has served in the uniform of our country" and "As you know, we have thousands of veterans living and working in the Statesboro/Bulloch County area. Many of them served our country at a very unpopular time. . . . I believe this would be a fitting way to finally say 'Thank You.'"[59]

Running throughout these statements is a belief that naming the perimeter could correct an unequal relationship between veterans and the larger community. But supporters of Martin Luther King Jr. also used this type of argument. Although writing in very subtle terms, the author of the following mail-in suggestion defined the legitimacy of naming a road after King in terms of its ability to inscribe a new vision of race relations into the landscape: "I want to convey my personal suggestion to name the road: Martin Luther King Parkway. I agree that this naming would affirm an important segment of our Statesboro and county population and would be a healing and unifying act."[60] The implication here is that attaching King's name to the perimeter highway will "unify" and "heal" the rift between African Americans and the larger city and county population. In order for street naming to facilitate such healing, people must personally identify with the social group and their commemorative cause. Building public identification with the past is not simply a matter of defining the legitimacy of a commemorative movement. As argued in the next section, it is also a matter of resonance.

The Resonance of Commemoration

In struggling to name streets, African American activists confront the barrier that not everyone feels that King's commemoration has resonance or relevance in their lives. Resonance, as Michael Schudson has pointed out, is a key factor in shaping the ultimate power of a cultural object.[61] The extent to which the reputation of a figure resonates with the public determines, in large measure, the cultural influence of that historical representation and the population that will have its identity defined by this commemoration. Events in Bulloch County illustrate how variation in public identification with King affected the struggle to rename a street after him.

The importance of resonance to the commemoration was evident in comments presented earlier. According to veterans Godfrey and Hendrix, each of their respective suggestions would represent a wider population than if the road were named for King. Godfrey, for example, stated that he wanted to name the perimeter in such a way as to honor "the veterans of both races." Hendrix, in advocating "Veterans Memorial Parkway," stated that veterans "represent all people." These comments imply that naming the perimeter after King is a symbol that resonates only with African Americans. In contrast, naming the perimeter in honor of veterans, they insist, is a biracial or multicultural symbolic project. The idea that the commemorative cause of veterans cuts across race and other lines of identity was articulated very well in an anonymous suggestion to the perimeter-naming committee: "To be fair and impartial to all peoples, I suggest we go with the name of 'Veterans Memorial Parkway.' This name would be all inclusive of males, females, all races, color, creeds, and all wars and skirmishes. With this name no one could claim they have been left out or not considered, for all families have, or have had a veteran in their family at some time."[62]

Thus, "Veterans Memorial Parkway" was represented as a "one-commemoration-fits-all" type of naming, one that would unify rather than divide the city and county's population. Of course, the implication, then, is that naming the perimeter after King would not offer such unity. The widespread nature of this belief was further substantiated when I interviewed a Statesboro city planner, who also serves as a pastor in one of the county's African American churches:

> *Alderman:* Why did the city council vote to name the perimeter for veterans rather than for MLK?
>
> *City Planner:* Members [of the city council] felt veterans represented a larger community than King. However, Dr. King stood for everyone, fighting for the poor. Poverty knows no race.[63]

The reputational politics of commemorating King through street naming are shaped by a prevailing assumption that his historical relevance is limited to the black community and that streets named for him represent only African Americans. As illustrated in the city planner's comments, however, African Americans countered by emphasizing the universal importance of King's legacy. This city planner built a class-based reputational account of the civil rights leader, reminding us how issues of poverty and economic inequality dominated the last years of King's life and career. For blacks in Bulloch County as well as across the country, the politics of commemorating King are about building an image of the civil rights leader that resonates across racial boundaries. Another anonymous letter sent to the perimeter-naming committee put forth the idea that King's importance was not limited to one race or even one country: "I think that Martin Luther King had profound effects on *all of America*. He was an inspirer and friend whose love helped to change the *attitudes of the world*. He has enlightened so many lives with his on-living dream. I think the road should be named MLK Drive. Having the Drive named such would express the thanks he deserves."[64]

In the struggle to define the public resonance of commemorating veterans over King, even timing played an important role. The deadline for submitting perimeter-name suggestions to the Bulloch County government ended on June 1, 1994, only a few days after Memorial Day. More important, however, June 6, 1994, marked the fiftieth anniversary of D-day. The local newspaper carried veterans-related articles in the weeks preceding and coinciding with the D-day anniversary. One of the anonymous suggestions submitted to the perimeter-naming committee on May 30, 1994, reflected how the naming of the perimeter was considered in close relation to the veterans' holiday: "As we have participated in our local observation of Memorial Day and seen it celebrated nationwide, what better tribute we can pay the memory of those who have served and died than to name this road in their honor? *It seems a right time.*"[65]

It is quite possible that the Memorial Day celebration and the anticipation of the D-day anniversary expanded the resonance of honoring veterans due to the power of holidays to focus briefly, but intensely, public attention and identification. In this instance, street naming has to be examined within the larger commemorative genre that it shares with holidays. Of course, African Americans have used this same relationship to their own commemorative advantage. For instance, the original request by African Americans to name the perimeter after King took place on February 1, 1994, only two weeks after the celebration of the King federal holiday.

The Hybridity of Commemoration

Lawrence Berg and Robin Kearns have suggested that the positions and identities of cultural actors involved in place naming are often ambiguous, complexly intertwined, and sometimes contradictory.[66] There can be hybridity and interdependence in people's geographic interests, thus leading to some rather unexpected political formations. The politics of naming Bulloch County's perimeter road cannot be understood without considering the multipositionality of African Americans within the debate to memorialize Martin Luther King Jr. versus military veterans. King's memory, while certainly important, was not the only commemorative cause that African Americans had an interest in pursuing.

In my informal conversations with African American leaders in Bulloch County, few criticized the right of veterans to be commemorated through street naming, although many asserted the greater necessity of memorializing King. Some African Americans found themselves in a difficult ideological position as supporters of honoring both King and veterans. According to a local American Legion leader, many black men signed letters of support for naming the perimeter for veterans.[67] Further, women accounted for the majority (or 66 percent) of the nonanonymous suggestions sent to the naming committee and many of the suggestions came from women's organizations such as the Negro Business and Professional Women Club and the Rain or Shine Social Club. Historically, women have often taken a leading role in commemorative campaigns. However, the weak presence of suggestions sent by men may be indicative of the commemorative tug-of-war in which African American veterans found themselves.

This issue of commemorative hybridity was brought into sharper focus during an interview with an African American pastor who had spoken in support of naming the perimeter highway for Martin Luther King Jr. at county commission and city council meetings. He described the difficulty in "placing" himself within the debate over commemorating veterans versus King:

> *Alderman:* How did you feel about the perimeter being named for veterans instead of King?
>
> *African American Pastor:* I wanted King's name on the perimeter road but I couldn't feel bad about honoring veterans. . . . When they named the perimeter for veterans, I was touched. I am a veteran and I have people [family] who were killed in war. . . . We walk around this country free because somebody died. When you come up with something for veterans, there are not many people who are going to fight that, even though you want the other part [King's commemoration]. . . . We should honor those who sacrificed so much.

Alderman: When you see Veterans Memorial Parkway, do you identify with it?

African American Pastor: You believe it! And not just me. A lot of black veterans identify with it. You are not going to find a young man who served [in the military] who doesn't.[68]

These comments illustrate how the politics of naming streets after King were complicated by the fact that some reputational entrepreneurs found themselves caught in the middle of two commemorative campaigns with which they identified and that they perhaps supported.

In the case of the pastor I interviewed, the reputational politics of naming the perimeter became so hybrid and intertwined that he saw similarities in both commemorative causes, drawing strong connections between King's quest for justice and the role of veterans in fighting for freedom. On this point he said, "Dr. King wanted justice and he gave his life for it. That is what the soldier was fighting for. If that man Hitler had won, we wouldn't have any justice. That's why I went [to war]. I went because I wanted my children to live in a free country. And that's what he [King] was doing. It's the same thing. Rather than being a war in a foreign country, it was someone working for peace right here in the U.S."[69] The pastor did not recognize the potential contradictions of comparing King's efforts to achieve peace—based on a philosophy of nonviolence and passive resistance—with the efforts of veterans to win peace through violent warfare. Nor did he mention King's controversial opposition to the Vietnam War. Instead, he created a reputational account that found commonality in King's death for freedom and the personal sacrifice of military veterans, making an analogy between the fight for civil rights in the United States to the fight in Europe to topple Hitler. Regardless of whether these comments are representative of other African Americans or not, they provide keen insight into how one black veteran interpreted and represented the meaning of King's legacy and reputation in the face of choosing between two commemorations near and dear to his heart. From a political standpoint, the representation of King as another soldier in the war against injustice and oppression poses problems to the extent to which African Americans can represent the civil rights leader's legacy as more legitimate and more resonant than the memory of military veterans. It is perhaps important to recognize that the reputational politics of memorializing King, or any historical figure for that matter, is a path-dependent process, in which commemorative images of the past are constructed and realized dialogically in the context of other memorials.[70]

Three years after their struggle with military veterans, black leaders again pursued the naming of a street after Martin Luther King Jr. Like the first attempt, this one also proved unsuccessful. The second naming campaign resurrected many of the same questions faced by activists in 1994, particularly: how is the politics of memorializing King a struggle to establish the historical legitimacy and cross-racial resonance of the civil rights leader? In their second time around, however, African American leaders encountered at least three additional issues that shaped the "reputational politics" of naming a road for King—location, economics, and race.

Rather than competing for the right to name a new road, African American leaders in 1997 faced the challenge of choosing a street to *rename*. They chose a large commercial thoroughfare (Northside Drive), resisting calls from many whites and some blacks to rename a smaller street largely within the black community. In the eyes of many of these activists, the renaming of a prominent road was appropriate given the historical importance they placed on King and his achievements. In contrast, renaming a smaller, less-visible street represented a degradation of King's commemorative image. Clearly, location played a key role in defining the historical reputation of the civil rights leader and the social importance of his commemoration.

In contrast to the first street-naming attempt, African American activists in 1997 encountered great opposition from nonresidential and business interests. In fact, several business owners along Northside Drive circulated a petition that completely disrupted plans to name the street for King. While these owners cited the economic cost of changing their addresses, they also expressed fear that having a MLK address would hurt business activity because customers might see their commercial establishments as being located in a "black" part of the city. Whatever the motivations or stated reasons, opponents weighed or appraised the reputation and image of King in direct relation to how it might affect economic development and the flow of capital along the road in question.

Race-based interpretations of King's importance certainly played a role in the failure of the first street-naming attempt in Bulloch County. Yet, participants in the second debate addressed the issue of racism much more explicitly. When a local leader of the NAACP officially proposed that Northside Drive be renamed, he represented King's commemoration as a way of correcting a long-standing imbalance in power between blacks and whites in the county. In asserting the legitimacy of King to the public, this same activist cited examples of local roads that bore the names of white figures from the past. Ironically, claims of racism did not come just from blacks in Bulloch County. Some outspoken whites represented the second street-naming proposal as a racist act by African Americans, equating it to what they saw as other preferential, "color-conscious" practices such as affirmative action.[71] Although there is a danger in analyzing King's commemoration through street naming in strictly racial terms, there are certainly instances in which racism and ideas about race play important roles.

The events in Bulloch County are not necessarily indicative of struggles found in all communities that pursue the commemoration of King through street naming, and this case study should be seen as illustrative rather than representative. This chapter raises some questions that, for the most part, require additional investigation in a variety of empirical contexts. Commemorative street names—like the roads they identify—traverse numerous social actors and groups—all of which hold different and sometimes competing interpretations of the past and its meaning to them. Although less ornate and ostentatious than other memorials to the civil rights movement such as monuments and museums, naming streets after Martin Luther King Jr. gives insight into how the historical memory of the movement has been incorporated into the very language of the city and its inhabitants. Moreover, the politics of these streets also help in evaluating society's relative progress in fulfilling the civil rights leader's "dream" of racial equality and social integration.

On the one hand, the widespread presence of MLK streets across the United States, particularly in places where African Americans have a

Perhaps no intersection so clearly encapsulates the tensions and contestations that occur in the arena of street naming as this crossing of Martin Luther King Street and Jeff Davis Avenue in Selma, Alabama. Here an effort to commemorate the best-known leader of the civil rights movement coexists with a public celebration of the president of the Confederate States of America. (Courtesy of Owen J. Dwyer)

significant presence, is a testament to the increased cultural and political power of the black community as well as the liberalization of white attitudes. On the other hand, naming a street for King is often contentious, particularly when it challenges long-standing racial and economic boundaries—the very same boundaries that civil rights leaders such as King had hoped to destroy. The contested nature of street names prompts one to consider how the civil rights movement, both in terms of how it has changed society and how it is remembered, is an evolving and unfinished project. Indeed, remembrance of Martin Luther King is still not complete in Bulloch County, even though government officials and African American leaders worked together in 2002 to finally rename a street for him. While many people thought a named street was long overdue, some opponents questioned the extent to which the chosen street (located in a poor, largely African American part of Statesboro) was prominent enough to bear King's name.[72] This street, like many others across America, is more than just a static monument to the civil rights movement; it is also an arena for people to actively define and debate the movement's legacy.

Notes

This essay was published in an earlier form in *Historical Geography* 30 (2002): 49–120. It has been reprinted and revised with permission. I wish to thank

Daniel B. Good, who assisted me in conducting interviews and carrying out archival research in Bulloch County, Georgia. Finally, I owe a debt of thanks to Andrew J. Herod, Barry Schwartz, Donna G'Segner Alderman, and Dydia DeLyser, who read and commented on earlier drafts of this manuscript.

1. Derek H. Alderman, "A Street Fit for a King: Naming Places and Commemoration in the American South," *Professional Geographer* 52, no. 4 (2000): 672–84.

2. Data collected in 2004 by Matthew Michelson, Christopher McPhilamy, and Derek H. Alderman from *American Business Disc*, http://www.mapblast .com, and http://www.melissadata.com.

3. Roger W. Stump, "Toponymic Commemoration of National Figures: The Cases of Kennedy and King," *Names* 36, no. 3/4 (1988): 215.

4. Joseph Rhea referred to this ongoing movement to recognize minority heritages as the "Race Pride Movement." He suggested that African Americans were the "initial catalyst for the Race Pride Movement and their impact on American collective memory has been greater than any other (racial/ethnic) group." Joseph Tilden Rhea, *Race Pride and the American Identity* (Cambridge, Mass.: Harvard University Press, 1997), 113.

5. Frank Newport, "Mother Teresa Voted by American People as Most Admired Person of the Century," *Gallup News Service*, December 31, 1999, http://www.gallup.com/poll/releases/pr991231b.asp (accessed May 2002).

6. Derek H. Alderman, "Street Names and the Scaling of Memory: The Politics of Commemorating Martin Luther King Jr. within the African American Community," *Area* 35, no. 2 (2003): 163–73.

7. Maoz Azaryahu, "The Power of Commemorative Street Names," *Environment and Planning D: Society and Space* 14 (1996): 311–30; Maoz Azaryahu, "German Reunification and the Politics of Street Names: The Case of East Berlin," *Political Geography* 16, no. 6 (1997): 479–93.

8. Azaryahu, "The Power of Commemorative Street Names," 321.

9. Barbara A. Weightman, "Sign Geography," *Journal of Cultural Geography* 9, no. 1 (1988): 53–70.

10. Alderman, "A Street Fit for a King," 672–84.

11. Brenda S. Yeoh, "Street-Naming and Nation-Building: Toponymic Inscriptions of Nationhood in Singapore," *Area* 28, no. 3 (1996): 298–307.

12. J. Carlos Gonzáles Faraco and Michael Dean Murphy, "Street Names and Political Regimes in an Andalusian Town," *Ethnology* 36, no. 2 (1997): 123–48.

13. Amana Seligman, "The Street Formerly Known as Crawford," *Chicago History* 29, no. 3 (2001): 36–51, 37.

14. Ramón Chacón, "Cesar Chavez Boulevard: Efforts to Suppress a Commemoration and Chicano Political Empowerment in Fresno, California," *Latino Studies Journal* 6, no. 2 (1995): 73–93.

15. Rhea, *Race Pride and the American Identity*, 5–7.

16. Melvin Dixon, "The Black Writer's Use of Memory," in *History and Memory in African American Culture*, ed. Geneviève Fabre and Robert O'Meally (New York: Oxford University Press, 1994), 18–27, 20.

17. Barry Schwartz, "Memory as a Cultural System: Abraham Lincoln in World War II," *American Sociological Review* 61, no. 5 (1996): 908–27; Barry Schwartz, "Memory as a Cultural System: Abraham Lincoln in World War I," *International Journal of Sociology and Social Policy* 17, no. 6 (1997): 22–58.

18. Gary A. Fine, "John Brown's Body: Elites, Heroic Embodiment, and the Legitimation of Political Violence," *Social Problems* 46, no. 2 (1999): 225–49, 226.

19. Gary Daynes, "History, Amnesia, and the Commemoration of Joseph McCarthy in Appleton, Wisconsin," *Locus* 8, no. 1 (1995): 41–64; Lori J. Ducharme and Gary A. Fine, "The Construction of Nonpersonhood and Demonization: Commemorating the Traitorous Reputation of Benedict Arnold," *Social Forces* 73, no. 4 (1995): 1309–31; Schwartz, "Memory as a Cultural System: Abraham Lincoln in World War II"; Fine, "John Brown's Body."

20. Gary A. Fine, "Reputational Entrepreneurs and the Memory of Incompetence: Melting Supporters, Partisan Warriors, and Images of President Harding," *American Journal of Sociology* 101, no. 5 (1996): 1159–93.

21. Fine, "Reputational Entrepreneurs and the Memory of Incompetence," 1161–62.

22. Ibid., 1160.

23. Kenneth Foote, *Shadowed Ground: America's Landscapes of Violence and Tragedy* (Austin: University of Texas Press, 1997).

24. Foote, *Shadowed Ground*, 75.

25. Nicholas O. Alozie, "Political Intolerance and White Opposition to a Martin Luther King Holiday in Arizona," *Social Science Journal* 32, no. 1 (1995): 1–16; Erik D. Potholm, "Passing the King Holiday in Arizona," *Campaigns and Elections* 14, no. 4 (1993): 26–27; "New Hampshire Governor Signs MLK Holiday into Law," *Boston Globe*, June 8, 1999, sec. B, 8.

26. "Honoured But Still Controversial," *Economist*, October 22, 1983, 23–24.

27. Gary Daynes, *Making Villians, Making Heroes: Joseph R. McCarthy, Martin Luther King Jr. and the Politics of American Memory* (New York: Garland, 1997).

28. Quoted in "Many Measures of King's Legacy; Day Viewed as American 'Paradox,'" *Boston Globe*, January 19, 1998, sec. A, 1.

29. "Outrage Expressed over King Labeling," *Chicago Defender*, January 18, 1989, 3.

30. "Newsmakers," *Jet*, May 15, 2000, 34.

31. National Public Radio Morning Edition, "Martin Luther King Holiday," January 19, 1998, transcript #98011903–210 (available through LexisNexis).

32. "City Council Won't Touch Parade Feud: Two MLK Events Set, But Only One Has Permit," *Houston Chronicle*, January 7, 1998, sec. A, 15.

33. John Paul Jones III, "The Street Politics of Jackie Smith," in *The Blackwell Companion to the City*, ed. Gary Bridge and Sophie Watson (Oxford: Blackwell, 2000), 448–59.

34. The author visited and interviewed Jacqueline Smith on December 23, 1995. At that time, Smith had been engaged in her sidewalk protest for almost 2,900 days. Before becoming a museum, the Lorraine Motel had served as housing for low-income people. Jacqueline Smith was the last resident of the Lorraine Motel before its closure and conversion into a museum and state-owned tourist attraction.

35. Owen J. Dwyer, "Interpreting the Civil Rights Movement: Place, Memory, and Conflict," *Professional Geographer* 52, no. 4 (2000): 660–71.

36. Stephen G. N. Tuck, *Beyond Atlanta: The Struggles for Racial Equality in Georgia, 1940–1980* (Athens: University of Georgia Press, 2001).

37. Derek H. Alderman, "Creating a New Geography of Memory in the South: (Re)Naming of Streets in Honor of Martin Luther King Jr.," *Southeastern Geographer* 36, no. 1(1996): 51–69.

38. "Back Streets Get King Name," *Atlanta Journal Constitution*, September 12, 1993, sec. F, 1; "Failure to Name Street to Honor MLK May Bring Boycott," *Atlanta Journal Constitution*, November 28, 1992, sec. B, 9.

39. "King's Fight Still in the Streets: Re-Naming of Roads Incites Controversy," *St. Petersburg Times*, April 23, 1990, sec. B, 1.

40. Judith Kenny, "Making Milwaukee Famous: Cultural Capital, Urban Image, and the Politics of Place," *Urban Geography* 16, no. 5 (1995): 440–58.

41. "Street's Name Switch Riles Portland Residents, Fierce Public Backlash to Avenue Named after Martin Luther King Jr.," *Seattle Times*, March 4, 1990, sec. D, 5.

42. Alderman, "A Street Fit for a King," 676.

43. Hal Gulliver, "King Took America to the Mountaintop," *Georgia Trend* 15, no. 5 (2000): 11–19.

44. "The Many Signs of MLK," *Atlanta Journal-Constitution*, January 17, 1999, sec. A, 1.

45. Bruce B. Williams and Bonnie Thornton Dill, "African Americans in the Rural South: The Persistence of Race and Poverty," in *The American Country Side: Rural People and Places*, ed. Emery Castle (Lawrence: University Press of Kansas, 1995), 339–51.

46. Alderman, "A Street Fit for a King," 677.

47. Tuck, *Beyond Atlanta*, 1–8.

48. *Minutes of the Bulloch County Board of Commissioners*, February 1, 1994; "County Asked to Withdraw Endorsement," *Statesboro Herald*, March 2, 1994, sec. A, 11.

49. "Main Street Makes Request to Council," *Statesboro Herald*, May 18, 1994, sec. A, 1, 11; "Perimeter Road Name Ideas Rolling In," *Statesboro Herald*, May 20, 1994, sec. A, 1, 6.

50. "Perimeter Road Naming Deadline Nears," *Statesboro Herald*, June 6, 1994, sec. A, 1, 8.

51. *Minutes of the Bulloch County Board of Commissioners*, June 21, 1994; "City, County to Settle Debate over Naming Perimeter Road," *Statesboro Herald*, June 21, 1994, sec. A, 1, 3.

52. *Minutes of the Bulloch County Board of Commissioners*, June 21, 1994; "City and County Differ on Name of New Road," *Statesboro Herald*, June 22, 1994, sec. A, 1, 8.

53. The interpretation of the suggestions was inspired by Lawrence D. Berg and Robin A. Kearns, "Naming as Norming: 'Race,' Gender, and the Identity Politics of Naming Places in Aotearoa/New Zealand," *Environment and Planning D: Society and Space* 14, no. 1 (1996): 99–122.

54. Dydia DeLyser, "Authenticity on the Ground: Engaging the Past in a California Ghost Town," *Annals of the Association of American Geographers* 89, no. 4 (1999): 602–32.

55. "Recognize Accomplishments of King by Naming Road for Him," *Statesboro Herald*, May 22, 1994, sec. A, 4.

56. "Name Road for Veterans," *Statesboro Herald*, May 29, 1994, sec. A, 4.

57. "City and County Differ on Name of New Road," *Statesboro Herald*, June 22, 1994, sec. A, 1, 8.

58. *Minutes of the Bulloch County Board of Commissioners*, June 21, 1994.

59. *Suggestions Submitted to Perimeter Naming Committee*, Bulloch County, Georgia, April 1–June 1, 1994.

60. Ibid.

61. Michael Schudson, "How Culture Works," *Theory and Society* 18, no. 2 (1989): 153–80.

62. *Suggestions Submitted to Perimeter Naming Committee*, Bulloch County, Georgia, April 1–June 1, 1994.

63. Interview with Statesboro city planner, by author, City Hall, Statesboro, Georgia, May 18, 1997.

64. *Suggestions Submitted to Perimeter Naming Committee*, Bulloch County, Georgia, April 1–June 1, 1994 (emphasis in original).

65. Ibid. (emphasis added).

66. Berg and Kearns, "Naming as Norming," 99–122.

67. Interview with American Legion Leader, by author, April 13, 1998.

68. Interview with African American pastor, by author, Statesboro, Georgia, May 18, 1997.

69. Ibid.

70. Jeffrey K. Olick, "Genre Memories and Memory Genres: A Dialogical Analysis of May 8, 1945, Commemorations in the Federal Republic of Germany," *American Sociological Review* 64, no. 3 (1999): 381–402.

71. "Women's Shelter Former Employees Allege Discrimination," *Statesboro Herald*, April 3, 1997, sec. A, 1, 6.

72. "City Approves Martin Luther King Jr. Drive," *Statesboro Herald*, December 5, 2002, sec. A, 1, 8.

RENEE C. ROMANO

Narratives of Redemption

The Birmingham Church Bombing Trials

and the Construction of Civil Rights Memory

On September 15, 1963, in what is commonly regarded as the most tragic and heinous crime of the civil rights era, a bomb exploded under the steps of the Sixteenth Street Baptist Church in Birmingham, Alabama. Birmingham had been the center of the civil rights movement since April 1963, when Martin Luther King and his organization, the Southern Christian Leadership Conference, had come to town to help local leader Fred Shuttlesworth fight against segregation and white violence. By May of that year, Birmingham had become the symbol of entrenched white resistance to racial change, as Police Chief Bull Connor used high-powered fire hoses and police dogs to break up the nonviolent demonstrations. Birmingham was a tough town; antilabor, pro-Klan, and anti-integration. The city, nicknamed "Bombingham," had been the site of over two dozen unsolved bombings from the late 1940s through the early 1960s.[1] But none of the earlier bombings had such a blatant intent to kill people as this one, which took place at 10:20 AM on a Sunday as the church prepared for its "Youth Day" services. In the downstairs ladies lounge, five young people were preparing for the service—Carole Robertson, Cynthia Wesley, Denise McNair, Addie Mae Collins, and her sister, Sarah. When the explosion ripped through the bathroom, four of the five were killed instantly; Sarah Collins survived, although she was seriously injured and was permanently blinded in one eye.

In his eulogy for those killed in the bombing, Martin Luther King insisted that the responsibility for the deaths of the four black girls did not lie with the bombers alone. As he told the grieving audience, the girls' deaths had "something to say to every minister of the gospel who has remained silent behind the safe security of stained-glass windows." They had something to say "to every politician who has fed his constituents with the stale bread of hatred and the spoiled meat of racism" and "to a federal government that has compromised with the undemocratic practices of southern Dixiecrats and the blatant hypocrisy of right-wing northern Republicans." King warned his audience that they must be concerned "not merely about who murdered" the girls, but also about "the system, the way of life, the philosophy which produced the murderers."[2]

King's eulogy indicted not just the individuals who planted the bomb that killed four black girls in church on a Sunday morning, but the racial climate, both in the South and nationwide, that allowed such a ghastly hate crime to occur. For a crime like this, it was not enough to blame individuals, King suggested. Responsibility also lay with the social environment that produced the murderers and, King might have added if he had lived longer, would enable them to avoid prosecution for their crime for decades.

Birmingham mayor Albert Boutwell made a very different argument about who, or what, was to blame for the bombing. The night of the bombing, Boutwell declared of city residents, "All of us are victims, and most of us are innocent victims." The people of Birmingham, he continued, had to work to punish those responsible and he insisted that the city would do its part: "No stone will be left unturned. . . . No effort or expense will be spared to accomplish that."[3] By declaring all citizens of Birmingham victims of the racist bombing, Boutwell sought to distance himself, other civic leaders, and his fellow white residents of Birmingham from the crime, and certainly from the few guilty perpetrators. In the immediate aftermath of the bombing, the city assumed a mantle of victimhood and innocence; whatever wrongs had happened in the city would be righted by zealous prosecution of the bombers.

Despite Boutwell's claim that "no effort or expense" would be spared to capture and convict the bombers of the Sixteenth Street Baptist Church, it would take fourteen long years for even one man to be brought to trial for the crime. In 1977, prodded by driven, young Alabama Attorney General Bill Baxley, an Alabama jury found Robert Chambliss guilty of one count of murder for his role in the bombing of the church. Another twenty-three years would pass before two more alleged bombers would be asked to answer for their crimes. In 2001, nearly forty years after King's eulogy, an Alabama jury convicted Thomas Edwin Blanton of four counts of murder. Bobby Frank Cherry was convicted for his role in the bombing in 2002.[4]

These three trials—in 1977, 2001, and 2002—offer an extraordinary site for the exploration of the construction of civil rights memory. Indeed, since 1990, the reopening of unsolved cases of crimes of the civil rights era has become one of the key arenas in which the American public is asked, even encouraged, to engage with the past. In the last fifteen years, approximately twenty civil rights cases have been reopened, resulting in at least ten trials thus far, including the high-profile conviction of Byron de la Beckwith for the 1963 murder of Medgar Evers. The United States Justice Department has recently reopened an investigation into the 1955 lynching of Emmett Till, and in June 2005, Edgar Ray Killen was convicted for his role in planning the executions of civil rights activists Mickey Schwerner, Andrew Goodman, and James Chaney in Mississippi in 1964.[5] Most of these trials have received extraordinary attention from the media. During the recent church bombing trials, for example, newspapers around the county editorialized about the decision to indict the two men and about their eventual convictions. Major stories related to the trials appeared in magazines as diverse as *Newsweek*, *Time*, *Essence*, *Glamour*, and *People*.[6] Television and radio coverage was equally intense, from hour-long programs on NPR's *Talk of the Nation* to features on national evening news.

With stories about old crimes from the civil rights era in the newspaper, on television, and on radio, these trials today are helping to educate the general public about the events of the 1950s and 1960s. The trials do not represent the only site in which Americans can engage with the history of the movement, but they are more likely to reach a broader audience than many of the institutional and educational sites devoted to the modern freedom struggle. While the civil rights movement is enshrined in public memory in monuments, museums, and representations of popular culture, most Americans will probably never visit a civil rights museum. Many will choose not to watch civil rights dramas; the majority of Americans probably mark Martin Luther King Jr. Day by shopping or enjoying a day off from school or work, not by attending a memorial service or a celebration in King's honor. In contrast, the extensive media coverage of the reopened cases from the civil rights era has the potential to bring the movement and its history into people's homes and everyday lives.

But what history of the civil rights era is being disseminated in these trials? This chapter contends that the contemporary trials of civil rights–era crimes are doing far more than simply providing contemporary Americans with a site to reflect about the events of the 1950s and 1960s; the trials are actively constructing a particular narrative about the past that may well influence both how people remember the movement and what they think about race relations in the present. In other words, the church bombing trials—the lawyers' arguments, the media coverage, the fictionalized accounts of them—are helping to shape the historical memory of the civil rights era, and especially of the nature and extent of white resistance to blacks' struggle for equality.

This chapter explores the narrative that has emerged in the church bombing trials. Just as narrative is deployed in film or in literature, legal cases also often rely on familiar storylines that can help make sense of complex events.[7] Although there are many facets to the "trial narrative" in the bombing cases, three stories or themes in particular stand out. First, echoing a common trope in civil rights memory, the trial narrative portrays whites as heroes and blacks as long-suffering victims. Like many civil rights films and dramas, the church bombing trials downplay the importance, and even the existence of, black activism, while offering images of whites who are committed to racial justice. Second, the trials pit these white heroes against individual evil racists, portraying the men who bombed the church as personally responsible for the racial hatred of the South while ignoring the larger culture of racism of the time. The Birmingham church bombing trials, and others like them, thus effectively remove civil rights crimes from their historical context.

Finally, the trials tell a critical story about how much the nation has changed since the civil rights era. By focusing on those responsible for the church bombing as individual racist men who are now archaic symbols of a time long gone, the trials suggest that racism is a thing of the past and that whites' racial attitudes have changed dramatically from the 1960s. Indeed, state prosecutors have been willing, even eager, to reopen cases like the Birmingham church bombing in part because they offer the southern justice system an excellent opportunity to highlight how much it has changed since the 1960s. In their zealous pursuit of the individuals who committed the racial crimes of the sixties, southern authorities can showcase how they have purged themselves of racism. Through these trials, the conviction of the church bombers comes to represent the final task needed to enable Birmingham, the South, and the nation more generally to achieve a form of closure and to move beyond the racial crimes of the past. As a result, the trials themselves have become a crucial part of a national narrative of redemption and atonement, proof of the immense changes that have taken place in the racial politics in the United States since the 1960s. But this narrative of redemption places no burden of responsibility for the bombing on city police or politicians from the time, on the FBI, or on the larger political and social structures of the South and the nation. It thus reinforces Albert Boutwell's picture of an innocent Birmingham tarnished by a few unusual racists and effectively erases Martin Luther King's understanding of the church bombing as an expression of a much larger system of organized white supremacy.

The "Trial Narrative" and the Construction of Victims and Heroes

When the film *Mississippi Burning* was released in 1988, the reviewer for the *Washington Post* summed up the pointed criticism of the film with his remark, "it's the right story, but with the wrong heroes."[8] The film took an actual crime—the murder of three civil rights activists in the midst of the voting registration movement in Mississippi in 1964—but focused on the zealous investigation of the murders by two fictional FBI agents. In focusing on white FBI investigators who break all the rules in their efforts to find the murderers, the film, NAACP Executive Director Benjamin

Hooks said at the time, "reeks of dishonesty, deception and fraud."[9] The FBI, as all civil rights activists who were in Mississippi during the summer of 1964 knew, had been neither their protector nor their advocate. But in this film, whites are the heroes, and blacks are the passive victims, for the most part suffering in silence as whites fight in their name. To *Time* reviewer Richard Corliss, the film caricatured both the white murderers, as rednecks with low IQs, and blacks, as "martyrs, sanctified by centuries of suffering." *Mississippi Burning*, black *New York Times* columnist Brent Staples argued, implied that "white Americans would shudder at the idea of heroes not cast in their images."[10]

Mississippi Burning is perhaps the most blatant example of the tendency of the mass media and popular entertainment to craft depictions of the movement that portray whites as heroes and blacks as victims, but this tendency extends far beyond this particular film. Indeed, the media coverage of the Birmingham church bombing trials presents a very similar story to that told in *Mississippi Burning*. The church bombing trials have proven particularly well suited to a simplistic storyline of white heroism and noble, but passive, black martyrdom. This storyline downplays black agency and takes attention away from the black activism and leadership that was at the center of the civil rights movement at the same time that it helps focus attention on whites who are driven by their sense of morality and justice to stand up for blacks.

The story of the bombing of the Sixteenth Street Baptist Church to some extent automatically casts blacks in the role of victims. These killings took place in a church on Sunday morning and all of the victims of the bombing were young women who had done nothing more than go to Sunday school that day. Given the nature of the crime, it is no surprise that the victims of the bombing have been remembered and memorialized in song, sculptures, plays, and novels, almost from the moment the bombing took place.[11] The Sixteenth Street Baptist Church has become a national historic site, and visitors can take tours and see where the bombing took place and the plaque that memorializes the victims. The bombing victims have also been remembered through memorial scholarship funds. The Jack and Jill Foundation created the Carole Robertson scholarship in 1966, and the *Birmingham News* began granting a scholarship in honor of the four girls in 1983. Villanova University has recently announced the creation of the Denise McNair Memorial Scholarship.[12] Spike Lee's 1997 documentary *Four Little Girls* put the story of the bombing and its victims back on the agenda of the national media. Lee's film sought to make each of the four victims come alive as an individual by focusing on family members and friends recounting their memories of their murdered loved ones. The state of Alabama is currently raising money to erect a memorial to the four victims at the Sixteenth Street Baptist Church, and Birmingham's congressman Earl Hilliard has asked the U.S. Postal Service to issue stamps in honor of the church bombing. Although Hilliard's recommendation was not adopted in time for the fortieth anniversary of the bombing, it might be accepted in the future.[13]

The heinous bombing crime took the lives of four young black teens and injured over twenty others, and it is fitting that any account of the bombing highlights the tragic loss of life and the humanity of those killed. But it in no way demeans those who lost their lives to explore the ways in which the trial narrative presents those who were killed as innocent, and largely passive, victims. The phrase that is most commonly used to describe the bomb's victims, "four little girls," is telling in that it emphasizes the two attributes of the victims—their youth and their gender—that make them particularly attractive to the media. Americans might not recognize the names of Cynthia Wesley, Addie Mae Collins, Denise McNair, and Carole Robertson, but the collective description of "four little girls" is well known. The victims have been memorialized under the moniker "four little girls" in countless media articles, in public monument, and in Spike Lee's film of that name. The general public, too, tends to remember the church bombing victims collectively with this phrase. Over a third of the Birmingham residents interviewed about the church bombing in a 2000 survey described the victims as "four little girls."[14]

Yet why "four little girls" when three of the four were fourteen years old at the time they were killed (the fourth was eleven)? The four might perhaps be more accurately described as the "four teen girls," but they are never referred to as teenagers. The constant invocation of the term "little" to describe the victims suggests their status as particularly blameless victims. Yet other black victims of white violence of the same age are not necessarily remembered in the same way. Emmett Till, a fourteen

This Associated Press photo collage of the four bombing victims has become an iconic image of the civil rights era. The four are, from the left, Denise McNair, eleven; Carole Robertson, fourteen; Addie Mae Collins, fourteen; and Cynthia Wesley, fourteen. (AP/Wide World Photos)

The thousands who gathered at a New York City rally on September 22, 1963, protested the death of all six black children who died on September 15 in Birmingham, not just the four girls killed in the bombing. The girls in the foreground hold a white "coffin," symbolic of the dead children of Birmingham. (© Bettmann/Corbis)

year old who was lynched in Mississippi in 1955, is not regularly referred to as a "little boy," perhaps because, innocent as he was, his lynching is usually explained as the result of an action on his part (either lisping in a way that sounded like a whistle or in fact whistling at a white woman in a store).

The phrase "four little girls" also highlights the gender of the victims. The fact that all of those killed in the bombing were girls seems to have played an important role in ensuring that the four would be remembered long after other victims of white violence in the South had been forgotten. Indeed, two other Birmingham teens who died on the same day as the four bombing victims, thirteen-year-old Virgil Ware and sixteen-year-old Johnnie Robinson, have not been accorded a central place in the nation's historical memory. These two black boys are certainly not known by their individual names. But neither have they been accorded any collective moniker, despite that fact that both died on September 15, 1963, in the aftermath of the bombing. Ware, in a crime that certainly seems as worthy of press attention as the church bombing, was shot and killed as he rode on the handlebars of his older brother's bike. The shooter was a white teenager, an Eagle Scout, who was driving home after attending a segregationist rally. Police shot Johnnie Robinson in the back after he threw stones at a white segregationist's car during the melee that followed the bombing.[15]

In the aftermath of the bombing, civil rights activists linked Ware's and Robinson's deaths with that of the four girls. When the National Women's Committee for Civil Rights wrote an open letter to the women of Birmingham, they expressed their grief for the six black children who died that day.[16] Similarly, the *Washington Post* reported that 10,000 people marched in Washington, D.C., on September 22 to mourn the "six Negro children killed by bombs and bullets in Birmingham a week before," while the *New York Times* noted that protest rallies were designed as "a memorial to six Negro children killed by a bomb and shooting in Birmingham, AL."[17] But the media quickly forgot the two boys, implicitly deeming their deaths to be less compelling than those of the four bombing victims. Since 1963, most of the retrospective media coverage of the tragic events in Birmingham has focused almost exclusively on the four girls who were killed. Perhaps the erasure of these two black boys from the nation's collective historical memory suggests that it is easier to paint girls as uncomplicated victims. If four young black men, aged eleven to fourteen, had been killed in that church basement instead, would they be remembered and memorialized as "four little boys"?

If media coverage is any indication, the girls' gender seems particularly important to their canonization as martyrs. Articles, for example, frequently discuss what the girls were wearing, in language that suggests both the girls' purity and their helplessness. A *U.S. News and World Report* article from 2000 describes how the four were "found dead in their Sunday white dresses, their bodies huddled together beneath the debris." A 2000 article from *People* magazine drew a vivid picture of "four girls, all in white party dresses and patent-leather shoes," while *American Lawyer* described the girls as "all dressed in white," in imagery reminiscent of brides. Some articles go so far as to describe the girls as angels. To a *Ms.* columnist, the bombing "interrupted four angels who had just found their wings and were poised to fly."[18] In this coverage, the victims are recognized not for humanity or their individual qualities; they are grouped together as generic victims, made especially innocent because of their age, their location at the time of their murder, and their gender.

For the prosecutors in all three of the church bombing trials, emphasizing the innocence of the "four little girls" proved a key strategy in the courtroom as they sought convictions from a jury. Alabama Attorney General Bill Baxley, one newspaper reporter noted during the 1977 Chambliss trial, "seldom misses a chance to refer to 'the church bombing in which four little girls were killed.'"[19] Baxley structured his closing argument around the fact that November 17, 1977, the date on which he presented his summation, would have been Denise McNair's twenty-sixth birthday. He also reminded the jury in his summation, "Those girls weren't out on the streets demonstrating. They were in the sanctuary of their church."[20] Trial consultants for the prosecutors in the Blanton and Cherry cases held focus groups and did jury questionnaires to determine the best themes to highlight in the courtroom. The consultants advised lead prosecutor, Doug Jones, to focus on the bombing only as the murder of four young girls rather than as an attack on the civil rights movement.

Consultant Andrew Sheldon helped Jones put together his dramatic closing argument, suggesting he use the line, "A mother's heart never stops crying." One of the last things the jury heard in the case was Jones's emotional appeal to them to find Blanton guilty: "We come here in this time and place to do justice. . . . And we come here because there were four children who died and the world changed and we changed. And we come here because a mother's heart never stops crying."[21]

The emphasis in the trials on martyrdom of the four girls serves to downplay the equally compelling story of black activism. These trials do not want to link the "four little girls" to the civil rights activism of the time and therefore perhaps complicate the question of their ultimate "innocence."[22] They weren't out on the streets demonstrating, as Bill Baxley made sure the jury knew. Nor do the trials in any way suggest, unlike some other representations of the church bombing, that the experience of black victimization requires blacks to become active in fighting against the forces that victimize them. In the trials, as we shall see, white lawyers come to avenge the death of the four young girls. In contrast, black poet Dudley Randall's 1969 poem "Ballad of Birmingham" suggests that blacks must become active in the struggle precisely because there is no space for them safe from racial violence. In the poem, a mother refuses to allow her daughter to join the freedom marches in Birmingham:

> "No, baby, no, you may not go,
>   for the dogs are fierce and wild, and clubs and hoses, guns and jails
>   ain't good for a little child."

When the daughter persists, her mother tells her she may instead go to church to "sing in the children's choir."[23] Of course, her daughter is killed in the bombing; no black mother, however loving and careful, could protect her child from becoming the potential victim of white violence. For Randall, the only hope to protect one's children was to allow them to put themselves in harm's way by fighting for their freedom in marches and demonstrations; events like the church bombing made black activism an absolute necessity.

The trials, and the media coverage of them, not surprisingly, do not make this link, presenting blacks as innocent, suffering, and, perhaps most important, passive victims. In the church bombing trial narrative, it is whites who are the heroic actors, either in their roles as informants against the bombers or for the part they played in reopening these cases and ultimately bringing the bombers to justice. Whites who cooperated in the investigations—such as Elizabeth Cobbs, a niece of Robert Chambliss, and Bobby Frank Cherry's son, Tom, and granddaughter, Teresa Stacy— have received a great deal of media attention, being featured in popular media outlets such as *Glamour* magazine and on the Oprah Winfrey show. These family informants not only provide a sense of drama, but they can also be used to showcase the transformation of whites' attitudes since the bombing. A lengthy article in *Glamour* highlighted Teresa Stacy's efforts to "cleanse herself of her family's racist legacy" and describes in detail her transformation from a runaway, drug-addicted stripper to an upstanding young wife and mother. On the day she testified against her grandfather, Stacy "cut herself loose from the racism she had absorbed as a child."[24] Articles about Tom Cherry emphasized how he was torn between loyalty to his father and his suspicion that his dad might be a murderer.[25] The media saw this story of a son coming to terms with the truth about his father as so compelling that it was even fictionalized in the FX Original TV movie *Sins of the Father*.[26] In these media representations the dramatic hero of the church bombing trials becomes the white family member whose moral values ultimately triumph over his or her sense of fear or family loyalty.[27]

The lead prosecutors of these cases, and sometimes the investigators as well, have also been awarded hero status. Bill Baxley, the young Alabama attorney general who successfully prosecuted Robert Chambliss in 1977, was celebrated in the media for his obsessive drive to bring the bombers to justice. Newspapers at the time described how the bombing in 1963 made Baxley physically ill and how he vowed at the time to do something to atone for it. The first thing he did after taking the office in 1971 was write the names of the four bombing victims on his state phone card, so that he would be reminded of the four girls whenever he placed a call.[28] The *Washington Post* praised Baxley for his dogged pursuit of the bombers and reminded its readers that "ten years ago it would have been inconceivable that a white 'native son' of Alabama would vigorously conduct so relentless an investigation of so racially motivated a crime." Baxley's pursuit of the bombers became a symbol of how much the South had changed. Thus the *Nation* editorialized that "the social transformation that produced Bill Baxley also gives hopes that some day racism will disappear in fact, as already it has been banned by law."[29]

In the two more recent cases, the media has focused on Doug Jones, U.S. Attorney for the District of Alabama, who served as lead prosecutor in the Blanton trial. As a law student, Jones skipped class so he could watch Bill Baxley prosecute Robert Chambliss in 1977. Noted for his perseverance in reinvestigating the bombing in the 1990s, Jones received a special designation as a state prosecutor in order to lead the case for murder against Blanton in state courts. The FBI agents in Birmingham who reopened the investigation in the 1990s have also garnered their share of praise. These white investigators and lawyers have received numerous awards and honors for their service. The SCLC thus awarded Doug Jones and one of the jury consultants in the bombing cases their annual Drum Major for Justice Award in 2003. Jones also received the 2002 FBI Director's Community Leadership Award for sending a message that "hate crimes will not be tolerated." Two of the FBI agents involved in the investigations of the Blanton and Cherry cases were named Federal Employees of the Year in 2002 and were selected to receive Service to America Medals, in recognition of government employees who directly improve people's lives.[30]

Although whites have been active figures in making these trials possible and certainly deserve praise for doing so, the relentless and narrow focus on the heroics of white actors represents a rewriting, or at least ignoring, of history. For one thing, this focus on white heroes largely obscures the actions of blacks who were instrumental in getting these cases reopened. Although Bill Baxley was largely responsible for launching the investigation that ultimately convicted Robert Chambliss in 1977, the more recent investigations began in large part because of black activism. In 1993, black ministers from Birmingham, especially Abraham Woods, the head of the local chapter of the SCLC, asked the local FBI agent to reopen the case. Pursuing the church bombers, they told him, was the single most important thing the FBI could do to gain the trust of the black community in Birmingham.[31] The Justice Department, meanwhile, moved to restart their investigation of the bombing shortly after the release of Spike Lee's documentary about the crime. The film helped put the bombing case back on the national agenda and it created pressure to bring the bombers to justice.[32] And when it appeared that Bobby Frank Cherry might not be tried for the church bombing because a judge had ruled he suffered from dementia, black activists, including Woods and Martin Luther King III, organized public protests and demonstrations. Convinced that Cherry was faking dementia in order to avoid having to face charges (which indeed turned out to be the case), Woods and others insisted that the judge's ruling be reversed, charging that the state had been willing to try mentally retarded black men.[33] While the media has not wholly ignored these black actors, it has paid far more attention to the actions of whites. Indeed, after Cherry was convicted in 2002, the *Birmingham Post-Herald* noted that "history would thank" those who helped bring the bombers to justice, a list that included only whites, like Bill Baxley, Doug Jones, and the FBI's Rob Langford.[34]

The emphasis on heroic whites also completely erases the actual history of stonewalling by white authorities that kept these cases from going before a jury in the years immediately after the bombing. The reopening of the Birmingham church bombing case in the mid-1970s and again in the early 1990s was not due to any new breakthroughs in the case. Robert Chambliss, Tom Blanton, and Bobby Frank Cherry were the prime suspects in the church bombing case even in 1963 (along with a fourth man, Herman Cash, who died before he could ever be brought to trial). All four were active in the Ku Klux Klan; indeed, they were members of a particularly violent wing of the Klan known as the Cahaba Boys. The FBI, which held a massive investigation into the bombing, identified these four men as suspects very early on. The local and state authorities in Alabama knew too that they were the likely bombers. But neither state nor federal authorities took steps to hold these men accountable for their crime during the 1960s. Instead, in an effort to derail the federal investigation, Alabama's Commissioner of Public Safety Al Lingo (the same man who ordered a posse of armed whites to attack unarmed marchers on the Edmund Pettus Bridge in Selma in 1965) had Chambliss and another suspect arrested and tried on the relatively minor charge of possession of dynamite, thus making it harder for the government to try them for the church bombing.

Although murder is a state crime, a 1960 law made it a federal crime to bomb an inhabited building, so the church bombers could have been tried in federal courts. The FBI, previously lax in investigating bombings in Birmingham, did a thorough investigation into this bombing. By 1965, agents on the ground believed that they had a strong case and that "there was a climate of public opinion favoring prosecution."[35] When they presented the evidence to FBI Director J. Edgar Hoover, however, he balked and refused to take it to trial. Hoover's defenders insist that he knew that there was little chance that an Alabama jury would convict white men for a racially motivated murder and that he didn't want to make it impossible to ever try them again at a later date. But there is no evidence that Hoover, or that anyone else in the FBI, sought to reopen the case before the statute of limitations on the federal crime expired. Indeed, when Alabama Prosecutor Bill Baxley asked the FBI for their records on the bombing in the 1970s, long after the federal statute of limitations had expired, the FBI stalled for years, only providing Baxley with some of the records after he threatened to expose their stonewalling in the press. Even then, the FBI failed to give Baxley the audiotapes that would be used years later to convict Tom Blanton.[36] When the tapes were finally turned over to Alabama prosecutors in 1997, a livid Baxley charged that the FBI had given Blanton a twenty-year "get out of jail free card." Why, Baxley asked in a *New York Times* column, would the "FBI aid Klansmen in avoidance of prosecution?"[37]

Given Hoover's well-known antipathy to the civil rights movement, he may have felt no sympathy for the Birmingham cause. He perhaps believed that finding the killers would aid Martin Luther King, a man he hated deeply. Hoover might have feared being embarrassed if he lost this high-profile case before a white southern jury. He may have refused to pursue the case because any trial would likely have required the testimony of FBI informant Gary Thomas Rowe, who was a member of the same Klavern as the men ultimately convicted of the church bombing. If Rowe had testified, it would have deprived the FBI of a key informant, and perhaps more significantly, it might have led to increased scrutiny of the ways in which the FBI chose and used informants. Rowe actively participated in many of the violent events of the civil rights movement, including beating up Freedom Riders in 1961, and when his identity and activities became known in the 1970s, it caused a scandal for the FBI.[38] Whatever the reason, none of the four suspects was brought to trial during the 1960s, and if the FBI had continued in its unwillingness to share documents, Robert Chambliss would never have been convicted in 1977, nor Tom Blanton in 2001.

Yet today this history of stonewalling, cover-ups, and the intransigence of white authorities has virtually been erased from the historical record, so much so that the defense attorneys in the Blanton case asked the judge to dismiss the charges against him on the grounds that the prosecution had *purposefully* waited decades to bring the bombing suspects to trial in order to gain a "tactical advantage." Blanton's attorneys charged that the state waited thirty-seven years to try Blanton because they thought it would be easier to get a conviction after a number of key potential witnesses for the defense had died.[39] In this scenario, the long delay in bringing the bombers to trial represents not the racism of the American justice system, but the fervent desire of those in the legal system to make sure that the alleged bombers would ultimately be convicted. "So maybe," one editorial after Blanton's conviction explained, "J. Edgar Hoover was, in the very long run, right."[40] The FBI and other white authorities were, in this reading of the case, prescient to delay the case because they knew they could not get a guilty verdict in the 1960s. Delay becomes proof of desire to see justice done, not a sign of the limitations of the legal system for black Americans.

That "Old-Time Racism"

With whites as the heroes in the trial narrative, the main "plot" of the trials pits these young white lawmen against old, unrepentant racists, effectively telling a story about the ways in which the South has left behind its racist past. It is a story, moreover, that resonates with common tropes in civil rights dramas and that has wide public appeal. In her 2001 work *Framing the South: Hollywood, Television, and Race during the Civil*

Rights Struggle, Alison Graham argues that the southern "cracker" has become the modern civil rights drama's raison d'être: "He (and it was always a 'he') would initiate and complicate the action, and he would be vanquished at movie's end by the only character capable of driving a stake through the heart of a Delta racist: his alter-ego, the man of law, the redeemed southern white man."[41] The civil rights drama, she insists, refuses to question institutional racism. Instead, these dramas focus on the redneck "cracker" as the villain, with the decent southern lawman redeeming his home and his race by ridding society of this form of "diseased whiteness."[42]

The mass media and the prosecutors in the church bombing cases may not have read Graham's book, but they have certainly internalized this civil rights genre script. In these trials, this story of lone rednecks being brought to justice by upstanding white men of the law becomes not just a representation of the past, but the actual narrative of the present. The heroics of the white investigators and prosecutors, nearly all native sons of the South, provide one half of this dramatic staging. The construction of the bombers as lone rednecks who do not represent the larger views of the South completes the script. In the trial narrative, moreover, this traditional script becomes an argument about the changes that have occurred in the South and among whites, as those bringing the bombers to justice come to represent the current and the modern, while the bombers come to represent the past. Even the visual images presented in the trials, where teams of vigorous, young, white lawyers take on decrepit, old men, suggest that racism, too, is old and beyond its prime.[43]

Of course, the prosecutors in these cases do not want the jury to think of the defendants as feeble old men suffering from various health problems, but as the "punks" that they were in 1963.[44] In all three of the bombing trials, the prosecution focused especially on the defendants' virulent racism and their intractable hatred of blacks. The emphasis on the personal attitudes of these men makes legal sense. In these cases, the evidence is old and circumstantial, and prosecutors have needed to make a compelling argument about the alleged motive for the bombing. Trial judges have therefore allowed them to bring in extensive evidence about the defendants' racial attitudes and their membership in the Klan

By the time the church bombers were brought to trial, they had become old men. Some observers argued that little purpose was served by putting elderly men in jail, but their age in some ways made them ideal for prosecutors, who could easily paint the defendants as archaic symbols of a racist past. In this photo, Bobby Frank Cherry sits in the courtroom during his 2002 trial, flanked by his attorneys, Mickey Johnson and Rodger Bass. (AP/Wide World Photos)

in order to shore up the circumstantial case against them. Thus in the Chambliss case, Baxley laid out a damaging picture of Chambliss as a racist man full of hatred of blacks. He had witnesses testify to the kinds of things Chambliss said in the 1960s, when he talked about the "god-damned niggers" and the need to "keep the niggers in their place."[45] In the Blanton case, Doug Jones and his legal team recounted conversation after conversation where Blanton reportedly said he hated black people and he wanted to kill them. An old girlfriend testified that Blanton had once tried to run down an old black man with his car. And, as one of the prosecutors probably unnecessarily reminded the jury, Tom Blanton didn't use the term "blacks": "He had names for black people and they were hateful names. Profane names."[46] Prosecutors and witnesses portrayed Bobby Frank Cherry, meanwhile, as a man who liked to dance around in his Ku Klux Klan robes in front of his family.[47] With much of the testimony in the cases focusing on the language the defendants used to describe blacks and their support of segregation, these three men effectively became the face of evil. They were easy men to prosecute, as one of Bobby Frank Cherry's lawyers explained, "the human equivalent of a cockroach."[48]

With prosecutors using reports about the defendants' conversations and views of blacks to paint them as unrepentant and hateful racists who despised blacks so much they were willing to kill four little innocent girls, defending lawyers had the thankless job of trying to put these men's speech acts in their historical context. While prosecutors sought to present the racist beliefs of these men as proof of their involvement with the bombing, defendants instead countered that such racial attitudes were widely shared and were not unusual at the time. Robert Chambliss's attorney thus urged the jury in his closing arguments to put themselves back in 1963 in order to understand Chambliss's comment that he had "stuff" that would make black people "beg" to segregate: "Rough talk does not make a verdict. Mr. Chambliss didn't have any monopoly on rough talk in those days. How would you like to be judged on things that were said then around your kitchen table. That was a normal, human, thing to say."[49] He reminded the jury that the use of the word "nigger" was common in 1963, and that Alabama Governor George Wallace also said that he was fighting to save segregation.[50] After prosecutors rested their case against Tom Blanton, his attorney, John Robbins, asked the judge to dismiss the charges because the state had only proven that "my client had a big mouth and had racist tendencies."[51] Robbins reminded the jury that Blanton's racial views did not automatically make him a murderer. "You're not going to like Tom Blanton. You're not going to like some of the things he says," Robbins argued in his opening statement, but "just because you don't like him, just because you don't like the views he espoused doesn't make him responsible for this tragedy." Although many of those who testified against Blanton had also been in the Klan, none of the witnesses seemed to want to admit that they had felt similarly toward black people, Robbins pointed out. "They want you to believe only Tom Blanton was the bad guy in Birmingham. He was the only racist in Birmingham. He was the only segregationist back then."[52]

While there is no doubt that these men were (and are) repugnant, they were not, as John Robbins noted, the "only segregationists" back then. Focusing on their racist attitudes outside of any larger context of the political culture of the times ignores the ways in which their views were not, in fact, an aberration and that the bombing was not an isolated act. Diane McWhorter, a white Birmingham native who for years struggled to discover her own father's possible connection to the bombing, has laid out most clearly the ways in which this bombing was more than simply the act of a few rabid individuals. *Carry Me Home*, her outstanding book about the civil rights movement in Birmingham, documents ties between the Klansmen who bombed Sixteenth Street Baptist Church and Birmingham city government. In their efforts to uphold their own business interests and to prevent unionization in Birmingham, city elites had long turned to the Klan as a vigilante group to protect their own economic dominance. Although the "Big Mules" of Birmingham eventually disavowed their Klan henchmen when the Klan's violence grew beyond their control, McWhorter demonstrates that the city fathers nurtured the Klan and created the conditions that allowed the bombing to take place. Describing the elite Birmingham Mountain Brook Club on the morning of the bombing, McWhorter writes: "Not that anyone standing in the buffet line that Sunday had anything to do with the lethal package planted during those dark hours before the blast, when no sensible white person would be found in the colored section of downtown. The fuse had been lit years earlier, in the broad daylight of community approval, and even the cleanest hands at the Mountain Brook Club did their bit to keep it dry as it sizzled through bad neighborhoods and across many decades before it blew up four black Sunday school girls on September 15, 1963."[53]

Similarly, for Elizabeth Cobbs, Robert Chambliss's niece whose testimony at his 1977 trial was probably responsible for his conviction, any version of the church bombing that ignored the ways in which the bombers had been applauded and supported by those with political power in Birmingham was woefully inadequate. Her uncle, she insisted, was no "freak of society," but a man who worked as a vigilante for politicians and the police.[54] His job maintaining cars for the city was widely believed to be a reward for his efforts to prevent the integration of the Fountain Heights neighborhood, an effort that involved bombing the houses of black residents. When he had been arrested earlier on other bombing charges, Birmingham Police Commissioner Bull Conner ordered his release. Chambliss, Cobbs argued, enjoyed "protection from prosecution and outright patronage from law enforcement."[55] She ends her memoir with a series of unanswered questions about the bombing that implicate many more people than simply the bombers, including asking what role Governor George Wallace played in impeding the bombing investigation, and why the Alabama attorney general elected after Bill Baxley immediately closed the bombing investigation. Wallace might be forgiven for his role as "enabler of the violent and vicious," but how could we forgive ourselves, Cobb asks, "for not asking the questions—and insisting on the answers" to these larger questions about the bombing.[56]

The trial narrative for the most part depicts these three men primarily as lone virulent racists, not as part of a larger terrorist apparatus that was used to maintain segregation in the South. In these trials, there is little, if any, sustained discussion of how the politicians of the time or the police, or the city fathers, might share some burden of responsibility. The impulse for both the prosecutors and the defending attorneys in these cases was to keep the focus firmly on the bombing and not to explore the crime in a larger context. Prosecuting attorneys did present brief history lessons explaining to the jury the civil rights struggle in Birmingham in 1963, but only so as to make clear the bombers' motivations for blowing up a church. Otherwise, prosecutors limited their narrative to the complicity of these men in the deaths of the four girls. The defense also wanted to focus solely on the events of the church bombing and not on all the "peripheral stuff" like marches that happened in 1963.[57] To the defense attorneys, the story of white resistance to the movement only further implied that their clients were guilty because they were racists who wanted to uphold segregation. Their best hope of acquittal lay in sticking very closely to what facts were known and what the evidence proved about the actual events on September 15, 1963.

As a result, the trials ignore the context of elite support for the Klan, and whites' widespread support for segregation. The church bombing trials took place around the same time that the notorious Mississippi

Sovereignty Commission Papers were opened to the public. These papers demonstrated that Mississippi's elected officials had engaged in illegal activities to maintain segregation, and that their actions were largely embraced by many whites. Alabama had its own state spy agency with the mandate of upholding segregation, the Alabama Legislative Commission to Preserve the Peace, founded by Alabama Governor George Wallace in 1964, in the aftermath of the church bombings.[58] But these trials do nothing to expose the web of white supremacy in the South in the 1960s or continued existence or legacies of institutional, structural, and legal racism. They have not provided space for any kind of conversation that reaches beyond the question of the individual guilt of these particular men. And this very narrow understanding of the crimes of the civil rights era has made the trials—with their image of righteous white men working diligently for years to bring these horrific bombers to justice—particularly useful symbols of the atonement and redemption of the legal system and the white South more generally.

Seeking Redemption: The Trial Narrative and Atonement

With these men, and the racist hate they symbolize, firmly ensconced in the past, the bombing trials became a platform to demonstrate just how much has changed in Birmingham, and the nation, since 1963. The trials, and the media coverage of them, argue that whites today have shed the racism of the past, in large part because of the impact of the bombing. Media coverage about the bombing frequently paints it as a singular event that led whites to a moral awakening, a tragedy that "galvanized a horrified nation behind the civil rights movement."[59] Whites who had been indifferent to, or apathetic about, the movement supposedly now became convinced of the moral righteousness of the cause. An Associated Press article from 2002 contains a typical representation about the bombing's impact: "The bombing on September 15, 1963, was an epochal event both for the city once known as 'Bombingham' and for a nation defending its creed of equality. In the aftermath of the atrocity, racial moderates came off the sidelines in Birmingham and elsewhere to hasten the transition away from segregation across the South."[60] In this simplified historical narrative, the bombing becomes almost a moment of triumph and growth for whites, when four "unwitting martyrs . . . forced most of America to recognize black America's struggle for civil rights." Other descriptions draw a direct line from the bombing to the legislative achievements of the civil rights movement. The bombing, one 2001 editorial explained, "focused the attention of a nation on the atrocities being committed within its own borders against its own people, and forced politicians to take a stand. As a result, Congress passed the Civil Rights Act of 1964 and the Voting Rights Act of 1965."[61] Arguments such as this ignore the intense black activism required to pass these laws, and the controversy that surrounded their passage. In this narrative, the death of "four little girls" was enough to show whites the error of their ways and to lead the nation to support the black freedom struggle.

In the bombing trials, prosecutors have emphasized the ways in which the bombing changed Birmingham by suggesting that the city's racist history was from such a distant past that jurors were probably unfamiliar with it. Doug Jones thus explained to the jury in his opening statement in the Blanton trial that some of the testimony would be about what Birmingham was like in 1963, a world that he suggested would be foreign to them. "As much as we find it hard to believe today," he told the jury, "there was separate lunch counters and separate restrooms and there was separate water fountains for black people and white people."[62] It seems unlikely that a jury comprised of adults from Birmingham would truly find it hard to believe that less than forty years earlier segregation had been practiced throughout their city, but Jones wanted to signal how much Birmingham had changed since the 1960s.

For the residents of Birmingham, these trials have become an important step in moving beyond their past, and especially in putting the stigma of living in "America's most segregated city" behind them. The bombing, and the images of fire hoses and police dogs being unleashed against nonviolent demonstrators, became what people knew about Birmingham. Richard Arrington, Birmingham's first black mayor, elected in 1979, came to see firsthand how the bombing "dragged the city's image to the very bottom." In trying to convince businesses to relocate to Birmingham, he discovered that most people outside the city "only knew about the water hoses used on marchers and that four little girls were killed in a church bombing."[63] The bombing trials sometimes made the explicit case that bringing the bombers to justice would help lay Birmingham's painful past to rest. In his closing summation in the Chambliss case, Bill Baxley thus told the jury that the church bombing "was not just heard in Birmingham but was heard around the world, and the people of Alabama have been a long time recovering." Finding Chambliss guilty is "not going to bring those little girls back, but it will show the world that this murder case has been solved by the people of Alabama."[64] Prosecutors in the Blanton case were less direct, but they too suggested a guilty conviction could help Birmingham achieve closure. "Don't let the deafening blast of this bomb be what's left ringing in our ears," one attorney told the jury. Doug Jones told them, "It's never too late. It is never too late for the truth to be told. It is never too late for wounds to heal."[65]

The sense that convicting the church bombers would help redeem Birmingham of its racist past was so widespread that the defense attorneys felt they had to address it directly. Tom Blanton's defense attorney reminded the jury this case was not about "removing the tarnished image that Birmingham may have or you may feel Birmingham has had as a result of what happened in the sixties."[66] Finding Blanton guilty would not atone for Birmingham's racist past, he insisted: "This case is not a case so we'll all feel good about ourselves by convicting Tom Blanton and then somehow we can go off and somehow Birmingham, if its image is tarnished, can be somehow washed away and the rays of sunshine will shine down on this state and this city and everything will be all better."[67]

Yet despite these protestations, the media has also argued that the trials not only atone for Birmingham's past but also demonstrate the extent of racial progress since 1963. After the Chambliss trial in 1977, the *Birmingham Post-Herald* argued that the trial symbolized the "monumental changes in attitude" that had taken place in the last sixteen years, a "cycle of change that would never have moved so fast without the bombing of the Sixteenth [Street] Baptist Church." *Nation* claimed that "fourteen years of shame came to a symbolic end" on the day Chambliss was convicted.[68] The later trials were viewed in the same light. The *San Francisco Chronicle* thus declared the conviction of Cherry, a "self-avowed racist," by a largely white jury "a remarkable measure of social achievement," while the *Columbus Dispatch* wrote that with Cherry's conviction, "justice was done in a state of Alabama that the girls would have trouble recognizing."[69]

In some cases, media accounts went beyond simply interpreting the meaning of the trials to more actively rewriting past history. Some newspaper accounts implied that the trials represented the culmination of a long quest by Americans to see justice done in this case. Only the bombing trials could satisfy "Birmingham's craving for justice," the *Birmingham News* claimed, while another editorial insisted that Americans would be watching the trials closely and "demanding a dose of justice." An editorial in the *Cleveland Plain Dealer* went further, suggesting that the people of Birmingham had been waiting thirty-eight years for "justice to rain down" on those who bombed the church. "They waited for a time when their murderers would rue the day they donned their white Ku Klux Klan robes."[70] Such language suggests that there had been a groundswell of popular support for pursuing the church bombing case in 1963 and reopening it later, an interpretation that, while flattering to whites, is simply untrue.

The prosecutors' and the media's insistence that the church bombing trials are helping to redeem the city, the South, and even the nation makes clear that they are in part show trials, or "atonement trials," in the words of historian Jack Davis.[71] They allow the city of Birmingham, and the white South more generally, to feel good about themselves for finally bringing these killers to justice. Doug Jones, the lead attorney in the Blanton case, made it his mantra that "justice delayed is not justice denied." In other words, although justice was slow in coming in this case, eventually the court system and white southerners proved that they were not willing to tolerate whites who terrorized blacks. The major story of the trial narrative thus becomes that of noble whites using a slow, but fundamentally sound, criminal justice system to punish wrongdoers even years after their crime. For the editorial writers at the *Tampa Tribune* the lesson of the trial was that "the system came through for the four little children, even if justice has been long delayed."[72] A line in a *Glamour* magazine article about the bombing perhaps best sums up the thrust of this narrative: "Racism has given way to a desire to see justice done."[73]

Robert Chambliss, Tom Blanton, and Bobby Frank Cherry were white supremacists who were very likely responsible (probably with others) for planting the bomb at the Sixteenth Street Baptist Church. The men have never admitted their guilt, and they have never repented for their role in the church bombing. Indeed, until his death in 1985, Robert Chambliss reportedly prayed every night in his prison cell that God never forgive Bill Baxley, the man who put him in jail.[74] Yet this very unwillingness to repent has allowed them to become symbols of all that was wrong with the South that the region has moved beyond today. By telling a particular story about how bad these men were, and how archaic they are in the modern South, the rest of the white South can be redeemed for its racist past. As *Newsweek* informed readers in the wake of the conviction of Bobby Frank Cherry, "In the thirty-eight-plus years since the bombing of Birmingham's Sixteenth Street Baptist Church, Alabama has been reborn. And in the process, Bobby Frank Cherry, once a lord of his universe, became an embarrassing relic of a shameful past. . . . In this enlightened age of tolerance and presumed equal opportunity, even most of Cherry's fellow Southerners consider him to be one step removed from excrement."[75] As "embarrassing relics of a shameful past," these men become almost like displays in the museum case, to be dusted off for their national display in these trials. By emphasizing how far we've come since 1963 and how very different these men are from "us," the trials and the media suggest that the nation has fully reckoned with the racial crimes of the past.

"Fixing" History

The trial narrative most effectively places racism in the past, both literally and symbolically, by focusing on the racial hatred of a few individuals outside any larger context of the era in which they lived. The simplistic story these trials tell, however, reflects neither the complexity of the historical record nor the understanding of the events at the time in which they occurred. Ray Jenkins, who covered the 1977 trial for the *Montgomery Advertiser*, was reminded of the Nuremberg war crimes trials as he watched the Chambliss case: "In Nuremberg, men were being tried for doing what they thought they were expected to do. In a way, that was how I felt about

Chambliss. He was a thoroughly depraved man, but he thought he was doing what his political leaders wanted him to do."[76] Little other press coverage, however, has attempted to place the bombers in the larger political context of their day. Neither the lawyers prosecuting these cases nor the journalists covering them have used the bombing trials as a place to explore the ways in which the political and legal system in Birmingham and elsewhere colluded to uphold white supremacy, or the ways in which the Ku Klux Klan was aided and abetted by those in "responsible" positions of power.

Yet this larger context was frequently remarked on in 1963, at the time of the bombing. The day after the bombing, President John F. Kennedy issued a public statement that suggested that Alabama Governor George Wallace's "public disparagement of law and order" had encouraged violence and was at least partially responsible for the church bombing.[77] Atlanta Congressman Charles Weltner called on southern white moderates, including himself, to take on part of the blame for the bombing. This bombing took place, Weltner charged, "because those chosen to lead have failed to lead. Those whose task it is to speak have stood mute."[78]

White Birmingham lawyer Charles Morgan infamously charged an even wider web of responsibility for the bombing in his speech to the Birmingham Young Men's Business Club on the day after the bombing. "We all" threw the bomb, he told his audience. "The 'who' is every little individual who talks about the 'niggers' and spreads the seeds of his hate to his neighbor and his son." It is "every Governor who ever shouted for lawlessness and became a law violator," the courts "that move ever so slowly," newspapers that "defend the law," white ministers, the timid mayor, and the distant business community. "Every person in this community who has, in any way, contributed during the past several years to the popularity of hatred is at least as guilty, or more so, than the demented fool who threw that bomb."[79] Morgan held the entire white community and political structures of Birmingham responsible for the bombing, much like Martin Luther King did in his eulogy of the four slain girls.

Newspaper editorials at the time also spread the blame for the bombing widely. The *New York Times* declared the bombing "a conspiracy" and argued that the responsibility for the bombing rested not just with the actual perpetrators but also "upon those who incite and encourage and direct. It is the merest hypocrisy for Governor Wallace and his political associates to offer rewards for the capture of the criminals who shamed his state and our country." Public officials and leading citizens created a "receptive atmosphere" for the crime, the *Times* charged, by not investigating past bombings and by not condemning violence. "This is the pattern of a police state, not of a state of the Union."[80] The *Washington Post* not only held Governor George Wallace "a party to this monstrous crime" but also declared Alabama's entire congressional delegation responsible for the climate of hate that allowed the bombing to take place.[81]

By focusing solely on the question of the provable guilt of individual men, the church bombing trials have not satisfied some activists in Birmingham who want to see a fuller and deeper reckoning with, and atonement for, the past. The Reverend Fred Shuttlesworth, the legendary Birmingham civil rights activist, insists that the city will only be able to achieve any real sense of closure when discussions of guilt reach well beyond the story of these few men. "Birmingham needs to make a statement, if not a confession," Shuttlesworth argued on the eve of Tom Blanton's trial. The trial, he insisted, would only produce "tidbits" of truth about the past, not a complete picture of what had gone on in Birmingham in the 1960s: "We can't put it behind us as long as tidbits are put before us."[82] Cynthia Tucker, a Birmingham native and editorial page editor of the *Atlanta Constitution*, agreed, noting that the bombings were aided and abetted by the Birmingham police department and tolerated by Birmingham's white middle class. Although the court could not legally condemn these more sophisticated bigots, there "can be no healing until the historical record reflects not just the misdeeds of the Klan's flunkies, but also the implicit endorsement of their deeds by people in positions of authority," she wrote in 2000.[83] In this same vein, several newspaper editorials called for a more serious reconsideration of J. Edgar Hoover's national reputation in light of his stonewalling of the church bombing investigation. Why is Hoover's name still "emblazoned at the entrance of the FBI building," one asked, while another charged that Hoover's name "should be stripped off the FBI headquarters' building and stored in the same deep recesses where he hid the evidence against the Birmingham church bombers."[84]

Other city residents insisted that the triumphant trial narrative of progress minimized the continuing racial problems in Birmingham and elsewhere. Noting that 80 percent of the people on death row in Alabama are convicted for killing a white person, even though 65 percent of Alabama murder victims each year are black, a *Birmingham News* editorialist argued that the Blanton trial would have the consequence of convincing the world that a still racially biased Alabama criminal justice system treats blacks and whites equally.[85] Myrna Jackson, the vice president of the Birmingham NAACP, saw the verdict as an attempt to "pacify" blacks in the short-term while the city continued to ignore the economic and educational inequalities between black and white residents.[86] For Horace Huntley, the director of the Oral History Project at the Birmingham Civil Rights Institute, these trials could not address or make up for the fact that blacks in Birmingham were still largely poor and economically disadvantaged compared to whites. Huntley instead believed that what Birmingham really needed was an "American-style Truth and Reconciliation commission" like that in South Africa. Such a commission could ask why blacks still faced unequal conditions in schools and housing and could explore the continued economic legacies of slavery and segregation.[87]

Truth and reconciliation commissions provide a forum for victims of oppression to tell their stories and to name their abusers publicly and for abusers to apologize for their crimes. Although the South African Truth and Reconciliation Commission has been criticized for its policy of granting amnesty to those who confess their crimes, others insist that the TRC allows for a larger telling of truths about the past that is a perquisite to ever moving beyond it and achieving a sense of closure.[88] These trials serve an opposite function: in holding a handful of individuals responsible, they do nothing to force other whites to come to terms with their own complicity with the racist practices of the past. As Diane McWhorter notes, no one repented at these trials, neither the bombers nor white southern society more generally. Unlike in South Africa, blacks in Birmingham were never able to extract confessions of wrongdoing from their white oppressors. In Birmingham, McWhorter writes, "black people are asked to forgive sins that white people have not yet gotten around to apologizing for." While the trials served to restore "the damaged virtue of white America," they did little to challenge whites to confront the legacies of America's racist past.[89]

And more than this, the trials perhaps have made it easier for Americans to feel that they *have* fully confronted the legacies of America's past racial practices. The narrative that has emerged from these trials holds that whites have atoned for their past sins and moved to correct them by hunting down the men responsible for violent racist crimes. Here the American legal system is sound, strong, and unbiased, and ultimately delivers justice. The trial narrative, however, has not begun a conversation about the web of deceit that allowed crimes like the church bombing to take place or about the state actors who protected the men who committed such crimes. It has not raised disquieting questions about government-sanctioned white supremacy or about the government's willingness to condone terrorist acts as long as they were committed against blacks. And it does not draw connections between the racial inequalities of the past and those of today. Yet by putting men like Robert Chambliss, Tom Blanton, and Bobby Frank Cherry in jail years after their crime, we as a nation can tell ourselves that we have achieved racial justice, that we have closed the door on the past, and that, indeed, we have been redeemed.

In writing about Birmingham's difficulties in atoning for its past, journalist Frederick Burger notes, "History is a hard truth to erase or forget, particularly in a multi-media age. That's been the curse of Birmingham's past. The old images—of attack dogs and fire hoses being turned on children protesting segregation in Birmingham in 1960s and the startling vision of rubble at a bombed church—keep being recycled in movies and on TV and in books."[90] It has been difficult for the city of Birmingham to erase the stigma of its racist past because that past has been so well documented in the historical record, especially through now iconic photos and videos. But these trials help illustrate that whatever kind of truth history is, "hard" is arguably not it. History, or our telling, retelling, and interpretation of the past, is a soft truth at best, subject to revision, contestation, and outright manipulation by those with a stake in the consequences of a particular historical representation. The 1977, 2001, and 2002 trials of the Birmingham church bombers offer compelling evidence of the ways in which past events are shaped and given meaning according to current beliefs, values, and political desires. In their insistence that convicting the Birmingham church bombers is a sign that justice has finally been achieved, and is an act that will help rehabilitate Birmingham's reputation and provide a sense of "closure" on the past, these trials argue for a particular version of the history. That version, which focuses on the bombing as the evil act of a small group of avid racists, emphasizes how much has changed since the civil rights era and showcases the ultimate victory of justice within the American legal system. If Martin Luther King Jr., who held the entire social and political structure of Birmingham responsible for the bombings, and Albert Boutwell, Birmingham's mayor at the time who insisted on the city's innocence, are taken as providing two competing interpretations of how to think about this crime, the contemporary trials are playing a crucial role in enshrining Boutwell's versions of the past into the historical record. They are, on many levels, "fixing" history by making what was not necessarily viewed as true in 1963 the "popular" truth today.

Notes

1. For in-depth discussion of the many bombings in Birmingham, see Diane McWhorter, *Carry Me Home: Birmingham, Alabama, the Climatic Battle of the Civil Rights Revolution* (New York: Simon and Schuster, Touchstone Book, 2001).

2. Martin Luther King, eulogy for Addie Mae Collins, Denise McNair, and Cynthia Wesley, delivered at Birmingham's Sixth Avenue Baptist Church, September 18, 1963, reprinted in *A Testament of Hope: The Essential Writings and Speeches of Martin Luther King, Jr.*, ed. James M. Washington (San Francisco, Calif.: Harper and Row, 1986), 221.

3. *Birmingham News*, September 16, 1963, 21.

4. The author was able to read the trial transcripts of the 1977 Chambliss trial and the 2001 Blanton trial. The transcript of *State of Alabama v. Thomas E. Blanton Jr.* is available at Jefferson County Courthouse in Birmingham, Alabama. The transcript of the Chambliss trial is available on microfilm at the Birmingham Public Library. Unfortunately, the court stenographer did not transcribe the opening and closing arguments from the Chambliss trial, so information about them is available only from media sources and the personal recollections of those who were in the courtroom.

5. The number of twenty reopened investigations comes from the Southern Poverty Law Center. Others who have been tried for civil rights–era crimes include Bobby Frank Cherry and Tom Blanton, both convicted for the bombing of the Sixteenth Street Baptist Church; Sam Bowers (convicted in 1988 of the 1966 murder of Vernon Dahmer); and J. B. Stoner (convicted in the late 1970s for the 1958 bombing of Bethel Baptist Church in Birmingham).

6. See, for example, "At Long Last," *People Weekly*, June 5, 2000, 133–36; "Echoes of a Klan Killing," *Newsweek*, May 29, 2000, 32.

7. For more on legal cases as a form of narrative, see Robert Weisberg, "Proclaiming Trials as Narratives: Premises and Pretenses," in *Law's Stories: Narrative and Rhetoric in the Law*, ed. Peter Brooks and Paul Gewirtz (New Haven, Conn.: Yale University Press, 1996), 61–83.

8. *Washington Post*, July 27, 1989, sec. C, 7.

9. Martin Kasindorf, "Winner, Best Brouhaha: The Fireworks over 'Mississippi Burning' Have Generated Unexpected Publicity and a Box Office Boost," *Newsday*, February 12, 1989, 3.

10. Richard Corliss, "Mississippi Burning," *Time*, January 9, 1989, 56–62; Brent Staples, "'Mississippi Burning': Generating Heat or Light? Cinematic Segregation in a Story about Civil Rights," *New York Times*, January 8, 1989, sec. 2, 1.

11. Some examples include John Waddell's sculpture *That Which Might Have Been*, created shortly after the bombing; Sena Naslund's 2003 novel, *Four Spirits*; and Darrah Cloud's 1991 play, *The Stick Wife*. Christopher Paul Curtis's young-adult novel *The Watsons Go to Birmingham—1963* (1995) centers on the Birmingham church bombing.

12. Angela Davis, "Remembering Carole, Cynthia, Addie Mae, and Denise," *Essence*, September 1993, 92; Frank Sikora, *Until Justice Rolls Down: The Birmingham Church Bombing Case* (Tuscaloosa: University of Alabama Press, 1991), 167; "Villanova University Names Scholarship for 1963 Birmingham Church Bombing Victim Denise McNair," *Jet*, February 18, 2002, 20.

13. *Birmingham News*, September 16, 2002; "Hilliard Seeks Bombing Anniversary Stamps," *Birmingham News*, August 9, 2001. The postal service receives 50,000 proposals a year for subjects for postage stamps, so it isn't surprising that Hilliard's proposal was not accepted.

14. In one sample of responses to the very generic question of what they recalled hearing about the bombing, 26 of 72 (or over one third) remembered the "four little (or innocent) girls." The use of this phrase is quite specific; only 3 of the 76 responded that they remembered "four black girls" were killed, and only four replied that "those girls" or "some girls" had been killed. No, what people knew is that there had been four girls killed, they were little, and their race was usually not specified. Reporter's Official Transcript, affidavit of Natalie M. Davis, sample

survey and sample verbatim answers, *State of Alabama v. Thomas E. Blanton Jr.,* Tenth Judicial Circuit, Jefferson County, Alabama, April 16–May 5, 2000, 312–57 (hereafter referred to as trial transcript, *State v. Blanton*).

15. In recent years, the media has paid some attention to the killing of Virgil Ware, in particular. This attention stems, in part, from the renewed interest in Birmingham's history as a result of the church bombing trials. But it is also due to a recent scandal, where U.S. District Court Judge James Ware was found to have lied by claiming to have been Virgil Ware's brother. Although Judge Ware shares the name of Virgil's brother and also grew up in Birmingham, he is of no relation to Virgil Ware's family. For press coverage, see "California Judge Up for Federal Appeals Bench Withdraws Nomination after Admitting to Lie," *Jet*, November 24, 1997, 8; "Cribbing a Civil-Rights Tragedy," *Newsweek*, November 17, 1997, 41; Tim Padgett and Frank Sikora, "The Legacy of Virgil Ware," *Time*, September 22, 2003, 53–59.

16. "Bomb Tragedy Is Their Clarion Call," *Washington Post*, September 20, 1963, sec. D, 2.

17. "Alabama Race Victims Are Mourned by 10,000," *Washington Post*, September 23, 1963, sec. A, 1; "Rallies in Nation Protest Killing of Six in Alabama," *New York Times*, September 23, 1963, 1.

18. Angie Cannon, "Justice at Long Last?" *U.S. News and World Report*, May 29, 2000, 23; *People Weekly*, June 5, 2000, 133–36; Ann Woolner, "Still Burning," *American Lawyer*, January 2000 (available through LexisNexis); Patricia Smith, "Girls, Interrupted," *Ms.*, August/September 2000, 92.

19. "Legal Infighting at Chambliss Trial Goes On before Jury, in Private," *Birmingham News*, metro edition, November 16, 1977, 3.

20. "Chambliss Guilty, Gets Life," *Birmingham News*, November 18, 1977, 1.

21. Kevin Sack, "Research Guided Jury Selection in Bombing Trial," *New York Times*, May 2, 3001, sec. A, 12; Trisha Renaud, "Juries and Beyond," *National Law Journal*, July 30, 2001, sec. A, 1; "Report of Sheldon Associates, Trial Consultants," Summer 2002, http://bellsouthpwp.net/s/h/sheldtc/articles/pdfs/ SA%20NL%20Summer%2002-Web.pdf (accessed January 22, 2003); trial transcript, *State v. Blanton*, 1853.

22. Although none of the four girls actually participated in the "children's crusade" in Birmingham, at least one (Denise McNair) had begged her parents to allow her to march, and others were involved in other activist organizations that were seeking to foster integration in Birmingham. Davis, "Remembering Carole, Cynthia, Addie Mae, and Denise," 92; McWhorter, *Carry Me Home*, 532.

23. Dudley Randall, "Ballad of Birmingham," in *The American Reader*, ed. Diane Ravitch (New York: HarperCollins, 1990), 336.

24. Barry Yeoman, "A Hideous Hate Crime: It's My Family's Secret No More," *Glamour*, August 2000, 225, 251.

25. See particularly Pamela Colloff, "The Sins of the Father," *Texas Monthly*, April 2000, 130–37, 150–54. See also "The Ghosts of Alabama," *Time*, May 29, 2000, 54–55.

26. *Sins of the Father*, directed by Robert Dornhelm (2002: Artisan, Fox Video).

27. Other informants have also been given their due. Elizabeth Cobbs wrote a memoir about her experience with the Chambliss trial, which she discussed on *Oprah*. Although she never publicly admitted her role, it is widely believed that Flora "Tee" Chambliss, Robert Chambliss's wife, was an FBI informant and that her information about her husband helped convict him in 1977. For a discussion, see Howell Raines, "The Birmingham Bombing," *New York Times Magazine*, July 24, 1983, 12–13, 22–29. The play *The Stickwife* focuses on the feelings of the bombers' wives and their potential to turn them in.

28. "One Southerner's Determination," *Washington Post*, May 23, 1976, 4; "The South: Arrest in Birmingham," *Newsweek*, October 10, 1977, 32; "Indictments Recall Terror of Birmingham Sunday in 1963," *New York Times*, October 4, 1977, 18. For a lengthy article on Baxley's role in the trial, see Joseph P. Blank, "The Day They Bombed the Church," *Reader's Digest*, November 1978, 112–20. For a particularly celebratory account of Baxley and of his investigative team, see Sikora, *Until Justice Rolls Down*.

29. "Southern Justice," *Washington Post*, September 28, 1977; "Birmingham Clears Its Name," *Nation*, December 3, 1977, 579.

30. "SCLC Honors Nunn, Lawyer," *Birmingham News*, April 5, 2003; "The Digest," *Birmingham News*, December 17, 2002; "FBI Agents in Church Bomb Investigation Get Top Awards," *Birmingham News*, November 14, 2002. One of the FBI agents, Bill Fleming, also received the 2002 award for "Excellence in Law Enforcement" from the attorney general of the United States. "The Digest," *Birmingham News*, July 12, 2002.

31. Associated Press, "Seeds of Church Bombing Indictment Sown in Meeting between FBI, Blacks," PM cycle, May 19, 2000; "Ex-Klansman on Trial for Infamous 1963 Church Bombing in Alabama," *Jet*, April 30, 2001, 6–7.

32. "FBI Reopens Church Bombing Probe at Debut of Spike Lee's Film," *Jet*, July 28, 1997, 11.

33. "Second Ex-Klansman Convicted in Deadly 1963 Church Bombing; Third Trial Uncertain," *Associated Press State and Local Wire*, May 2, 2001; "King to Join Cherry Trial Backers," *Birmingham News*, August 5, 2001.

34. *Birmingham Post-Herald* quoted in the *Associated Press State and Local Wire*, May 23, 2002.

35. Howell Raines, "The Birmingham Bombing," *New York Times Magazine*, July 24, 1983, 23.

36. For more on the FBI's foot-dragging in this case, see Howell Raines,

"Rounding Up the Sixteenth Street Suspects," *New York Times*, July 13, 1997, sec. E, 16; Raines, "Federal Report Says Hoover Barred Trial for Klansmen in '63 Bombing," *New York Times*, February 18, 1980, sec. A, 1. *San Diego Union-Tribune*, May 5, 2001, sec. B, 8.

37. DeWayne Wickham, "Hoover Role in Bombing Case Deserves Our Condemnation," *USA Today*, May 8, 2001, sec. A, 13; Bill Baxley, "Why Did the FBI Hold Back Evidence?" *New York Times*, May 3, 2001, sec. A, 25.

38. Gary Thomas (Tommy) Rowe was a Birmingham resident who was recruited by the FBI to join the Klan as an undercover agent in 1959. His identity was revealed when he testified against Klansmen accused of the murder of white civil rights activist Viola Liuzzo in 1965. A 1978 investigation into the FBI's covert domestic counterintelligence program, however, revealed that Rowe had personally engaged in violence against civil rights demonstrators while working for the FBI. A special report about Rowe's activities was undertaken in 1978, shortly after Rowe himself was accused of murdering Viola Liuzzo. An investigation discovered that Rowe's FBI handlers had covered up his violent activities. See Gary Thomas Rowe Jr., *My Undercover Years with the Ku Klux Klan* (New York: Bantam Books, 1976); Jared Taylor, "The Many Deaths of Viola Liuzzo," *National Review*, July 10, 1995, 38–39; "Hoover Withheld Data in Klan Case," *Washington Post*, February 19, 1980, sec. A, 1.

39. *Thomas E. Blanton v. State of Alabama*, Appeal to Alabama Court of Criminal Appeals, "Motion to Dismiss," volume 1, 106–18; Associated Press, "Defense: Prosecution Intentionally Delayed '63 Church Bombing Case," BC cycle, November 15, 2000.

40. "Time Catches Up with a Killer," *Omaha World Herald*, May 5, 2001, 16.

41. Alison Graham, *Framing the South: Hollywood, Television, and Race during the Civil Rights Struggle* (Baltimore, Md.: John Hopkins University Press, 2001), 148.

42. Ibid., 154.

43. Bill Baxley was in his midthirties at the time of the Chambliss case, and Doug Jones was in his midforties when he tried Tom Blanton, while Chambliss was seventy-three when convicted and Cherry was seventy-one when he was brought up for trial. Although Tom Blanton was the youngest of the suspects, only sixty-two at the time of his trial, longtime journalist Howell Raines recalled his shock at seeing a picture of Thomas Blanton after his arrest. When Raines had last interviewed Blanton in 1978 he had the "swagger of a honky-tonk tough," but by 2000, he appeared "a puffy old man." See Howell Raines, "Alabama Presses the Klan to Answer for its Most Heinous Bombing," *New York Times*, May 21, 2000, sec. 4, 16.

44. "Thirty-nine Years Later, Last Suspects Trial Begins," *Birmingham News*, May 5, 2002.

45. Sikora, *Until Justice Rolls Down*, 138, 141.

46. Trial transcript, *State v. Blanton*, 1776.

47. Rick Bragg, "Witnesses Say Ex-Klansman Boasted of Church Bombing," *New York Times*, May 17, 2002, sec. A, 18.

48. "Ex-Klansman's Fate in Jury's Hands," *CNN.com/Law Center*, May 22, 2002, http://www.cnn.com/2002/LAW/05/21/church.bombing.trial/.

49. "Case Goes to Jury in Birmingham in '63 Church Bombing Fatal to Four," *New York Times*, November 18, 1977, 18.

50. Elizabeth Cobbs/Petric Smith, *Long Time Coming: An Insider's Story of the Birmingham Church Bombing that Rocked the World* (Birmingham, Ala.: Crane Hill, 1994), 175. Elizabeth Cobbs underwent a sex-change operation and became Petric Smith in 1981, and she used both names when she wrote the book.

51. Associated Press, "Defense to Try to Unravel Government's Case in Church Bombing Trial," BC cycle, April 30, 2001.

52. Opening Argument by John Robbins, trial transcript, *State v. Blanton*, 913.

53. McWhorter, *Carry Me Home*, 25.

54. Cobbs/Smith, *Long Time Coming*, 20.

55. Ibid., 61. Cobbs also claims that local police had informants who reported to them on Klan activities, but this information never went anywhere or stopped any crimes. Cobbs charges not only that the Birmingham police did nothing even though they were tipped off to the bomb at the Sixteenth Street Baptist Church by an informant hours before it exploded but also that at least one Birmingham police officer (who was Chambliss's nephew) helped with the bombing in some capacity. State authorities also attempted to stymie the FBI investigations by charging Chambliss and others with possession of dynamite, tying up any investigation of the actual bombing with these lesser charges (90–91, 96, 102).

56. Ibid., 186.

57. Trial transcript, *State v. Blanton*, 907.

58. David Garrow, "Mississippi's Spy Secrets," *Newsweek*, March 30, 1998, 15; Claude Sitton, "Alabama Compiling Files on Civil Rights Advocates," *New York Times*, February 17, 1964, 1.

59. *San Diego Union-Tribune*, May 5, 2001, sec. B, 8.

60. Jay Reeves, Associated Press, "Verdict in Klan Bombing Trial Doesn't Heal All Church's Wounds," May 25, 2002. While there is some truth to this claim that the church bombing shocked whites and led them to become more vocal in their criticisms of southern segregation, it ignores the very complex history after

the bombing, and especially the fact that the 1964 Civil Rights Act, which outlawed segregation, was highly contested and probably only passed as a memorial to slain President John F. Kennedy.

61. "Distant Times Still Linger," *New Orleans Times Picayune*, April 17, 2001, 4; "Justice in Alabama," *Buffalo News*, May 7, 2001, sec. B, 4.

62. Trial transcript, *State v. Blanton*, 887.

63. "Tragedy Soiled City Image," *Birmingham News*, May 18, 2000.

64. *Washington Post*, November 19, 1977, sec. A, 1; *New York Times*, November 18, 1977, 18.

65. Trial transcript, *State v. Blanton*, 1828.

66. Opening argument by John Robbins, trial transcript, *State v. Blanton*, 915.

67. Trial transcript, *State v. Blanton*, 1793.

68. "Chambliss Trial Recalls '61 Election," *Birmingham Post-Herald*, November 21, 1977, sec. A, 6; "Birmingham Clears Its Name," *Nation*, December 3, 1977, 578.

69. "Birmingham Justice Delayed," *San Francisco Chronicle*, May 24, 2002, sec. A, 30; "Justice at Last," *Columbus Dispatch*, May 7, 2001, sec. A, 8.

70. *Birmingham News*, May 19, 2000; *San Francisco Chronicle*, May 19, 2000, sec. A, 28; "Justice Rains on a Parched Land," *Cleveland Plain Dealer*, May 26, 2002, sec. H, 2.

71. Davis quoted in Rick Bragg, "In One Last Trial, Alabama Faces Old Wound," *New York Times*, May 12, 2002, 16.

72. "Justice Delayed in Birmingham Case," *Tampa Tribune*, May 20, 2000, 14.

73. "A Hideous Hate Crime," *Glamour*, August 2000, 226.

74. This was reported by J. B. Stoner, another segregationist convicted on other bombing charges, in 1980. Stoner and Chambliss shared a cell for several months. Sikora, *Until Justice Rolls Down*, 164.

75. Ellis Cose, "A Reckoning in Birmingham," *Newsweek*, June 3, 2002, 31.

76. Bob Johnson, Associated Press, "Second Church Bombing Trial Revives Memories of the First," BC cycle, April 14, 2001.

77. "Kennedy Decries Racial Bombings; Impugns Wallace," *New York Times*, September 17, 1963, 1.

78. "Mourning of Bomb Victims Asked; Representative Blames Moderates," *Washington Post*, September 18, 1963, sec. A, 5.

79. "Lawyer in Birmingham Blames Whites, Saying 'We All Did It,'" *New York Times*, September 17, 1963, 24.

80. "The Blame—and Beyond," *New York Times*, September 17, 1963, 34.

81. "Reaping the Whirlwind," *Washington Post*, September 17, 1963, sec. A, 12.

82. Stephen Merelman, "An Opportunity to Erode Myths, Write New History," *Birmingham News*, April 15, 2001.

83. Cynthia Tucker, "A Step Toward Healing," *Birmingham News*, May 21, 2000.

84. Colbert King, "No Thanks to Hoover," *Washington Post*, May 5, 2001, sec. A, 19; DeWayne Wickham, "Hoover Role in Bombing Case Deserves Our Condemnation," *USA Today*, May 8, 2001, sec. A, 13.

85. Jack Davis, "Blanton Conviction Does Not Mean Justice," *Birmingham News*, May 6, 2001.

86. Cose, "A Reckoning in Birmingham," 31.

87. Horace Huntley, *Talk of the Nation*, National Public Radio, May 21, 2002.

88. The TRC only offers amnesty to those whose crimes were politically motivated. For criticism of the TRC, see Wole Soyinka, *The Burden of Memory, the Muse of Forgiveness* (New York: Oxford University Press, 1999), 13, 27–29. For support of the commission, see Donald Shriver, "Where and When in Political Life Is Justice Served by Forgiveness?" in *Burying the Past: Making Peace and Doing Justice after Civil Conflict*, ed. Nigel Biggar (Washington, D.C.: Georgetown University Press, 2001), 23–39.

89. Diane McWhorter, "No Trial Closes Injustice's Wounds," *USA Today*, May 22, 2002, sec. A, 12; McWhorter, "The Way We Live Now," *New York Times*, July 29, 2001, sec. 6, 11.

90. Frederick Burger, "Closure in Birmingham?" May 7, 2001, http://www.africana.com/DailyArticles/index_20010507.htm (accessed January 22, 2003).

PART TWO

VISUALIZING MEMORY

The civil rights movement was incredibly photogenic, staging demonstrations and revolutionary performances that heightened the drama of the struggle for national and international audiences. Images brought people into sympathy with the movement. Images embarrassed the U.S. government in the international arena. And images foreground the violence that pervaded the lives of African Americans. Film, television, and photography, in other words, proved central to the emergence of the 1960s African American freedom struggle. As each of these essays in this section elucidates, these visual media have been central to the production, circulation, elaboration, and, in many cases, the containment and sanitizing of the movement's memory in subsequent years.

From *Forrest Gump* to Apple computer ads, from *Time* to *NBC News*, Edward P. Morgan's incisive survey of mass media portrayals of the civil rights movement both in its moment and in the decades that have followed begins this second section. If consensus memory of the civil rights movement presents a facile, easily consumable narrative of living heroes, bygone villains, canonized martyrs, and steadfast success, Morgan cautions us that it is the mass media that provides the enduring images to fix those depictions in the national imagination. He identifies and outlines perhaps the most pervasive and pernicious narrative of civil rights memory: the Manichaean battle between the "good" movement and the "bad" movement. The corporate-run mass media, Morgan tells us, needs the threats of liberal outsiders Malcolm X and James Earl Ray in order to set the sanctified and "sanitized" Martin Luther King Jr. into high relief.

Such a juxtaposition is necessary to "forge the hegemony of late capitalist consumer culture." What such binary memory forgets is the radical democratic vision that guided the civil rights movement in its moment.

Jennifer Fuller's essay continues this interrogation of the kinds of narratives the mass media produces and perpetuates about civil rights by turning her lens specifically to films and television of the 1990s. In a decade fraught with the racial tensions engendered by the Los Angeles uprising and the O. J. Simpson trial, the mainstream media sought to make sense of the "failures" of the civil rights movement amid this wave of national fracture along racial lines. Many of these texts, like the film *The Long Walk Home* and the television show *Any Day Now*, turned to the civil rights movement as "a barometer of racial progress." For contemporary viewers, the civil rights movement is thus produced as a site of nostalgia for a "simpler" heteronormative, black/white racial political landscape confined to the borders of the United States. Moreover, civil rights dramas of the 1990s function as enactments of racial reconciliation. Significantly, Fuller urges us to consider the gendering of this reconciliation, astutely observing that many of these texts place the burden of racial and national healing on the interpersonal relationships between black and white women.

The final two essays in this section attempt to trouble the boundaries of consensus civil rights memory by asking how memory narratives of the civil rights movement change when they are juxtaposed with memorializations of the Black Power movement. Tim Libretti carefully considers independent filmmaker John Sayles's 2002 film, *Sunshine State*, while Leigh Raiford offers an analysis of the various restagings of Black Panther photography from blaxploitation film to *Vibe* magazine. Both authors consider the Black Power and anticolonial struggles of the late 1960s to be an integral part of the long civil rights movement. However, in consensus memory, as Morgan points out, these movements are set in opposition to one another. Libretti's reading of *Sunshine State* suggests that the somewhat uneasy tensions between the two divergent ideologies are resolved in the ways contemporary activists choose to recall them. But for contemporary commodity culture, which attempts to maintain the dichotomy, Raiford argues that Black Power presents a more confounding though no less consumable memory than the civil rights movement.

EDWARD P. MORGAN

The Good, the Bad, and the Forgotten

Media Culture and Public Memory

of the Civil Rights Movement

As millions of American moviegoers know, the beguiling morality tale of *Forrest Gump* is set against a backdrop of familiar 1960s sounds, images, and stories. Early in the film, a young Gump innocently ventures, with the aid of computer enhancement, into the grainy black-and-white footage of George Wallace resisting the tide of desegregation on the steps of the University of Alabama. Several years later, after his improbable service in Vietnam, Gump encounters his best friend, Jenny, amid a secretive gathering of sixties revolutionaries—most notably a threatening assembly of black leather–jacketed, Afroed, and gun-toting Black Panthers who defiantly spit their manifesto against white America in Gump's face.

Gump's popular representation of this bygone era dichotomizes the past into a "good" and a "bad" sixties—the triumphant southern civil rights movement and a hopeful young president on the one hand; on the other, a stereotyped Black Panther, a war in which Americans suffer at the hands of invisible Vietnamese, an abusive Students for a Democratic Society leader who denounces Gump as a "baby-killer," and an excessively self-indulgent counterculture that deteriorates into hard drugs and eventually, in the case of Jenny, death from AIDS. Coinciding as it did with the 1994 Republican party "contract with America," the film's dichotomy complements the prevailing ideological revisionism occurring in American politics at the time.[1]

The racial imagery in *Gump* is telling because it reflects broader treatment of 1960s racial liberation movements throughout mainstream, mass media culture.[2] As with the 1960s generally, public memory of the civil rights struggle has been the site of contested interpretations of the meaning and lessons of the past. Whereas the study of history has traditionally been understood as an empirical and rational undertaking and memory a more subjective phenomenon, increasing interest in terms like *public history*, *collective memory*, and *public memory* suggests that the distinction between history and memory may no longer be so clear. In her study of the construction of the Pearl Harbor attack in "American memory," Emily Rosenberg has argued that "especially in the media nation of post–World War II America . . . memory and history are blurred forms of representation whose politics need to be analyzed . . . as interactive forms."[3] Rosenberg suggests that the media plays a crucial role in the construction of this recent past, since they "provide the matrix that collects and circulates diverse memories in America, shaping them in various ways and keeping some alive while burying others." As she puts it, "Forgetting is the condition of media death (no matter how 'alive' certain memories may be within individuals)." In America, "there is increasingly no effective memory or history outside of media, broadly defined."[4]

I suggest, however, that there is a significant, qualitative difference between what I call the *public memory* of the civil rights movement retained within the market-driven mass media culture and what I would call a *democratic exchange* about the past that respects evidence and tries to understand the subjective dimension of interpretation. Mass media's construction of the past is governed first and foremost by the imperative of maximizing audiences and readers. Their selective memory, then, invariably reflects fundamental economic, organizational, and ideological forces at work within a capitalist economy. As such, the mass media plays a crucial role in creating the foundations of *common*, or near universal, public discourse and public memory within a culture.

Counterpoints to the prevailing themes in mass media culture persist in historical books or documentaries like *Eyes on the Prize*, critical independent media, conferences, university courses, public lectures, and the like. Here, too, the civil rights struggle and the 1960s are contested, with, however, one crucial difference. One can find in these realms an identifiable interpretation of the past—or more accurately, an exchange among various interpretations—that has vanished from mass media culture. Or, to use Emily Rosenberg's term, it is a perspective that has suffered mass media death.

Public memory of the civil rights movement, then, is qualitatively different from the process of assembling collective history of the movement. First, instead of being an investigative undertaking that examines the relationship between evidence and historical interpretation, mass media's public memory draws heavily on the very stories, events, and personalities that prevailed in past media accounts. Subject to intervening influences, the frames of public memory resemble those that permeated media interpretation *during* the civil rights and other 1960s social movements.[5] Moreover, the *form* in which the past is typically preserved in mass media reflects the market-driven imperatives of mass enterprise. The mass media engages its viewers by playing on emotion rather than engaging in a dialogue that interacts with viewers' experiences. With a function of entertaining rather than educating its viewers to a broader understanding of themselves and their world, the mass media simplifies the past in a way that is inherently ideological, even though it seeks impartial balance between competing viewpoints, typically presented as two sides of a conflict. It gives serious consideration to credible voices, while helping to delegitimize "newsworthy" manifestations of systemic criticism or outsider opposition. While there is no media conspiracy to silence radical critiques of the American system, the media routinely reduces radical ideas to barely credible conspiracy theories. By reinforcing the ideological boundaries of conventional public discourse and turning public affairs into consumable entertainment, the mass media thereby helps to forge and sustain the hegemony of late capitalist consumer culture.[6] In the process, the mass media culture undermines the very possibility of the kind of democratic community envisaged by civil rights activists in the past.

The effort of a social movement like civil rights to contest the hegemony of dominant elites and their ideology required that movement activists utilize the mass media to get their message across to a wider, supportive audience. Of all the 1960s movements, the civil rights movement was probably the most successful in using the media to mobilize sympathetic national support for its cause. This success, however, reveals the distinctive way in which the cultural institutions of capitalism deal with contested hegemony. The mass media attended to new voices, at least when they were deemed newsworthy. Outsider challenges could be seen. But the grievances that were alive in the movements' free spaces found their way into mainstream discourse only in terms that were compatible with the ideological foundations of that culture. Outsider critics were, in effect, absorbed into the culture, absent their threatening criticism.

To discern mass media themes about the civil rights struggle of the 1960s, I have reviewed weekly news magazine and some newspaper accounts of major civil rights anniversaries. The public memory that emerges elevates some aspects of the struggle to the level of iconic myth, attributes others to demonic forces that seem beyond comprehension, and obscures portions of the civil rights struggle that challenge hallowed beliefs about American traditions of tolerance and equality. The iconic figure of Martin Luther King Jr. towers over this public memory. I reflect on the origins of this public memory in news magazine accounts of civil rights events during the 1960s. I then examine the way the boundaries of mass media discourse are sustained through other media, such as popular films, news media coverage of urban riots, and television's treatment of America's racial divide.[7]

Three recurring themes characterize mass media culture's public memory of civil rights. First, the "good" civil rights text retells the story of a regional struggle in the South in ways that legitimize rather than challenge national traditions and institutions. Second, persistent national issues like racial inequality are interpreted through a bounded discourse in which critics of national institutions are either rendered invisible or are relegated to a status of illegitimate Other. Third, the civil rights story, like the contemporary media discourse on race, reduces the public to spectators identifying with or cheering for one or another public representation of conflicting sides. Both the content and form of media discourse, then, contradict the powerful democratic assertiveness that lay at the heart of the civil rights struggle.

At the Center of Public Memory: Martin Luther King Jr. as Icon

One occasion that brings the media torrent's content critics into public view is the national holiday honoring Martin Luther King Jr. Typically, university campuses around the country host lectures that purport to resurrect King's historical legacy, in contrast to the typical media culture celebration. It is a day in which private memories and serious historical analysis are shared with wider audiences. On these occasions, some will hear of the King who lauded Malcolm X on the occasion of his death in 1965, the King who took his campaign to Chicago in 1966 and encountered in his own words the "worst racism" of his experience, the King who condemned the United States as the "greatest purveyor of violence in the world" when he spoke out against the Vietnam War in 1967, or the King who criticized capitalism as the root of the inequality he confronted in the Poor People's Campaign of 1968.

These are representations of a political King who has virtually disappeared from mainstream mass media accounts. Public memory's Martin Luther King Jr. has been ideologically sanitized, detached from his own politics and their more radical, or system-critical, implications. The elevation of King to iconic representation of the civil rights movement has obscured a movement built on the courageous and determined efforts of thousands upon thousands of everyday people—a revision of the past that removes the struggle for justice, and its potential continuity with today's world, from the realm of what "the people" can do. As Fred Powledge has observed, "In the minds of untold numbers of Americans, for example, the Reverend Dr. Martin Luther King, Jr, *was* the civil rights movement. Thought it up, led it, produced its victories, became its sole martyr. Schoolchildren—including Black schoolchildren—are taught this."[8]

Like anniversaries of the civil rights leader's assassination or other momentous events from that era, the King holiday is an occasion that prompts mass media culture to revisit and make sense of the past. Typically the media revisits King's "I Have a Dream" speech and asks how far America has come in realizing King's powerful oratorical challenge of 1963. So pervasive is the 1963 image of King addressing the March on Washington that it led Vincent Harding to bemoan, "Brother Martin

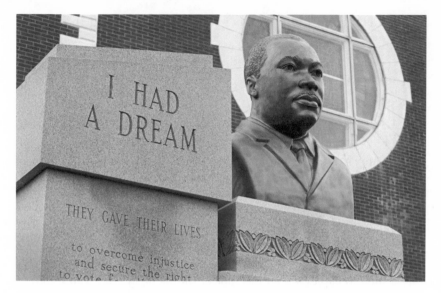

This memorial, which sits in front of the Selma, Alabama, church that served as headquarters for the Selma-Montgomery marches of 1965, literally freezes Martin Luther King's famous dream speech in stone. The inscription on the bust transforms King's oft-quoted line into the past tense, which could suggest either the fulfillment of King's ideals or the lost opportunity to realize King's dream. (© Owaki/Kulla/Corbis)

spent a fair amount of time in jail, but his worst imprisonment may be how his own nation has frozen him in that moment in 1963."[9] This is the Martin Luther King Jr. whose place in public history has been cemented as America's conscience.

For example, on the twentieth anniversary of the March on Washington, a feature-length *U.S. News and World Report* article examined "King's Dream: How It Stands Twenty Years Later."[10] Similarly, *Newsweek* chose the twentieth anniversary of King's death to assess the state of "Black and White in America." After reviewing the balance sheet of gains and losses in racial equality, the magazine observed that "there are signs of a revival of interest in the unfinished civil-rights revolution." The magazine noted further, "Television, newspapers, and magazines are observing the twentieth anniversary of King's death with a fresh look at the problems of blacks," suggesting the self-referential way the media confuses the virtual reality of media discourse with the everyday life of the citizenry.[11]

In between these accounts, the inaugural celebration of the King holiday led *Time* to salute "Justice's Drum Major" with references to the "prominent visitors" to King's hometown and their recollections of King. In a manner that typifies its retrospective accounts of the 1960s generally, *Time* placed the celebration in "historical" context by recalling a brief collage of civil rights–era imagery: "The ceremonies became occasions to recall one of the most painful and dramatic eras of American history. Segregated schools, lunch counters and bathrooms. Freedom riders. Churches bombed and civil rights workers murdered. Helmeted police wading into demonstrators with attack dogs, tear gas, hoses, guns and bayonets. Then the fight to win passage of the 1964 Civil Rights Act and the 1965 Voting Rights Act."[12] Some civil rights veterans took the occasion to observe that President Reagan had initially opposed creation of the King holiday along with civil rights legislation in the 1960s. With the detached journalistic "balance" typical of mass market media, *Time* then cited comments by Reagan's attorney general, Edwin Meese, to the effect that the administration's opposition to affirmative action policies was "very consistent with what Dr. King had in mind" when speaking of a "color-blind society." Without checking this claim for historical validity, the article concluded with reference to King's "true legacy," tracing the "distance the United States has traveled toward an integrated society."[13]

Three years later, a *U.S. News* column opined that, in contrast to his "prime" when King was "perceived as a threat by practically all segments of society," his reputation had revived to the point that "people of all persuasions now have a sense that he challenges them to be at their best and that he's articulating principles they believe in that are larger than race."[14] *U.S. News* happened to be the national news weekly most prone to viewing King as threatening in the 1960s.[15] By 1989, however, King had been sufficiently domesticated to the point that racial conflict was subsumed in the broader dream of national harmony—something that can presumably be achieved if we are all "at our best." With King's own political actions removed from the *U.S. News* record, "our best" would not seem to include going to jail in the cause of confronting oppressive or unjust government policy.

If these news media accounts weren't enough to indicate King's safe, sanctified status, a second indicator can be found in ways in which association with the King image has itself become a marketing phenomenon. In 1999, with approval of the Atlanta-based King Center, Apple computer featured King in magazine and billboard ads as part of its "think different" campaign, in effect translating determined political opposition into creative entrepreneurship. In 2001, against an image of King speaking (to an empty mall) from the steps of the Lincoln Memorial in 1963, a television voice-over suggested to viewers, "Before you can inspire, before you can touch, you must first connect. And the company that connects more of the world is Alcatel, a leader in communication networks." Without Alcatel's communications technology, presumably, even King's powerful oratory would fail to reach today's audiences.[16]

So vapid is the sanitized King that it has drawn the occasional content critic into the mainstream media. One of the more assertive voices has been that of Michael Eric Dyson, who in 2000 penned an editorial column in *Newsweek* decrying the King who had become "frozen in myth." Dyson argued that "America has forgotten King's radical legacy. We have banished him to blandness, turning his fountain of rage against injustice into a faucet of polite protest."[17] By the late 1990s, in fact, the news weeklies were taking note of a public contest over King's legacy. Their responses to this contest are instructive, for they illustrate the way meanings of the past *are* hotly contested within mass media, yet this contestation takes place within a discourse that omits more system-challenging perspectives. The more consistently King-friendly *Newsweek* addressed "The War over King's Legacy" in 1998. The occasion was the thirtieth anniversary of King's assassination, which occurred at a time when, according to *Newsweek*, King's "Dream was turning dark. Worried about poverty and Vietnam, he was growing more radical." Noting that King's "popular beatification" began with his death, *Newsweek* juxtaposed this King legend against an "assault" from "King's own family and many of his aging lieutenants." However, the counterpoint to the beatified King, it turns out, was a conspiracy theory on a par with Oliver Stone's account in *JFK*—namely, that King was killed because of his effort to "build an interracial coalition to end the war in Vietnam and force major economic reforms." Thus the effort to rehumanize King and assert his radical politics was subsumed within dubious assertions of massive conspiracy leading to King's assassination.[18]

Apparently it did not occur to *Newsweek*'s writers that the radical King may have been more effectively contained by the media culture's sanctification than his politics could have been by an alleged conspiracy to kill him. Belying its "balance," the magazine repeatedly weighed in with open skepticism toward the antibeatification critics, once again finding America's intransigent racial divide at its heart. In the magazine's glib generalization, blacks, it seems, view King differently from whites. Asking "who was the real Martin Luther King, Jr.—the integrationist preacher or the leftist activist of the spring of 1968," the article suggests that "many whites want King to be a warm civic memory, an example of the triumph of good over evil," whereas for many African Americans the "sanitizing of King's legacy, and suspicions about a plot to kill him" resonate with the "larger forces" that "hijack their history and conspire against them." Once again drawing on another popular "reality" of media culture, the article asserts that ultimately the war over King's legacy mirrors the biracial reading of the O. J. Simpson trial. The article concluded by speculating about the King who would have grown older had he lived. Noting that King's "I Have a Dream" speech would not resonate with the "Malcolm X–saturated hip-hop generation," *Newsweek* concluded that King would have "stood by liberalism" and remained a hero for the "upwardly-mobile, assimilated black youth," a perspective that, as King chronicler Taylor Branch points out, obscures the fact that, at the end of his life, "King was not in the company of white presidents or black elites, but marching with the garbagemen of Memphis."[19] The radical King's removal from history receives *Newsweek*'s blessing.

Time also inquired into the legacy of a contested King, observing that King "is still regarded mainly as the black leader of a movement for black equality," a characterization that *Time* rejected as "far too restrictive." Instead of considering the more radical King, who criticized the economic inequality built into capitalism, however, the article observed that "for all King did to free blacks from the yoke of segregation, whites may owe him the greatest debt, for liberating them from the burden of America's centuries-old hypocrisy about race." As a result, the United States "can claim to be the leader of the 'free world' without inviting smirks of disdain and disbelief."[20] The movement that King led swept away all traces of the oppressive Jim Crow system in the South. This was its defining "victory."

For *Time*, the contest over King's legacy arose because his "most-quoted line" from 1963, when he dreamed of a nation where black children would "not be judged by the color of their skin but by the content of their character," was "kidnapped" by the opponents of affirmative action. The contested King, in other words, is, for *Time*, a safely contained, integrationist King versus a right-wing version linked to efforts to roll back the liberal legacy of 1960s public policy. Such are the boundaries of mass media discourse.

In short, *Time* substitutes its kidnapping of King's legacy for the right-wing's claim. For *Time*, King's radicalism lay not in his political viewpoint but in his "sense of urgency" in confronting racial inequality; his victory should be appreciated by whites because it legitimized the United States dominion over much of the world, dominion that the more radical King challenged in 1967. *Time's* framing echoes earlier characterizations of King's contribution emanating from the Reagan and Bush administrations. In 1988, as civil rights veterans gathered to commemorate the twenty-fifth anniversary of the March on Washington, President Reagan issued a statement praising the progress that had been made toward "fully achieving Dr. King's dream of a color-blind society" and observing that the United States "is an even more brilliant beacon of freedom and hope" as a result.[21] Less than a year after the first Persian Gulf War, Deputy Secretary of State Lawrence Eagleburger invoked King's "message to the world" to "make real the promise of democracy."[22] The iconic King is thus claimed to support just about any cause justifiable within the boundaries of mainstream ideological assumptions.

Media Culture and Coverage of King in the 1960s

Both the safely domesticated King and the heroic figure eclipsing much of the civil rights struggle echo ways the mass media covered the civil rights struggle at the time it was occurring.[23] These were, and are, grounded in three defining characteristics of mass media culture as it was evolving through the sixties spectacle into its current form. First, the mass media embraced a market-driven emphasis on personality as a key signifier of political meaning. Second, the media followed market-driven codes and biases with respect to protest activity, violence, drama, and dichoto-mous conflict. Finally, the mass media turned to an ideologically bound discourse for interpreting or explaining the meaning of events, one that Stuart Hall and others have referred to as the media's common discourse, or that Noam Chomsky has termed the "bounds of the expressible" or the "bounds of thinkable thought."[24]

The heroic icon reflects not only Martin Luther King Jr.'s significant leadership role and his power as a public figure but also mass media's tendency to personalize news stories as a way of reducing the complex-ity of events and attracting audience notice. The market-driven push to maximize profit margins has a great deal to do with the elevation of public figures to celebrity status. The violent death of significant figures such as King only compounded this media tendency. The elevation of leaders into larger-than-life celebrities has left the rest of us, in effect, waiting for a new King.

Violence, dramatic action, personalized or partisan conflict, and evoc-ative imagery are common features in the news media's packaging of events to maximize audience size or readership.[25] All featured promi-nently in mass media's coverage of the civil rights struggle during the 1960s.[26] The emergence of television, combined with powerful imagery of civil rights struggle and the telegenic young president and the emo-tional power of his assassination, helped to launch the public-affairs-as-spectacle phenomenon that prevails today. The events that evoked most powerfully the "great moral dramas" of civil rights, in Richard Lentz's phrase—Birmingham's police dogs and fire hoses, the March on Washing-ton, and Selma's "Bloody Sunday"—have themselves become icons of the historical struggle, revisited by mass media on significant anniversaries.

Even more crucial, perhaps, is the mass media's tendency to frame the news in system-reinforcing ways. Reflecting the journalistic credo of balance and impartiality, reporters are supposed to let their subjects speak, balancing one speaker against another in order to avoid taking sides. The meaning of events is thereby reduced by the media's inclination to present social and political issues as conflicts between two—and usu-ally no more than two—concrete interests or perspectives. Throughout the civil rights movement, protest coverage and media attention accorded to King were persistently juxtaposed against some competing interest or voice in the struggle. The selection of these voices or actors reveals the media's sympathies toward or against King, as well as the crucial boundaries of legitimate discourse about the public meaning of events.

In the cases that have become the signal stories of public memory, King and the movement were juxtaposed against violent white racists in the South. These were the straightforward good-versus-evil stories that readily lent themselves to binary media simplification. Thus, when the national media lenses captured nonviolent activists under violent attack by police dogs and fire hoses in Birmingham, or mounted, billy club–wielding police in Selma, a sympathetic national audience was instantly mobilized. In many respects, this response echoed that of northern journalists sent south to cover civil rights, reporters who, in ABC reporter Paul Good's words, received "invaluable on-the-job training on the subject of racism."[27] Sympathetic media coverage also helped to spread the contagion of sit-ins in 1960 and proved a boon to recruitment of new activists.

Civil rights activists themselves came to recognize the enormous importance of this media spotlight, for it reinforced the principle of effective protest politics: making one's audience feel psychologically closer to the protester than to the target of the protest. From the activists' perspective, media coverage of early sit-ins and the violence of Bull Connor's police in Birmingham taught powerful lessons about the importance of mass media and its dichotomous treatment of "good" and "evil." As the white Birmingham lawyer David Vann reflected on the Birmingham experience, "It was a masterpiece [in] the use of the media to explain a cause to the general public."[28] National media planning became an increasingly significant part of civil rights and other protests. In Staughton Lynd's account of the planning sessions for the 1964 Mississippi Freedom Summer, a great deal of attention was given to the strategic advantage of inviting northern white students to participate because, as the notes of Student Nonviolent Coordinating Committee (SNCC) worker Mendy Samstein recounted, "it was clear from the nature of the publicity derived from the Freedom Vote campaign that the press would respond to the beating of a Yale student as it simply would not do to the beating of a local Negro."[29]

As a consequence, media coverage of protest activities invariably involved (and involves) an interaction between protesters efforts to "get their message across" and the imperatives and systemic predispositions of mass media. As protesters' grievances shifted from the blatant racism of the South to national institutions steeped in legitimizing ideology, their grievances invariably were minimized, typically replaced by a pejorative focus on the protesters themselves. This interaction helped to set in motion a dynamic that effectively *widened* the psychological distance between protesters and broader national audiences.[30]

When Martin Luther King Jr. emerged as a civil rights leader in the Montgomery bus boycott of 1955–56, both *Time* and *Newsweek* found him to be an intriguing new voice of patient persistence and promise. In fact, *Time* placed King on its cover for the first time in February 1957. In both the 1963 Birmingham and the 1965 Selma protests, however, the national news magazine's response was more varied. In the early days of each campaign, both magazines expressed considerable skepticism about King's (and the Southern Christian Leadership Conference's) timing, echoing sentiments expressed by the *New York Times* and officials in the Kennedy and Johnson administrations. In Birmingham both magazines juxtaposed King and the SCLC against the voices of white moderates in the community. Similarly, in early 1964, *Time*'s coverage of its "Man of the Year" included excerpts from King's letter from the Birmingham jail— minus the segment in which King wrote of his great disappointment with "white moderates" who preferred a "negative peace which is the absence of tension to a positive peace which is the presence of justice."[31] In the case of Selma, the magazines decried the "unnecessary confrontation" caused by the leader who was "determined to create a crisis" that might rankle the sympathetic Johnson administration.

However, as Richard Lentz has observed, King "got his crises, when the dogs were loosed in Birmingham, when the mounted possemen thundered down on the marchers at the Edmund Pettus Bridge," and as a result "*Time* and *Newsweek* were forced to reinterpret King," this time placing him on the side of good against the savage racist attack led by Birmingham's Bull Connor and Selma's Jim Clark.[32] In the aftermath of King's leadership in the Birmingham struggle and his stirring oratory at the March on Washington, *Time* crowned King "Man of the Year." By the end of 1964, King's leadership earned him the Nobel Peace Prize. Shortly after Selma's aptly named "Bloody Sunday," however, both magazines once again began to distance themselves from King, criticizing his insistent efforts to remobilize the march to Montgomery while speaking sympathetically of Selma's public safety director, Wilson Baker, who was "desperately trying to keep the peace in the strife-stricken town."[33]

The mass-market magazines also contained innumerable examples of a "good" King juxtaposed against civil rights activists whom the national media deemed unsavory. Younger, more rhetorically militant civil rights activists, like those of SNCC, repeatedly fared poorly in comparison to King. When the Mississippi Freedom Democratic Party was offered what it considered a patronizing compromise at the Democratic National Convention of 1964, King joined with a variety of Johnson loyalists to urge the MFDP to accept the offer of two at-large votes. The liberal *Newsweek* embraced the position of "black moderates" like King while distancing from the powerful oratory of Mississippi activists like Fannie Lou Hamer. In an account that may have also reflected class and gender biases, *Newsweek* reported that, according to civil rights leaders, "Fannie Lou Hamer, the Freedom Democrat's leading mouthpiece, is showing disturbing demagogic tendencies—attacking middle-class Negroes and whites, American policy in Vietnam, and Martin Luther King."[34] A year later, in the aftermath of the Selma march, even the normally skeptical *U.S. News* saluted the moderate King while denigrating the angry responses of SNCC director James Forman.

Perhaps the starkest contrast came in news magazine accounts that juxtaposed King against Malcolm X. In 1964, *Newsweek* compared a moderate King to Malcolm ("a man with a menacing word for every occasion") and King's followers, who believed in a "middle way," to Malcolm's followers, who were drawn to him because of "little more than the anger in their hearts."[35] On the occasion of Malcolm's murder, *Time* dismissed Malcolm as a former "pimp, cocaine addict, and thief" who had been transformed into an "unashamed demagogue" who preached hatred and violence. The magazine criticized King not only because he failed to denounce Malcolm as a radical but also because he had "sanctified" him as a "brilliant" leader who had "moderated" his extremist views.[36]

Finally, the mainstream mass media treated King himself in a dichotomous manner, in effect pitting a good King against an undesirable

King. The latter was the civil rights leader who ventured outside the boundaries of conventional ideological consensus to attack national institutions and policies such as white racism in the North, the war in Vietnam, and capitalism's link to class and poverty. This "bad" King is, of course, the invisible King in today's public memory. The dichotomous coverage of the two Kings reveals ideological biases that inform mass media and limit the range of acceptable meanings.

The national news magazines, for example, were openly skeptical about King's activism in Chicago. The SCLC campaign in Chicago focused on educating the public about the appalling conditions of ghetto life in northern cities, organizing tenants to make demands on absentee landlords, and eradicating segregated housing in the North. *Time* viewed urban segregation largely as a function of "free choice" in the real estate market and thus the magazine was skeptical about the contribution a southern integrationist preacher like King could offer the urban North. When two riots marred the early days of the Chicago operation, one in the Puerto Rican district, the other in the black ghetto, *U.S. News* blamed them on King's aggressive, unsettling message. *Time* and *Newsweek*, on the other hand, criticized the Chicago police and an unresponsive Richard Daley administration. As the campaign evolved, however, both magazines began to characterize open-housing marches as ineffectual because they triggered a violent response, a dramatic departure from their take on Selma a year earlier. In the end, *Newsweek* applauded the campaign's gains but distanced itself from King's tactic of "provocation."[37]

Media skepticism toward King's participation in northern cities also reflected the fact that ghetto life was depicted within the narrowed ideological framing of mass media: ghetto problems were a function of the presence or absence of government supports and the quality of interaction between city governments and inner-city minority populations. King's exploration of a broader economic framework for understanding ghetto life remained obscured by the media's prevailing image of King as the southern integrationist.

When King raised his voice to challenge the Vietnam War, the national media responded emphatically and in unison. King's advocacy of a moderate "bombing halt" in 1965 was attacked by all three news magazines. *Newsweek* tried to rescue King from the "peaceniks" and the "hypermilitant" SNCC by urging him to stick to "his issue" and fight "one war at a time." These commentaries, however, paled in comparison to the national media's response to King's 1967 Riverside Church speech against the war. The *Washington Post* editorial of April 6 typified the media's condemnation: "Dr. King has done a grave injury to those who are his natural allies in a great struggle to remove ancient abuses from our public life; and he has done an even graver injury to himself. Many who have listened to him with respect will never again accord him the same confidence. He has diminished his usefulness to his cause, to his country, and to his people."[38] Similarly, the *New York Times* decried King's "disastrous" attempt to link "his personal opposition to the war . . . with the cause of Negro equality," noting this would "lead not to solutions but to deeper confusion."[39]

In August 1967, in the aftermath of the massively destructive Newark and Detroit riots, King announced his most radical campaign, the Poor People's Movement, which was designed to unite the poor of all races in a campaign of disruption, school boycotts, factory sit-ins, and a massive march on Washington by the unemployed. In effect, the Poor People's Movement represented a frontal attack on an economy that King had been criticizing privately as the root of the inequalities plaguing Americans. The now unsympathetic news magazines dismissed King's plans as a desperate effort to take the initiative away from militant extremists like SNCC. In Richard Lentz's analysis, both *Time* and *Newsweek* "wanted King back in the South." As Lentz put it, "*Time*, no less than *Newsweek*, needed to demonstrate that the System was working."[40] After he was killed in the midst of the struggling Poor People's Campaign, all three magazines froze King in the role of the great leader of the southern movement.

Public Memory of Civil Rights: Preserving the Boundaries of Discourse

As it has with Martin Luther King Jr., mass media's public memory of the broader era of civil rights struggle reinforces the boundaries of public discourse by legitimizing national institutions and stigmatizing voices critical of those institutions. The end result, a kind of self-contained media "reality" designed for mass consumption, reinforces the hegemony of consumer capitalism. Several themes seem to dominate this consumable past. Civil rights struggle, to the degree that it is depicted, involved the effort to erase a regional deviation from the national ideal in which all are "created equal." The horrors of racial oppression occurred in the South. They were erased when civil rights activists appealed to the national conscience and the government to override the peculiar institutions of Jim Crow. The federal government played the crucial role in righting these wrongs, thus removing America's great hypocrisy, at least in its most blatant form.

This does not mean that racial inequality and racial polarization have disappeared. It means they are *national* phenomena and are therefore treated quite differently by national media. The national creed is grounded in equal rights, legitimizes the national government as a potential instrument for righting social wrongs, and embraces the market economy as an important foundation for individual freedom and social mobility. Consequently, approaches to the "unfinished agenda" of civil rights are limited to the familiar "liberal" and "conservative" polarities of mainstream political discourse.

One crucial characteristic of this discourse is that voices from "outside" this spectrum are, quite simply, not part of the discourse. Expressions of "outside" perspective are often seen in the frightening visual representations of outsiders like Malcolm X or the Black Panthers, but their meaning is interpreted through the assumptions of mainstream discourse. They become part of the spectacle, for the most part harmlessly consumed by mass audiences. A few examples, drawn from different media, can illustrate the boundaries of this discourse.

Popular entertainment film, as opposed to historical documentary, is one medium that contains public discourse even as it dramatizes the past and engages viewers with personalities who may, in fact, have been radical critics of mainstream institutions. Hollywood's depiction of the civil rights era seems to "bring history to life." Yet while providing an opening for counterhegemonic expression, the net effect of civil rights at the movies—like that of *Forrest Gump*—is to reinforce the framing of media culture's discourse and to set that discourse in the context of consumption and spectatorship.

One cannot, of course, expect an authentic political portrayal of an explosively divisive issue from Hollywood studios seeking to maximize their mass appeal. But with respect to media culture, that's exactly the point. Where *mass* appeal counts—that is, in any medium competing for a mass market—the media produce entertainment that teaches a safe political lesson. Mass media are the media of *common* discourse, as distinct from the largely invisible islands of subcultural criticism and subjective response. In this case, our common history is reduced to a commodity to be consumed. Potential activists in the audience are turned into spectators watching a movie that provides them with no call to action other than, perhaps, imitation.

Because other chapters in this volume concentrate on civil rights films, I will only comment on two popular film representations of the civil rights era, *Malcolm X* and *Panther*, both films that sought to center the lesser-known stories of 1960s black radicals. Spike Lee's 1992 film *Malcolm X* drew heavily on Malcolm's *Autobiography* in a conscious effort to provide an authentic portrayal of the powerful leader whose voice was widely demonized in mass media culture during and since the 1960s. Yet the mass-market film reflected a tension between a "constant quest for legitimacy and the need to quell and displace fears at the same time that it calls them forth."[41] Lee's Malcolm seemingly appealed to two kinds of audiences: those who sought to redress mass media stereotypes, including the mass media's reduction of Malcolm to racist demagogue, and those in inner-city audiences who could heed Malcolm's life lessons about self-assertion through self-reflection, study, and hard work. The appealing, fleshed-out Malcolm helped to redress stereotypical treatments, yet the apply-yourself lesson he seemed to teach left Lee open to critics who argued that his Malcolm was an overly conventional, commercially acceptable figure befitting the Hollywood market.[42] Not surprisingly, one by-product of the film was a renewed burst of "Malcolm-mania" already occurring in rap music, the widespread commodification of Malcolm X's image on sweatshirts, jackets, refrigerator magnets, and the like, along with the ubiquitous X-marked baseball caps. *Malcolm*'s 1992 inner-city audience could hardly be blamed for latching onto commodities that seemed to express some of their alienation, thereby conforming to the media culture's prevailing mode of discourse: a politics-of-expression that leaves political structures intact.

A similar fate seemed to befall Mario Van Peebles's film *Panther*, a 1995 effort to tell a partially fictionalized but essentially authentic story of another iconic outsider group from the 1960s. While the film's historical accuracy has been criticized on several fronts, *Panther* accurately corrected mass media distortions about the Black Panther Party's historical origins, its community service dimension, and the government's effort to eradicate the group. However, the film introduced the seemingly ubiquitous conspiracy dimension to the latter, suggesting an improbable collaboration between organized crime and the federal government to introduce hard drugs into the inner city to pacify inner-city youth and eradicate the Panther element. While the influx of heroin and later crack cocaine into the inner cities from the late 1960s on clearly had a deleterious effect on inner-city youth, and the question of federal intent has never been fully invalidated, it is notable that the only plausible way systemic forces can be explained in the individualistic language of mass media is through conspiracy. It is precisely this collaboration that seems most improbable and thus readily dismissible by mainstream media critics. The film, not surprisingly, ends with a shoot-out.

While trying to counter the media culture's longtime condemnation of the Panthers with a corrective narrative, Peebles was, in a way, imprisoned by the very dramatic symbolism used by the historical Panthers—the guns, the black berets and leather garb, the battles with police—symbolism that was also the focal point of 1960s media distortion and political attack. Thus it is not surprising that several years before the release of *Panther* a group calling themselves the "New Black Panthers" expropriated the symbolism of the original group to preach a black nationalist, anti-Zionist message filled with references to "white devils" and "bloodsucking Jews." Nor is it surprising that, as former Panther Bobby Seale has charged, the New Black Panthers don't "understand our history."[43] Thus it is that *Panther*'s reliance on Black Panther Party symbolism spoke loudly to audiences of inner-city youth, while it was precisely the film's efforts to expand the meaning of the symbols that provoked a new round of public condemnation.[44] On the one hand, once youthful audiences have consumed the heavily symbolic *Panther*, they are left with no course of *action* except imitation. On the other, the effort to convey the meaning of that symbolism is widely denounced in the mass media.

Media coverage of the 1992 riot in Los Angeles also demonstrates the boundaries of media discourse. For many Americans, one of the more frightening phenomena of 1960s racial struggle were the so-called "long, hot summers" from 1964 to 1968 in which ghetto residents from Rochester and Harlem to Watts, Cleveland, Chicago, Newark, Detroit, Washington, D.C., and many others exploded in violent insurrection. The early riots, as they were commonly called, helped to trigger parts of the Johnson administration's "War on Poverty." More generally, however, the riots were widely viewed as a "revolution of rising expectations" aroused, and disappointed, by a combination of the awakening of civil rights struggle in the South, fury at the racist attacks on the nonviolent civil rights activists, and long-simmering frustration at the apparent political invisibility of inner-city hopelessness.[45] More concretely, riots were sparked by acts of police brutality against a backdrop of heightened aggravation caused when the more radically empowering Community Action Program fell far short of its promises.

In 1992, young Americans had a chance to experience feelings of horror and fascination comparable to their counterparts in the 1960s when South Central Los Angeles exploded in fury that matched the scale and intensity of the worst of the 1960s riots. In its efforts to make sense of this violence by some inner-city racial minorities, media coverage of the 1992 conflagration resembled media coverage of the earlier era, with the exception that, in 1992, the media had to ask why the violence occurred after years of public policy that allegedly, in one way or another, had responded to the sixties riots and dealt with inner-city poverty.

The explanation of the South Central riots immediately devolved into a debate between the Reagan-Bush approaches to urban policy and those of the Johnson administration's Great Society. Bush administration officials were quick to seize on the riot as evidence of "failed" federal policies that created massive dependency and stagnation among poverty-stricken inner-city residents. Liberal defenders of past government policy countered by claiming that the riots reflected the years of "benign neglect" toward racial minorities in particular and the inner-city poor generally, from the Nixon administration through the Reagan and Bush administrations. The meaning of the 1992 riot, in other words, was framed in classic liberal-conservative terms.

The policy debate over the inner-city revolt was notable for what it left out, namely any reference to the history of the Community Action Program or any other grassroots organizing efforts that occurred in the 1960s. While powerlessness and empowerment were deemed relevant in some way to the explosion of inner-city rage, these terms were defined in ways entirely compatible with prevailing political and economic institutions. Liberals spoke of the need for a new resurgence in government programs designed to improve deteriorating public schools, counter drug dependency, and train the unemployed, which would presumably help to "empower" those stuck in inner-city hopelessness. Conservatives criticized the way in which government "handouts" created a dependency on government largesse among a victimized population, arguing instead for renewed "enterprise zones" that would presumably encourage job creation, thereby "empowering" the poor to take action to improve their personal livelihood.

It is noteworthy that neither of these positions paid the slightest attention to efforts to involve the inner-city community in its own collective empowerment during the civil rights era. A LexisNexis search of all newspaper accounts of the 1992 riots revealed but a single mention of the Community Action Program (simply listed as one of the poverty programs). Yet as originally conceived, the Community Action component of the War on Poverty provided federal funds directly to community action agencies and mandated that at least 50 percent of the agency members had to be the indigenous poor themselves. Funds could be used for purposes articulated by these communities in grant applications, and they were widely used to organize inner-city residents to tackle the issues that were most salient to them, such as horrible housing conditions caused by negligent absentee landlords, a lack of jobs and job training, and brutal oppression by an unaccountable and largely white police force.

Needless to say, these efforts brought the inner-city poor into volatile conflict with city officials and social service providers. After about a year of varying levels of conflict in the nation's cities, the mostly Democratic mayors appealed to the Johnson administration to remedy the Community Action Program so it would work in a manner more typical of American big city politics. The membership of Community Action agencies, like those of the successor Model Cities program, were subsequently appointed by city hall, thereby augmenting rather than detracting from the power of urban mayors. In the case of Newark, at least, the growing frustrations over city hall intransigence in the face of Community Action demands helped to fuel the explosion of 1967, yet this perspective on empowerment was entirely absent from mass media accounts of the 1992 revolt.

Civil Rights and the Rise of Spectator Democracy

The prevailing message of the media culture's reflective civil rights treatment reinforces the view that there is a national consensus about civil rights grounded in ideals about racial tolerance and opportunity. The old southern apartheid system violated this national consensus, so once it was brought to the nation's attention, this wrong was righted, albeit at considerable cost to individuals involved. This very history reinforces national beliefs about the United States as a "special" nation. It has been claimed as such by the very forces that resisted these advances. Icons from this era remain to remind us what the nation went through during that turbulent time. Figures like Martin Luther King Jr., Rosa Parks, and other notables in King's entourage still figure prominently in the media during Black History Month and on anniversaries of notable civil rights events. Media spectacles from the 1960s like the Birmingham fire hoses and police dogs, the March on Washington, and the Selma march are reminders of the violence of the white South, the nonviolence of civil rights petitioners, and the benign response of the federal government. Americans are encouraged to revisit this past in our cultural museums—notably the very bus in which Rosa Parks refused to give up her seat in Montgomery and the Smithsonian exhibit of the Greensboro, North Carolina, Woolworth lunch counter where four students sparked the sit-in movement that spread across the South. Much of this revival of the past legitimately conveys good feelings about being American.

As a result of the media culture's public memory, national myths are strengthened, and the popular base of southern civil rights activism largely disappears. At most, critical films seem to invite expressive emulation from audiences for whom they resonate emotionally, rather than suggesting context-relevant forms of political action. They certainly don't invite critical reflection about the media culture's role among the many who lack personal memory or book knowledge of sixties events. Like much of the rest of this culture, they invite us to sit back and *feel* the various emotions they exploit. While arguably more entertaining than most media accounts of 1960s relics, they become part of the overwhelming media torrent that renders the past turbulent but ideologically safe, and seemingly impenetrable. Instead of active, discursive democracy, we get spectator democracy. And we get the illusion that spectator democracy—which offers something for everyone—*is* democracy. One way this is manifested is in the apparently easy integration of multiracial, mostly middle-class faces and voices into the media culture itself. However, what it took to get them there—the living, breathing history of civil rights—is obscured by the very media that offers us these integrated faces.

To some degree, the *success* of civil rights struggles reflected their ultimate compatibility with capitalism's marketplace. After all, racial integration incorporated formerly excluded Americans into the mainstream culture and added potential consumers and competitors for available jobs, and there's nothing anticapitalist about that. However, these victories didn't occur because capital *welcomes* change; they came about because capital was threatened with economic loss via boycotts, or disruptive direct confrontation. In effect, capitalism prefers what Martin Luther King Jr. called "negative peace," or the absence of struggle and confrontation that can produce embarrassment and loss of revenue.[46] Thus it is hardly surprising in the era of neoliberalism to find both Republican and Democratic presidents endorsing a revitalization of volunteerism, capitalism's compatible substitution for the confrontational political action of an earlier era. On the King holiday in 2001, the *Boston Globe* ran a full-page ad that satirized, yet epitomized, the era of spectator democracy. The page was divided into two columns, one featuring "Martin Luther King Jr.," the other "Most People." On the King side, the paper published the famous "I Have a Dream" speech. On the other side, it listed the dreams "most people" apparently have: dreams of winning the lottery, owning a nice home and car, and becoming a movie star. The now legendary character of King had not only eclipsed the courageous efforts of everyday people engaged in the civil rights struggle but it had apparently become inconceivable by 2001 that most people could share in his dream of a just world. Instead, the *Globe* ad suggests, the most we can hope for is to take time from our pursuit of material dreams to consume the inspiring message of this heroic figure.

And yet, America's racial dilemma remains intransigent, as media references to an "unfinished revolution" attest. Thus mass media accounts triggered by the King holiday or civil rights anniversaries struggle to make sense of this unfinished revolution in conventional terms. Every year, the media produces statistical updates on segregation or black-white income gaps near Martin Luther King Day, yet they continue to puzzle over the lack of public will to complete King's dream. Incidents of racial hostility erupt into public view as white communities beat back invading outsiders or police engage in excessive brutality. In the wake of the long-running O. J. Simpson court saga, the media was transfixed by the inexplicable polarization between black and white responses to the verdict.

When the members of the media themselves zero in on the continuing problems associated with race and racism, however, they become part of the problem. In one rare, notable case, NBC broadcast a ninety-minute documentary on America's racial problem in 1981, entitled *America—Black and White*. In his review essay, television critic Mark Crispin Miller observed that, despite the program's serious intent to uncover the problem of racism, it embodied all the landmarks of television: "strong contrasts, lots of pathos, easy distinctions between weak (good) and strong (bad)." Miller's essay examined the program's variety of "contrived dramatic situations" representing the variety of problems faced by black

Americans and found a repeated "dual caricature in which all whites were equally devious, heartless, and remote, united in their groundless 'prejudice.'" African Americans, on the other hand, were "time and again" reduced to a "single pitiable figure—the Black, an eternal victim who suffers beautifully." Miller concluded that the program "told us little about racism in our society" but "revealed a lot more about the subtle sort of racism that pervades television news" that "usually belittles blacks in the very act of taking their side, while dismissing whites entirely."[47]

Television's reductionist dichotomy between racist whites and victimized blacks was an exact echo of the mass media's most sympathetic accounts of the civil rights struggle during the 1960s. Once again, the media employed its typical binary approach to interpreting the meaning of events.[48] Of course, in other dichotomized media representations, black voices angrily denouncing white racism are typically dismissed as too militant or impatient. The crucial disempowering impact of this presentation is, in Miller's view, the "guiding assumption" of the NBC show: "'If *you* would *feel* the problem, then *we* would not *have* a problem as a *race!*' Not only is this formula naïve, implying that one's emotional response can overcome political and cultural realities; but it is profoundly slavish. It suggests that blacks are obsessed by whites, the weak waiting angrily for the strong to do something; and so it bespeaks the surrender of all responsibility in an outburst of blame and self-pity: 'All my problems are your fault.'"[49]

Ultimately, the media culture revolves around *how we feel* in response to the media stories we encounter, for those feelings have a great deal to do with the size of corporate media's audience. Whether we are moved by a retrospective tribute to great moments in civil rights history, visit the cinema complex to view *Malcolm X*, or watch NBC's serious documentary, we are encouraged to react emotionally to one side or the other. Yet rarely do we get a glimpse of the ways in which ordinary people took it upon themselves to rise up and challenge the racial oppression that surrounded them, nor are we likely to hear arguments that suggest the applicability of similar acts of collective self-empowerment in this day and age, an era, like that of the pre–civil rights South, when many find the prospect of significant transformation inconceivable. Instead spectator democracy systematically erodes a common conversation among citizens where we can come to an understanding of the varieties of ways in which racism, and other wounding forms of domination, oppression, or exclusion, affect us all. Instead, the media culture "torrent" pushes the civic task of understanding, debating, and using our history off into privatized enclaves.[50]

It's hard to tell which characteristic of this media culture is more damaging to critical public discourse about civil rights: the exclusion or marginalization of critical voices that address systemic problems or the systematic ways in which the form of media culture itself erodes public conversation, balkanizes the population in think-alike enclaves, and undermines political action. The fact that the media culture does both reveals the troubled condition of today's democracy.

Notes

1. See Edward P. Morgan, "Who Controls the Past? Propaganda and the Demonised Sixties," *Irish Journal of American Studies* 5 (December 1996): 33–57. More generally, this dichotomy so completely reflects postsixties media discourse about the 1960s that *Gump's* director, Robert Zemeckis, maintained that he chose the familiar sixties imagery to give Gump's story "realism." See Edward P. Morgan, "Democracy in Eclipse? Media Culture and the Postmodern 'Sixties,'" *New Political Science* 40 (Summer 1997): 5–31.

2. Douglas Kellner has written of a commercial media culture in which "images, sounds, and spectacles help to produce the fabric of everyday life, dominating leisure time, shaping political views and social behavior, and providing the materials out of which people forge their very identities." Douglas Kellner, *Media Culture: Cultural Studies, Identity and Politics between the Modern and the Postmodern* (London: Routledge, 1995), 1.

3. Emily S. Rosenberg, *A Date Which Will Live: Pearl Harbor in American Memory* (Durham, N.C.: Duke University Press, 2003), 5.

4. Ibid., 4.

5. See especially Charles Payne, *I've Got the Light of Freedom: The Organizing Tradition and the Mississippi Freedom Struggle* (Berkeley: University of California Press, 1995), chap. 14.

6. By hegemony, I refer to ways in which elites are able to dominate mass publics through their *consent* rather than through force—a phenomenon first explored in the prison writings of the Italian Marxist Antonio Gramsci. See Quintin Hoare and Geoffrey Nowell Smith, eds., *Selections from the Prison Notebooks of Antonio Gramsci* (New York: International Publishers, 1971).

7. While each of these media represents a distinct form of expression with a distinct purpose, audience appeal, and use of communication conventions, my emphasis in this chapter is on the *common* themes across these diverse media. The weekly news magazines are a particularly fertile source for investigations like this because, as Richard Lentz has observed, "Making sense of the world is something all journalistic media must do, but it is the *raison d'être* of the news weeklies. . . . That readers of *Time* (and its competitors) got their news first from the fleeting images of television or the jumbled patterns of a newspaper page mattered little; what mattered a great deal to the news magazines was to impose order on what they reported." Richard Lentz, *Symbols, the News Magazines, and Martin Luther King* (Baton Rouge: Louisiana State University Press, 1990), 4.

8. Fred Powledge, *Free at Last* (New York: HarperCollins, 1991), xiv.

9. Vincent Harding, "The Road to Redemption," *Other Side*, January/February 2003, 12.

10. *U.S. News and World Report*, August 29, 1983, 47–48.

11. David Gelman, et al., "Black and White in America," *Newsweek*, March 7, 1988, 18–23.

12. Jacob V. Lamar, "Honoring Justice's Drum Major," *Time*, January 27, 1986, 24–25.

13. Ibid.

14. Alvin P. Sanoff, "The Greening of a Martyr," *U.S. News and World Report*, January 23, 1989, 22.

15. During this entire period, except when King was being compared to more militant (i.e., "radical") black leaders, *U.S. News* maintained a consistently skeptical stance toward King. It fact, in Richard Lentz's account, *U.S. News* "consistently damned King and his cause." Lentz, *Symbols*, 339.

16. In its effort to make King's legacy publicly accessible, even the King family has been drawn into the market's cultural commodification, producing a King "autobiography" and an animated video about King and offering to sell the King Center, his home, and hundreds of memorabilia to the National Park Service.

17. Michael Eric Dyson, "The Truth about Martin Luther King, Jr.," *Newsweek*, January 24, 2000, 57. See also, Michael Eric Dyson, *I May Not Get There with You: The True Martin Luther King, Jr.* (New York: Free Press, 2000).

18. Vern E. Smith, et al., "The War over King's Legacy," *Newsweek*, April 6, 1998, 42–47. My point is not to dispute the possibility of wider involvement in King's assassination but to note how the news weekly treats his radical politics. In effect, absent the institutional framework of analysis that lies outside the boundaries of conventional ideology, the mass media are only able to represent

"radicalism" in one of two ways: either as conspiracy theory, or as a form of militant extremism.

19. Ibid.; Taylor Branch, "Uneasy Holiday: How Should We Honor a Man We Still Don't Know?" *New Republic*, February 3, 1986, 22–24.

20. Jack E. White, "Martin Luther King" in *"Time* 100: Leaders and Revolutionaries of the Twentieth Century," *Time*, April 13, 1998, 160.

21. *New York Times*, August 28, 1988, 20.

22. *U.S. Department of State Dispatch* 3, no. 8 (February 24, 1992): 137.

23. One telling instance of this treatment was *Newsweek*'s use of King as the focal point for much of its coverage of the student-generated sit-ins of 1960. *Time* was initially more inclined to focus on the compelling morality play in the struggle between the idealistic young and the "familiar flotsam" [the "duck-tailed, sideburned swaggerers, the rednecked hatemongers, the Ku Klux Klan"] who attacked them. See Lentz, *Symbols*, 42–51.

24. Chomsky uses these terms in *Necessary Illusions: Thought Control in Democratic Societies* (Boston, Mass.: South End Press, 1989) and "The Bounds of Thinkable Thought," *Progressive*, October 1985, 28–31.

25. See W. Lance Bennett, *News: The Politics of Illusion*, 3rd ed. (White Plains, N.Y.: Longman, 1983), 48–52.

26. ABC reporter Paul Good's account of his years of reporting on the southern civil rights movement documents ways in which the network's interest in covering the movement revolved around the presence or absence of action and violence (or potential violence). See Paul Good, *The Trouble I've Seen: White Journalist/Black Movement* (Washington, D.C.: Howard University Press, 1975).

27. Ibid., 4.

28. Quoted in Juan Williams, *Eyes on the Prize: America's Civil Rights Years, 1954–1965* (New York: Viking/Penguin, 1987), 191. In effect, this interaction with national media was a kind of learning experience for both parties.

29. See Lynd's second chapter, entitled "Freedom Summer: A Tragedy, Not a Melodrama," in Staughton Lynd, *Living Inside Our Hope: A Steadfast Radical's Thoughts on Rebuilding the Movement* (Ithaca, N.Y.: Cornell University Press, 1997). Samstein is quoted on 29.

30. For documentation of this effect with respect to media and the antiwar movement of the sixties era, see Todd Gitlin, *The Whole World is Watching: Mass Media in the Making and Unmaking of the New Left* (Berkeley: University of California Press, 1980), and Edward P. Morgan, "From Virtual Community to Virtual History: Mass Media and the American Antiwar Movement of the 1960s," *Radical History Review* 78 (Fall 2000): 85–122.

31. Lentz, *Symbols*, 116–18.

32. Ibid., 340.

33. Ibid., 146.

34. "Waving the Red Flag," *Newsweek*, April 12, 1965, 28. ABC reporter Paul Good contended that the northern media generally treated the MFDP challenge in a patronizing and inaccurate manner—a tendency he attributed in part to their arrogance and in part to a "subjective identification with the White House Establishment." See Good, *Trouble I've Seen*, 206, and Payne, *I've Got the Light of Freedom*, 399.

35. "Calculated Risk," *Newsweek*, July 13, 1964, 28–29.

36. Lentz, *Symbols*, 147–48.

37. Ibid., 225–33.

38. *Washington Post,* April 6, 1967, sec. A, 20.

39. *New York Times*, April 7, 1967, 34.

40. Lentz, *Symbols*, 239, 245.

41. Herman Gray, "Television, Black Americans and the American Dream," *Critical Studies in Mass Communication* 6 (1986): 376–86.

42. See for example, J. Emmett Winn, "Challenges and Compromises in Spike Lee's Malcolm X," *Critical Studies in Media Communication* 18 (December 2001): 452–65; Donald Bogle, *Toms, Coons, Mulattoes, Mammies and Bucks: An Interpretive History of Blacks in American Films*, 3rd ed. (New York: Continuum, 1996); Michael Eric Dyson, *Making Malcolm: The Myth and Meaning of Malcolm X* (New York: Oxford University Press, 1995).

43. Among other things, according to a 2002 *New York Times* report, the New Black Panther Party is listed by the Southern Poverty Law Center as an active "hate group." Dean E. Murphy, "Graying Black Panthers Fight Would-Be Heirs," *New York Times*, October 8, 2002, http://www.nytimes.com/20 . . . ANT.html?pagewanted=print&position=top.

44. While even some former Panthers criticized the accuracy of Peebles's rendition, it was the relatively authentic features that stirred up "a chorus of discontent" that branded the film as "lopsided, revisionist history" in a *Boston Globe* account. *Time* suggested that offering "the Panthers as idealists and as objects of veneration to today's youth" was "criminal naiveté," while the right-wing Center for the Study of Popular Culture attacked the film as a "two hour lie." See Richard Corliss, "Power to the Peephole," *Time*, May 15, 1995, 73.

45. See, for example, the *Report of the National Advisory Commission on Civil Disorders* (New York: Bantam, 1968), widely known as the "Kerner Commission" report.

46. In one telling account of the struggle to break down rigid segregation in the deep South, Steven Classen describes the efforts by black students at Tougaloo College to enlist the cooperation of popular culture figures like the stars of television's *Bonanza*, the cast of *Hootenanny*, and the popular trumpet player

Al Hirt to withdraw from booked appearances at segregated facilities in Jackson, Mississippi. In effect, the cultural celebrities were employed as leverage to force the integration of these facilities. When celebrities demurred, however, the students threatened to sit-in during their appearances, thereby creating a potentially embarrassing confrontation. These threats "forced" figures like *Hootenanny's* Glenn Yarborough and Hirt to withdraw. Steven Classen, "Southern Discomforts: The Racial Struggle over Popular TV," in *The Revolution Wasn't Televised: Sixties Television and Social Conflict*, ed. Lynn Spigel and Michael Curtin (New York: Routledge, 1997), 305–26.

47. Mark Crispin Miller, "Black and White," in Miller, *Boxed-In: The Culture of TV* (Evanston, Ill.: Northwestern University Press, 1989), 135–49.

48. For example, Paul Good maintained that most of the journalists traveling to Mississippi to cover Freedom Summer were seeking stories of "violence, police brutality, volunteer heroism, Negro suffering." Good, *The Trouble I've Seen*, 255. More generally, see the discussion of the construction of meaning through "The Spectacle of the 'Other,'" in Stuart Hall, *Representation: Cultural Representation and Signifying Practices* (London: Sage, 1997), chap. 4.

49. Miller, "Black and White," 143 (emphasis in original).

50. In one compelling account of this balkanized culture, Cass Sunstein documents ways in which the Internet-driven culture creates a phenomenon he calls the "daily me," in which citizens are increasingly able to screen out interaction with all issues, ideologies, and groups that differ from their own. See Cass Sunstein, *republic.com* (Princeton, N.J.: Princeton University Press, 2001).

JENNIFER FULLER

Debating the Present through the Past

Representations of the Civil Rights

Movement in the 1990s

There are currently more than forty-five films and television programs that dramatize the civil rights movement, and more of them were released in the 1990s than in the 1960s, 1970s, and 1980s combined. In the 1990s, fears of racial fracture and desires for racial reconciliation converged in ways that made the civil rights movement a site of intense ideological struggle. As a major turning point in American race relations, the movement was constantly used as a reference point for judging the state of contemporary race relations and for defining what constituted racial progress. Civil rights drama became an arena to explore these issues and to articulate competing political ideologies. This chapter looks at political, academic, and popular discourse about race in the 1990s.[1] Using examples from civil rights dramas, coverage of the fortieth anniversary of the Central High crisis, and other examples from popular culture, it argues that the racial context of the nineties made media representations important sites of struggle over meanings of the civil rights movement.[2]

Television scholar Herman Gray has argued that representations of the civil rights movement convey "contemporary political and cultural hopes and longings," in particular, the belief that America has transcended racism.[3] This chapter focuses on how representations of the civil rights movement were vital at a time when racial conflict jeopardized this belief in the end of racism. Fears of a racial split in the nation were accompanied by concerns about the fate of integration and re-examination of the goals of the civil rights movement in general. "The problem today," a 1991 *Newsweek* article thus suggested, "is shattered dreams. After all the high hopes and genuine progress of the past 30 years, people on both sides of the color line feel they've reached an impasse, and that things are getting worse."[4] In the 1990s, growing concerns about a racial divide would be articulated, criticized, and considered through civil rights dramas.

Race Discourse in the 1990s

Media and political discussions of race in the 1990s were dominated by a discourse that might be best characterized as fear of a "racial divide." Again and again, journalists and commentators lamented that the races still didn't understand each other, even after thirty years of integration. Just three days after the dramatically different racial reactions to the acquittal of black former football star O. J. Simpson in the slaying of his white ex-wife and her friend, an editorial cartoon depicted Uncle Sam seated at a piano with a cloud of despair hanging over his head. He couldn't play the national anthem because the white keys and the black keys were piled up at opposite ends of the keyboard.[5] This image of Uncle Sam perplexed by a split nation illustrated anxieties about the racial divide that was widely discussed at the time. The 1990s were marked by the concern that despite the changes brought by the civil rights movement of the 1960s, blacks and whites lived separate and perhaps irreconcilable realities. Two years before the Simpson verdict, *Newsweek* noted, "When it comes to discussing race, Americans might as well be watching different movies. Confronted with everything from the Reginald Denny beating trial to the Ted Danson jokes, whites see one reality, blacks see another. And the fact that both have such a hard time talking straight about their grievances only makes matters worse. How can we move the racial debate to more realistic—and honest—ground?"[6]

The deep contradictions in racial "progress" that were a distinguishing feature of the 1990s fueled concerns about the racial divide. While the goals of multiculturalism and diversity had become accepted by many individuals and institutions, events such as the 1991 Rodney King beating and the 1992 Los Angeles uprisings made racial strife hypervisible. The nineties saw the ascendance of a sizeable black middle class as well as the growth of the so-called black "underclass." Interracial marriages and transracial adoptions were on the rise, but so were hate crimes. In the 1990s racial strife captured the national imagination in ways that it had not in the seventies or eighties. For example, in 1992, the *Progressive* announced: "It's out in the open again. The racism that has haunted America for three centuries never really went away. It hid like an iguana, and now it's sunning itself on the rocks of economic distress."[7]

The contradictions of race in the 1990s led many to contemplate whether or not American society had achieved the racial equality that civil rights activists had fought for in the 1960s. An article appearing a week after the Million Man March explored this issue. Writer Howard Fineman observed, "In entertainment, advertising, sports and most workplaces, integration is the order of our day. In films, Denzel Washington commands millions for roles that have nothing to do with skin color. . . . A black middle class thrives in the suburbs. But in politics, the ideal of integration is a spent force. Americans of all colors seem exhausted by the effort to come this far, and embittered by the new brand of race-based obsessions that have developed along the way."[8]

These racial discourses highlighted a fear that discord between blacks and whites could endanger the nation. Clearly, the nineties was not the first era in which people feared that the nation was somehow "falling apart." Racial inequality has always been a crack in the nation's foundation, whether or not that fact is articulated. But in the decades since the civil rights movement, the nation had prided itself on extending equal rights to all of its citizens; the movement had supposedly led to a new racial unity. The "rediscovery" of racism and a racial divide between blacks and whites threatened America's new sense of itself as a successfully integrated nation.

Magazines and newspapers made clear this growing fear that racial tensions could literally tear the nation apart. In 1992, an editorial cartoon reprinted in *Newsweek* showed the impact of the blows dealt by police officers during the Rodney King beating exacerbating a "Racial Fault Line" zigzagging across the country. Near the beating, a sign warned "Severe Pounding May Cause Quakes."[9] A 1995 cartoon in the conservative *National Review* similarly showed a map of the United States behind two seismographs; the jagged lines on one, labeled "Quake Action," were outdone by the violent tremors of the seismograph labeled "Affirmative Action."[10] Either racial violence or racial politics threatened to quite literally rupture the nation.

The racial "divide" discourse peaked following the Los Angeles uprisings and again after the Simpson trial. In an article on postriot Los Angeles, *Time* magazine used the refrain from the song, "This Land Is Your Land" to illustrate what it called "the Two Americas." Across a double-truck photograph of blacks and Latinos walking in front of a burned out South Central Los Angeles block, the headline read "This Land Is Your Land." On the next two pages, in an identical layout, under the headline "This Land Is My Land," was a photo of two white women walking along the sidewalk of a middle-class suburb. *Time's* account of contemporary white flight to the suburbs provided a visual refutation to the song's claim that "From California, to the New York Island . . . this land was made for you and me."[11] After the Simpson verdict, articles and illustrations alike portrayed the much-lamented racial divide as gaping chasms and wide gulfs. "They [Americans] were united, briefly, in an anxious silence of the heart," wrote Roger Rosenblatt in *Time*. But, "as soon as the verdict was read, however, they split apart; they could watch themselves do it on the split screens. On one side jubilation, on the other dismay." The dramatic differences between black and white reactions to the Simpson verdict led to many observations that linked this difference with the nation. Rosenblatt continued, "Afterward it was said that Americans should have seen this coming, that the division of the races cut so deep, it ought to have been obvious that two nations had always been hiding in one."[12]

If the increasingly visible rift between blacks and whites was caused by a gap in understanding, then the obvious solution was to foster more cross-racial conversation. After the O. J. Simpson acquittal, a writer put a positive spin on the racially divided reactions, saying that although it was painful, "the fact that both whites and blacks felt so free to vent their frustrations represented a kind of progress in a nation where for so long both groups have been afraid to confront each other with their true feelings."[13] A *Wall Street Journal* columnist meanwhile argued, "We know exactly how to heal our racial divide: by getting to know each other as individuals."[14] The desire to talk things out would be made official in 1997, when President Bill Clinton's administration created an advisory board to start a national conversation on race. A Clinton pollster found that Americans were "quite open to taking another look at race in America."[15] But rather than advocating policy changes, such as creating new jobs and housing, the administration instead began "town hall" meetings around the country, led by a tightly controlled Advisory Board on Race. Although the panel opened discussion about race in the mass media, ultimately the racial initiative was regarded as a failure.[16]

Writer Benjamin DeMott has noted that "at the heart of today's thinking about race lies one relatively simple idea: the race situation in America is governed by the state of personal relations between blacks and whites."[17] DeMott calls this racial ideology "the friendship orthodoxy." The belief that persistent racial problems such as discrimination and economic inequality are caused by personal attitudes and are not a matter of public policy became "common sense" in the nineties. The "friendship orthodoxy" of race was endorsed by the left as well as the right. Proponents of racial reconciliation, in the form of the president's advisory board and others, seemed to take as a given that the legal goals of the civil rights movement had been met, and any lingering racism was more a result of personal attitudes than deeply entrenched structures and institutional practices. In this view, the era of civil rights legislation was past; at best, changing racial attitudes was beyond the scope of the law, and at worst, such policies violated individual rights. Even as President Clinton announced his One America initiative, he said, "Money cannot buy this goal. Power cannot compel it. Technology cannot create it. This is something that can only come from the human spirit."[18]

By the end of the twentieth century, the dominant understanding of "racial progress" had shifted from creating social *equality* through policy to fostering racial *harmony* between individuals. Up until the late 1980s, "racial progress" had primarily referred to minority advancement in areas such as economics, politics, and education. In this tradition, a 1979 special issue of *U.S. News and World Report*, "Blacks in America: Twenty-five Years of Radical Change," focused on post–*Brown v. Board of Education* changes in socioeconomic indicators such as poverty rates, income levels, political participation, and performance in public schools and higher education. Beginning in the late 1980s, however, discussions of progress placed more emphasis on efforts toward interracial understanding. For example, a 1988 special issue of *Newsweek* asked "How Integrated Is America?" and looked at affirmative action–related tensions among workers, a laboratory in which whites are given a glimpse of what it is like to be black, and experiments at creating integrated churches and neighborhoods. In the nineties, many analyses of "race relations" seemed to take the term quite literally; there were several investigations of whether or not blacks and whites were "getting along," particularly in high schools and on college campuses.

The Civil Rights Movement in Racial Divide Discourse

The civil rights movement was central to discourses about racial progress. The concern about the continued racial rift in the country led many in the media to question the accomplishments of the movement in the 1950s and 1960s. The *Economist* opined that the Simpson verdict was an illustration of how, in spite of civil rights gains, "America is steadily resegregating."[19] Similarly, *U.S. News and World Report* observed that "forty years after the Supreme Court ordered the nation's schools integrated, thirty years after Congress passed the Voting Rights Act, white and black Americans—even successful blacks—live in the same country but in different worlds."[20] With open questioning of the movement's legacies, even the movement's key ideal of integration came under new scrutiny in the 1990s. The NAACP, which successfully argued against segregationist laws in the 1950s, reconsidered its position on school integration during this decade. When black students organized their own prom at a Chicago prep school, it attracted national attention. In the *New York Times*, a professor at Northwestern University suggested that the controversy might actually be beneficial: "For 20 years we have had a kind of token integration. . . . Now what we're getting is a real debate. What does integration mean and when has it really occurred? It is one of the most fundamental questions facing America right now."[21]

People's views on racial reconciliation depended in large part on how they viewed the history of the civil rights movement. The widespread acceptance of racial reconciliation discourse is linked to a hegemonic view that the civil rights movement succeeded in dismantling racist structures and in guaranteeing equality before the law. Those who believed that civil rights struggles were no longer necessary found proof of the movement's success in the growing black middle class and the crossover popularity of black public figures such as Oprah Winfrey, Michael Jordan, Bill Cosby, and Colin Powell. In this view, what was left to be achieved was "true" integration, which meant close relationships between whites and blacks. Thus a 1996 article in *New Democrat*, argued that civil rights reforms "succeeded, but they also failed. *De jure* segregation is dead. But, due to the continuing desires of whites and blacks to associate with persons of their own choosing, *de facto* segregation is very much alive."[22]

The fortieth anniversary of the 1956 desegregation of Central High School in Little Rock, Arkansas, became a key moment for supporters of racial reconciliation to send a message about the need for better interpersonal relations between blacks and whites. In 1957, a federal court had ordered nine black students in Little Rock, Arkansas, to be admitted to the all-white Central High School. When the Arkansas governor fought integration and encouraged a mob to prevent their entry in the school, the story drew national and international attention as a state government challenged the legitimacy of the federal government. President Eisenhower eventually had to send the U.S. Army's 101st Airborne Division to escort the Little Rock Nine into the school and to protect them from violent segregationists. In 1987, the thirtieth anniversary of the Central High crisis received little national attention, being commemorated quietly by the NAACP, and then by Governor Clinton, who hosted some of the Little Rock Nine at the governor's mansion.[23] By 1997, however, the national media and federal government seized on the fortieth anniversary of this event as an opportunity for the nation to take stock of how far it had come and how far it had to go in race relations since the 1950s. Clinton's speech at the commemoration of the Little Rock crisis argued that efforts at racial reconciliation were needed to fulfill the promise of the legal desegregation of the fifties and sixties: "Today, children of every race walk through the same door, but then they often walk down different halls. Not only in this school but across America, they sit in different classrooms, they eat at different tables. . . . Indeed, too many Americans of all races have actually begun to give up on the idea of integration and the search for common ground. For the first time since the 1950s, our schools in America are resegregating." Segregation may no longer be the law, Clinton claimed, "but too often separation is still the rule."[24] To make desegregation meaningful, blacks and whites would have to learn how to work together, play together, and speak to each other.

All of the major news outlets devoted a great deal of coverage to the anniversary, with many reports focusing on the story of Elizabeth Eckford, one of the Little Rock Nine, and Hazel Bryan Massery, a white woman who had taunted Eckford. A famous photograph shows taut-faced Eckford clutching her notebook as she walks through a jeering crowd; Massery is directly behind Eckford, her face contorted in a scream. Eckford's composure in this moment has been portrayed as the epitome of the courage, dignity, and determination of civil rights activism, and Massery's grimace came to symbolize the ugliness of racial hatred. Massery, in her own words, became "the poster child of the hate generation."[25] In 1997, Massery and Eckford were important symbols of race relations in America for another key reason: they were a real-life example of the racial reconciliation that Clinton was championing. Five years after the famous picture was taken, Massery called Eckford and apologized to her. Every major broadcast and print story about the anniversary celebration focused on the 1957 incident and Massery's apology. Massery's contrition became emblematic of Little Rock's and the nation's remorse for racism; as a CNN reporter said, "Little Rock is seeking redemption for an ugly chapter in its history. . . . So far, though, she's been the only white person to publicly say she's sorry."[26] The reconciliation between Massery and Eckford symbolized the commemoration's theme of racial healing. The two women met for the first time in 1997, when photographer Will Counts, who won national acclaim for his pictures of Massery and Eckford forty years earlier, brought them together for a new photograph showing them embracing in front of Central High School.

Elizabeth Eckford taunted by Hazel Bryan Massery, Little Rock, Arkansas, September 6, 1957. (Will Counts, *A Life Is More than a Moment*, Bloomington: Indiana University Press, 1999)

Elizabeth Eckford and Hazel Bryan Massery publicly reconciled at the fortieth anniversary commemoration of the Central High School integration, in Little Rock, Arkansas, in 1997. (Will Counts, *A Life Is More than a Moment*, Bloomington: Indiana University Press, 1999)

The staged photo was one of many gestures and images that were to represent the contemporary unity of blacks and whites. At the commemorating ceremony, two girls—one black, one white—sang the national anthem together, and Clinton held open the door of Central High School for the Little Rock Nine. Clinton closed his speech with a reversal of Alabama Governor George Wallace's famous 1963 "segregation forever" proclamation: "One America today, one America tomorrow, one America forever."[27]

Civil Rights Melodramas and the Quest for Racial Reconciliation

Discourses around civil rights drama in the nineties often contained similar messages about interracial cooperation and reconciliation. Those narratives were often gendered female; I call such texts "civil rights melodramas." The best of example of this was Lifetime's original television series *Any Day Now* (1998–2002), a drama about a black woman and a white woman in their forties who were childhood friends in 1960s Birmingham. In the series, the two women had a bitter argument when they were nineteen and parted ways. Rene, the black woman, became a corporate attorney in Washington, D.C., and Mary Elizabeth ("M.E."), the white woman, became a housewife and stayed in Birmingham. The women are reunited when Rene comes home for her father's funeral and decides to stay. *Any Day Now* switched between the women's present lives and their memories of the sixties. While the contemporary story lines were typical of women's television dramas in their focus on relationships and parenting, the faded-color flashbacks centered on how the girls dealt with key moments in history, such as the Cuban missile crisis and the March on Washington.

Any Day Now was remarkable in that it lasted for four seasons with strong civil rights and otherwise racial themes. Its success stands in contrast to NBC's *I'll Fly Away* (1991–93), which, despite critical acclaim and viewer campaigns, was cancelled after two seasons of unsatisfactory ratings. *Any Day Now's* success can be partly attributed to the fact that because it was on cable it didn't have to attract a mass audience; it only had to draw Lifetime's target audience of educated urban women, which it did successfully. *Any Day Now* highlights the centrality of women and women's stories to many civil rights dramas in the 1990s. The idea that racism was about interpersonal relations, and the rise of the racial reconciliation discourse in the nineties, made the melodrama an apt genre for talking about as feminized a concept as "healing" racism. Lorraine Touissant, who portrayed Rene, said: "This show works on so many different levels. We're beginning to access the racial healing that is so prevalent in this country; I know we're attempting to do it from a woman's perspective—but I think that's where the healing is going to come from."[28] Annie Potts, the other star of *Any Day Now*, concurred. According to her, the show is "not just based on entertainment, but on healing." She remarked, "America was built on the issue of race. We're just beginning to learn how to deal with it. I believe this show is a catalyst for a dialogue in the workplace and in the community."[29]

Herman Gray notes that representations of the fifties and sixties are "engaged in a kind of recuperative work, a kind of retrospective production of raced and gendered subjects who fit the requirements of contemporary circumstance."[30] While civil rights melodramas were generally liberal and often feminist, they also fit conservative efforts to assert the continuity and primacy of the middle-class nuclear family, and they often placed the impetus for social change on the individual and the family rather than on social movements and institutions. Lifetime, *Any Day Now*'s creator, and its stars said the show's goal was to improve race relations; its construction of femininity was central to this. In Touissant's words, *Any Day Now* "can be helpful . . . [and] informative . . . in a way only women can, with the kind of honesty and emotionality, coming from a feeling place and a thinking place."[31]

The figure of woman is key to navigating the choppy waters of race and nation. In America, black-white racism is often framed as a struggle between black and white men, while white women are relatively innocent of racism and black women aren't its "real" victims. In her essay "'No Longer in a Future Heaven': Gender, Race, and Nationalism," Anne McClintock argues that women are politically marginal yet central to the national imagination: "Excluded from direct action as national citizens, women are subsumed symbolically into the national body politic as its boundary and metaphoric limit. . . . Women are typically constructed as the symbolic bearers of the nation but are denied any direct relation to national agency."[32] McClintock's analysis applies to many civil rights dramas in that even as black and white American women are often denied agency and/or subjectivity in regards to racism (not its "real" victims or perpetrators), they are repeatedly depicted as leading the nation into a less racist future. According to McClintock, nationalism's contradiction between nostalgia and progress is resolved by representing time in gendered terms. Women, represented as "inert, backward-looking, and natural," symbolize continuity, and men, constructed as "forward-thrusting, potent, and historic," represent progress.[33] *Any Day Now* and other civil rights melodramas negotiate between the overt racism of the past and the "less racist" present by suggesting that while racial conflict was raging in the streets, women were forging bonds with other women in their homes.

Indeed, Rene and M.E.'s friendship bridges the civil rights era and today in ways that suggest that while there has been conflict in the public sphere between men, interracial harmony was always possible in the domestic sphere, among women.[34] For example, in one episode, M.E.'s mother rushes into a white hospital bearing an unconscious and bloodied Rene in her arms. When the doctors refuse to treat Rene, Catherine insists: "If you don't help this girl, I will call President Kennedy, Martin Luther King, the NAACP, and every other colored church in Birmingham and see to it that a demonstration happens in front of your hospital that will make last month's march on Birmingham look like a picnic."[35] In another episode, Catherine's mother (Grandma Otis) gives her a copy of Betty Friedan's feminist text *The Feminine Mystique*. When Grandma Otis asks her if she's read the book, Catherine dismisses the book's claims. However, the issue of Catherine's liberation gets contradicted quickly. In the same scene, M.E. sees on the news that Rene's church, the Sixteenth Street Baptist Church, has been bombed. M.E. begs her mother to take her to Rene's house, but her father, Matthew, forbids it, saying it would be dangerous for them to venture into a black neighborhood on that day. Catherine, concerned with consoling her weeping and anxious child, defies her husband and takes M.E. to see if Rene is alright. At the Jackson home, Rene and M.E. hold each other, weeping. Rene's father keeps his distance, but Catherine tentatively reaches for Rene's mother's arm in consolation.[36] The formal feminism of Friedan may be unnecessary, but when it comes to protecting the children, sisterhood is powerful.

Two feature films about the civil rights movement that came out just as the racial divide discourse was emerging focused on white women awakening to racism and sexism. In 1989, Ally Sheedy starred in *Heart of Dixie*, a film about a white college student who becomes aware of racial injustice in 1950s Alabama. The lead character falls in love with a movement photographer and gets expelled from school for writing an article sympathetic to the civil rights movement. When she leaves school she also leaves behind her sorority sisters and fiancé and the racism and sexism that they espouse. *Heart of Dixie* did not fare as well at the box office as did *The Long Walk Home* (1990), which starred Whoopi Goldberg and Sissy Spacek as, respectively, a maid participating in the Montgomery bus boycott and her middle-class employer who gets involved with the protest. The film's producers sought to give equal screen time to its white and black heroines, and they made sure to invite Rosa Parks to the premiere. At the premiere, Parks said: "The tone is right, the events could have happened, but to my knowledge, there were no white women who actually drove in the carpools."[37] A New Visions Pictures spokesperson later responded to Parks's concerns, saying that Spacek's character was "an amalgam of white men and women who took various actions in support of the boycott. . . . If white women didn't drive, then we have documented evidence that white males did. It's a movie, and the ending was a dramatic choice—a conglomeration of real-life incidents."[38] By focusing on the private lives of wholly fictional characters, the film suggested that while black and white men were in conflict in the streets, black and white women were friendly (or at least not antagonistic) in their homes. Even though no white women drove in the car pools, *The Long Walk Home* avoided considerable challenges to its credibility by depending on the idea that women are more capable of interracial cooperation than men, and by shifting the story from docudrama to drama, from public space to domestic space.

Contesting the Reconciliation Narrative

Just as the media and popular culture provided sites to articulate the need for racial reconciliation through representations of the civil rights movement, these same outlets provided some space to those who resisted the dominant emphasis on reconciliation, notably many black activists and political progressives. For example, when they were interviewed by CNN, two of the black students who desegregated Little Rock's Central High made clear that important racial change was about access to resources, not about socializing. Ernest Green, the first of the Little Rock Nine to graduate from Central High, said their struggle "was not about sitting next to white students. It was about widening opportunity, getting the best preparation that we could."[39] In another CNN report, a correspondent observed that "after forty years of court-supervised racial integration . . . [black and white students] studied together but often socialized apart." Thelma Mothershed, another member of the Little Rock Nine, then remarked: "It's all right not to sit together as long as they're getting the same education. They don't really have to socialize, just get the education that they deserve, and that they're seeking for themselves."[40]

Progressives and civil rights activists argued that the dominant view of the civil rights movement as about racial harmony gutted its revolutionary content; they pointed to persistent discrimination and economic inequality and argued that there was a great deal of work left to be done to achieve the goals of the civil rights movement. Spike Lee hoped that his 1989 film *Do the Right Thing* would "generate discussion about racism because too many people have their head in the sand about racism. . . . They feel that the problem was eradicated in the 60s when Lyndon Johnson signed a few documents."[41] In an article that ran in *Nation* and was circulated widely in the black press, Congressman Jesse Jackson Jr. (D-Ill.) criticized the concept of racial reconciliation as policy, arguing that it marginalized civil rights goals such as equality in education, wealth, and income.[42] Adolph Reed, writing in the *Progressive*, also argued that a national conversation on race failed to deal with the pressing issues of economics and political power:

The problem isn't racial division or a need for healing. It is racial inequality and injustice. And the remedy isn't an elaborately choreographed pageantry of essentializing yackety-yak about group experience, cultural difference, pain, and the inevitable platitudes about understanding. Rather, we need a clear commitment by the federal government to preserve, buttress, and extend civil rights, and to use the office of the Presidency to indicate that commitment forcefully and unambiguously. As the lessons of the past three decades in the South makes clear, this is the only way to change racist attitudes and beliefs.[43]

Popular culture texts also contained readings of the civil rights movement that resisted hegemonic constructions. There were texts in the nineties that denied a neat ending to the civil rights struggle by bringing the civil rights movement into the present. Rap group Public Enemy, which was famous in the eighties and nineties for its black nationalist lyrics, recorded the theme song of the *Do the Right Thing* soundtrack, "Fight the Power." The extended version of the video, directed by Spike Lee, is an excellent example of challenges to the dominant meaning of the civil rights movement. The video begins with one-minute edit of a Universal International Newsreel of the 1963 March on Washington. Over images of smartly dressed black and white marchers, the announcer asserts: "They come united in one cause, to urge Congress to pass a civil rights bill to end forever the blight of racial inequity." He describes the "growing animation" of the crowd and how peaceful it was in the city that day. Over the sounds of marchers singing "We Shall Overcome," the announcer declares that the protesters needed no more "stimulants" than freedom songs. As King stepped up to the platform, the announcer proclaims: "Washington, D.C., 1963. Democracy Speaks in a Mighty Voice." The newsreel ends, complete with credits. Then, Chuck D, lead rapper of Public Enemy, is shown looking into the camera as he addresses a crowd: "Yo, check this out man. We rollin' this way. That march in 1963, that's a bit of nonsense. We ain't rollin' like that no more. Matter of fact, the young black America, we rollin' up with seminars, press conferences, and straight up rallies, am I right?" The crowd roars in response. "We gonna get what we got to get comin' to us. Word up. We ain't goin' out like that '63 nonsense." The video is a documentary of sorts, showing images from the Young People's March on Brooklyn to End Racial Violence, an event orchestrated by Spike Lee in part to serve as a backdrop for Public Enemy's performance, and behind-the-scenes material. Images of Chuck D and Flavor Flav rapping are intercut with crowd scenes and shots of people getting ready for the march and rally.

What does Chuck D mean when he says "we ain't rollin' like that"? There are key differences between the video and the 1963 march. Most visible is the video's black nationalist bent. When the music starts, Chuck D and Flavor Flav are on stage with the S1Ws (Security of the First World), a group of black men who dress in all-black fatigues and berets and perform Nation of Islam–style militaristic drill steps to the beat of the music. Behind them are two huge images side by side: a picture of Malcolm X and the Public Enemy logo—a silhouette of a rapper in the sights of a rifle. The rally is not the quiet, "dignified" protest like the one in the newsreel. This crowd of young people in hip hop fashions is not as disciplined as the 1963 marchers: they dance and chant and they wave and cheer when the camera passes them. In addition, there do not appear to be any whites in this rally.

It would be easy to conclude that Public Enemy is rejecting the March on Washington and the movement that sparked it. However, the rally in the "Fight the Power" video contains many markers of the earlier march. First of all, the name of the march echoes that of the 1963 March on Washington for Jobs and Freedom. While symbols of black nationalism are most prominent, they are alongside markers of the civil rights movement. In fact, as Chuck D calls the 1963 march "a bit of nonsense," behind him is a poster that says "Remember Selma," referring to the famous 1965 conflict between civil rights activists and the police during a voting rights march. However, the poster has "Fight the Power" across the bottom and depicts a black man holding aloft a rifle. The marchers carry small black liberation flags as well as signs that read "Register to Vote." Although Malcolm X's visage looms largest over this rally, posters of liberal civil rights activists such as Medgar Evers, Jesse Jackson, and Martin Luther King float above the crowd next to posters of radicals such as Angela Davis and Marcus Garvey. In one shot, small signs bearing the Public Enemy logo are hoisted around a poster of Harriet Tubman. The marchers hold signs similar to the tall, triangular placards that delegates carry at national political conventions; here, the locations on the signs are sites of racial violence. These signs bring together the past and the present, as they bear the names of places such as Brooklyn, Montgomery, Birmingham, Miami, and Little Rock. The imagery in this video is a mélange of historical moments and political philosophies that defies the clear distinction between past and present that conservatives espouse.

Although not a rap video, the HBO docudrama *Boycott* (2001) was marketed as a civil rights drama "for the hip hop generation." Director Clark Johnson wanted the movie about Martin Luther King and the Montgomery bus boycott to inspire young black viewers by demystifying King—the movie portrays King when he was a young minister in his twenties, with doubts and fears. The movie also decenters King by showing that the Montgomery Improvement Association, which organized the boycott, was already underway when King became its president. *Boycott* was praised for its portrayal of rarely represented boycott leaders such as E. D. Nixon and Jo Ann Robinson. The movie also was noted for its acknowledgment that influential civil rights activist Bayard Rustin was gay.

The desire for the film to reach younger viewers is exemplified in a scene that, like the "Fight the Power" video, brings the racial past into the present. At the end of *Boycott*, several activists celebrate their victory by going on a ride on a city bus. King (played by Jeffrey Wright) decides not to board the bus. The activists get on board to the tune of "Ella's Song." The song, which has the refrain "we who believe in freedom cannot rest until it comes," was also used in an episode of *Any Day Now* during a re-enactment of the Birmingham Children's March in 1963. Although it was composed in 1983 by former Student Nonviolent Coordinating Committee (SNCC) activist and founder of the singing group Sweet Honey in the Rock, Bernice Johnson Reagon, as a tribute to civil rights activist Ella Baker (the refrain is a quote of hers), it has the simple folksy and spiritual sound of a sixties' protest song. The anachronistic use of "Ella's Song" heightens the cinematic device that follows. The bus pulls away and as King stands there watching it, an unmistakably contemporary gospel song starts. The song continues as the 1956 scene dissolves into a present-day city street. A traditional-style church is reflected in the mirrored walls of a skyscraper, and the camera tilts down to capture King walking past, still outfitted in his same suit and hat. King walks against the traffic on the sidewalk, an angle that allows us to see the faces of the diverse crowd. King passes between a young Asian family and a black man with a bleached-blond Afro. The black man, who is on a cellular phone, turns to give King a familiar smile. King stares at the man's hair, puzzled and amused. Next, a Latina girl, holding the hand of a younger boy, freezes, staring at King in awe. King ruffles the boy's hair and continues his walk. He is spotted by a group of young black men who are hanging out on the street. The men seem to listen with interest as King chats with them, affecting their stance as he leans against the wall with them. A police car stops in front of them, and the officers, a black man and a white woman, point at the men (including King) with two fingers in a gesture that is part greeting and part warning. King continues to talk with the young men as the screen fades to black.

By seeing King in the present, where racial debates are more complex than black and white, and where racial problems still exist (dramatized here by the police officers' vague greeting/warning), the viewer can speculate on how King might react to contemporary racial issues. This ending resonated with a viewer who posted this at HBO's bulletin board for the movie: "the ending made tears run down my face to think that if Dr. King would have lived that he would have walked down the streets of today."[44] Another viewer praised the ending using words from King himself: "I thought the ending of the film was PURE GENIUS, during the last scene when Dr. King transcended time and walked into the New Millennium! Now that was righteousness flowing like a MIGHTY STREAM!"[45] This ending is quite different from the 1978 miniseries *King*, which closed with his autopsy. Similar to the ending of Spike Lee's *Malcolm X* (1992), in which several people, including Nelson Mandela, announce "I am Malcolm X!" this strategy denies the death of the leader by insisting on the continuation of his spirit.[46]

Boycott was also part of a conscious effort on the part of producers to represent the civil rights movement in ways that privileged black characters. These characters could be leaders, like King, but they often were lesser-known activists or fictional private citizens. The shift to private and often fictional people allowed the texts to foreground personal relationships. Even though *Boycott* was about King, it represented activists who had previously had little or no representation in docudramas, and it privileged King's private side, such as his doubts, fears, and his relationship with his wife.

Boycott took movies like *The Long Walk Home* one step further: while *The Long Walk Home* featured a black maid, it gave equal screen time to her white employer. *Boycott* did not feel the need to bring in white costars for equal screen time. In part, this move toward more active black characters can be traced back to the controversy surrounding the film *Mississippi Burning* (1988). *Mississippi Burning* is the most studied and perhaps best-known civil rights drama. In fact, it was the first film to be widely described as a "civil rights drama." Despite its box office success, the film was pilloried for making the FBI the heroes of the civil rights movement as they tried to solve the Freedom Summer triple homicide without much help from local blacks, who were too scared and too unorganized to act on their own behalf. Even though the murder victims had been activists, civil rights activists were marginalized in *Mississippi Burning*.[47]

In the nineties, civil rights drama started to focus more on black characters, first with texts that featured both white and black costars. *The Long Walk Home* did this in 1990, as did *Murder in Mississippi*, an NBC made-for-TV movie that was framed as presenting the "real" story depicted in *Mississippi Burning*. *Murder in Mississippi* emphasized the difficult development of a friendship between a black Mississippi native and a white northern student who was there for Freedom Summer, men who would be two of the three victims of the infamous triple homicide in 1964. It ended with the murders; the final shot is of the two men lying next to each other, with their blood running together.

As the 1990s progressed, the terrain of racial representations in civil rights drama shifted even more, so that white centrality to civil rights texts came under intense scrutiny. Criticism was especially heated for Rob Reiner's 1996 film *Ghosts of Mississippi*, which sought to tell the true story of Bobby DeLaughter, an assistant district attorney who, with the help of Myrlie Evers-Williams, successfully prosecuted Byron de la Beckwith in 1994 for the 1963 murder of civil rights activist Medgar Evers. Unlike what happened to *Mississippi Burning*, critics of *Ghosts* rarely attacked Reiner's film on historical grounds. Rather, the main criticism was that like *Mississippi Burning* and other films, *Ghosts* marginalized black actors in the civil rights movement and focused on a white character as a savior. As one reporter pointed out, the actor who portrayed Evers in *Ghosts of Mississippi* was listed twenty-third in the film's credits.[48]

The opening sentence of *Variety*'s unfavorable review of *Ghosts* was quoted in several articles about the film: "When future generations turn to this era's movies for an account of the struggles for racial justice in America, they'll learn the surprising lesson that such battles were fought and won by square-jawed white guys."[49] This criticism, which was taken up by white and nonwhite critics alike, would not likely have been as dominant prior to the nineties. Director Rob Reiner himself expressed the doubts he had as a white man creating a film with a civil rights angle. He cringed at mention of Myrlie Evers's disappointment in the final product, but argued that his focus on DeLaughter was "the only way as a white man that he could feel comfortable approaching the story."[50] The focus on the white character was often seen as part of the usual demands of Hollywood that compromised the claims to history, but in the eyes of some, this focus breached *Ghosts*'s promise to tell a true story. For example, one reviewer wrote that the film "captures the history but misses the point. . . . Like a lot of movies before it, 'Ghosts of Mississippi' uses the white point of view to hook moviegoers. So even in director Reiner's obsession with detail . . . the real story is buried, revised, however innocently, with an eye to the majority perspective." The reviewer speculates about the reasons for such evasions: "Maybe it's just economics. Maybe the market can handle only one 'Malcolm X' a decade. But I wonder when white America will be willing to see history through the eyes of the history makers, even when they don't look like us."[51]

In the nineties, white coming-to-consciousness about racism was still important and often central to civil rights drama, but white main characters tended to be portrayed more as sympathizers (either as activists or in spirit) and less often as leaders of the civil rights struggle. Texts with white lead characters tended to have black costars, such as *Any Day Now*. *I'll Fly Away* was as much about a white prosecuting attorney sympathetic to civil rights as it was about his black maid who was an activist.

The end of the decade witnessed perhaps the first mainstream civil rights drama that was told from the perspective of local activists on the ground. In February 2000, the basic cable channel Turner Network Television aired the original movie *Freedom Song*.[52] This fictional drama focused on the tensions that build between a father, Will Walker (Danny Glover), and his son, Owen (Vicellous Reon Shannon), who becomes involved in SNCC. Director Phil Alden Robinson and other producers of *Freedom Song* emphasized getting the story "right" and even framed the movie as a corrective to previous civil rights dramas. They aimed to accurately represent SNCC and give the organization proper credit for its role in the civil rights movement. The producers also wanted to show that the black community was on the front lines of the struggle, but had not been given its due by Hollywood, or even by history. Actor Stan Shaw, who portrayed Archie, a character modeled after former SNCC chairman Chuck McDew, articulated the need for *Freedom Song*:

> We are portraying people who didn't get a lot of credit for their involvement in the SNCC movements. It's very humbling. I said to Chuck, "We know Rosa Parks, we know Martin Luther King, Jr. and we know Ralph Abernathy. Why don't we know you?" He said he was holding out for someone to portray the story accurately. So when Phil Robinson got involved, they trusted him enough to give them their babies, so to speak. Through the eyes of those individuals, this country and other countries will understand SNCC and what they did in basically creating the Civil Rights Movement.[53]

McDew told the *New York Times* that *Freedom Song* was the first movie "ever made that captures the spirit and integrity of the people involved in the movement." According to McDew, *Freedom Song* told "the real story," unlike *Mississippi Burning*, which "was really like an old-fashioned buddy drama of two white guys coming in and saving the trembling natives. Well, back then the F.B.I. was a bunch of good old boys, and to make them heroes was ridiculous."[54]

Freedom Song represented real-life activists and supportive members of the community in several ways. The main character, soft-spoken, philosophical activist Daniel Wall, was patterned after Bob Moses, who worked on voter registration in Mississippi in the 1960s. The character Wall was a teacher from the North, as was Moses. Wall wore the same horn-rimmed glasses and overalls that Moses was often photographed in. Barber and advisor T-Bone Lanier seems to be based on the real-life Curtis C. Bryant, who ran a barbershop in the front of his home and helped civil rights activists who came to McComb, Mississippi.[55] The character Jonah Summer, a fearless NAACP leader, seems to be a composite of activist E. W. Steptoe and a farmer named Herbert Lee. Summer, like Lee, is shot to death by a white man because he registered to vote.[56] *Freedom Song* makes the point that even when they weren't involved in sit-ins or marches, or even if they didn't attempt to register to vote, the older generation provided a network of support for political action: Miss Cole's restaurant fed SNCC workers, another woman provided lodging, T-Bone's barbershop offered haircuts and advice. *Freedom Song* was also dedicated to the memories of less-celebrated activists who worked for civil rights in Mississippi, including Ella Baker, Amzie Moore, W. E. B. Owens, Herbert Lee, Louis Allen, and Fannie Lou Hamer.

Freedom Song was praised in the press. Several critics even suggested that this "fictional" text was more real than previous docudramas about the movement. A positive review of *Freedom Song* in the *New York Times* highlighted how "real" the movie seemed: "Mr. Alden took a fictional route to present . . . a microcosm of the civil rights movement (although he employed S.N.C.C. veterans as consultants)."[57] One reviewer found *Freedom Song* a "refreshing" change from the racial dramas that are paraded during black history month: "It's not to say that stories like these should go untold; certainly a large part of the preservation of the freedom wrought by the civil rights movement is rooted in remembering the struggle. But that struggle, at times, can be taxing. Yet, by focusing on 'the little people' behind the movement, 'Freedom Song' manages to offer a new take on an often-told tale."[58]

Robinson, like the directors of *Mississippi Burning* and *Ghosts of Mississippi*, is white. Perhaps to counter criticisms based on his race,

Robinson's credibility was constantly asserted in promotional material for the movie and interviews with the cast and crew; Robinson's ability to create a civil rights drama was based on the research he'd done, his interviews with activists and Mississippi residents, and on the endorsements of *Freedom Song*'s stars Glover and Shannon.[59] A related strategy was to portray Danny Glover, one of the film's executive producers, as the spirit or the guiding force of the work. Glover was credited with helping TNT convince Robinson to create his then-titled "Mississippi Project" for that cable channel.[60] Glover is a source of credibility for the movie for several intertwined reasons. As an older black man, he can presumably vouch for the authenticity of a representation of the civil rights movement. He is a respected actor and a veteran of several historical dramas about race such as the feature film *Beloved* (1998), TNT's *Buffalo Soldiers* (1997), and HBO's *America's Dream* (1996). Glover also served as an executive producer for the latter two movies. Finally, Glover is outspoken about racism. In 1999, Glover filed a complaint with New York City's Taxi and Limousine Commission because of what he argued was discriminatory treatment.[61] Locally, Glover's complaint led to political and police action against the commission.[62] Nationally, because Glover's experience had been shared by many others, a black person—particularly a black man—not being able to flag down a cab, despite his wealth or celebrity status, became a symbol of the persistence of racism in the late twentieth century.[63]

The struggle between the father and son in *Freedom Song* mirrors and seemingly addresses contemporary young blacks' criticisms of the civil rights generation for not doing enough to change the racial order. The final scene of the film shows the father and son building the frame of their new home, a home that would replace the one that was foreclosed on almost fifteen years earlier, when white supremacists closed the father's business and put the family into poverty. This house signified a new beginning, and the father used it at one point to try to convince Owen not to get involved with the movement for fear that he would lose this chance. At the end of the film, however, the Walkers are more confident about their future. Owen, through a voiceover, says that his father never "got involved" and didn't register to vote until 1966 (which would have been a year after the Voting Rights Act of 1965); however, he remained vital to the struggle. Owen looks at his father proudly as his father hammers nails into the frame, connecting one wall to another: "Good and strong," his father says. Owen's voiceover and the action portray the actions of the pre–civil rights movement generation as essential to providing a strong framework for the freedom struggle. By extension, it can be seen that SNCC laid a foundation that later generations can build on.

Into a New Racial Era: The Move Away from Civil Rights Dramas

The civil rights movement's role in national identity has shifted since the nineties, a decade permeated by a widespread concern that the foundation that the movement laid for contemporary race relations was cracking. This anxiety was apparent in discourses about racial reconciliation, celebrations that tried to reconcile the racial past, and the rise in civil rights dramas in this decade. Rodney King's plea during the 1992 Los Angeles uprisings, "Can we all get along?" has been widely ridiculed, but its sentiment resounded in popular and political discourses throughout the nineties.[64] Unlike in previous decades, the primary measure of "racial progress" lay in how well people of different races were "getting along." This "progress" was constantly measured against different meanings of the civil rights movement.

The rise of civil rights drama that occurred in the nineties seems to have peaked in 1999. There were a few afterward, but to date, the last was in 2002. Race, national identity, and what constitutes a threat to national unity have become increasingly reformulated as national borders, and therefore international histories and relations, have become the focus of anxieties about the nature and future of "America." This new construction of the fragility of race and nation has been created by Latinos becoming the nation's largest minority (partly through immigration), and by the ways in which fundamentalist Islam has captivated the American imagination and public policy after terrorist attacks on American targets in 2001 and U.S. attacks on Afghanistan and Iraq. These changes have reconfigured "us" versus "them" in ways that don't square as easily with the civil rights struggle as hypervisible black-white conflicts did in the nineties.

Struggles over the meaning of "America" and what it means to be "American" have since begun to focus more on national origin and religion. The concern with national origin has been influenced by the terrorist attacks and the wars in the Middle East, as well as by the economic downturn of the early 2000s, which has fueled existing fears about immigration (legal and illegal) and the "outsourcing" of jobs to Asia. Racial difference didn't go away; the threats of terrorism, immigration, and outsourcing have all been racialized. But this racialization marks a shift from the black-white tensions of the nineties to "Americans" (usually understood as white) versus East Asians, South Asians, Middle Easterners, and Mexicans. In addition, after the 2004 presidential election, the "blue state/red state" trope became a prominent way of understanding differences within the nation, especially in regard to social issues of particular interest to the religious right, such as abortion and gay rights. Although these concerns have been debated in terms reminiscent of the nation's history of racial struggle, such as bigotry, civil rights, and human rights, the civil rights movement has not emerged as a dominant metaphor for understanding them. This may be attributed to the black-white focus of the movement, or to the inability of the notion of "reconciliation" to resonate in a time when the desire to police the borders of territories as well as of identities has become paramount.

The movement has not been forgotten, however. Mississippi Senator Trent Lott's comments at South Carolina Senator Strom Thurmond's one hundredth birthday party in late 2002 made the movement central to contemporary politics again. While praising Thurmond, Lott proclaimed that when Thurmond ran for president in 1948 "we voted for him. We're proud of it. And if the rest of the country had followed our lead, we wouldn't have all these problems over all these years, either."[65] Thurmond had run for president on a segregationist platform, and Lott's comments were criticized as nostalgic for the Jim Crow era. The history of Lott's racial views and politics became a matter of contemporary concern; he was Speaker of the House and his critics charged that his comments exposed the racism of contemporary Republicans. Covers of *Newsweek* and *Time* juxtaposed Lott with his, and the nation's, past in interesting ways: *Newsweek* represented him with his 1962 University of Mississippi yearbook picture, with the headline "The Past That Made Him—And May

Undo Him; Race and the Rise of Trent Lott." *Time* ran a recent color picture of the senator, set against black-and-white images from the civil rights movement, including black activists being sprayed by water hoses, a group of whites holding a Confederate flag, and pictures of Rosa Parks and Martin Luther King. The cover headline, "Whitewashing the Past," referred to how Lott was trying to distance himself from his past racial views and from anti-integration sentiment in general. Lott made public apologies, including in an interview on Black Entertainment Television; ultimately, he stepped down as Senate Majority Leader. As *Time* declared, Lott was "tripped up by history." Although civil rights drama is not as popular as it was in the mid- to late nineties, events such as this remind us that, in many ways, the past continues to catch up with the present.

Notes

1. I use the word "discourse" to refer to how utterances (statements, media texts, and so on) are organized in ways that both influence and are influenced by social structures and power relations.

2. Some of the texts that are most closely analyzed in this chapter appeared in 2000 or afterward; I do not consider such texts to be outside the scope of my analysis. These turn-of-the-century texts are excellent examples because they are responding to a range of events, discourses, and other civil rights dramas from the 1990s proper.

3. Herman Gray, "Remembering Civil Rights: Television, Memory and the 1960s," *The Revolution Wasn't Televised: Sixties Television and Social Conflict* (New York: Routledge, 1997), 351.

4. Mark Whitaker, "A Crisis of Shattered Dreams," *Newsweek*, May 6, 1991, 29.

5. Nick Anderson, cartoon, *Louisville Courier-Journal*, October 6, 1995, as reproduced in *Best Editorial Cartoons of the Year*, ed. Charles Brooks (Gretna, La.: Pelican, 1996), 111.

6. Mark Whitaker, "White and Black Lies," *Newsweek*, November 15, 1993, 52.

7. "Racism Resurgent," *Progressive*, January 1992, 7.

8. Howard Fineman, "Grappling with Race," *Newsweek*, October 23, 1995, 32.

9. Mike Luckovich, cartoon, *Atlanta Constitution*. Reprinted in *Newsweek*, May 11, 1992, 23.

10. Dick Locher, cartoon, *Chicago Tribune*. Reprinted in *National Review*, March 20, 1995, 46.

11. Richard Lacayo, "This Land Is Your Land, This Land Is My Land," *Time*, May 18, 1992, 28–33.

12. Roger Rosenblatt, "A Nation of Pained Hearts," *Time*, October 16, 1995, 41–42. See similar sentiments in Anthony Lewis, "Abroad at Home," *New York Times*, October 6, 1995, sec. A, 31.

13. Mark Whitaker, "Whites v. Blacks," *Newsweek*, October 16, 1995, 35.

14. Hugh Pearson, "After O.J., Racial Divide Simply Grows," *Wall Street Journal*, October 11, 1995, sec. A, 14.

15. James Carney, "Why Talk Is Not Cheap," *Time*, December 22, 1997, 32.

16. Clinton's focus on race also waned during investigations into his former relationship with White House intern Monica Lewinsky.

17. Benjamin DeMott, *The Trouble with Friendship: Why Americans Can't Think Straight about Race* (New York: Atlantic Monthly Press, 1995), 7.

18. "Excerpts from Clinton's Speech on Race in America," *New York Times*, June 15, 1997, sec. A, 16.

19. "Two Nations, Divisible," *Economist*, October 7, 1995, 8.

20. Jerelyn Eddings, "Black and White in America," *U.S. News and World Report*, October 16, 1995, 33.

21. Isabel Wilkerson, "Separate Senior Proms Reveal an Unspanned Racial Divide," *New York Times*, May 5, 1991, sec. A, 1.

22. Glenn Loury, "Shall We Overcome? The Future of Integration," *New Democrat*, July/August 1996, 10.

23. "1957's Little Rock Nine Return to Central High in Joy, Sadness," *Los Angeles Times*, September 23, 1987, sec. A, 1.

24. "Excerpts from President's Comments on School Desegregation," *New York Times*, September 26, 1997, sec. A, 20.

25. Helen E. Starkweather, "Crisis at Central High," *Smithsonian*, February 2002, 20.

26. CNN Early Edition, September 25, 1997, transcript (accessed through LexisNexis).

27. Muriel Dobbin, "One America Forever," *Denver Rocky Mountain News*, September 26, 1997, sec. A, 2.

28. Michael Starr, " 'Any Day' Boss Spells Out Thanks for Stars," *New York Post*, August 30, 1998, 107.

29. John Kiesewetter, "Remember to Watch Any Day," *Cincinnati Enquirer*, March 1, 1999, sec. C, 1.

30. Gray, "Remembering Civil Rights," 353.

31. Eric Deggans, "Lifetime Doesn't Play It Safe," *St. Petersburg Times*, August 18, 1998, sec. D, 1.

32. Anne McClintock, " 'No Longer in a Future Heaven': Gender, Race, and

Nationalism," in *Dangerous Liaisons: Gender, Nation, and Postcolonial Perspectives*, ed. Anne McClintock, Aamir Mufti, and Ella Shohat (Minneapolis: University of Minnesota, 1997), 90.

33. Ibid., 92.

34. My use of the term "public sphere" here is not completely within Jurgen Habermas's definition of a civil space in which the public arrives at consensus about political issues. I am using the phrase to refer to those heavily mediated demonstrations, talks, and negotiations between civil rights activists and white police, politicians, and other citizens.

35. "I Feel Awful," *Any Day Now*, episode 13, December 8, 1998.

36. "I'm Not Emotional," *Any Day Now*, episode 20, February 16, 1999.

37. Elaine Dutka, "Driving Miss Odessa," *Los Angeles Times*, December 20, 1990, sec. F, 1. Parks also said that the ending, in which black women keep a racist mob at bay with their singing, was improbable.

38. Ibid.

39. James Jefferson, "Little Rock Nine Revisit Central High," *Memphis Commercial Appeal*, August 17, 1997, sec. B, 1.

40. CNN World Report, September 28, 1997, transcript (accessed through LexisNexis).

41. Michael T. Kaufman, "In a New Film, Spike Lee Tries to Do the Right Thing," *New York Times*, June 25, 1989, sec. H, 1.

42. Jesse L. Jackson Jr., "Why Race Dialogue Stutters," *Nation*, March 31, 1997, 22.

43. Adolph Reed Jr., "Yackety-Yak about Race," *Progressive*, December 1997, 19.

44. iwillbthere4u, bulletin board, *Boycott*, March 4, 2001, www.hbofilms .com (accessed March 9, 2001).

45. gcooke, bulletin board, *Boycott*, 29 March 2001, www.hbofilms.com (accessed April 1, 2001).

46. Lee's multiplication of Malcolms at the end of *X* is similar to strategies he used in *A Huey P. Newton Story*, the first original movie for the Black Starz! cable channel. The "A" in the title suggests that there are many stories to be told about Newton. Also, the style of the film, a one-act play with media images in the background, constantly contradicted the insecure, stuttering, addicted Newton with bolder, invulnerable images of him and his supporters.

47. Making whites central to the civil rights struggle and explicitly or implicitly denying black agency is a part of racial ideology that makes blacks marginal to American history and culture, even when that history explicitly concerns them. Kelly J. Madison argues that by highlighting the sacrifices of sympathetic whites and marginalizing black agency, "anti-racist-white-hero films" co-opt struggles

against apartheid, slavery, and segregation in order to create "a more flattering mirror for whiteness than the one originally created by the movements." According to Madison, whiteness now suffers from a "legitimation crisis" because black struggles in the fifties and sixties helped to name and question the dominance of white supremacy and patriarchy. *Mississippi Burning* is Madison's primary example of how these "anti-racist-white-hero films" shore up white identity and legitimate white domination by constructing revisionist narratives of black struggles for equality in which passive "black children" could not have succeeded without the aid of "the white Father." Mark Golub defines "Hollywood redemption histories" as films about white men who awaken to and struggle against oppression. Among Golub's examples are *Amistad*, *Mississippi Burning*, and *The Long Walk Home*. Films in this genre are intended to be antiracist, yet their focus on the salvation of the white hero marginalizes the history of the oppressed group. Using theories of memory and trauma, Golub argues that these films depict painful moments of the racial past in order to enact "the ritualized forgiveness that white audiences long to hear." Golub calls these films "irresponsible" history because they absolve their audience of responsibility for the racist past and present by framing racism as firmly in the past and by encouraging identification with a white hero whose redemption becomes their own. See Kelly J. Madison, "Legitimation Crisis and Containment: The 'Anti-Racist-White-Hero' Film," *Critical Studies in Mass Communication* 16 (1999): 413; Mark Golub, "History Died for Our Sins: Guilt and Responsibility in Hollywood Redemption Histories," *Journal of American Culture* 21 (Fall 1998): 29.

48. James Verniere, "Miss. Trial," *Boston Herald*, January 3, 1997, sec. S, 3.

49. Godfrey Cheshire, "Ghosts of Mississippi," *Variety*, December 16, 1996, 78.

50. Peter Howell, "Hit and Myth," *Toronto Star*, December 20, 1996, sec. D, 1.

51. T. D. Mobley-Martinez, " 'Ghosts of Mississippi' Blanches History for Mass Consumption," *Albuquerque Tribune*, January 3, 1997, sec. B, 6.

52. *Freedom Song* was one of several original civil rights dramas that Turner Network Television aired in the 1990s. TNT ran the made-for-television movies *Hope* (1997) and *Passing Glory* (1999), as well as the biographical *George Wallace* (1997). *Hope* was a fictional drama about a girl whose town and family were being changed by the civil rights movement. *Passing Glory* was based on the true story of a basketball game between an all-black and an all-white school in New Orleans amid civil rights struggle in the 1960s. *George Wallace* highlighted Wallace's fight against the civil rights movement and his later regrets about his segregationist views.

53. "Q and A with Stan Shaw," *Freedom Song* press packet, n.d.

54. Bernard Weinraub, "Standing Up for His Film and for Real Black Heroes," *New York Times*, February 24, 2000, sec. B, 3.

55. Curtis C. Bryant, "Oral History with Curtis C. Bryant," interview by Jimmy Dykes, November 11, 1995, University of Southern Mississippi Center for Oral History and Cultural Heritage, http://www.lib.usm.edu/spcol/crda/oh/bryanttrans.htm.

56. Charles M. Payne, *I've Got the Light of Freedom: The Organizing Tradition and the Mississippi Freedom Struggle* (Berkeley: University of California Press, 1995), 104–31.

57. William McDonald, "On the Road to Freedom, United Yet Also Split," *New York Times*, February 26, 2000, sec. A, 29.

58. Denene Miller, " 'Freedom Song' Rings with Glover," *New York Daily News*, February 27, 2000, sec. New York Vue, 3.

59. Robinson's credibility was also often linked to the success of his film *Field of Dreams* (1989).

60. Jefferson Graham, " 'Freedom Song' Fulfills a Dream," *USA Today*, February 23, 2000, sec. D, 4.

61. Monte Williams, "Danny Glover Says Cabbies Refused to Stop for Him," *New York Times*, November 4, 1999, sec. B, 8.

62. Elisabeth Bumiller, "Cabbies Who Bypass Blacks Will Lose Cars, Guiliani Says," *New York Times*, November 11, 1999, sec. A, 1.

63. Glover's sympathizers pointed out that the fact that many of the cab drivers were nonwhite and immigrants was proof of the pervasiveness of racial stereotypes about blacks.

64. "Riots in Los Angeles: A Plea for Calm," *New York Times*, May 2, 1992, sec. A, 6.

65. Don Goodgame and Karen Tumulty, "Tripped Up by History," *Time*, December 23, 2002, 24.

TIM LIBRETTI

Integration as Disintegration

Remembering the Civil Rights Movement

as a Struggle for Self-Determination in

John Sayles's *Sunshine State*

John Sayles's 2002 film, *Sunshine State*, tackles vital social issues facing contemporary American society. As his films typically do, Sayles addresses these current issues through a confrontation with the past and the historical conditions that have led to our present situation. *Sunshine State*, which focuses on how corporate power and greed are undermining democracy and freedom in the United States, turns to the civil rights movement, both to seek models for resistance to contemporary developments and to diagnose why that important liberation struggle fell short of establishing meaningful economic freedom. Sayles's investigation of the civil rights era highlights that multiple struggles for civil rights took place, each of which had different concepts of freedom, endorsed different means of seeking it, and transmitted to us differing legacies of political activism. These various struggles also produced quite divergent memories of the civil rights movement in terms of who its actors were, what it sought, and who inspired it.

Introduction: Learning to Remember the Civil Rights Movement

Reflecting on the state of contemporary Asian American activism and its connection to the civil rights movement, Glenn Omatsu questions the recent generation's historical consciousness of the civil rights movement in a way that is instructive for a discussion of issues of historical memory in *Sunshine State*. Curious as to the staying power and resonance of key political concepts that gave coherence to the Asian American movement of the 1960s and 1970s, he complains that a generation raised on the "Asian American code words of the 1980s," such as *advocacy*, *access*, and *legitimacy*, have a hard time understanding "the urgency of Malcolm X's demand for freedom 'by any means necessary,' Mao's challenge to 'serve the people,' the slogans of 'power to the people' and 'self-determination.'" But it was these ideas, Omatsu argues, that "galvanized thousands of Asian Americans and reshaped our communities. And it is these concepts that we must grasp to understand the scope and intensity of our own movement and what it created."[1]

I begin this essay with Omatsu's assessment for two reasons: first, because he directly raises the question of exactly if and, perhaps more important, how the "new generation" of activists and citizens remembers the history, organizational models, and political lessons of the civil rights movement; and, second, because he links the Asian American movement with Third World nationalist movements (the Chicano movement, the American Indian movement, black nationalist movements) more generally. Omatsu views all of these movements as factions of the larger struggle for civil rights in a way that challenges the contemporary association of the civil rights movement primarily with African Americans and perhaps even more narrowly with the leadership of Dr. Martin Luther King Jr. When Omatsu asks if concepts such as self-determination remain relevant to Asian Americans today, if they can find any legacy in the struggles of the 1960s and 1970s, and if "the ideas of the movement [are] alive today" or have instead "atrophied into relics—the curiosities of a bygone era of youthful and excessive idealism," he raises important questions about how we remember the struggle for freedom and, in fact, define freedom itself.[2]

Indeed, Omatsu's own experience of learning the history of the Asian American movement and, by extension, the civil rights movement, highlights the often impoverished and narrowly selective memory of the civil rights movement, which tends to marginalize the history of nationalist political action by people of color in the United States. In discussing how scholars have come to reinterpret the movement "in narrower ways" over the last twenty years, he relates his own experience in an Asian American studies class at UCLA:

> The professor described the period from the late 1950s to the early 1970s as a single epoch involving the persistent efforts of racial minorities and their white supporters to secure civil rights. Young Asian Americans, the professor stated, were swept into this campaign and by later anti-war protests to assert their own racial identity. The most important influence on Asian Americans during this period was Dr. Martin Luther King, Jr., who inspired them to demand access to policymakers and initiate advocacy programs for their own communities. Meanwhile, students and professors fought to legitimize Asian American Studies in college curricula and for representation of Asians in American society.

While the lecture was well organized and well received, Omatsu remembers, there was a crucial problem: "the reinterpretation was wrong on every aspect." The Asian American movement grew not out of the early civil rights movement but out of the later demand for black liberation, Omatsu charged, and the key influence on the movement was not Martin Luther King Jr. but Malcolm X. Those who took part in the Asian American struggles in the 1960s and 1970s surely knew "that the focus of a generation of Asian American activists was not on asserting racial pride but reclaiming a tradition of militant struggle by earlier generations; that the movement was not centered on the aura of racial identity but embraced fundamental questions of oppression and power; that the movement consisted of not only college students but large numbers of community forces, including the elderly, workers, and high school youth; and that the main thrust was not one of seeking legitimacy and representation within American society but the larger goal of liberation."[3]

Omatsu's story telescopes many of the issues this chapter takes up, as it points out the distortions history undergoes in the process of remembering and rewriting. In particular, he highlights how history is repackaged in ways that make its memory less threatening to the fundamental organizing structures of American life. Here the civil rights movement is homogenized as "a single epoch" as opposed to a movement composed of many factions that emerged, evolved, and transformed over time and that espoused, as did Martin Luther King Jr. and Malcolm X, radically divergent political philosophies.

Omatsu writes against the popularized memory of the Asian American movement, and the civil rights movement more generally, as struggles for integration and representation in American society. Instead, he stresses those elements of the movement that were more militantly nationalist and fundamentally challenged an American system they saw as unjust to the core. Put another way, instead of seeking the right to be allowed to play by the pre-established rules of American society, the Third World movements—such as the various black nationalist movements, the Chicano movement, the American Indian movement (AIM), and the Asian American movement—sought the right to determine the rules by which they would govern their lives. Omatsu's memory of this political moment underscores the history of the struggle for self-determination that is often left out of a historical memory of the civil rights era that foregrounds the struggle for integration and excises the more "extreme" politics of nationalism and anticolonialism.

In this chapter, I explore the ways in which the film *Sunshine State* invokes this alternative historical consciousness of the civil rights movement expressed in the 1960s through Third World nationalist movements in the United States that organized, first and foremost, not for integration but for self-determination and liberation. *Sunshine State* not only shows the ways in which recurring colonizing practices throughout Florida's history influence the state today but also figures freedom as entailing and necessitating ownership and control over resources and over political decisions that impact people's lives. John Sayles's version of freedom as a kind of participatory democracy is often absent from our consciousness, displaced by conceptions of democracy based on access to consumption.

This chapter also seeks to contextualize *Sunshine State* in relation to other narratives that question the outcomes of integration, such as Toni Morrison's novel *Sula*. Sayles's analysis of the limitations of integration is not new, as the discussion of *Sula* demonstrates, but he suggests that remembering the struggle for self-determination by people of color during the civil rights era is crucial for a cross-racial populace. Ultimately,

Sayles suggests that the movements by people of color in the 1960s, properly remembered, provide important models for political liberation for all people in the present.

Political Evolution in the Films of John Sayles

Sunshine State distinguishes itself from Sayles's other films in its more direct and detailed invocation of a civil rights memory. Many of John Sayles's movies treat such themes as the quest for social justice and resistance to tyranny and oppression, the formation of racial identity and divisions in the United States, the abiding role of history in the present and the recovery of historical consciousness, and the formation of self-active, self-governing communities. Indeed, Sayles claims, "A lot of my movies are about community. Their culture is an attempt at community culture rather than mass culture."[4] In *Sunshine State*, however, in contrast to his other films, Sayles directly cites the civil rights era and the movement for economic, social, and spiritual self-determination as providing concrete models and viable directions for achieving genuinely democratic communities. In his 1984 film *The Brother from Another Planet*, which recast a slave narrative in the present, Sayles highlighted the persistence of racial economic oppression, but the film did not directly offer a viable historical model of liberation. Likewise, *Return of the Secaucus Seven* (1980) featured a group of former sixties radicals reflecting nostalgically on their political pasts but, somewhat like Kasdan's *The Big Chill*, did not urgently press for the reapplication of those activist politics to the present. *City of Hope* (1991) also tackled political issues resonant with the civil rights movement in its treatment of urban political corruption and the quest for racial progress. By his own admission, however, Sayles felt unable to address economic issues of racial oppression in *City of Hope*. As he said of the film, "A more important factor than the fragmentation of the black community is just brute economic factors, and there isn't much chance for me to talk about that in the film."[5]

The analysis Sayles offers in *Sunshine State*, however, suggests that the fragmentation of the black community and "brute economic factors" cannot be discussed independently of one another. Rather, economic factors are precisely responsible for this fragmentation. It is for this reason that recalling the civil rights politics of self-determination is so urgent, and it is in this regard that *Sunshine State* constitutes a development and deepening of John Sayles's thinking about freedom and social justice.

A comparison with Sayles's very popular 1996 film *Lone Star* is instructive for highlighting this development. *Lone Star* dealt with issues of racial division, social justice, and multiculturalism but fell short of the vision presented by *Sunshine State* in terms of the depth of analysis and the referencing of historical models of political possibility and liberation. One of the film's central plots features the sheriff of a Texas town, Sam Deeds, who begins to investigate a possible murder case when the skull of a former sheriff is unearthed in the desert. The case implicates his deceased father, former legendary sheriff of the town whom Sam Deeds succeeded. Sam's investigation of the crime requires a reconstruction of the past both in familial terms and in a larger historical sense, exploring the dynamics of race relations, immigration, and colonization that characterize the foundation of the community. His quest to solve the crime, if one in fact occurred, however, is figured as motivated not only by a desire for justice but also by a desire, embedded as he is in a Freudian family romance, to undermine his father's legendary status in the community: "If it's built on a crime, [the people] deserve to know," he tells one character in the film. This statement applies as much to the American nation as it does to Sam Deed's father, however, as his investigation of the crime is simultaneously an inquiry into the genocidal and racist crimes that define the colonialist founding and formation of the U.S. nation-state. But, Sayles suggests, just as Sam Deed's oedipal bitterness toward his father threatens to distort his investigation of the crime, racial bitterness threatens to distort the larger reconstruction of U.S. history itself by overaccentuating the role of race and the process of genocide in national development. Thus, in this film, Sayles seems to offer a vision suggesting that the focus on "race" in U.S. society and history is a contemporary phenomenon that distorts the past and needlessly threatens in the present the national unity symbolized in the trope of the lone star.

This element of the film is developed most evidently in the reconstruction and adult re-emergence of the adolescent romance between Sam Deeds and his teenage sweetheart Pilar. Sam's father had insistently forbidden the romantic relationship between Sam and Pilar, and looking back both Sam and Pilar attribute this intolerance of their relationship to racial prejudice. Yet we learn at the end that the two were kept apart not because of racial prejudice or miscegenation fears but rather because of an incest taboo, as we discover that Pilar is actually the product of an extramarital affair between Sam's father and Pilar's mother. Even after they learn the truth, Pilar and Sam decide to pursue a romantic if incestuous relationship, believing that they can put the past behind them, that they can, as Pilar's pithy imperative concludes the movie, "Forget the Alamo."

Through this resolution the film seems to suggest that an obsession with "race" in U.S. society has less to do with the material effects or reality of racial discrimination than with the complex neurosis of the national psyche that has obsessively focused on the genocidal history of the United States as a means of disgracing our forefathers. This theme is allegorically dramatized in Sam's oedipal quest to rewrite history in a way that criminalizes his otherwise glorified father. Both Sam and Pilar misinterpret their enforced separation as motivated by racial prejudice when in fact, Sam's father loved Pilar's mother and also, we learn, cared for his daughter. Moreover, the interracial relationship between Sam's father and Pilar's mother, Pilar's bicultural identity, and the incestuous relationship between Sam and Pilar, which keeps it "all in the family," forward the notion that we are already, individually and collectively, a hybridized, multicultural nation. Additionally, the concluding imperative to "forget the Alamo" exemplifies a repression of history and historical consciousness. It suggests that forgetting history rather than confronting its lasting effects might be a plausible solution to social strife.[6]

Sayles himself saw the ending of *Lone Star* as an evasion of rather than a solution to the historical legacy of racial oppression. In discussing the ending in which Sam and Pilar decide that it is acceptable for them to break the taboo of incest because they do not plan to have children, Sayles comments that while

> they choose to cross the border of moral opinion . . . it is only an individual accommodation, and that was a lot of my point with the ending, it's not going to change society. They're going to have to leave the society they're in, they can't stay in that town. You may be very nonracial, you

may be married to a black person, but if you're in the middle of the Watts riots, that's not going to help you. That individual accommodation you made has not changed the social situation, or hasn't changed it enough so that what society is still doing is going to honor your change.[7]

Thus, while the film offers a critique of society's stubborn resistance to change and even perhaps of the limitations of individual forms of resistance to effect significant alterations in power dynamics, *Lone Star* falls short of providing any effective historical models for working toward social transformation and liberation.

Sunshine State constitutes an evolution in Sayles's thinking. While Sayles saw *Lone Star* as "so much . . . about the burden of history," *Sunshine State* understands history as not just a burden but also a key repository of important models of political struggle that provide a sense of possibility for addressing current social ills.[8] In *Sunshine State* Sayles recuperates the memory of the struggle for self-determination during the civil rights era as a necessary and useable politics for populist multiracial challenge and resistance to the new colonizing practices of contemporary corporations. The memory Sayles recuperates, however, is a contested one that is frequently marginalized in favor of less threatening avenues of political change that do not fundamentally alter the distribution of social power and capital.

Sunshine State and Multiple Memories of the Civil Rights Movement

At one point in *Sunshine State*, the young, professional African American Bostonian Dr. Reginald Perry, who has come to Florida with his wife, Desiree Stokes Perry, to visit her mother, runs into the elderly Dr. Lloyd on the oceanfront of Lincoln Beach. Dr. Lloyd has been organizing to save the city of Lincoln Beach from what the city council benignly calls "incorporation" and what he calls "expropriation." Dr. Lloyd invites him to attend the protest he is organizing, but Dr. Perry defers, explaining that he is "just visiting." Nonetheless, he inquires about the nature of the protest, wondering if it is an "ecological thing." "They're trying to save an endangered species," Dr. Lloyd answers, "Us." Elaborating on the significance of the protest and its historical underpinnings, he then meaningfully elaborates: "In the forties and fifties, Lincoln Beach was it—all the oceanfront in three counties we were allowed to step foot onto. Black folks, I'm talking about the pillars of the community, got together and bought this land, built the houses. You'd drive through a couple of hundred miles of redneck sheriffs, park your ride on the boardwalk, step out, and just breathe."[9]

When Dr. Perry asks what happened, Dr. Lloyd offers the young anesthesiologist the following analysis: "Civil rights happened. Progress. Used to be you were black, you'd buy black. In the Jim Crow days, you'd need a shoe shine, wanted a taxi ride to the train station, wanted some ribs or a fish sandwich, chances are a black man owned the place you bought 'em at. Nowadays the drive-throughs serve anybody, but who owns them? Not us. All our people do is wear paper hats and dip out them fries. Only thing we got left are funeral parlors and barbershops." Confused, if not unconvinced by this analysis, Dr. Perry replies half-questioningly, "But now we can do anything." Somewhat despondently Dr. Lloyd qualifies this reply, "Them that can get over do fine. Them that can't are in a world of trouble."

In many ways this scene centers the film's memorial invocation of the civil rights movement. Dr. Lloyd assesses not only the gains the movement made in achieving integration ("Now the drive-throughs serve anybody"), but also the pitfalls and continuing challenges that resulted from the success of that struggle. Integration fell short of, and perhaps even hindered, Dr. Lloyd suggests, the achievement of social, political, and economic self-determination for African Americans and others ("but who owns them?"). Indeed, in dramatizing this conversation between an African American professional of the post–civil rights movement generation and an older professional of the civil rights generation, who still has roots in the movement and who still responds to injustice with the impulse for activism, this scene depicts what has been lost in terms of a legacy and historical consciousness of the civil rights movement for the next generation. Reginald's memory seems vague at best. In measuring historical transformation by his own mobility, status, and achievement, he comprehends the movement as a success ("But now we can do anything") and seems to understand the struggle for civil rights as primarily having been centered on integration. That he sees the civil rights movement as already having succeeded in achieving freedom and equality is itself disarming, the film suggests, precisely because this vision stops short of understanding freedom as entailing some ownership of the world that empowers people to make decisions central to the governance of their lives. Instead, Reginald understands freedom primarily in terms of economic opportunity, which might allow him to succeed individually in the terms of the U.S. capitalist system but not to have a say in how that system is organized and operated. Thus, in this conversation between the two doctors, Sayles presents us with two memories or legacies of the civil rights movement that also entail two very different conceptions of freedom.

Moreover, these two characters also embody divergent ways of imagining the relationship between the individual and the larger community. While Dr. Lloyd is concerned about those in the African American community who have not succeeded, Reginald seems alienated both from the larger black community, particularly those of the working and lower classes, and from the tradition of self-activity, organizing, and protest. As he notes, he is "just visiting" Lincoln Beach and thus will not take part in the protest. The scene registers the breakdown of community among African Americans and the extent to which integration has been accompanied by the assimilation of African Americans into the individualistic ethos of U.S. capitalist culture to the detriment of the collective ethos Dr. Lloyd represents. Integration, the film implies, contributed ironically enough to the *disintegration* of the African American community by, one, dispersing the community and thereby eroding the conditions of propinquity and of place that enable the development of community relationships (both Reginald and his wife Desiree Stokes left the South) and, two, by superseding or displacing the objective of self-determination.

Critiquing Integration: *Sula* and Beyond

This analysis of the detrimental effects of integration not only rehearses the arguments of Eldridge Cleaver and others who saw integration as part of "the mother country's" strategy to maintain colonial domination over

African Americans but also resonates strongly with Toni Morrison's depiction of the consequences of integration in *Sula*.[10] The novel ends in 1965 with Morrison representing the integration of the new generation of African Americans as part of the same process of their dispossession from their neighborhood in the Bottom. She writes,

> Nobody colored lived much up in the Bottom any more. White people
> were building towers for television stations up there and there was a
> rumor about a golf course or something. Anyway, hill land was more
> valuable now, and those black people who had moved down right after
> the war and in the fifties couldn't afford to come back even if they
> wanted to. Except for the few blacks still huddled by the river bend,
> and some undemolished houses on Carpenter's Road, only rich white
> folks were building homes in the hills. Just like that they had changed
> their minds and instead of keeping the valley floor to themselves, now
> they wanted a hilltop house with a river view and a ring of elms. The
> black people, for all their new look, seemed awfully anxious to get to the
> valley, or leave town, and abandon the hills to whoever was interested. It
> was sad, because the Bottom had been a real place. These younger ones
> kept talking about the community, but they left the hills to the poor,
> the old, the stubborn—and the rich white folks. Maybe it hadn't been a
> community, but it had been a place. Now there weren't any places left,
> just separate houses with separate televisions and separate telephones
> and less and less dropping by.[11]

Morrison, too, questions the efficaciousness of integration for achieving genuine liberation for African Americans, interrogating the narrative of progress informing integrationist civil rights historiographies. Like Cleaver, she suggests that whatever progress integration might have constituted, one of its consequences, unintended or otherwise, was the solidification of a colonial relationship between African Americans and whites. In Morrison's representation, African Americans not only still suffer economic disparities, but have now lost the conditions that made community possible. Achieving integration instead led to an erosion of community that alienated black people from each other, just as Reginald Perry is alienated from his community in *Sunshine State*.

Indeed, as Morrison opens the final section of *Sula*, titled "1965," she highlights the apparent hallmarks of progress but calls into question the true nature of change: "Things were so much better in 1965. Or so it seemed. You could go downtown and see colored people working in the dime store behind the counters, even handling money with cash-register keys around their necks. And a colored man taught mathematics at the junior high school."[12] The economic opportunities opened by the success of the civil rights movement, Morrison suggests, did not equal substantial change. Rather, integration of African Americans into American capitalism on still largely unequal terms effectively reritualized colonialism and dissolved the political cohesion of African Americans. Evident in the writings of Cleaver and Morrison is a vision of the struggles for civil rights consistent with that of Dr. Lloyd in *Sunshine State*, as Morrison, Cleaver, and Sayles point out that just because some African Americans might have achieved the status of doctor or mathematics teacher does not mean that the problem of racial inequality has been solved. Even more important, such a fact certainly does not mean that self-determination—what these artists seem to define as the real meaning of freedom—has been achieved.

In *Sunshine State*, recalling and ratifying this vision of civil rights struggle as the quest for self-determination is important not just to refresh the memory of people of color; rather, Sayles seems to want to mobilize this memory in the service of a broader populist agenda. He suggests that the majority of people living in the United States are deprived of the opportunity to meaningfully participate in the governing of the nation. Moreover, he suggests most Americans lack a memory of the movements that could provide a catalyst to help them rethink what constitutes genuine freedom and democracy.

Viewed in the light of this critical perspective on the civil rights era, Dr. Lloyd represents an alternative and often forgotten element of the civil rights movement frequently obscured or glossed over in historical accounts that foreground the organizing of King and the integration struggle. Lloyd gives voice to the sector of the civil rights movement that saw the philosophy of integration as insufficient and instead argued for the necessity of nationalism or national liberation, a philosophy given voice by such prominent black nationalist activists and writers as Malcolm X, Eldridge Cleaver, Angela Davis, George Jackson, and Amiri Baraka in addition to many voices in the Chicano, American Indian, and Asian American movements. These Third World national liberation movements stressed the need for people to have a land of their own as the basis not just for democratic self-rule but for the free and full development of their identity.

Indeed, in his attempt to protect the land of Lincoln Beach and the fading legacy of black ownership and community control from predacious land "developers," Dr. Lloyd uses words that clearly recall the words and ideals of these activists. When he stands before his church and tells the congregation that "the matter I came to discuss is not exactly religious, but it is a matter of the spirit," he strongly echoes, for example, Malcolm X, who similarly spoke of the spiritual element of economic self-determination central to the black nationalist agenda: "The social philosophy of black nationalism only means that we have to get together to remove the evils, the vices, alcoholism, drug addiction, and other evils that are destroying the moral fiber of our community. We ourselves have to lift the level of our community, the standard of our community to a higher level, make our own society so that we will be satisfied in our own social circles and won't be running around here trying to knock our way into a social circle where we're not wanted."[13]

This social philosophy, of course, has a requisite economic agenda, too, in order to provide the necessary material basis for this spiritual renewal:

So the economic philosophy of black nationalism means in every church,
in every civic organization, in every fraternal order, it's time now for
our people to become conscious of the importance of controlling the
economy of our community. If we own the stores, if we operate the
businesses, if we try and establish some industry in our own community,
then we're developing to the position where we are creating employment for our own kind. Once you gain control of the economy of your
own community, then you don't have to picket and boycott and beg
some cracker downtown for a job in his business.[14]

We can also hear LeRoi Jones (Amiri Baraka) identifying land ownership as the necessary basis for healthy emotional, psychic, and spiritual development. As he wrote in an essay in *Home* in 1968, "The Black Man will always be frustrated until he has land (A Land!) of his own. All the thought processes and emotional orientation of 'national liberation movements'—from slave uprisings onward—have always given motion to a Black National (and Cultural) Consciousness. These movements proposed that judgments were being made by Black sensibility." [15]

For Jones, as for Dr. Lloyd, freedom is not realized simply through having a better job or becoming a professional, as it seems to be in the thinking of Reginald Perry. Rather, the politics of Third World nationalisms, for Jones and I think for Dr. Lloyd, imagines freedom in more complex and fundamental ways in terms of a people's ability to make judgments and govern its life in its enlightened interest as a community.

Jones's formulation of the differences between nationalism and integration as delineated in the following passage is useful here for understanding the historical depth in the dialogue between Dr. Perry and Dr. Lloyd:

> What I am driving at is the fact that to me the Africans, Asians, and
> Latin Americans who are news today because of their nationalism,
> i.e., the militant espousal of the doctrine of serving one's own people's
> interests before those of a foreign country, e.g., the United States, are
> exactly the examples the black man in this country should use in his
> struggle for *independence*. (And that is what the struggle remains, for
> independence—from political, economic, social, spiritual, and psy-
> chological domination of the white man. Put more simply, the struggle
> moves to make certain that no man has the right to dictate the life of
> another man. The struggle is not simply for "equality," or "better jobs,"
> or "better schools," and the rest of those half-hearted liberal cliches; it
> is to completely *free* the black man from the domination of the white
> man. . . .) [16]

This concept of self-determination is central to nationalist politics in Dr. Lloyd's valorizations of formerly black-owned Lincoln Beach as a sanctuary for African Americans. Lincoln Beach affords them the kind of independence of which Jones speaks in this passage. It is this sense of freedom as independence from domination that is absent from the young doctor's belief that African Americans are now free because "now we can do anything," or because, in Jones's terms, they can have "better jobs."

This worldview underscoring the relationship between land ownership, the ability to control one's life, and healthy spiritual, emotional, and intellectual growth characterized a range of Third World movements in the United States by peoples of color who understood their struggle as one of decolonization. In "El Plan Espiritual de Aztlan," the manifesto of the Chicano Movement, for example, it is stated,

> Economic control of our lives and our communities can only come
> about by driving the exploiter out of our communities, our pueblos, and
> our lands and by controlling and developing our own talents, sweat, and
> resources. Cultural background and values which ignore materialism
> and embrace humanism will contribute to the act of cooperative buying
> and the distribution of resources and production to sustain an economic
> base for healthy growth and development. Lands rightfully ours will be
> fought for and defended. Land and realty ownership will be acquired by
> the community for the people's welfare. Economic ties of responsibility
> must be secured by nationalism and the Chicano defense units.[17]

"El Plan Espiritual" made clear that the civil rights movement was not just an African American struggle, and it emphasized that land ownership was necessary for the ideal self-determination that was the informing objective of so many liberation struggles. People must have a material stake in the world, the theory goes, in order to ensure that they can participate in making decisions regarding how society is organized and how resources are allocated. Only when these conditions are met can a people develop spiritually and creatively.

The Persistence of Colonialism and the Necessity of Self-Determination

In this sense, the scene I have been discussing at length as central to the film's memory of the civil rights movement demonstrates not just what we remember of the movement but, more important for Sayles, what lessons and principles we have forgotten as well as what the consequences of that amnesia are. Sayles represents contemporary life in Florida as conditioned by its colonial history, suggesting that the same practices of piracy, conquest, and colonization practiced against indigenous populations in the past exist in the present in the form of corporate plunder and piracy. The objective of this corporate colonization, however, is not to subjugate only people of color but the working-class and middle-class population as a whole across racial lines. Sayles seems to suggest in part that the inability of that movement to achieve genuine democratic empowerment of not just racial minorities but the populous as a whole rests in the failure to comprehend class and racial inequality as an experience of colonization. This inability, consequently, results in the failure to conceptualize movements for liberation as struggles for decolonization and self-determination as opposed to struggles for integration.

In many ways the film echoes and shares the analysis of the integration solution voiced by Eldridge Cleaver in his 1968 essay "The Land Question and Black Liberation," where he writes, "The basic flaw in the analysis and outlook of the white liberals, radicals and the black bourgeoisie is that the concept of the American melting pot completely ignores the distinction between the white mother country and the black colony. And the solution of Integration, based on this false outlook, was doomed from the beginning to yield only a deceptive and disillusioning result. Black people are a stolen people held in colonial status on stolen land, and any analysis which does not acknowledge the colonial status of black people cannot hope to deal with the real problem."[18] Sayles too suggests in *Sunshine State* that "to deal with the real problem" entails addressing the colonial history of Florida, and by extension, of the United States. The objective in doing so is to understand the inequality and exploitation of the present and the cultural practices that perpetuate and even celebrate such relationships. For Sayles, as for Cleaver, restoring freedom and equality to the oppressed and exploited necessitates identifying and eliminating the operative mechanisms that create, organize, and reproduce the exploitative deprivation of freedom and equality.

The opening scenes of the film make painfully clear the ways in which Florida's history of conquest, plunder, and genocide is celebrated and marketed in a way that implicitly validates colonialism. Additionally, these scenes explore the ways in which that history and those cultural practices are cognitively divorced from the present, mystifying any causal relation-ship or continuity between past behaviors and the current predicament in which those behaviors and values are reritualized in different forms. The first shot of the movie features the troubled African American teen Terrell Bernard burning down the *Freebooter*, the model pirate ship built for the Buccaneer Days festival celebrating Florida's history. Later, we see Francine Pinckney, the festival's organizer, declare the arson a "shock and an outrage" and a "senseless act of vandalism." The film's narrative, how-ever, implicitly suggests that the burning of the pirate ship—a symbol of colonial conquest, slavery, and plunder—makes sense when Terrell's dif-ficulties are contextualized in the history of colonization, created in part as they are by the influx of drugs in the African American community and by the general disintegration of a community that could support him.

In these scenes, Sayles dramatizes the persistence of imperialist val-ues as demonstrated in the celebration of Florida's buccaneer history and also the blindness toward the effect of persisting and reritualized colonial relationships on the African American community. Terrell's setting the pirate ship aflame is senseless only if one forgets the significance and im-pact of the colonial history that is, ironically, at the same time persistently celebrated and put before one's eyes. Indeed, Sayles attempts to bring his audience beyond what Eldridge Cleaver called the "false outlook" of integration that could "yield only a deceptive and disillusioning result" and to recall the alternative and oft-forgotten memory of the civil rights movement represented by the likes of Cleaver and other Third World activists and thinkers.

The struggle for memory is further accentuated later in the film when Terrell appears before a judge for his juvenile court hearing. The judge admonishes Terrell, telling him, "When somebody destroys something that stands for a group of people, that's called desecration." We see here how the legal and juridical discourses and practices underwrite and ratify a colonialist mentality and cultural vision. The continuing colonialist as-pect of current cultural, legal, and economic practice is highlighted again when Eunice Stokes visits her deceased ancestors in an African American cemetery where, among others, slaves are buried. A golf course has been built around the cemetery, and Eunice complains to her daughter as she cleans gravesites littered with golf balls: "They don't belong here. It's bad enough we have to pass through all this security to visit our dead. It's a resting place, not a playpen." This scene underscores how the desecration of African American sacred historical monuments that contain important personal and collective historical memories is sanctioned while the legal system intervenes when a wooden pirate ship representative of enslavement and genocide is destroyed. Once again, Sayles points out how the dominant U.S. culture marginalizes and indeed forgets the history of those negatively impacted by the genocidal colonial processes of U.S. nation formation at the same time that it valorizes those who took part in perpetrating the colonization.

The effect, the film suggests, of this celebration of colonialism—cleansed of the ugly truths of slavery, genocide, land expropriation, and brutal exploitation—is not just that such behaviors and values are perpetuated but that they are normalized so that as a culture we take them for granted and fail to recognize the operations of contemporary capitalism as mechanisms of conquest and colonization. It is precisely this normalization of colonization that necessitates the recuperation of a civil rights memory informed by a politics of decolonization and an analytical framework that allows us to identify the operations of colonialism. Dr. Lloyd, for example, protests the city council's zoning decisions allowing for the "incorporation" of Lincoln Beach by developers by labeling it an "expropriation" of "land with important historical significance to this community . . . a history this commission," he asserts, "has repeatedly ignored." When the commission responds by invoking the legality of the concept of eminent domain, he retorts that the concept of eminent domain "is a weapon you people have used to undermine the well-being of our people." In this scene, Dr. Lloyd unmasks the city council's behavior with its legal underpinnings as a recurrent contemporary form of colonization, the intent of which, similar to that of the pirates of old in search of gold, is to dispossess the people from their lands in the pursuit of accumulating wealth.

This representation of the continuity between the colonization of Florida in the past and the present is suggestively framed and set up in the beginning of the film with the transition from the opening scene in which Terrell burns the pirate ship to the second scene featuring four white men applauding their roles in developing Florida as they golf. Standing at the tee surveying the fairway, Murray Silver depicts himself as the master of his own creation myth, exclaiming, "In the beginning there was nothing." "Wilderness," one of his cohorts responds. "Worse than wilderness," Silver insists. "This was land," he continues, "populated by white people who ate catfish. We created this." "Golf courses?" his cohort asks. "Nature—on a leash," Silver clarifies. The developer Silver rehearses the same rationalizations used to justify colonization that early settlers in the United States did, that of the territory being a "virgin land" that is basically uninhabited, except, of course, for the catfish-eating white people. Even this last contradiction replicates early American colonial discourses that figured the land as uninhabited in the same breath that Indians were mentioned.[19] Immediately juxtaposing this scene with that of Terrell setting fire to the pirate ship, a monument to conquest and plunder, Sayles highlights the relationship between imperialist history and the persistence of a colonial mentality and of colonizing practices in the present that generally go by the name of "development."

In this respect, again, the film underscores how the celebration and romanticization of the brutal and genocidal history of colonial conquest promote and validate like behavior in the present that might manifest itself in different forms whose brutality is less visible to us as such. Silver embodies this romantic connection to the past, as he returns in the last scene of the movie again standing at a golf tee waxing nostalgic about Ponce de León and the romance of questing for gold. He laments the lack of poetry in our times, wondering, "What do our young people dream of?" As he hits the ball, the camera pulls back to show him standing in the middle of an urban thoroughfare teeing off into an ugly and unappetizing row of fast food restaurants and strip malls. Thus, the movie ends by drawing a connection between the brutal colonial projects of the past and the modes of development and capital accumulation in the present, suggesting that the two are more similar than they might initially appear and that contemporary capitalist "development" constitutes a continuation of piracy.

This final scene brings us back full circle to Dr. Lloyd's conversation with Reginald Perry and to the film's central theme of our inability as a culture to recognize the illusory aspect of the so-called "democratic" institutions of "American" society. Indeed, just as Reginald Perry believes that "now we can do anything" without recognizing that lack of access to capital limits people's ability genuinely to shape their world, so Sayles suggests that the American people as a whole labor under the illusion of living in a democracy without fully recognizing its subjection to capital and its lack of self-determination. When Murray Silver talks about developing a land "that was populated by white people eating catfish," Sayles makes clear that the experience of colonization is not exclusive to people of color in the United States. He thus adopts a unique populist stance by creatively extending models of colonization to comprehend the experience of both whites and people of color in the United States in their relationship to capital in a corporatized U.S. culture and political economy.

This colonial subjection, the film suggests, is kept in place because people buy into the marketing of democracy and freedom as defined by access to consumption rather than by ownership of the means of production that would ensure the right of self-determination. This distortion of democratic values is dramatized in the film when different developers are vying to purchase the Temples' oceanfront motel. One developer attempts to persuade Marly Temple to sell to him instead of the Exley Plantation development because, he explains, "Exley Plantations are only for the rich. We have a democratic development in mind." Marly queries whether that means fast food restaurants and strip malls. The developer replies that there would probably be some of that. We see here that what is meant by democratic development is creating cheap and accessible consumption for the mass of ordinary citizens, as opposed to making the ownership of capital and by extension the decision-making process accessible to the mass of ordinary citizens so that they could have some control in directing their lives by having a say in how resources are developed and used. Again, this is precisely Dr. Lloyd's point when he reminds Dr. Perry that while drive-throughs now serve anybody, African Americans do not own them.

Recovering Memory

Recovering a memory of the civil rights movement as a struggle for self-determination is important for Sayles because that memory provides a model for political activism and possibility for all people. The civil rights memory embodied in the character Dr. Lloyd refocuses political activism on the struggle for self-determination that entails the necessity of having ownership of one's world. *Sunshine State* also features white characters as political subjects seeking self-determination. Delia Temple, the owner of the Temple family motel, surprises a greedy land developer when she demands in addition to a flat fee to sell the hotel, a continuing interest in whatever enterprise the developers pursue. Through her experience running community theater, she has developed the financial savvy to know how to protect the rights of the community and to make sure she maintains a stake in the running of it. In this sense, Delia becomes Sayles's figure for an effective activist who understands the necessity of ownership in order to guarantee the right of self-determination.

Like Dr. Lloyd, Delia has a clear sense of connection to the community and does not suffer the sense of alienation and powerlessness that the characters from the younger generation in the film seem to experience. She is contrasted with the character of Flash Phillips, a former college football star who now works for a car dealership. Flash's employers are using him as a front to try to buy up Lincoln Beach. Flash justifies his behavior to Desiree Stokes, rationalizing, "It's a handful of people who run the whole deal, and then there's the rest of us who do what they tell us and get paid for it." As with Dr. Lloyd and Dr. Perry, Sayles here juxtaposes characters from different generations to highlight the post–civil rights movement generation's distance from the politics of self-determination and their assimilation into individualist capitalist values. As we see here with Flash Phillips's defeatism, Sayles represents capitalist individualism as disempowering in its surrendering acceptance to the system as it is as opposed to the community ideals and sense of collective empowerment Delia Temple and Dr. Lloyd hold because of their experience and memory.

Integration, *Sunshine State* suggests, unfortunately also entailed assimilation into individualist values that eroded a community sensibility and fostered a condition of alienation for African Americans. The film also highlights that white citizens who supposedly live freely in the democratic capitalist United States also suffer from this alienation. Indeed, the film critiques American democracy for failing to offer the majority of people meaningful freedom and a voice in their world. Sayles clearly illustrates the stakes in how we remember the civil rights movement, invoking a memory of the struggle for self-determination in ways that recall other definitions of freedom and democracy that genuinely empower the individual in a collective context. Because it is the colonizing practices of contemporary U.S. capitalism that need most urgently to be resisted, the models of political activism and thinking developed by the Third World movements of the 1960s offer, Sayles seems to suggest, the most useful lessons for directing popular movements in the struggle for self-determination and the genuine cultivation of freedom and democracy.

Notes

This chapter is dedicated to Caleb.

1. Glenn Omatsu, "The 'Four Prisons' and the Movements of Liberation: Asian American Activism from the 1960s to the 1990s," in *The State of Asian America: Activism and Resistance in the 1990s*, ed. Karin Aguilar-San Juan (Boston, Mass.: South End Press, 1994), 21.

2. Ibid., 21.

3. Ibid., 20–21.

4. Diane Carson, ed., *John Sayles: Interviews* (Jackson: University Press of Mississippi, 1999), 166.

5. Ibid., 148.

6. For a more extensive reading of *Lone Star* in the context of an analysis of "postethnic" theory, see my "Against Premature Internationalism: Reasserting the Necessity of Nationalism for Socialist Liberation in the Age of Post-Theory," in *Re-Reading Global Socialist Cultures after the Cold War*, ed. Dubravka Juraga and M. Keith Booker (London: Praeger, 2002), 27–54.

7. Carson, *John Sayles: Interviews*, 216.

8. Ibid., 220.

9. *Sunshine State*, written and directed by John Sayles (2002: Sony Pictures).

10. Eldridge Cleaver, "The Land Question and Black Liberation" in *Post-Prison Writings and Speeches*, ed. Robert Scheer (New York: Random House, 1968), 59.

11. Toni Morrison, *Sula* (New York: Plume, 1973), 166.

12. Ibid., 163.

13. Malcolm X, "The Ballot or the Bullet," in *The Heath Anthology of Amer-*

ican Literature, 2nd ed., vol. 2, ed. Paul Lauter et al. (Lexington, Mass.: Heath, 1990), 2505.

14. Ibid., 2506.

15. LeRoi Jones, "The Legacy of Malcolm X, and the Coming of the Black Nation," in *Home: Social Essays* (New York: William Morrow, 1968), 244.

16. LeRoi Jones, "Black Is a Country," in *Home*, 84.

17. "El Plan Espiritual de Aztlan" in *Aztlan: Essays on the Chicano Homeland*, ed. Rudolfo Anaya and Francisco Lomeli (Albuquerque: University of New Mexico Press, 1989), 2.

18. Cleaver, "The Land Question and Black Liberation," 61.

19. See, for example, Henry Nash Smith, *Virgin Land: The American West as Symbol and Myth* (Cambridge, Mass.: Harvard University Press, 1950).

LEIGH RAIFORD

Restaging Revolution

Black Power, *Vibe* Magazine, and

Photographic Memory

In 1970, Angela Davis was perhaps the most visible underground insurrectionary intellectual in the country. Davis fled the law and charges of murder, conspiracy, and kidnapping in connection with the failed attempt to free prisoner and Black Panther George Jackson and two other inmates known collectively as the Soledad Brothers in August 1970. During the two harrowing months Davis spent dodging the FBI, her photographic image bombarded the United States in the form of FBI wanted posters and newspaper and magazine articles, including a *Life* magazine cover story, which prominently displayed Davis's headshot on newsstands worldwide. Davis's likeness also appeared on posters, buttons, and leaflets, which called for an immediate end to the hunt and for all charges against her to be dropped. "Taken by journalists, undercover policemen, and movement activists," these myriad photographs, Davis acknowledges, "played a major role in both the mobilization of public opinion against me *and* the development of the campaign that was ultimately responsible for my acquittal."[1] She is acutely aware of how the familiar image of her face became infused with political meaning, simultaneously framed to signify an armed and dangerous black militant Communist or a strident and dynamic revolutionary. Both images resonated loudly in the charged polit-

WANTED BY THE FBI

INTERSTATE FLIGHT - MURDER, KIDNAPING

ANGELA YVONNE DAVIS

FBI No. 867,615 G

Photograph taken 1969   Photograph taken 1970

Alias: "Tamu"

DESCRIPTION

Age:	26, born January 26, 1944, Birmingham, Alabama		
Height:	5'8"	**Eyes:**	Brown
Weight:	145 pounds	**Complexion:**	Light brown
Build:	Slender	**Race:**	Negro
Hair:	Black	**Nationality:**	American
Occupation:	Teacher		
Scars and Marks:	Small scars on both knees		

Fingerprint Classification: 4 M 5 Ua 6

I 17 U

CAUTION

ANGELA DAVIS IS WANTED ON KIDNAPING AND MURDER CHARGES GROWING OUT OF AN ABDUCTION AND SHOOTING IN MARIN COUNTY, CALIFORNIA, ON AUGUST 7, 1970. SHE ALLEGEDLY HAS PURCHASED SEVERAL GUNS IN THE PAST. CONSIDER POSSIBLY ARMED

The FBI issued this wanted flyer on August 18, 1970, after adding Angela Davis to its "Ten Most Wanted Fugitives" list. (© Bettmann/Corbis)

ical climate of the late 1960s and early 1970s, when the Black Panthers represented both a tremendous threat and a revolutionary opportunity.

Twenty-five years later, Davis confronted many of these same photographs as, what she called, a "commodified backdrop for advertising" clothing. In its March 1994 issue, *Vibe* magazine, founded by entertainment mogul Quincy Jones, produced an eight-page fashion layout entitled "Free Angela: Actress Cynda Williams as Angela Davis, a *Fashion Revolutionary*" (emphasis mine). The layout combined re-creations of pictures of Davis from the early 1970s and a pastiche of Black Panther and Third Worldist iconography, specifically black men with large Afros wearing leather jackets and sunglasses.

The photographs were taken by Albert Watson, a middle-aged white Swiss-born photographer born blind in one eye, who has since achieved high praise from the art world. Watson is perhaps best known for his images of black men, including Tupac Shakur, Bobby Brown, and Mike Tyson. Watson's work has been celebrated as testimony to the "power of the fetish."[2] Another critic, in an unfortunately titled article, "Albert Watson: One Eye on the Prize," wrote, "While photographing celebrities in a way that turns them into icons standing in for themselves, Watson depicts objects by searching beneath their surface for what they actually represent."[3] But what do these subjects actually represent and *for whom*? In the case of the photographs of both famous and unknown black men, Watson transforms his subjects into stereotypes, drawing from and feeding into the river of ideas and ideologies regarding black male identity. Shot from behind, faces completely concealed from the viewer (as in the Brown and Tyson photographs) or posed with "a short, blunt pistol" under the "fiendish garb" of a dark hoodie (as in the Tupac photograph), these men are reduced to their bare backs and signifying props.[4] They are hypervisible in the camera's lens yet entirely unknowable and inapproachable, specters that both haunt and entice the white imagination. As Maurice Wallace astutely points out, Watson's photographs function as "metapicture[s], representation[s] of . . . representation[s]," which offer up Tyson, Tupac, Brown, and others as "specimens" of an *idea* of dangerous and inscrutable black male identity. Watson's Davis layout offered a similar kind of hypericonization in which viewers were presented with the restaging of representations.[5]

Vibe touted its "Free Angela" spread as " 'docufashion' because it uses modern clothing to mimic Angela Davis's look from the '70's."[6] This hybrid term proves fitting in that fashion is propelled by a quest for the cutting edge, an eternal new in which consumers live only in the present state of their own desires, a sort of antimemory. Following the prefix "docu-," however, such a layout depends on the vérité of the past it mimics while also documenting its own materialization as spectacle. "Free Angela" relies on the familiarity of its young post–Black Power audience with the icons of Black Power without recounting the history of those icons.[7]

Davis was angered by the transformation of her legal case into contemporary fashion, as a vehicle for rampant consumerism. "The way in which this document [her photograph] provided a historical pretext for something akin to a reign of terror for countless young black women is effectively erased by its use as a prop for selling clothes and promoting a seventies fashion nostalgia," she charged.[8] Davis noted the multiple political uses to which her photographic image was put: to discredit and incarcerate her, to liberate and venerate her, and ultimately to depoliticize and commodify her work. Not unlike photographs of Martin Luther King Jr. delivering his "I Have a Dream" speech at the 1963 March on Washington representing McDonald's present-day equal opportunity (read: low wages/no benefits) hiring practices, in the *Vibe* spread, the photograph frees Angela from the political exigencies of 1970 yet imprisons her in the outward appearances of that earlier moment.

The genesis and transformation of Angela Davis's "Wanted" photograph offers a useful entry point into a consideration of the cultural life of social movement photography, specifically photography of the Black Panther Party and Black Power movement, and how such images shape memory of the 1960s African American freedom struggle. The transformation, or restaging, of Angela Davis's image begs specific questions about what happens when these images travel through time. Why and how has Black Power and Black Panther social movement photography resurged in particular moments and what messages and meanings do they carry in these new contexts?

This chapter considers how this specific archive of social movement photography has moved through time and in what ways and to what ends these photographs have mobilized present-day memories of Black Power politics and culture. When first created in the late 1960s and early 1970s, Black Panther photographs, as I demonstrate, imaged the revolutionary possibilities of the moment and the power that lay in re-visioning black identity. At the same time, the images of mass protests, militarized formation, charismatic leaders, and committed rank and file members captured numerous contradictions within the party and its politics. Such photographs encapsulated, widely disseminated, and ultimately iconized Panther style as well as the Panthers themselves. These icons came to stand in for and symbolize a wide range of complex ideas and competing ideologies around the party and Black Power more generally. As time passed, as the Panthers were crushed from both within and without, many of these icons—dress, style, rhetoric—could be called on by myriad sources to invoke not only Black Power but the structure of feeling of the late 1960s.

Perhaps no other source summoned up Black Power icons as vigorously or as clumsily as Hollywood. During the blaxploitation film cycle of 1969–75, moviemakers animated Panther social movement photographs for the big screen. Angela Davis was metamorphosed into Foxy Brown; the collective anti-imperialism of "All power to the people," became the individual vigilantism of an (white) eye for an (black) eye, and Hollywood effectively mobilized black rage into easy rides and quick returns at the box office. Through a reading of the film *Foxy Brown* (Jack Hill, 1974), I also explore how blaxploitation employed the visual icons of Black Power to both celebrate and lampoon the movement, especially its black female leaders, confining to memory prematurely the radicalism of Black Panther politics even as the party continued to struggle offscreen for its survival and the survival of the communities it served.

Blaxploitation represents a significant bridge between social movement photography in the service of the Black Power movement and the harnessing of those images to contemporary popular commodity culture. This is not to suggest, however, that the magnetism of the Panthers lay purely in its politics and had nothing to do with image. Black Power, and the Panthers especially, were rife with visual appeal and aesthetic allure— raised fists and crisp uniforms that signified collective solidarity and organization, big Afros and serious countenances manifested the ethos "Black

Is Beautiful." Indeed, it is this allure that has made the party so fascinating to its own and subsequent audiences, that has enabled such effective iconization and reproduction in films, music videos, and advertising. Nor do I want to preclude these sites as effective media for inspiring political change. Yet, as Angela Davis, advises us: "Where cultural representations do not reach out beyond themselves, there is the danger that they will function as surrogates for activism, that they will constitute both the beginning and end of political practice."[9] The journeys of Black Power social movement photography, of cultural representations of political activism, point to the spaces the movement has come to occupy, and what of Black Power remains, in our national memory.

Social Movement Photography and the Black Panther Party

Let me begin with a definition of social movement photography. With this term, I refer to the voluminous body of images maneuvered specifically for the purpose of recording, describing, and advancing social movements. Snapshots of lynchings placed at the center of antilynching pamphlets transformed lynching photography into antilynching photography.[10] Photographs of casual community conversations appearing in movement organization newspapers, documents of demonstrations transformed into posters and books, carefully composed portraits of movement leaders metamorphosed into icons, each constitute an element of social movement photography.

Social movement photography describes not simply photographic subject but political project, more than visual documentation but also cultural labor. In this way, the term differs from and expands on the more common "documentary photography" in its explicit acknowledgment and inclusion of the politics—of creation, of distribution, of reception—that stir the image. Social movement photography is concerned with the creation *and* mobilization of photography by movement organizers first and, to a lesser extent, the response and application—both material and imaginative—of these images by movement constituents and observers. Social movement photography recognizes the marriage of form and function, a union that also illuminates the inextricable link between representation in the cultural sphere and representation in the political sphere. This relationship is one that continues to both animate and beleaguer African American quests for justice.

Photojournalists, movement organizers and participants, observers and artists, wielded cameras to document the many shapes and phases of the African American freedom struggle. They did so for purposes political and public, private and domestic, artistic and journalistic, for reportage and for agitprop. Looked at individually and closely, these photographs confound our notions about various moments and manifestations of African American quests for justice and the documentary impulse generally. Taken together, they complicate our ideas and memories, many received visually, of these movements themselves. A closer examination of perhaps the most iconic image of the Black Panther Party reveals how we can begin to interrogate the uses and abuses of Panther memory.

In early May 1967, Huey Newton, cofounder and minister of defense of the six-month-old Black Panther Party (BPP), assembled with Bobby Seale, the party's cofounder and chairman; Eldridge Cleaver, the recently named minister of information; Kathleen Cleaver, former Student Nonviolent Coordinating Committee (SNCC) member and soon-to-be BPP communications secretary; and a photographer named Brent Jones. This group met in the San Francisco apartment of white attorney Beverly Axelrod.[11] The primary purpose for this gathering was to make a photograph of Newton that could then be transformed into a poster to raise funds for and awareness about the nascent BPP. Through community police patrols as well as other "survival programs," the party gained a regional reputation as defenders of black communities. Only a few days before the meeting at Axelrod's home, the Panthers achieved national attention when on May 2, 1967, they took a cadre of twenty-four men and six women and the organization's Ten Point Platform to Sacramento, California's capital. Now as their reputation grew, Eldridge Cleaver urged the Panthers to begin fashioning and projecting an image entirely of their own making.

Keenly aware of the power of image and the power of personality through his own experiences as a journalist, Cleaver posed Newton in a wicker fan chair on top of a zebra rug in Axelrod's living room. Newton wore the Panther uniform of black beret (modeled after those worn by

Here Huey Newton sits in front of the famous 1967 Black Panthers poster of him in the fan chair. (© Ted Streshinsky/Corbis)

French Nazi resisters Newton and Seale had once seen in a movie), black leather jacket, crisp powder blue shirt, and pressed black slacks. Cleaver gathered a number of objects to serve as props. He stood a rifle in Newton's right hand and placed one of Axelrod's African spears in his left. He leaned two of Axelrod's African shields against the walls, one on either side of Newton. Bobby Seale later wrote of the significance of the spear and shields, "Huey would say many times that long, long time ago, there was a man who invented a spear, and he frightened a whole lot of people. But, Huey said, the people invented a shield against the spear. . . . So this is what Huey P. Newton symbolized with the Black Panther Party— he represented a shield for black people against all the imperialism, the decadence, the aggression, and the racism in this country."[12] Jones took several shots of a still and stern Newton, his face partially obscured in shadow.

Through the visual dramaturgy of this image, Newton seemed to capture and clarify many of the ambiguities and competing strains of "Black Power" that had adhered around the discourse. The African artifacts symbolized cultural nationalism, a philosophy defined by a glorified African past and the unifying force of a monolithic black culture. The rifle and the shells collected at Newton's feet signified revolutionary nationalism, an ideology culled from the influential writings of Frantz Fanon, an identity that emerges from armed active struggle against a group's oppressor. Newton himself, minister of defense of the self-proclaimed vanguard organization of the black movement in the United States, personified black nationalism, a conviction that only black people can best lead black communities. The photograph also revealed more than intended. A sort of black capitalism, a breed of Black Power vociferously eschewed by the Panthers, can be inferred from the polished attire and expensive setting.

Like the shields surrounding him, Newton marked a necessary invention of "the people," the physical manifestation of their anger and frustration into a structured and creative force mobilized to counter the oppression of the state. This photograph came to exemplify black American revolution and came to embody the black American revolutionary. Transformed into a poster, it emerged as wildly popular with rank and file Panther membership, as well as radicals of other groups. This photograph is perhaps the most well-known and most often reproduced image of Huey Newton and, by extension, of the Black Panther Party to date.

The production and dissemination of this image illuminates several contradictions about the party and the various ways in which it chose to represent itself and be represented by those around it. First, by focusing the camera on Huey Newton alone, Cleaver and those who circulated the poster placed an emphasis on the leadership of the party rather than the rank and file membership or the communities the Panthers served. This focus would later prove crucial in the years 1968 to 1970 when the party's work centered on freeing Newton from jail and the real threat of the gas chamber for the murder of white Oakland police officer John Frey in October 1968. Newton, in this photograph with spear and rifle and uniform, projects and defines a militarized, hypermasculine leadership seemingly willing to give up his life for the revolution and for the people he served. Yet here the leader is seated, enthroned like a monarch, with his back to an undecorated wall. Rather than appearing in active defense of the people, Newton looks as though he is waiting for the people to come to him. Moreover, with his face partially shrouded in shadow, he figures not as open and approachable but as somewhat mysterious and inaccessible. The credence surrendered to leadership in this photograph reveals a tension between the power of the vanguard, chosen to both serve and lead the people, and the power of the people themselves.

In many ways, the poster, as part of a concerted effort to raise awareness and support for the "Free Huey" campaign, did bring the people to Huey, or as close to his words and image as they could come to the imprisoned leader. The party's membership grew from a couple hundred to the thousands during the period of Newton's incarceration, due in large part to the tireless organizing efforts of the party for Huey's release. Officially, the party viewed cultural forms and the media as little more than tools that needed to be harnessed if the Panthers, as individuals and as an organization, were to survive. When Kathleen Cleaver began working with the party officially in November 1967, she found herself thrust into the maelstrom created by Newton's incarceration. From her experience working with SNCC, Cleaver "created the position of Communications Secretary based on what I had seen Julian Bond [SNCC Communications Secretary] do. . . . I sent out press releases, I got photographers and journalists to publish stories about us. . . . I designed posters."[13] The photographs and posters, though popular and significant in mobilizing interest in the party, were understood in strictly quotidian terms—generating awareness and fundraising—as opposed to the higher purpose of revolution and liberation.

The image projected around the country and around the world was one Newton himself did not like. According to Kathleen Cleaver, Newton often complained that the photograph misrepresented both the party and him.[14] Others, like Stew Albert, a white radical and early friend of both Eldridge Cleaver and the party, felt similarly ambivalent about the image. Albert recalls, "Cleaver showed up at my pad and wanted to put a large personality poster of Huey seated in a wicker chair . . . up on my wall. Because Eldridge was so happy with his new friends, I agreed." Albert's alacrity, however, quickly changed to diffidence: "But when he gave me a bunch of posters for my 'associates,' I felt unspoken reservations about their corniness. Besides, personality posters were relatively new. Even our new San Francisco rock stars hadn't as yet made use of them. They seemed narcissistic and quasi-cultic, not really ideal food for egalitarian revolutionaries." Despite Newton's protests, Cleaver, along with countless others who possessed and displayed the poster, remained enthusiastic about it. According to Albert, "the Newton trial made the spear poster chic."[15]

The spear poster demonstrates the power of the image to supersede even a leader's wishes. It further elucidates the struggle between Newton and Cleaver over meaning and direction of the Black Panther Party. Additionally, if we consider how "chic" the poster would become with Newton's incarceration, we can begin to understand the struggle that took place on the broader terrain of visual representation. The poster functions as a snapshot of a clash between the range of images that various constituencies wanted to see or hoped to project.

These various constituencies—Newton, Cleaver, branches around the country, rank-and-file membership, the media, the state, everyday people who supported or opposed the Panthers or wrestled with something in between—each infused the image of Newton with their own political meaning. This is evidenced by the appearance of the photograph in many forms and locations. The poster could be found in the front windows of Panther offices from Oakland to Harlem to Algiers. The party's newspaper, the *Black Panther*, reproduced the photograph a number of times on the cover and within the publication. Protesters attached the poster to sticks and raised it above their heads at "Free Huey" demonstrations. College students of all races and ethnicities hung it on their dorm room walls. The image traveled internationally as well: the Organization of Solidarity of the Peoples of Africa, Asia, and Latin America (OSPAAL), for example, incorporated the photograph into posters and postcards of their own.[16] Likewise, the dominant press replicated the image. And the FBI remarked on the photograph and others in reports on the Panthers.[17] Many observers and participants viewed the Panthers' style, rhetoric, and image as circulated through photography as the outward manifestation and best representation of the party's political platform.

Perhaps one of the most striking and most compelling contexts in which the image signified lies is its reproduction in a 1969–70 photograph taken of the poster in the window of the Oakland BPP office.[18] Made by Stephen Shames, a young white man from Berkeley, California, and a close ally of the Panthers, the photograph shows the poster of Newton sitting in a cracked window shot full with bullet holes. Behind the fractured but not quite broken glass, the minister of defense sits full frame in the wicker chair. As the front page of the February 21, 1970, special issue of *Black Panther* on "Evidence and Intimidation of Fascist Crimes by U.S.A." attests, the tattered poster represents the extensive written and visual list of murdered and incarcerated Panthers, as well as attacked and destroyed BPP offices. Despite the FBI-police assault on the party, Newton and the party he leads remain stoic and resolute. The reproduction of this photograph of a photograph reveals that the Panthers understood not only themselves as under attack but also their icons and their image. The realm of the visual—of image, of performance, of culture—here emerges as a battleground as significant as the field of politics.

Photography provided a space of imagination, documentation, and creativity, one in which "evidence" could be refigured and recontextualized to tell an alternative tale of repression and terrorism.[19] Here we witness the concept of an "alternative practice of photography," a practice that begins to defy and undermine the cultural logic of late capitalism, even as it makes use of its protocols.[20] Panther posters often embodied such creative performances, employing postmodern aesthetics such as cut and paste and montage. The utilization of segments of the image of Huey Newton and Bobby Seale in front of the Oakland office reassembled as part of cheaply made and easily reproduced posters for the Chicago or New York offices, for example, enabled different and often divergent chapters of the party to lay claim to Panther leadership, to extend the protection of ghetto streets throughout the country, while imagining and performing the version of the Panthers they wanted. Such collage through the use of photographs of lesser-known Panthers, combined with quotes from Ho Chi Minh, also rendered visual international influences and gave voice to important figures beyond Newton and Seale.[21] Posters made use of striking and easily recalled images in order to compile, assemble, arrange, and ultimately create the organization they hoped to bring together and bring into being.

Perhaps no poster makes this more evident than one created for the Revolutionary People's Constitutional Convention. Heeding the call of the Panthers, between eight and fifteen thousand delegates from domestic and international liberation organizations came to Philadelphia to radically rewrite the U.S. Constitution over the weekend of September 5, 1970.[22] The RPCC documents, accepted by the five to six thousand people present at the final plenary session, called for an international bill of rights, international reparations, the abolishment of capitalism, the renunciation of U.S. nationhood, the destruction of nuclear weapons and the U.S. Army, support for gay and women's liberation, and an end to genocide. While broad and lofty in scope, the goals of the RPCC and the convention itself "shed light on . . . the aspirations of the 1960s [New Left] movement."[23]

A poster made for a second RPCC gathering reveals the breadth of domestic and international events and ideologies the convention was responding to and hoping to change or build on. A drawing made by Minister of Culture Emory Douglas of a revolutionary wearing a peasant hat and fatigues raising a Kalashnikov (the AK-47 assault rifle) in one hand and a grenade in the other—the weapons of choice for the Vietcong and guerrilla warriors worldwide—stands in the foreground. Behind him are cut-and-paste photographs of slain Panther Fred Hampton, the bullet-riddled poster of Newton in the fan chair, Panther rallies, various acts of police brutality, including the iconic image of the National Guard murders of students at Kent State earlier that year, riots, forlorn and weeping children from around the world, and all sorts of faces consumed with anger and frustration. These photographs are not merely assembled. Rather, all the components interact, witness, and even respond to each other's struggles. A young black child mourns over the body of the Kent State student. In the top right corner, a suited white man applauds the violence and misery, while to his left, a black man trains a handgun on this representative of imperialism and fascism. It is the communication between these juxtaposed figures that lends the poster its power, that suggests a broader context for the individual components. The poster visualizes the interconnectedness of each of these struggles and presents global revolution as the best and final solution. Its assemblage constructs the crucial living context for these images, which critic John Berger advocates presents them within "a radial system . . . so that [each] photograph . . . may be seen in terms which are simultaneously personal, political, economic, dramatic, everyday and historic."[24] The RPCC poster epitomizes the production of a radical form of photography that recorded and expanded the insurgent visibilities of the BPP while preserving the urgency and efficacy of this visibility.

But as Walter Benjamin reminds us, "the camera . . . need not respect the performance as an integral whole."[25] While the technology of photography presented new opportunities for visual intervention and self-representation, it also possessed the potential to delimit the power and efficacy of radical performances. The many indexical registers of the photograph, as document of truth, as construction of desire, as that which brings the viewer intimately close and yet keeps her permanently at arm's length, intermingle to create an image both fascinating and repulsive, both specific to a particular moment and historically transcendent. In a climate in which "the political" had become increasingly fashionable and readily transformed into commodity, in the era of "the society of the spectacle," we can also see how photography in some senses conquered the Panthers' insurgent visibility into a flattened two-dimensional reified and easily consumed package, distant from the revolution the Panthers were waging in the streets.[26]

Photographic Memory

Looked at in this way, how then do we understand the forms of memory of Black Power and the Black Panther Party engendered by these very complex images? How have these images engaged and/or mobilized memory in our contemporary moment? By memory, I refer to the process by which people recall, lay claim to, and understand the past. Memory is an active element in the composition of social and political communities. For social movements especially, memory is never an end in itself but rather a tool to make sense of history, declare lineages, clarify allegiances, and mobilize constituents. Memory implies the negotiation, the *use* of history for the present. Memory is about process: when that process ends, memory becomes either history—fact—or nostalgia—the failure to think historically.[27]

The deployment of social movement photography at the turn of the twenty-first century has engaged the process of memory in at least two distinct yet similar ways. First, social movement photography has been maneuvered to reanimate certain forms of political struggle through resuscitation of the icons that have come to signal such struggles. Second, social movement photography has encouraged the curtailment of political struggle and the reification of past social movements. Put another way, social movement photography can readily aid and abet a "Then as Now" narrative, a narrative that presupposes the similarities between past and present, or a "Past is Past" narrative, one that assumes history is over and gone.

In the first scenario, the reawakening of political engagement is achieved through acknowledgment and activation of what we might call the *spatiality* of the photograph, literally what inhabits the picture's frame. This spatiality is similar to Roland Barthes's definition of the *studium*, "the general enthusiastic commitment" on the part of the viewer for what the photographer has framed.[28] Here we pay attention to the fact of the image's subjects, the weight of their photographic presence across time, their intractability. Employed as document, the photograph can further be called on to illustrate the persistence and *unchanging* nature of black oppression: African Americans suffered then, at the hands of white Americans, as they do now. While photographs viewed through their spatiality may provide a framework for making sense of one's own moment and shaping future actions, one significant danger is a loss of historical specificity. Another danger lies in the limitations imposed on the strategies political protest might take. By considering the spatiality of the photograph, its subject, its *studium* only, viewers serve to resituate African American freedom struggles within or on the skin alone. Viewers are to take the political solutions represented within the space of the photograph, quite literally, at face value: black people alone can mount movements for social justice, movements whose strategies replicate those that proved successful in a previous social formation. Strategies for struggle often remain imprisoned within the past of the image itself.

For example, members of the New Black Panther Party (NBPP), formed in Texas in 1996, don black berets and carry arms in an attempt to "revive the radicalism" and potency of the earlier Black Panther Party.[29] However, the Anti-Defamation League and even the original Black Panther Party have accused the New Panthers of spouting racist and anti-Semitic rhetoric. Indeed the New Panthers have been quoted as inciting members to "send [crackers] to the cemetery."[30] The original Panthers, represented by the Black Panther Party, Inc., went so far as to sue the new organization in order to prevent use of the Panther name and logo, stating that they "do not wish to be confused with . . . a group preaching racial division and the inappropriate use of arms to promote social change."[31] The New Panthers encouraged African Americans to exhume old bodies and old politics without regard to the ways in which the meanings of black bodies and the American political landscape have changed over time, even as the practitioners of those former strategies call for new methods.

Likewise, a focus on a photograph's *temporality*, its pastness, its signification as artifact, can engender the limitation of political activity. This is a second mode through which photographic memory operates. Here, curators, politicians, popular culture makers, to name only a few groups, employ social movement photography to inform us that the black people who populate such images as victims, or as revolutionaries as in the case of Panther imagery, no longer exist. Likewise, their white oppressors are gone as well. Also vanished is the America that enabled such crimes or created the conditions for radical dissent. In these ways, social movement photography may provide solace and a pretext for inaction.

Narratives of Black Power: Foxy Brown

There exists a multiplicity of visions and voices today that compete for the hegemonic and popular memory of the civil rights movement of the 1960s. By emphasizing the temporality, the pastness, of these particular photographs—images of Martin Luther King delivering his "I Have a Dream" speech on the steps of the Lincoln Memorial, or the images of police dogs and fire hoses from Birmingham 1963, for example—all can be cast on the "right" side of the struggle, and a simple ending can be found for a history whose end is still being written.

The redeployment of Black Panther images mobilizes photographic spatiality, a picture's subject, and photographic temporality, a picture's pastness, in decidedly unique ways. This is due in large part to the very different kinds of narratives constructed about the Panthers and the Black Power movement as juxtaposed with those ideological framings of the civil rights movement of the early 1960s or even antilynching struggles of an earlier period. Popular narratives of the civil rights movement offer us a Manichaean tale in which the good guys, long-suffering pure-of-heart African Americans and their white supporters—including in some accounts the Kennedy administration and the FBI—vanquished the evil forces of fear, ignorance, and intransigence embodied by Klansmen, Bull Connor, and lone white gunmen.[32] It is an all-American story in which nonviolence and love conquer violence and hate, resulting in tangible so-called race-blind legislation. And now all of us, black and white, Jew and Gentile, and not least of all American democracy, emerge as victor. We have all overcome.

It is a neat and straightforward story, effortlessly recounted to schoolchildren and other audiences who can experience sadness, indignation, and ultimately pride in how far we have come. Clearly the story of the civil rights movement and its legacies are far more complicated. Yet it is the simplified narrative that has been visually perpetuated through film, through television, and of course through black-and-white photography. We are presented with the challenge of seeing beyond such visual narratives, of recognizing how the collective African American freedom struggle has continued to grow and redefine its goals when pictures "show" us how much individual African Americans have achieved, socially, economically, and politically.

Conversely, the story of the Black Panther Party is far more difficult to convey within a similar good versus evil paradigm. How do we find dignity and the best in the human spirit in stories of the federal government actively and aggressively "disrupting, discrediting and destroying" organizations that fed free breakfast to poor children?[33] Where does the transformation of the American soul take place in the premeditated murder and false incarceration of dozens of movement participants at the hands of local police acting under FBI directives? How do we construct a safe narrative to pass on to future generations out of communities of color choosing to fight systemic violence with guns and volatile rhetoric rather than a turned cheek and righteous indignation? Is it possible to locate victory for American democracy through the work of a movement that affected no changes in the law (unless we count the attention the Panthers brought to the FBI's abuses of their counterintelligence program, COINTELPRO) and cultivated alliances with armed anti-imperialist struggles throughout the globe? We keep these complexities sequestered from constructions of the struggles of the early 1960s, because such contamination would undermine the purity of our civil rights movement narratives.[34] Ultimately, there is no facile Black Panther narrative, because good and evil are compromised, not least of all because the Panthers themselves offered up such a stunning and alluring visual contradiction.

From this narrative that defies tidy endings and simple categorizations also emerges the possibility and potential of an unfinished revolution, the traces of which are handed down to us through a visual and photographic repertoire of style and gesture. This is what the blaxploitation film cycle of 1969–75 offered viewers on the cheap: a flashy and chic good versus evil narrative, but one that nevertheless robbed Black Power ideology of its political force.[35] "Good," whether sex workers–turned–rebels on the run, downtown detectives, beleaguered drug dealers, avenging soul sisters, or champions of the undead, wore big Afros and a changing array of the hippest fashions and were armed to the teeth in "defense" of the black community.[36] Above all, good was black and black was beautiful, bold, and badass. Conversely, "evil" was personified by white pimps, pushers, and pigs. In the world of mainstream Hollywood film, blaxploitation offered its target African American audience a chance to see black actors, often under black direction, conquer with style and soul, kung fu and a cool pose, the forces that oppressed the black community. Moreover, the films presented a vision of blackness more attuned to the political exigencies and cultural developments of the rebellious late sixties and early seventies than the integrationist social problem films of only a few years earlier, and certainly than Hollywood studio films before that.

Indeed, Richard Roundtree's tough talking and sexually aggressive John Shaft proved far more compelling than Sidney Poitier's oppressively perfect Dr. John Wade Prentice in Stanley Kramer's *Guess Who's Coming to Dinner* (1967), and Pam Grier's Foxy Brown served only her spirit of vengeance and her own sexual desires as opposed to Hattie McDaniel's Mammy, servile to the old plantation South.[37]

Blaxploitation simultaneously championed and cartooned Black Power; it made use of the language and impulse of Black Power while containing its force. As political scientist Cedric J. Robinson contends, blaxploitation's cinematic "translation . . . of mass black rebellion . . . transmuted liberation into vengeance, the pursuit of social justice which embraced race, class, and gender into Black racism, and the politics of armed struggle into systematic assassination."[38] Furthermore, this translation reduced black feminist activist-intellectuals like Angela Davis and Kathleen Cleaver to the hypersexual, constantly dressed and undressed, body of Pam Grier in particular.

Nowhere is this truer than in the 1974 film *Foxy Brown*, written and directed by Jack Hill. Pam Grier stars as Foxy Brown, a black woman whose federal agent boyfriend (Terry Carter) is ratted out to a drug and prostitution syndicate by Foxy's own ne'er-do-well, drug-dealing, numbers-running brother, Link, played by blaxploitation institution Antonio Fargas. When Foxy implores Link to straighten his life out, Link responds with the limitations placed on him as a black man: "Foxy, look, I'm a black man. And I don't know how to sing and I don't know how to dance. And I don't know how to preach to no congregation. I'm too small to be a football hero. And I'm too ugly to be elected mayor." Link wants Foxy to understand his failures as the product of his pursuit of a bastardized American Dream: "When I watch TV and I see all them fine people in all them fine homes they live in and all those fine cars they drive and I get all full of ambition. Now you tell me what I'm supposed to do with all this ambition I got?" But when Link passes on the whereabouts of Foxy's boyfriend, Mike, to the syndicate in exchange for his own life, Link's failure is not external limits placed on him, but his willingness to sell out his own people to "the Man." The Man is here represented by an underworld organization rather than the U.S. government. In *Foxy Brown*, as in *Cleopatra Jones* (Jack Starrett, 1973), *Superfly* (Gordon Parks, 1971), *The Mack* (Michael Campus, 1973), and others, the fight for black communities is waged against white crime syndicates rather than against the systemic racism and economic exploitation of the state. The state, and its ideological apparatuses that create unattainable "ambition" for people of color, is effectively erased from the blaxploitation filmic world.

After her man dies in her arms unable to complete his work securing a federal indictment, Foxy determines to take down the syndicate herself—not through community organizing or collective action but by way of good old-fashioned vigilante justice, "as American as apple pie." Robinson reminds us that "as the lone avenger . . . [Foxy Brown and other such characters] were estranged from community or political organizations."[39] Even so-called political organizations, signified by costume (Afros, sunglasses, and dashikis) and setting (hidden rooms full of weapons and posters of real-life Panthers), are themselves little more than vigilante avenger posses in the blaxploitation ghetto world. Following the lead of the local "neighborhood committee," a Black Panther–like group of black men whom we first encounter beating a black drug dealer down in the street and promising to run him out of town, Foxy concludes, "the only way to handle those smart-ass hoods is with a bullet to the gut."

Foxy's brand of vigilantism, we quickly find out, will bestow much more than just a bullet. Interrogating her brother with the aid of a small caliber bullet to the ear, Foxy learns that the syndicate is run by the controlling "Miss" Katherine Wall (Kathryn Loder) and her "private property" Steve Elias (Peter Brown). Elias handles the drug operation while Miss Katherine, through her modeling-agency front, provides protection with "the finest stable of high class call girls," exchanging sex for political favors. Foxy joins "the stable" and manages to humiliate a lascivious middle-aged white judge, help a black prostitute named Claudia (Juanita Brown) escape home to her husband and son, and beat down a barroom of white lesbians before finally being caught by Miss Katherine and Elias. These two then send Foxy to "the Ranch," a rundown shack where she is injected with heroin and repeatedly raped, beaten, and even cattle roped by a couple of "good ol' boys." Foxy's brutalized body—her bruised face, bared breasts, and needle-tracked arms—serves to individualize the systemic and collective dehumanization of African Americans at the hands of whites. So when Foxy ultimately and brutally vanquishes her adversaries—setting fire to the good ol' boys, overseeing the castration of Steve Elias, and delivering his genitals to Miss Katherine in a pickle jar— audiences are meant to cheer wildly Foxy's display of strength.

Foxy's victories are assured not simply through the use of firepower, but significantly by way of sexual wiles accentuated by changes of fashion. For example, when she goes undercover as a prostitute, Foxy wears low-cut evening gowns and long straight-pressed wigs. In the final sequences, her body is pressed into a tight black leather pants suit, and large gold hoop earrings hang from beneath her perfectly picked-out Afro. She is a precise vision of the stylized black revolutionary. This combination of fashion and sexuality signals the cooptation of the second-wave feminist movement in which a woman's power is embedded within (and bedded down by) her sexuality and her own willingness to utilize and manipulate her body and masculinist expectations for personal gain. It is this everyday or vernacular feminism that we witness at the beginning of the twenty-first century, especially in the music and visual culture of hip hop and R & B, including Britney Spears, Beyoncé, and namesake rapper Foxy Brown. Further, this vernacular feminism only serves to underscore a "fierce phallocentrism" in which a (black) man's power is dependent on simply having a penis, "where what the male does with his penis becomes a greater and certainly a more accessible way to assert masculine status."[40] Cultural critic bell hooks suggests that such phallocentrism emerged fully with the Black Power movement. Foxy's plot to have "neighborhood com-mittee" leader Oscar and his band of black male "revolutionaries" castrate the white male villain as Foxy looks on, later referring to Elias and his henchmen as "faggots" in her final confrontation with Miss Katherine, perpetuates on film the limited notion of Black Power as a (re)claiming by black men of power and control from white men. Black women, even at the center of the story, still help support such a narrative of Black Power.

Robinson reminds us how blaxploitation and its companion genre, "the Bad Black Woman narrative," "borrowed . . . directly from reality by snatching Angela Davis from the pages of newspapers, news maga-zines and law enforcement dockets," utilizing Davis's true-life struggle to extend the cycle of and hype around reel-time fantasy.[41] As Foxy talks with Oscar and waits to make her plea to the "neighborhood committee" to assist in her final effort to bring the syndicate down, a poster of Kathleen Cleaver sits just behind Foxy, looking over her like a guardian revolutionary. When Oscar moves to comfort her over the murder of Link at the hands of Elias's henchmen, he stands to reveal a poster of George Jackson. And when the door opens to let Foxy and Oscar inside the conference room, a poster of Angela Davis is fixed to a far back wall laden with a sizable cache of weapons. Foxy stands to make her case and for a split second is framed between Davis in the background and Cleaver in the foreground. The posters serve as mise-en-scène, providing atmosphere for the tight windowless meeting room in which these revolutionaries have gathered. But further, the posters of Davis and Cleaver are the only other women's faces—a poster of a woman's naked backside, looking uncannily like Foxy herself in earlier scenes, reads "Black Is Beautiful" and is placed on the closed door—besides Foxy's, present in the room. The presence of the two women, "two of the most familiar and alternative gender significations of revolutionary America," reinforces Foxy Brown's own signification as black woman revolutionary. In doing so, the images also serve to complete a seamless transition from black liberation as a struggle for justice, the aim of the activists frozen on the walls of the set, to black liberation as a mission for revenge. Foxy convinces the organization that such collusion is beneficial when she closes her case with, "You just take care of the justice, and I'll handle the revenge myself."

By watching "the gun-toting impersonation[s]" fight an individuated, depersonalized, ultimately degraded (and borderline pornographic) revolution onscreen, blaxploitation audiences, both in the genre's originary moment and in subsequent viewings, have been drawn "further away from the reality of the liberation movement."[42] Audiences may have been drawn further away but we are left with traces and reminders of the aura of the liberation movement. Indeed, we need to consider Black Panther and Black Power social movement photography as being refracted through blaxploitation film and emerging in a diffused form in "docufashion." The leap then from social movement photography to docufashion may not be so far after all, may not even be a leap. Rather, this move may be a different articulation of competing though not mutually exclusive elements—spectacle and revolution, consumer desire and political yearning—always within each other's presence yet differently articulated at various moments.

Dissecting Docufashion

The 1990s witnessed a resurgence in blaxploitaion and its aesthetics: bell-bottoms and big Afros, the music of Curtis Mayfield and Isaac Hayes, pimp culture and other cultures of black excess each experienced new life in film (thanks especially to Quentin Tarantino), music, and fashion. *Vibe*, chronicler of urban vogue, functioned as a producer, distributor, recorder, and perpetuator of this trend. From this nexus of black fact, fiction, and fashion, docufashion emerged. Over the past few years, docufashion has become a staple of *Vibe*'s fashion department, restaging well-known photographs from the past with up-and-coming or arrived young celebrities in the present to sell tomorrow's clothes. Spilling over into lead interview photographs as well as album covers and advertisements in the magazine's pages, Black Power imagery has emerged as a standard visual trope in *Vibe* magazine. We must ask: Why these images now? What do the icons signify and what feelings, political or otherwise, do they engender or mobilize in their viewers?

The June 2003 cover interview with hip hop artist Nas featured as its lead image a photograph of the rapper posed as Huey Newton in the fan chair. Complete with shields, spear, rifle, and zebra rug, the image nevertheless sampled on but distinguished itself from the original by eliminating the rifle shells from the base of the picture. An effort perhaps to counter the excessive violence that has marked and marred hip hop, the absence of the shells points to the artifice of the image and the distance between Nas, his audience, and the realities of armed revolutionary struggle. Further, Nas wears the urban "uniform" of crisp baggy pants and Timberland boots. Instead of the wide-lapelled black leather jacket, Nas sports a green militarized adaptation with epaulets and polished buttons. The open jacket reveals dog tags hanging from his neck. The transformation from black revolutionary uniform to U.S. military uniform is further emphasized in the next photograph, in which Nas wears head to toe green fatigues, accented by a huge belt that reads "WAR is not the answer." Speaking to the militarization of American culture, army camouflage collides with black leather jackets, and what was once the enemy becomes unified, overcome in the cultural landscape of contemporary hip hop. Nas's eyes are shrouded not by the shadow of the image but by a large pair of sunglasses. Further, a sizeable pinky ring, like those worn by movie gangsters, reminds us that the Black Panthers are not the only cultural influence on contemporary hip hop.

The centerpiece article, entitled "Of Love and War," within an issue dedicated to "peace and love," that hackneyed phrase from the sixties, describes Nas as a "revolutionary rapper" and details his "battle to save hip hop's everlasting soul."[43] Calling up the icon of Huey Newton as enthroned monarch and leader of "the people," photographer Robert Maxwell positions Nas as hip hop's vanguard doing the work of "saving hip hop" and its listeners from themselves.

In the November 2002 fashion spread entitled "Radical Chic," hip hop artists stic.man and M-1 of dead prez dress up in Armani and Dolce and Gabbana as Malcolm X and Fred Hampton respectively, Charli Baltimore dresses up in J.Lo as Kathleen Cleaver, and Joi dresses up in DKNY and FUBU as Angela Davis to perform revolution. Robert Maxwell posed Nas as Newton as a form of comparison, a juxtaposition of star personae, but "Radical Chic" photographer Daniel Hastings and stylist Michael Nash explicitly engaged in a commemorative project. " 'It wasn't just a fashion shoot, it was representing history,' says photographer Daniel Hastings, 33, of paying homage to civil rights icons for this month's VFashion.' "[44]

It would be entirely too easy to dismiss these images out of hand for their almost complete commodification of 1960s radicalism. We might consider that through a postsoul aesthetic, these images enlist social movement photography in such a way that takes both the spatiality and the temporality of the earlier photographs into account.[45] Social movement photography (by way of fashion photography) here becomes aware and self-conscious of the tension between its situatedness and its transcendence.

For example, how do we read the fact that these *Vibe* images are each restagings (pastiche? blank parody?) of iconic photographs rather than reproductions in the traditional sense? Is it possible to infer a kind of performative dialogic between the artists-cum-models and those they attempt to stand in for or represent? Through their participation in this "homage," dead prez, Joi, and Charli Baltimore are inscribed or hailed as revolutionary artists for performing a radical past. Simultaneously, the models refract the Black Power activists through a legible lens for contemporary audiences who know of dead prez as one of the few aboveground voices of "conscious" or political rap along with Mos Def, Talib Kweli, and the Coup, artists concerned with the rise of the prison industrial complex, economic exploitation, and persistent inequality. *Vibe* readers might be familiar with Joi through her song "Freedom," the theme of Mario Van Peebles's 1995 fictional film *Panther*, and as the artist whose unique blend of R & B, hard rock, and the occasional Catholic dirge has marginalized her in the music industry. Audiences may recognize Charli Baltimore as the Murder Inc. rapper discovered by the Notorious BIG who played Smooth Blak, a member of the parodic rap group the Mau Maus, in *Bamboozled* (2000), Spike Lee's unsparing satire of the commodification of black culture.

Here the lines between popular culture and political consciousness-raising are blurred yet again in the realm of hip hop. This is evident in the proliferation of phrases like "hip hop nation" or "hip hop revolution." Indeed, as former *Vibe* editor-in-chief Emil Wilbekin tells us, "Nas helps me feel empowered. . . . [Singer] Mary J. Blige's *My Life* inspires me to keep it moving. [Rapper] 50 Cent makes me feel radical and unstoppable."[46] Wilbekin confesses that "music is a temporary sedative. . . . And I keep wondering, Where's the political leadership among young people today?" Wilbekin looks back longingly to the political leaders and organizations of the 1960s and '70s that "offered direction, motivation, and a voice for troubled souls," the Panthers among them. For this moment, for the hip hop "revolution" his magazine publicizes, Wilbekin can only come up with a handful of rappers including dead prez. Wilbekin here expresses a desire that the revolutionary impact of hip hop on U.S. and even global economic, social, and cultural landscapes might translate into revolution in the formal political arena.

Wilbekin's doleful expression of political desire speaks to a pervasive disappointment and even apathy on the part of the postsoul generation regarding the cooptation and failures of the civil rights movement, including the persistent expansion of the prison system with black and brown bodies, the repeal of affirmative action policies, and continued economic and educational disparities based on race. Wilbekin also speaks to a yearning to remember, recuperate, and revitalize the radical energy of Black Power that offered a constructive response to collective black anger and riots in the streets. However, *Vibe* magazine and especially the format of fashion photography that foregrounds contradiction and ambiguity and revels in its own signifying meaninglessness in order to sell proves to be a difficult space for the transmission of past histories and future visions of political change. Indeed, even if "social consciousness goes deeper than fashion," as yet another *Vibe* fashion spread, entitled "Proactivist," informs us, it reaches only to the level of "lifestyle."[47]

We might turn once more to the admonition of Angela Davis, for whom 1970 only marked the beginning of her activist intellectual career: "Where cultural representations do not reach out beyond themselves, there is the danger that they will function as surrogates for activism, that they will constitute both the beginning and end of political practice."[48] If memory is indeed about constructing living contexts, about making use of the past for present and future struggles, we might add to Davis's caution that when cultural representations of the past do not reach out beyond themselves, when they function as surrogates for activism, they do not and cannot function as memory. They are merely nostalgia, the reification of the past for consumption and incorporation into one's "lifestyle." It remains to be seen if *Vibe* can reach beyond itself (and its parent company) and provide a true living context for the memory of Black Power.

Notes

1. Angela Y. Davis, "Afro Images: Politics, Fashion, and Nostalgia," in *Picturing Us: African American Identity in Photography*, ed. Deborah Willis (New York: New Press, 1994), 174.

2. James Truman, introduction to *Cyclops*, by Albert Watson (Boston, Mass.: Little, Brown, 1994), n.p., quoted in Maurice O. Wallace, *Constructing the Black*

Masculine: Identity and Ideality in African American Men's Literature and Culture, 1775–1995 (Durham, N.C.: Duke University Press, 2002), 22.

3. Karl-Peter Gottschalk, "Albert Watson: One Eye on the Prize," http://www .easyweb.easynet.co.uk/karlpeter/zeugma/inters/watson.html (accessed August 17, 2004).

4. Wallace, *Constructing the Black Masculine*, 22, 21. I am indebted to Wallace's profound reading of Watson's images.

5. By *icon*, I refer to an image or picture that stands in for or symbolizes something else. For more on the notion of the icon, see Vicki Goldberg, *The Power of Photography: How Photographs Changed Our Lives* (New York: Abbeville, 1991).

6. *Vibe*, March 1994, 16.

7. *Vibe* describes itself as follows: "Through the prism of Urban Music, VIBE chronicles the celebrities, sounds, fashion, lifestyle, new media, and business born from this art form. With an authoritative voice, VIBE creates trends as much as it records them. VIBE covers music, educates its readers, and gives back to the community. VIBE serves as a portal to a growing, young, trend-setting, multicultural audience. By being excellent journalists and innovative marketers, we are champions of urban music and culture." According to a Spring 2003 Marketing Research International report, "VIBE reaches more people of color age 18–24 than any other magazine," and 61 percent of all African American teens read the magazine. http://www.vibe.com (accessed August 16, 2004).

8. Davis, "Afro Images," 177.

9. Angela Y. Davis, "Black Nationalism: The Sixties and the Nineties," in *Black Popular Culture*, ed. Gina Dent (Seattle, Wash.: Bay Press, 1992), 324.

10. I discuss this in further detail in "The Consumption of Lynching Images," in *Only Skin Deep: Changing Visions of the American Self*, ed. Coco Fusco and Brian Wallis (New York: Harry N. Abrams, 2003).

11. Roz Payne, telephone interview with the author, April 2, 2002. For other accounts of this photo shoot, see Beverly Axelrod, video interview with Roz Payne, in Payne's archives, and Bobby Seale, *Seize the Time: The Story of the Black Panther Party and Huey P. Newton* (New York: Vintage Books, 1970). It is important to note that neither Payne nor Seale recall whether Jones was black or white.

12. Seale, *Seize the Time*, 182.

13. Kathleen Cleaver, "Women, Power, and Revolution," in *Liberation, Imagination and the Black Panther Party: A New Look at the Panthers and Their Legacy*, ed. Kathleen Cleaver and George Katsiaficas (New York: Routledge, 2001), 124–25.

14. Kathleen Neal Cleaver, conversation with the author, New Haven, Connecticut, October 7, 1998. See also Mario Van Peebles, Ula Y. Taylor, and J. Tarika

Lewis, *Panther: A Pictorial History of the Black Panthers and the Story behind the Film* (New York: New Market Press, 1995), 158.

15. Stew Albert, "White Radicals, Black Panthers and a Sense of Fulfillment," in *Liberation, Imagination and the Black Panther Party*, 189.

16. See Erika Doss, "'Revolutionary Art Is a Tool for Liberation': Emory Douglas and Protest Aesthetics at the *Black Panther*" in *Liberation, Imagination and the Black Panther Party*.

17. U.S. House of Representatives Staff Study by the Committee on Internal Security, *The Black Panther Party: Its Origin and Development as Reflected in Its Official Weekly Newspaper*, the Black Panther Black Community News Service, Ninety-first Congress, Second Session, October 6, 1970, Labadie Collection at the University of Michigan, Ann Arbor.

18. The *Black Panther*, February 21, 1970.

19. For more on Panther poetry see Regina Jennings, "Poetry of the Black Panther Party: Metaphors of Militancy," *Journal of Black Studies* 29, no. 1 (September 1998): 106–29. On BPP visual art, see Erika Doss, "'Revolutionary Art Is a Tool for Liberation': Metaphors of Militancy," *Journal of Black Studies* 29, no. 1 (September 1998): 106–29; and Elton C. Fax, *Black Artists of the New Generation* (New York: Dodd, Mead, 1977).

20. See John Berger, "Uses of Photography," in *About Looking* (New York: Vintage International, 1980), 52–67.

21. See, for example, "Black Power—Black Panther Party," Poster and Broadside Collection, Tamiment Library/Wagner Labor Archives, New York University.

22. For more on the RPCC, see George Katsiaficas, "Organization and Movement: The Case of the Black Panther Party and the Revolutionary People's Constitutional Convention of 1970," in *Liberation, Imagination and the Black Panther Party*, and Nikhil Pal Singh, "The Black Panthers and the 'Undeveloped Country' of the Left," in *The Black Panther Party Reconsidered*, ed. Charles E. Jones (Baltimore, Md.: Black Classic Press, 1998).

23. Katsiaficas, "Organization and Movement," 142.

24. Berger, "Uses of Photography," 67.

25. Walter Benjamin, "The Work of Art in the Age of Mechanical Reproduction," in *Illuminations: Essays and Reflections* (New York: Schocken Books, 1968), 228.

26. Guy Debord, *The Society of the Spectacle* (1967; repr., New York: Zone Books, 1995). I borrow the term "insurgent visibility" from Nikhil Pal Singh's important essay "The Black Panthers and the 'Undeveloped Country' of the Left," in *The Black Panther Party Reconsidered*.

27. For more on the relationship between history and memory, see especially

"Grounds for Remembering," special issue, *Representations* 69 (Winter 2000), and Raphael Samuel, *Theatres of Memory*, vol. 1, *Past and Present in Contemporary Culture* (New York: Verso, 1994). On nostalgia, see Frederic Jameson, *Postmodernism, or, The Cultural Logic of Late Capitalism* (Durham, N.C.: Duke University Press, 1991).

28. Roland Barthes, *Camera Lucida: Reflections on Photography* (New York: Hill and Wang, 1981), 26.

29. "Black Panthers: Old v. Young," *London Sunday Times*, March 16, 1997.

30. Khallid Muhammad, spokesman for the NBPP, quoted in "Black Panthers: Old v. Young."

31. *The Black Panther Party v. the New Black Panther Party*, quoted in "Black Panthers: Old v. Young."

32. See especially Edward P. Morgan's "The Good, the Bad, and the Forgotten: Media Culture and Public Memory of the Civil Rights Movement" in this volume.

33. Ward Churchill, " 'To Disrupt, Discredit and Destroy': The FBI's Secret War against the Black Panther Party," in *Liberation, Imagination and the Black Panther Party*. For more on the FBI's COINTELPRO campaign against the Panthers, see *The COINTELPRO Papers: Documents from the FBI's Secret Wars against Dissent in the United States* (Boston, Mass.: South End Press, 1990), and Churchill and Vander Wall, *Agents of Repression: The FBI's Secret War against the Black Panther Party and the American Indian Movement* (Boston, Mass.: South End Press, 1988).

34. Tim Tyson's seminal works *Radio Free Dixie: Robert F. Williams and the Roots of Black Power* (Chapel Hill: University of North Carolina Press, 1999), and *Blood Done Sign My Name* (New York: Crown, 2004), both describe the breadth and depth of Black Power in the South throughout the 1960s.

35. On Blaxploitation, see especially chapter five, "The Rise and Fall of Blaxploitation," in Ed Guerrero, *Framing Blackness: The African American Image in Film* (Philadelphia, Pa.: Temple University Press, 1993).

36. Take for example, Sweetback in *Sweet Sweetback's Baad Asssss Song* (Melvin Van Peebles, 1971); John Shaft in *Shaft* (Gordon Parks, 1971); Priest in *Superfly* (Gordon Parks Jr., 1972); any of the films starring Pam Grier, Tamara Dobson, or Gloria Hendry; and Manuwalde in *Blacula* (William Crain, 1972) and *Scream, Blacula, Scream!* (Bob Kelljan, 1973).

37. See Guerrero, *Framing Blackness*, as well as Vijay Prashad, "Bruce Lee and the Anti-imperialism of Kung Fu: A Polycultural Adventure," *Positions* 11, no. 1 (Spring 2003): 51–90.

38. Cedric J. Robinson, "Blaxploitation and the Misrepresentation of Liberation," *Race and Class* 40, no. 1 (1998): 5, 6.

39. Ibid., 7.

40. Bell hooks, "Reconstructing Black Masculinity," in *Black Looks: Race and Representation* (Boston, Mass.: South End Press, 1992), 94.

41. Robinson, "Blaxploitation and the Misrepresentation of Liberation," 11.

42. Ibid.

43. Rob Kenner, "Of Love and War," *Vibe*, June 2003, cover, 92.

44. "The Guest List," *Vibe*, November 2002, 40.

45. The term "postsoul" comes from black popular culture critic Mark Anthony Neal, who employs it as a means to describe a black postmodernism focused on the experiences and expressions of the generation of African Americans "born between the 1963 March on Washington and the [*Regents of the University of California v.*] *Bakke* case [of 1978, the first major challenge to affirmative action]." Mark Anthony Neal, *Soul Babies: Black Popular Culture and the Post-Soul Aesthetic* (New York: Routledge, 2002), 3.

46. Emil Wilbekin, "Follow the Leader?" *Vibe*, June 2003, 26.

47. Melvin Sokolsky and Kadi Agueros, "Proactivist," *Vibe*, June 2003, 142. The term "lifestyle" describes superficially the attitudes or values of a group of individuals reflected in their way of life, "elevat[ing] habits of consumption, dress, and recreation to categories in a system of social classification." The American Heritage Dictionary of the English Language, 4th ed. (New York: Houghton Mifflin, 2000). People who share a "lifestyle" often consider themselves as part of a social class, linked to consumerism, and devoid of politics.

48. Davis, "Black Nationalism: The Sixties and the Nineties," 324.

PART THREE

DIVERGING MEMORY

In the commonly accepted version of the movement today, black people, under the leadership of male elites, protested peaceably and patiently in their quest for basic civil rights, like the right to vote. Yet this narrative, which emphasizes the role of men, the nonviolent nature of black protest, and the importance of traditional political activity like voting, is incomplete. Although this account is not wholly fictitious, it overemphasizes certain historical acts and actors and dismisses other aspects of the movement, with the result that the movement is made to seem less controversial than it actually was. The two essays in this section explore how particular aspects of civil rights history, especially those related to the role and treatment of women in civil rights organizations, have come to be ignored or downplayed in contemporary historical memory of the movement.

In the first essay in this section, Kathryn L. Nasstrom examines how the contributions of women in a 1946 Atlanta voting registration campaign have been largely erased from a historical narrative that came instead to celebrate male leadership. Although women activists were recognized at the time as leaders of the voter registration drive, their participation was downplayed in later histories of the event, with the media and scholars choosing to locate the 1946 voting drive in a narrative about the rise of black elected officials in Atlanta. But by associating the civil rights movement exclusively with male leadership, Nasstrom warns, the historical memory of the movement comes to valorize electoral success over community organizing in ways that may well shape the future of activism in the United States.

In his essay on the gendered nature of the memory of the civil rights movement, Steve Estes moves beyond the question of what the traditional civil rights narrative ignores to instead examine the ways in which movement activists shape their own accounts of the movement in part in response to dominant historical memories and historiography. Focusing on the Student Nonviolent Coordinating Committee, especially in Mississippi, Estes explores how civil rights activists' descriptions of the gender relations in the movement have changed since the 1960s. White female activists, Estes argues, have come to downplay the existence of sexism that they charged they experienced in the 1960s out of fear of contributing to an official memory that would discredit the movement. Black male activists, he suggests, have begun to view their experience in the movement more in terms of the achievement of manhood as a result of the gender politics that emerged during the Black Power movement and continue today with events like the Million Man March. Estes' essay, especially in conversation with Nasstrom's piece, makes clear that historical memory evolves over time and that individuals who lived the movement have a complex relationship with the official narratives of its history.

KATHRYN L. NASSTROM

Down to Now

Memory, Narrative, and Women's Leadership

in the Civil Rights Movement in Atlanta, Georgia

On October 28, 1983, the Black Women's Coalition of Atlanta, a social service and advocacy organization serving Atlanta's African Americans, took time from its service work to present an awards ceremony honoring thirty-five black women for their significant contributions to the civic and political life of their city. The tribute included this pointed statement, in which the coalition linked the question of women's leadership to issues of historical memory and narrative: "The Black Women's Coalition of Atlanta is proud to provide an occasion to remember and to recognize a segment of Atlanta's Community which has been overlooked and under-acknowledged in the chronicling of our city's history. While much has been written and recorded about the men of that era, little (if any) recognition has been afforded those Black women who worked shoulder to shoulder with the 'Negro Leaders' of the late forties, fifties and the early sixties . . . thus we salute *Our Legacy!*"

As they enjoined their fellow black Atlantans "to remember," coalition women also objected to a particular "chronicling" of Atlanta's history that had celebrated "'*Negro leaders*'" (implicitly male) at the expense of "Black women." By underscoring the phrase "Negro leaders," they indicated that the concept was not of their making, but they also acknowledged that it had a widely recognized currency. Leadership in the decades of the civil rights movement had become associated largely with black men. Women's leadership, by contrast, remained to be recovered and interpreted, a task that the coalition began when it presented its Pioneer Awards. "Our Legacy" too, they claimed, "is Leadership."[1]

The Black Women's Coalition of Atlanta pinpointed a problem that scholars of the civil rights movement have since taken up as they document the nature and scope of women's leadership. The recovery of this previously obscured area of women's activism, which was just emerging as a subject of historical and sociological study when the coalition honored Atlanta's women, is now well underway. As our research on women's involvement grows, we are learning about areas, such as citizenship education and neighborhood organizing, for which women bore special responsibility.[2] Women were often pioneers, paving the way for actions that brought male leaders to prominence.[3] State and local studies, the locus of much recent scholarship, deepen our knowledge of women's participation, for this body of literature suggests that women were more active in local movements than in the more intensively studied national organizations and campaigns. Local studies, with their greater representation of women, also allow for a comparison of women's and men's activism.[4] One of the early conclusions concerning gender differences is that, in the succinct phrasing of one scholar of the movement, "men led, but women organized."[5] This is a very useful assessment, in part because feminist scholars have been concerned with revaluing the important contribution of female organizers. In recent scholarship organizing is being recognized as a critical movement activity in its own right and as an underappreciated form of leadership.

Organizing, this body of literature suggests, entailed a distinctive form of leadership. Organizing leaders focused on developing the potential for reflection and action in others and sought to involve as many participants as possible in the decision-making that shaped the movement's direction. While acting as leaders themselves, they sought to develop leadership potential in others. The contrasts between organizing leadership and more traditionally recognized forms of leadership are notable. Because organizing involved a dynamic of participation internal to a social movement, organizing leaders were less likely than traditionally recognized leaders to serve as spokespeople who interpreted strategies and goals to constituencies beyond the movement itself. While traditionally recognized leaders almost always held positions of formal authority, including high-ranking posts in the major civil rights organizations, such as the NAACP, SCLC, and SNCC, organizing leaders often operated without formal authority because of their deep ties to community groups and institutions. Rather than serving as central figures and the focus of attention themselves, organizing leaders worked at the juncture of the leaders and the led, blurring the distinction between the two.[6]

Scholarly redefinitions of leadership are important for the recovery of a lost political past, but they raise other questions, particularly about the relationship of the past and present. Why is it necessary to *revalue* this form of political activity? Why hasn't organizing been valued as much as leadership or seen as a form of leadership, and was it always this way? How did leadership in the civil rights movement become so thoroughly associated with men, and what are the consequences of that connection? These questions are all the more critical because the problem identified by the Black Women's Coalition of Atlanta is a problem of the civil rights movement writ large. For all that scholars have done to recover women's activism and redefine leadership, the association of leadership with men is an exceedingly stubborn one. As one scholar of the movement put it recently, "In the minds of untold numbers of Americans, for example, the Reverend Dr. Martin Luther King, Jr., *was* the civil rights movement. Thought it up, led it, produced its victories, became its sole martyr. Schoolchildren—including Black schoolchildren—are taught this."[7] The challenge, thus, is not simply to document women's activism but also to concern ourselves with the dissemination of knowledge regarding that activism.

The case study that follows, based on women's activism in a massive voting rights campaign in Atlanta in 1946, suggests that the question of women's leadership can be examined as a problem of historical memory and narrative. We have inherited a composite portrait of civil rights leadership that has a male face. If we go back to contemporary accounts, however, we see that women were often recognized as leaders, precisely because they were effective organizers. In the gap between participants' definitions of leadership and those that are still widely recognized today lies the history of women's leadership in the civil rights movement. To assert that historical memory is the issue is also to inquire into the meaning of the movement for our own time. This study, then, proceeds on two levels: first, it documents women's leadership in a voting rights campaign and contributes to the ongoing effort to recover and interpret women's activism; then, it identifies the concrete ways that knowledge of their leadership came to be "overlooked and under-acknowledged." This is at once a history of an organizing campaign and, more important, a history of that history as the event itself passed into memory and became incorporated into a narrative of Atlanta's history. I begin with a brief overview of treatments of the 1946 voter registration drive in order to establish the drive's central place in the post–World War II history of black Atlanta. A description of the drive follows, highlighting women's roles and the dynamics of community organizing. Next, I discuss how and why women's leadership was written out of an official history of the drive that emerged from the late 1940s through the mid-1970s. Finally, this chapter closes with remarks on the nature of memory and narrative and their relevance for writing the history of women's leadership in the civil rights movement.[8]

On July 17, 1946, Atlanta's African American citizens first voted in the previously all-white Georgia primary. Two years earlier, the U.S. Supreme Court had ruled in *Smith v. Allwright* that the white primary was unconstitutional. This method of disfranchisement, adopted throughout the South in the early twentieth century, limited participation in primary elections to white citizens, at a time when the heavily Democratic political makeup of the South made the outcome of primaries tantamount to election. As happened throughout the South, white Democratic party leaders in Georgia challenged the legitimacy of the decision for their state, but in time a local suit made its way through the courts and the ruling was upheld for Georgia as well.[9] The court's decision helped spur a massive seven-week voter registration drive in Atlanta's black communities. African American voters increased their number from approximately 7,000 registered voters (or 8 percent of the electorate) to 24,000 (or 27 percent of the electorate) at a time when blacks made up slightly more than one third of the city's total population of over 300,000.[10] When these voters went to the polls on July 17, A. T. Walden, an attorney and leader of the city and state black Democratic factions, declared it the "birthday of genuine democracy."[11] One Atlanta black leader, reminiscing in the late 1980s about the pivotal events forty years earlier, concluded: "That was the real beginning of black power."[12]

Scholars, for their part, have echoed this claim of a new beginning. One went so far as to conclude that the "political consciousness of Atlanta Negroes dated from 1946."[13] Historians have also mapped out a sequence of significant developments that followed, and these events form the core of a well-developed political history of black Atlanta. By the end of the 1940s, the Atlanta Negro Voters League, an outgrowth of successful voter registration, was marshaling the black vote in city elections and had established a pattern of biracial negotiations with the mayor. These conferences, and the voting power that backed them up, brought black police to the city in 1948, the first African American to the school board in 1953, and increasing numbers of blacks to elective and appointive city posts in the 1960s. In the history of black Atlanta, thirty years of political advancement connect the registration effort of 1946 with the election of the city's first African American mayor in 1973.

This interpretation, built up over the ensuing decades, constitutes what I call an official history of the drive, and it reinterpreted the event itself in light of these later developments. This history came to have such wide resonance in large part because its architects were many, varied, and mutually reinforcing. Atlanta's black leaders served as the earliest interpreters of the significance of these events; the media, first locally and later nationally, condensed them into a compelling story and disseminated it to an ever wider audience; and scholars extended the scope of analysis but relied extensively on original press coverage and the retrospective commentary of recognized leaders. In time, white city officials joined in propagating the story, for they found it advantageous to incorporate black political power into a narrative of post–World War II Atlanta as a distinctive southern city—"the city too busy to hate"—where whites and blacks advanced together. Eventually many powerful constituencies came to have a stake in the official story. In a diffuse form, the Atlanta story echoes down to the present day. Commenting on the Olympic Games in

Atlanta in 1996, the *New York Times* reported, "Atlanta won the Games in large part because it sold itself as a model of interracial harmony."[14]

Little evidence of women's participation survives in this cumulative rendition, but contemporary records of the drive—press reports, photographs, and the materials used to conduct the drive—yield a distinctly different perspective: the drive embodied the importance of community organizing around voting rights, and women were recognized, along with men, as leaders of the drive. This critical feature has been very nearly written out of the official history. Just a hint of the importance attached to community organizing remains in retrospective assessments, but at the time it was understood to be the core of the drive's significance, the very measure of its success. By attending closely to the conduct of the drive, it is possible to recover women's participation and examine the gendered dynamics of leadership that inhered in the drive.

Anticipating a favorable decision in the case that eventually upheld *Smith v. Allwright* in Georgia, African Americans in Atlanta, under the auspices of the newly formed All Citizens Registration Committee (ACRC), launched an extensive voter registration drive on March 6, 1946. ACRC's executive committee, chaired by C. A. Bacote, a historian at Atlanta University (AU), consisted of prominent citizens, including other faculty members from AU, a prestigious complex of black colleges and universities, and the leaders of the Atlanta Urban League and the local NAACP. Their goal was ambitious: to turn voter registration into a mass movement and register 25,000 new voters. The NAACP sponsored the registration committee, but the logistical work fell to the staff of the Urban League under Grace Towns Hamilton, its executive director.

As a member of ACRC's executive committee, Grace Hamilton was the most visible of the drive's female leaders. Her place on the executive committee reflected both her privileged status in Atlanta's African American community and a career path that emphasized community work. She was a member of Atlanta's black elite; her father taught at AU and her mother was deeply involved in civic and charitable work. Hamilton herself attended AU, and after a number of years with the YWCA she joined the Atlanta Urban League as its executive director in 1943. In Atlanta, as in many cities, the Urban League's program included a strong social work component and emphasized community self-help. This approach followed naturally from Hamilton's years at AU, where the Atlanta School of Social Work trained many generations of social workers and where she taught briefly, and from her work in the black YWCA, which sent social workers and volunteers into black communities at the same time that it battled discrimination within the larger, white-dominated YWCA movement. When she took over leadership of the Atlanta Urban League, Hamilton was ideally suited to the task of coordinating the community organizing component of the registration drive.[15]

The registration committee's elaborate plans called for a block worker for each city block on which African Americans lived. At the peak of the campaign, some 875 workers canvassed door to door to encourage registration. They distributed fifty thousand handbills, placed three hundred placards on buses and in business windows, and handed out thousands of stickers that declared, "We Are Registered Voters." The executive committee called on a host of black institutions, ranging from churches and schools to social clubs and labor unions, to urge their members to exercise their newly legitimated right to the franchise. A round of meetings, large and small, followed. Mass gatherings at Atlanta's largest black churches drew crowds to hear speakers, music, and prayer, while voter registration workers from ACRC's speakers' bureau fanned out across the city for meetings with individual organizations and clubs. Black-owned businesses encouraged their employees to join the effort, labor unions and college fraternities made registration their project for the year, and housing project managers oversaw the recruitment of their tenants. Closing its campaign on May 4, 1946, the last day to register for the upcoming primary, the registration committee fell just shy of its goal, having raised the black voter registration count to 24,137.[16]

The *Atlanta Daily World*, the city's black daily newspaper, offered powerful reinforcement to the voter registration campaign. Virtually every issue during the seven weeks of the drive featured front-page coverage, and in its editorials the paper exhorted black citizens to register at the same time that it kept tabs on the rising count. In a celebratory assessment of the drive on the day it ended, the *Atlanta Daily World* cited "effective cooperation" as the key to success. The editorial ended on this note: "The credit is ascribed to no one person or club, or church or school. It was the result of the effective, unselfish and wholehearted unit of everyone, young as well as old, literate as well as unlearned, well-to-do as well as poor, together with the church, the school, the clubs and various organizations, partisan and non-partisan, cemented by a flaming spirit of togetherness. . . . We congratulate Atlanta and the vision evidenced by these leaders."[17] Despite the reference to the drive's leaders, the editorial cited none by name. Instead the effort had taken on a life of its own, drawing the community into a "flaming spirit of togetherness." The significance of the voter registration drive lay in the cumulative impact of a single act repeated some 24,000 times.

The *Atlanta Daily World*'s emphasis on community "togetherness" spoke a fundamental truth: the key to success lay not with an individual or leader but in the dynamic relationship of individual acts and the communal context that invested them with meaning. Displaying a "We Are Registered Voters" sticker called public attention to individual action and encouraged others to follow. The registration committee explained the value of the vote in terms of community betterment and established the vote as a symbol of hope for a better quality of life. "Register Now," one poster urged, and it listed these as potential community improvements: "more and better schools, streets and lights, and police protection." The voter registration drive thereby held the individual and the community, as well as those who led and those who followed, in creative tension. Furthermore, the drive recognized leadership on several levels. Citizens volunteered to be block workers, precinct organizers, and ward leaders, with each successive position representing a greater degree of initiative and responsibility. At the successful completion of the drive, all voter registration workers, "even those that had a small part," received certificates of merit signed by the president of the NAACP and the chairman of the registration committee. These were presented at a final celebratory mass meeting to honor services rendered on behalf of the community. The conduct of the drive thus emphasized relationship and process above all else, and an effective leader was one who motivated others. The act of registering to vote was paramount, and recognition went to those who stood out less because of their own action than because they encouraged action in others.[18]

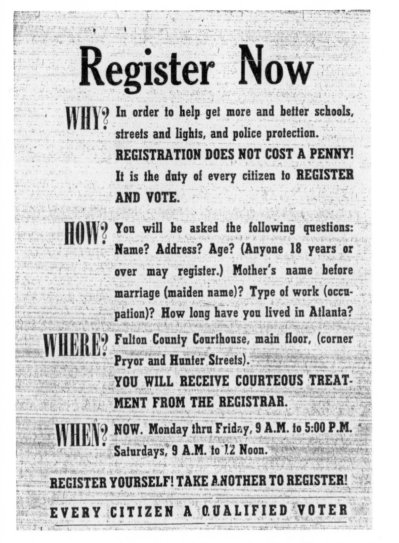

Register Now

WHY? In order to help get more and better schools, streets and lights, and police protection. **REGISTRATION DOES NOT COST A PENNY!** It is the duty of every citizen to **REGISTER AND VOTE.**

HOW? You will be asked the following questions: Name? Address? Age? (Anyone 18 years or over may register.) Mother's name before marriage (maiden name)? Type of work (occupation)? How long have you lived in Atlanta?

WHERE? Fulton County Courthouse, main floor, (corner Pryor and Hunter Streets). **YOU WILL RECEIVE COURTEOUS TREATMENT FROM THE REGISTRAR.**

WHEN? NOW. Monday thru Friday, 9 A.M. to 5:00 P.M. Saturdays, 9 A.M. to 12 Noon.

REGISTER YOURSELF! TAKE ANOTHER TO REGISTER!

EVERY CITIZEN A QUALIFIED VOTER

Register Now poster. (Kenan Research Center at the Atlanta History Center)

Photographs of the drive, in which black Atlantans recorded their effort for posterity, provide further evidence of the dynamic relationship between the individual and the community in the act of registering to vote. Long lines formed outside the courthouse as prospective voters waited for their turn to place their name on the roll. But the sheer number of registrants—"vast throngs," as the *Atlanta Daily World* reported—brought individuals into extended contact with each other as they sometimes waited several hours for their turn. The camera's eye captured a smile, a moment of conversation, the gaze or comment of a passerby, and thereby recorded the communal nature of voter registration. These were not single-file lines of individuals but clusters of citizens who had (or found) commonalities as they stood in line. Clothing, posture, and expression aggregated individuals into groups. Several men in overalls formed a tight circle of conversation, while farther down the line women in office attire sat on a cement ledge. Around the corner, a young man held forth in animated fashion, leaning forward, hand outstretched. Registrants' attire indicated that occupation and social class were the most likely reason for groups to form, while expression and conversation linked individuals into groups of the same gender and similar age. Participants in the early civil rights movement often donned their best attire in order to establish their respectability and readiness for the rights of citizenship, yet Atlanta's black registrants sported a range of fashions. Photographs of the drive provide visual evidence of social and occupational patterns within the black community as they were brought to bear on the registration effort.[19]

The historical record of the drive, from the rhetorical flourishes of newspaper editorials to the photographs, can be read as embodying a story that black Atlantans told themselves about the value of registering to vote, a story that the organizers of the drive designed and implemented but many black Atlantans carried out. The central action of the drive was the repetition, thousands of times, of the act of registering to vote. Taken together, however, these individual acts contributed to a rising registration count and built a powerful narrative of success. This narrative form, molding repetitive action into a story of progress, reflected the logic of a mass movement and the leadership of organizing. It allowed for the

Voter Registration Drive, Atlanta, Georgia, 1946. (Kenan Research Center at the
Atlanta History Center)

importance of many actors, while it also honored those who directed that
action.

No statistics survive to establish whether Atlanta's black women registered in numbers equal to men, but the photographic record of the
drive attests to the likelihood that they did.[20] The photographs show, at
least impressionistically, that women withstood rain and tired feet to join
the ranks of voting citizens just as men did, for the "vast throngs" contained as many women as men. The conduct of the drive at the level of
community organizations also suggested women's equal, and at times superior, contribution. Women's organizations were among the groups to
which ACRC made special appeals, and, when asked, women responded,
at times outdistancing the men. They became models held up for emulation. On February 20, 1946, the *Atlanta Daily World* reported that the
M.R.S. Club, a social club comprised largely of young working women,
became the "first 100% registered organizaztion."[21]

Schoolteachers made up the bulk of the M.R.S. Club's membership, and mobilizing teachers meant, by definition, mobilizing women, as 82 percent of Atlanta's black teachers were female.[22] The nature of teaching in Atlanta's black schools positioned teachers, and educators more generally, to be effective voter registration workers. Most immediately, teachers had direct access to a brand-new group of potential voters, as the voting age in Georgia had been lowered to age eighteen when a new state constitution went into effect in 1945. The teacher's reach, however, extended well beyond the classroom, as students who learned about citizenship in school might take the lesson home with them. Narvie J. Harris, a longtime educator, described the connection she used to encourage voter registration: "As a result of registering students, we started registering parents. So it was kind of a stairstep sort of a thing. If you can reach the child, you can reach the parent. And sometimes it is vice versa." Harris founded a PTA Council in the area she served in 1945, because she "saw the need for some adult education." She asked the principal of each school in her district to send a representative to meetings that featured speakers and demonstrations on topics ranging from public health to voting rights.[23]

As a committed black educator whose career spanned from the mid-1940s to the mid-1980s, Narvie Harris exemplified the multiple roles of African American educators and their deep connections to the communities they served. Working as a school administrator, Harris's main role was to "enhance instruction in the school system." Under that capacious goal fell many activities. She located needed educational materials for black schools and provided in-service training for teachers. As the schools themselves were often poorly maintained, many with "no running water, no paved streets, no lights in any school, none of the kinds of things that you would say would make a school," Harris worked with county agencies and private organizations to improve conditions. "I knocked on the doorsteps of the Red Cross, the Fire Department, Police Department, the Department of Family and Children Services." Some of the students who came to schools were poorly fed or housed, so Harris made home visits with a nurse and home demonstration agent to address family problems. Voter registration, then, was only one of many activities ancillary to children's schooling that consumed Harris's time, but her multiple roles and the connections she forged to families and organizations facilitated voter registration work. Furthermore, community betterment was at the heart of Harris's many activities, precisely the angle ACRC stressed in its appeals to citizens to register to vote. In all the tasks of their daily work, black educators embodied teaching as a leadership style that focused on the development of others.[24] The organizers of a mass meeting of voters recognized the leadership of educators when they issued this call: "The leaders of Negroes, particularly ministers and teachers, were called upon to lead their people out of the cultural, political and social wilderness on election day."[25] In this early mobilization for civil rights in the 1940s, female teachers were on par with ministers, the men who would come to be widely recognized for their leadership in the movement of the 1950s and 1960s.

The voter registration appeal also went out to the working class, and here too women emerged as key figures. At one voter rally, representatives of various constituencies in the black community were given the opportunity to speak on the value of the franchise for their group, and a domestic worker, representing approximately two thirds of all black females employed in Atlanta, was allowed the same three-minute speech as representatives of other groups.[26] Domestic workers had been organized during World War II by Ruby Blackburn, herself a former service worker, when she formed the Negro Cultural League to train domestic workers and help them find employment. Beyond the organization's central objective, which was "a fair day's pay for a fair day's work," lay, in the league's words, "grave civic duties and responsibilities that every citizen should be aware of."[27]

A working woman all of her life, first a maid at a black school and later proprietor of Ruby's Beauty Shoppe, Ruby Blackburn exhibited an unusual degree of commitment to the civic and political life of black Atlanta. During the Great Depression, she helped organize the TIC (To Improve Conditions) Club. Under this catch-all title, clubwomen worked on projects ranging from city beautification (they planted dogwoods along sidewalks) and education (they lobbied for more elementary schools in black Atlanta) to what would become Blackburn's main passion: voter registration and education. During World War II, Blackburn forged a commitment to the NAACP that would last the rest of her life, as she chaired both the wartime defense committee and the membership drive. An indefatigable NAACP worker, Blackburn delivered four speeches to churches and clubs on a single Sunday. As the NAACP merged its voter registration work into ACRC, Blackburn's participation grew. When the chairman of the registration committee singled out two Atlantans for their outstanding contributions to voter registration, one was Professor George A. Towns, a faculty member at Atlanta University and a member of Atlanta's black elite. The other was Ruby Blackburn. Blackburn went on, in the early 1950s, to establish the League of Negro Women Voters, whose motto was "that every woman and girl who becomes of age is registered"; the organization continued its work into the late 1970s.[28]

In the course of the voter registration drive, Atlanta's female leaders called attention to the political mobilization of their sex. As they worked to register and motivate the new voters of their race, they saw themselves as empowering black women as a distinct group. Mrs. W. A. Scott, of the Scott family, publishers of the *Atlanta Daily World*, spoke "for the women" at a registration rally; Julia Pate Borders, wife of a prominent Baptist minister, spoke to the Atlanta chapter of the National Council of Negro Women on the "ever-growing influence of women."[29] Mary McLeod Bethune, who had launched the National Council in 1935, was featured more often than any other national African American leader on the pages of the *Atlanta Daily World* during the period of the voter registration drive. The paper detailed her activities: on January 11, Bethune predicted that 1946 would be a "Woman's Year"; on February 1, she urged women to support the Fair Employment Practices Commission and its efforts to open new federal jobs to blacks; on April 5, she announced plans to organize the women of the South. On the particular task of registering new voters, Bethune had this to say: "We women will ring door bells, make house-to-house canvasses, work with the ministers and the churches, the good time clubs and the civic groups, the labor unions and the professional organizations of both races and all creeds." With the ballot as another tool, women would be able to do even more. In sentiments not dissimilar to those of early-twentieth-century suffragists, black women spoke of the potential the vote held for improving community life. Bethune declared that the vote would "bring victory" in many areas. Among these she listed, "The victory of progressive schools, vocational education, decent housing, opportunities for full and fair employment, participation in government locally and nationally, acceptable health standards and facilities, elimination of degrading segregation and all the other lacks in American life that today cry out for correction." In the end, she concluded, "women have a tremendous part to play."[30]

Calling on teachers and domestic workers, as well as businessmen and ministers, the drive depended equally on women and men to succeed and employed women's and men's differing networks of work and leisure. ACRC used these networks to reach and motivate voters, implicitly recognizing gender differences as they were embedded in the institutional pattern of the black community. Historians of African American life under segregation have shown how black institutions sustained the community through the abuses of Jim Crow. They also became, in 1946, important foundations for the post–World War II civil rights movement.[31] Moreover, these gendered networks presented a variety of opportunities for leadership, and ACRC capitalized on the unique position of an individual or group to provide service and leadership to the drive. Schoolteachers worked out of the classroom, while ministers exhorted from the pulpit. C. A. Bacote, a historian of political behavior, headed up ACRC, while Grace Hamilton, based in the Urban League, coordinated the community organizing campaign. When the measure of leadership was effectively mobilizing a constituency, Ruby Blackburn, a former domestic worker, could be recognized at the same level as George A. Towns, a university professor. For Atlanta's African Americans, the path to citizenship might be gendered, but the act itself was not; nor was leadership.

A brief sketch of the history of the Atlanta chapter of the NAACP and the local affiliate of the Urban League, the two organizations most responsible for launching ACRC and the voter registration drive, serves to highlight the historical roots of women's leadership and provide further context for claims, such as Julia Pate Borders's, of the "ever-growing influence of women." Both organizations are typically viewed, with good reason, as male dominated, but their history in Atlanta prior to 1946 suggests that both had significant female influences.[32]

The Atlanta NAACP established itself in 1916 and 1917 and almost immediately set to work on voter registration. In its first three decades, its leadership was decidedly male; the founders and early presidents included a minister, businessman, attorney, and newspaper editor. Lugenia Burns Hope, a teacher, social worker, and wife of John Hope, president of Morehouse College within the AU complex, was the exception to this pattern; she served as first vice president in the 1930s. In that capacity and as the head of the Citizenship Committee, whose goal was to "bring about a feeling of race consciousness with . . . reference to the ballot," Hope conceived of and established the chapter's citizenship schools. Over the courses of the 1930s, thousands of black Atlantans learned about the workings of government and procedures for voting. The committee also produced a primer on citizenship and both the primer and citizenship schools became models for similar programs around the country.[33]

Voter education was only a small part of Lugenia Burns Hope's civic work. She is more often remembered as the guiding force behind the Neighborhood Union, Atlanta's contribution to the settlement house movement of the early twentieth century. Established in 1908, the Neighborhood Union pioneered much of black social work in Atlanta. Beginning on the black West Side and eventually extending its program citywide, the union investigated a variety of social problems, including housing conditions and educational needs; established much-needed social services, such as a health clinic, playgrounds, and courses in hygiene, nursing, and infant care; and petitioned the city for sewers, street lights, and better schools.[34] For Hope, as for many black female reformers of the first half of the century, social work, education, and politics were all of a piece.[35]

The connection between social work and the formal politics of voting was even stronger in the case of the Urban League. The Atlanta affiliate dates from 1919, and, like the Atlanta chapter of the NAACP, had a history of male leadership, both on the Board of Directors that guided its development and within the paid staff. Grace Hamilton, when she took over as executive director in 1943, was the first female executive of the organization. Nonetheless, the Atlanta Urban League had a particularly female lineage, which also ran back to Lugenia Burns Hope. On the broadest level, the Neighborhood Union pioneered the social work methods of research, education, prevention, and advocacy that came to characterize the Urban League approach in Atlanta. More specifically, the Neighborhood Union functioned as an unofficial affiliate of the Urban League prior to the formal launching of the Atlanta league. Neighborhood Union leaders maintained close contact with the National Urban League staff in the 1910s and submitted annual reports on its programs. In short, the Atlanta Urban League, as it set out to improve schools, health care, housing, and recreation for the city's African Americans, followed the path cleared by the union.[36] When Grace Hamilton coordinated the community-organizing component of the 1946 voter registration drive, she was heir to Hope's pioneering efforts, and when ACRC's voter registration flyers urged citizens to register so as to obtain "more and better schools, streets and lights, and police protection," it likewise linked social work concerns with the call to citizenship rights, lending an explicitly political and electoral strategy to decades of community work.[37]

To acknowledge the historically female roots of the NAACP and Urban League program in Atlanta and to recognize their relevance to the voter registration drive of 1946 is not, however, to deny that formal authority remained a largely male prerogative. Both the NAACP and the Atlanta Urban League had women's auxiliaries, which functioned largely as fund-raising arms of the organizations and implicitly suggested that most women were helpmates, rather than equal partners, in the organizations' work. Leadership in partisan political activity was similarly dominated by men. Like the NAACP and Urban League, the Young Men's Republican Club maintained a women's auxiliary, and scattered evidence suggests that some women resented the limits placed on their activity and authority. Two of them, a social worker and an elementary school principal, founded the Woman's Civic Club in 1940, because they had "long been interested in political activity among Negroes" but "became disgusted with the men for doing nothing."[38] Grace Hamilton complained of the obstacles she faced as she took over leadership of the Atlanta Urban League: "There was not an expectation among the League's black leadership, men largely, that women deserved full and equal treatment."[39]

Black Atlantans, then, carried into the voter registration drive of 1946 strong traditions of male and female participation in political life, as well as a history of limitations on female leadership. Viewed against this backdrop, the 1946 effort represented a continuation of this heritage, both its strengths and its weaknesses. Women's contributions and leadership were widely recognized, yet they made up only ten to fifteen percent of the ward and precinct leaders selected by ACRC, and Grace Hamilton was the only female member of ACRC's executive committee.[40] As important as the distinction between formal and informal authority was (and it was important enough to elicit complaints from some women), the greater distinction came as the drive passed into memory and became enshrined in an official history.

The voter registration drive of 1946 became, and has remained, a significant event in the political history of black Atlanta. Its meaning, however, has changed over time. Narrative theory provides a useful tool for examining this shifting significance. Narratives, like memories, depend on selection and omission; they limit both action and actors to build a compelling story. Moreover, narrative form, rather than the discrete events themselves, conveys meaning. A narrative's overall structure places events in a causal sequence, thereby defining the relationship among them, and provides an explanatory system to call attention to the significance of central characters and events. The official history of the drive that developed after 1946 exhibited these features of a coherent narrative. The importance attached after the fact to the voter registration drive of 1946 was as a point of origin for the development of Atlanta's postwar black leadership as defined by achievement in the electoral arena. The growing power of the black vote and the movement of African Americans into significant positions in city government in the 1950s and 1960s, culminating with the election of an African American mayor in 1973, established benchmarks of progress within a narrative of leadership development. This official history developed in tandem with the rise of black electoral power in Atlanta and served to legitimate this particular form of black political activity above all others. Seen through feminist eyes, however, it obscured as much as it explained. Sparsely represented in the group of recognized black leaders, women were also effectively written out of this new, more narrowly focused narrative of leadership, and its form, a linear and progressive story line, did not do justice to the politics of organizing.[41]

The creation of an official history began soon after the drive was completed, and in its earliest renditions it was shaped largely by participants themselves. When A. T. Walden declared that the first primary day on which African Americans voted was the "birthday of genuine democracy," he signaled a recognition among the drive's leaders that the events of 1946 might be of historic proportion.[42] Walden and others set that vision of the future into motion when they formed the Atlanta Negro Voters League (ANVL) in the fall of 1949 in preparation for city elections. ANVL brought together the city's black Democrats, led by Walden, and its black Republicans, under John Wesley Dobbs, a retired railway mail clerk and Grand Master of the Masons, to marshal a unified black vote. In positions of formal authority, ANVL was, like its organizational predecessor, ACRC, predominately male. All the members of its executive committee were men, although several women, including Grace Hamilton, served on the campaign committee.[43] More important, ANVL placed emphasis on a decidedly different political note, on the outcome of the black vote. Celebrating the effect of ANVL's foray into electoral politics, the organization's executive secretary noted in the fall of 1949: "First and foremost among the accomplishments was the election of Mayor William B. Hartsfield. It is estimated that 10,000 Negroes voted in the Primary, and at least 8,500 of them cast their vote for Mr. Hartsfield. . . . [This] clearly indicates the effect of the Negro vote."[44] "First and foremost" signaled a new measure of significance for black political mobilization and shifted attention from internal black community politics to citywide, biracial politics.

Despite this noticeable shift in meaning, the early official history of the drive retained some emphasis on community organizing. In the first decade following the voter registration effort, the architects of the drive employed the memory of success in 1946 to urge similar community action. Consequently, the process of mobilizing voters retained for a time a prominent place in the narrative. C. A. Bacote, a key figure in both ACRC and ANVL over several decades, told a meeting of black voters in 1953 that they would be expected once again to "answer [the] call" when asked to serve as block workers in a new voter registration drive. The city's geographic limits had been enlarged in 1951, and new city residents needed to be encouraged to add their names to the roster. In a speech to the membership of ANVL in 1954, A. T. Walden urged his fellow black Atlantans to register, citing the registration effort of 1946 as evidence of what might be accomplished with renewed effort.[45] As the events of 1946 passed into the realm of historical memory, they became a collective recollection of political efficacy for Atlanta's black citizens. There was, however, a danger in dwelling on 1946 solely as past accomplishment, as when Bacote sent a mass mailing to the membership of ACRC in 1956 with this cautionary note: "Our registration campaigns in the past are a part of the past, we must develop new techniques, discover new leadership, generate new enthusiasm, enlighten the uninformed and unearth latent talent, to do the job ahead."[46] This dual emphasis on 1946 as a success of the past and a goad to future action marked the memory as still largely internal to black politics, reflecting, as the drive itself had, the aspirations of a people still not fully incorporated into the political life of the city. There remained a need "to do the job ahead," a call to collective action to improve the future for all black Atlantans.[47]

By the mid-1950s, the impact of the drive could be identified in increasingly tangible ways and the meaning attached to the drive became more firmly anchored in electoral politics. In 1953, Rufus E. Clement, president of Atlanta University, was elected to the Board of Education, and A. T. Walden and Miles Amos, a politically active pharmacist, joined the City Democratic Executive Committee, the first African Americans to serve in citywide posts. C. A. Bacote found in these electoral results the "climax of black political participation," a fitting tribute not only to community organizing but also to the growing influence of black votes. With the election of black city officials, the meaning of the past had changed. The voter registration drive became less important for the process it embodied than the outcome it enabled. Clement, Walden, and Amos marked a definitive break from the past, as they could be said to represent not only black Atlanta, but all of Atlanta. Nonetheless, Bacote took pains in 1953 to praise the block workers of the voter registration drive that had launched African American citizens on this path, those "whose names never got into the newspapers but who performed their assignments diligently." Those names, unrecorded at the time and slipping from memory as subsequent developments unfolded, became even more faintly remembered in the next decade.[48]

As the narrative of the drive evolved into its next stage, its primary disseminators were not participants themselves but observers, particularly the news media and scholars, who found that the notable achievements of Atlanta's African Americans warranted wider exposure. These political commentators of the 1960s largely left behind the story of effective organizing and focused on the efficacy of the black vote, elaborating a theme first articulated by ANVL. These concerns interjected a new frame of reference, comparison with white voters and the city's recognized white leaders, and on this account social scientists found Atlanta's blacks to be exceptional. The city's black citizens voted more regularly and more solidly than their white counterparts and as a result often influenced the outcome of elections, despite being a minority of the electorate. As their proportion of the Atlanta population grew, they also began to elect increasing numbers of black politicians to local offices.[49] The series of electoral firsts initiated by Clement, Walden, and Amos in 1953 accelerated during the 1960s: Leroy Johnson, a close associate of A. T. Walden, was elected in 1961 as Georgia's first black legislator since Reconstruction; Johnson and Walden together joined the State Democratic Executive Committee in 1963; Q. V. Williamson, a realtor, was elected in 1965 as the first black alderman in nearly a century; and eight African Americans went to the state legislature in the same year. By the mid-1960s, the story of Atlanta's black elected officials began to have a discernable plot, linear and progressive in form, as additional victories followed the precedent set in the previous decade. These later electoral victories made Clement's election all the more important for having been the first of several, and in time his election came to be a rival point of origin for black political advancement, one rooted in electoral politics rather than community organizing.[50]

A growing body of social science literature analyzed similar trends on a national scale and articulated a typology of black leadership. Most often, scholars constructed a dichotomous portrait that contrasted an older, accommodationist group of leaders with a younger faction more oriented to protest and militant action. The relationship of black leadership to the white city officials and business leaders who responded to the desegregation agenda of the civil rights movement framed this analysis. Atlanta was a success story in part because youthful militants pushed the civil rights agenda forward, while older leaders smoothed over the rough edges. This emerging typology of leadership did much to reveal the dynamic of desegregation protest, but rarely shed light on the politics of organizing.[51]

During the 1960s, popular commentary on the rise to prominence of Atlanta's black leadership proliferated, and the media came to play an important role in propagating the official history. The city became widely celebrated for having provided an unusual degree of leadership to the civil rights movement. Nationally and internationally, Atlanta's Martin Luther King Jr. represented the civil rights movement, but local leaders enjoyed their own, if lesser, reputations. A. T. Walden and Leroy Johnson were among the most well-known local leaders whose names became household words in Atlanta in the 1960s.[52] Equally important, the 1960s saw the rise of the student movement. The sit-in movement in Atlanta, as elsewhere, brought a younger generation of leaders to the fore and generated intense press coverage. Sit-ins in Atlanta speeded the process of desegregation and also the movement of African Americans into the political life of the city. Lonnie King and Julian Bond, both sit-in leaders and founders of SNCC, joined the local NAACP, while Bond and another student leader, Ben Brown, entered electoral politics by running successfully for the state legislature in 1965.[53] While still very much a minority, the number of black elected officials in Atlanta warranted examination, and press coverage of black political life became a regular feature in the city's white dailies. Even the Chamber of Commerce publication, once staunchly segregationist, often featured the city's black political leaders in its pages in the 1960s. The majority of these articles profiled individual male leaders and outlined similarities and differences between black and white leaders. The press relegated most citizens and voters to supporting roles, important only to the extent that they shed light on recognized leaders and how they operated in a biracial context.[54]

National television followed the lead of the local media. One ABC program, in a series on the state of race relations in the United States aired in 1969, portrayed Atlanta as the city where, in the program's title, "It Can Be Done," referring to the city's reputation for interracial cooperation. In that year, black representation on the school board and the aldermanic board approached one third, and the city elected a black vice-mayor. The program presented a panel of the city's African American male leaders, "and everyone a graduate of Morehouse except one." A respected local minister described Morehouse's importance: "And from that college, every man here got a kind of world view which qualifies him to be a significant contributor to the beautiful and just society. Now this makes Atlanta different." Graduation from Morehouse, the alma mater of Martin Luther King Jr. as well as of many of Atlanta's local leaders, had come to serve as a ticket to leadership in Atlanta by the end of the decade. The ABC program only made explicit what was often left implicit: Atlanta's black leadership was male.[55] By the end of the 1960s, Atlanta's politically sophisticated black leadership class had taken its place alongside the city's white leadership in a biracial story of the city as a place where black and white leaders, despite their differences, worked together. Some twenty-five years after a massive voter registration drive launched the post–World War II political participation of blacks, a narrative with origins in black community politics had taken on citywide significance and the story was so notable as to warrant national publicity. In this same period, the collective memory of political efficacy, established first within the black community, became a more general memory claimed by city officials for Atlanta as a whole. This transformation occurred because there had been discernible black political advancement but also because white city officials found that black political advancement reflected well on the city as a whole.

With an emphasis on the power of the black vote and black elected officials, community organizing, the centerpiece of the narrative in 1946, slipped from the prominent place it formerly had in assessments of the voter registration drive, and with it the fortunes of women slipped as well. The elision of women's leadership from memory was vital to the creation of an official history centered on electoral success, for only through a systematic amnesia about the full range of leadership exhibited in the past could such a celebratory official history be established.[56] To have traced the trajectory of women by the same standard would have yielded a more sober assessment of leadership development. Women were not moving into elective offices in large numbers. Grace Hamilton, elected to the state legislature in 1965 after a twenty-year career as the head of the

Atlanta Urban League, was the exception among women. While her position as a state legislator guaranteed her a degree of publicity, as the lone black female she could not represent a notable trend and a typology of leadership to be described and analyzed.

To say that women had not achieved as much as men in the electoral arena is not, however, to say they were inactive. Rather, the scholarly and popular attention paid to electoral leaders and the student movement obscured both the continuity of black women's activity and their progress in this decade. In the years following the voter registration drive of 1946, black women had moved increasingly into significant positions within ANVL and ACRC, both of which were still operating during the 1960s. For example, women made up less than one fifth of ward leaders in ANVL in 1951; in 1965 they constituted slightly more than one third.[57] The student movement was itself a catalyst not only for the college-aged women who organized sit-ins, marches, and demonstrations, but also for many older women. Among the most active in the field of voter registration was Ella Mae Brayboy, who was inspired by her own children, as they joined the Atlanta student movement, to launch her own activist career. She became the codirector of the first registration drives sponsored under the auspices of the Voter Education Project (VEP) of the 1960s and took as her mission a decentralization of voter registration activity so that poor Atlantans could register in their neighborhoods, housing projects, and senior citizen centers.[58] Brayboy was unique in the level of responsibility she assumed within VEP, but she had counterparts in many individual black neighborhoods. In Atlanta, SNCC undertook a community organizing and voter registration drive in several largely poor black neighborhoods, an urban parallel to its more well-known efforts in the rural Deep South. As SNCC workers moved into these communities, they discovered a network of black female community organizers already in place. As one SNCC worker put it in 1966, "I have found that the women tend to be much more active there than the men."[59] In the 1960s, then, women, and particularly women of the generation that had been active in 1946, fell through two cracks: they were increasingly marginalized by a black leadership discourse in Atlanta that traced the rise of black male electoral leaders, and by a new emphasis (in the sense that it was perceived at the time as being new) on organizing pioneered by a student generation. Neither framework adequately accounted for the fact that there was a great deal of continuity in women's leadership in community organizing over the decades of the 1940s, 1950s, and 1960s.

The decade of the 1970s brought a culminating event to celebrate the efficacy of the black vote and the rise of black elected officials in Atlanta: the election of a black mayor. Maynard Jackson's election in 1973 as the city's and the Deep South's first black mayor drew even more national attention to Atlanta, and the media took the city's narrative of progress and leadership to a new level of praise. "Black Mecca of the South," declared *Ebony* magazine; the *New York Times* labeled Atlanta the "capital of black-is-bountiful," as it located Jackson in a third wave of black leadership in the city. Maynard Jackson's election allowed Atlanta's blacks to claim a greater ownership in the political life of the city. Atlanta was no longer a city where blacks participated politically, but one in which they took leadership at the highest level of city governance. This was, as the *New Yorker* claimed, a "new politics" in Atlanta.[60]

Maynard Jackson's political lineage pointed directly back to the political awakening of the 1940s: his grandfather, John Wesley Dobbs, had been one of the organizers of ANVL. Thus it was possible to give his election a deep and compelling history. One historian, from the vantage point of 1977, summarized the evolution of that narrative—with 1946 as its point of origin—with this assessment: "The opening of [the white] primary, as well as general and special elections, to blacks was the foundation on which the black leadership of Atlanta built a citadel of political power. Seizing quickly upon the new freedom and opportunity, Atlanta's black elite influenced the city's black masses to flock to the registrar's booth and later, quadrennially, to the polls."[61]

The cumulative attention paid to leaders and the lack of attention to process had, by the 1970s, enacted a near complete reversal in the meaning of the voter registration drive of 1946. With Atlanta's unusually large group of African American elected officials established as the point of interest, the rank-and-file voters received little attention. Their actions remained important—without them no black leaders could rise—but the means by which they were mobilized did not receive careful scrutiny.

In the 1970s, attention was closely focused on the pinnacle of leadership, those in power and how they operated in the Atlanta context. Even though an unprecedented number of African American women ran for local offices, ranging from school board member to legislator, in the same election season as Maynard Jackson, the story of the first black mayor captured virtually all attention.[62] The official history had done much to broaden the story of Atlanta, bringing the city's African Americans into a biracial political history of the city, but it had not done this equally for men and women. It remained for the Black Women's Coalition of Atlanta, ten years after Maynard Jackson's election, to remind black Atlanta that there was an "old politics" of community organizing in Atlanta, in which women were central, and to reclaim that legacy as leadership.

To study women in the civil rights movement, and indeed to study the civil rights movement, we need to tell two kinds of stories.[63] The first is the many stories of women's leadership, such as that of Atlanta's voter registration drive, that remain to be recovered and interpreted. But, we also need to describe how and why women's stories came to be less well known than men's stories. Both the conduct of the drive and the ensuing official history of it describe black political mobilization in Atlanta and articulate why it is important and what it leads to. But they are otherwise very different stories: different in their narrative form, in the characters they place at the center of attention, and in the lessons about leadership they convey. When we consider these two kinds of stories in relation to each other, we see that the pre-eminence of a narrative tracing the rise of black male leadership came at the expense of a narrative that would have attended as well to women's leadership. Atlanta's narrative of leadership development was profoundly gendered, not only because women were under-represented in that group of visible leaders but also because that narrative wrote over another history, altering its meaning and diverting attention from women's forms of leadership.

By treating the civil rights movement from the perspective of memory and narrative, we call attention not only to activists in their own time but also in relation to the present and, implicitly, the future. The civil rights movement was not only a social and political struggle, but also an intensely documented and self-documenting process: widely reported by the media, closely scrutinized by scholars, and self-consciously preserved by participants. Although the heyday of the movement has passed, commentary continues on all of these levels. When we focus on the ongoing documentation and meaning of the movement, the disseminators of information themselves become historical actors who intervene between the past and present, continually reframing the movement. We are thereby encouraged to consider stories of women's leadership in relationship to men's, not only for the purposes of comparing male and female leaders (an important task in itself) but also to reveal the cultural production of leaders, how they are identified and how some leaders become more prominent than others, particularly when this designation takes place after the fact. This move does not allow the movement to be comfortably, or even uncomfortably, behind us; rather, it involves us in its evolving present. To honor the activists of 1946—or of any historical period—we should do no less. Certainly, this is what the Black Women's Coalition of Atlanta had in mind when it included this stanza in its poem of tribute:

> Through knowing our Sisters
> Our history comes clearer,
> Our cause stays in focus,
> The legacy grows dearer.[64]

The coalition honored women not simply to set the past record straight but also to inspire the future. In this, they prefigured a commentary on leadership offered by African American intellectuals today. Cornel West, for example, has linked the need for new models of leadership for the future to the paucity of knowledge about the variety of leadership exhibited in the past.[65]

Focusing on the cultural production of leadership can also help feminist scholars challenge the still stubborn association of civil rights leadership with men. The official history of the voter registration drive of 1946 in Atlanta is a cautionary tale of scholars' involvement in the process of defining leadership. At a critical juncture, social scientists aided the dissemination of Atlanta's official history by putting the imprimatur of scholarly analysis on a typology of black leadership that had little room for women. The feminist re-evaluation of women's leadership that is now underway brings organizing, and with it women, into this typology. Our goal, however, should not be simply to add women's stories, or to replace men's stories with women's stories, but, rather, to examine the complex relationship of women to an evolving discourse on African American leadership. Taking a cue from the Black Women's Coalition of Atlanta, we should note that it did not want to overthrow the existing narrative so much as reintroduce women to it and thereby change it. A complementary agenda for scholars would be to critique existing narratives of leadership even as we write narratives based on research on women's leadership. Both the historical actuality of women's leadership and the historical memory of it, and particularly the points of discontinuity between the two, are our legacies to analyze and interpret.

Notes

Originally published in *Gender and History* 11 (April 1999): 113–44. Reprinted with permission.

1. "The Legacy of Atlanta's Black Women Pioneers," Program for Awards Dinner, October 28, 1983, Ella Mae Brayboy Collection, Auburn Avenue Research Library, Atlanta, Georgia.

2. Donna Langston, "The Women of Highlander," and Sandra B. Oldendorf, "The South Carolina Sea Island Citizenship Schools, 1957–1961," in *Black Women in United States History*, gen. ed. Darlene Clark Hine, vol. 16, *Women in the Civil Rights Movement: Trailblazers and Torchbearers, 1941–1965*, ed. Vicki L. Crawford, Jacqueline Anne Rouse, and Barbara Woods (Brooklyn, N.Y.: Carlson, 1990), 145–67, 169–82; Sara Evans, *Personal Politics: The Roots of Women's Liberation in the Civil Rights Movement and the New Left* (New York: Knopf, 1979), chap. 6.

3. David J. Garrow, ed., *The Montgomery Bus Boycott and the Women Who Started It: The Memoir of Jo Ann Gibson Robinson* (Knoxville: University of Tennessee Press, 1987); Carol Mueller, "Ella Baker and the Origins of 'Participatory Democracy,'" in *Women in the Civil Rights Movement*, 51–70.

4. "Editors' Introduction," in *Women in the Civil Rights Movement*, xx. Charles Payne, *I've Got the Light of Freedom: The Organizing Tradition and the Mississippi Freedom Struggle* (Berkeley: University of California Press, 1995); John Dittmer, *Local People: The Struggle for Civil Rights in Mississippi* (Urbana: University of Illinois Press, 1994). Community studies provide an ideal setting for weighing the relative importance of various actors over time. See, for example, William H. Chafe, *Civilities and Civil Rights: Greensboro, North Carolina, and the Black Struggle for Freedom* (New York: Oxford University Press, 1980).

5. Charles Payne, "Men Led, But Women Organized: Movement Participation of Women in the Mississippi Delta," in *Women in the Civil Rights Movement*, 1.

6. This generalization about the nature of organizing as a form of leadership draws on insights from scholars of the civil rights movement specifically and social protest more generally. See Charles Payne, "Ella Baker and Models of Social Change," *Signs* 14 (Summer 1989): 885–99, esp. 897–99; Bernice McNair Barnett, "Invisible Southern Black Women Leaders in the Civil Rights Movement," *Gender and Society* 7 (June 1993): 162–82; Karen Bodkin Sacks, "Gender and Grassroots Leadership," in *Women and the Politics of Empowerment*, ed. Ann Bookman and Sandra Morgen (Philadelphia, Pa.: Temple University Press, 1988), 77–94.

7. Fred Powledge, *Free at Last? The Civil Rights Movement and the People Who Made It* (Boston, Mass.: Little, Brown, 1991), xiv.

8. Scholars have recently turned their attention to questions of periodization and, in the process, have established the beginnings of the civil rights movement in events of the 1930s and 1940s. My research supports that expanded periodization of the movement. On the need to recover the history of the civil rights struggles of the 1940s, see Robert Korstad and Nelson Lichtenstein, "Opportunities Found and Lost: Labor, Radicals, and the Early Civil Rights Movement," *Journal of American History* 75 (December 1988): 786–811. Critical events and trends of the 1930s and 1940s have recently received more attention. See Payne, *I've Got the Light of Freedom*; Dittmer, *Local People*; Adam Fairclough, *Race and Democracy: The Civil Rights Struggle in Louisiana* (Athens: University of Georgia Press, 1995).

9. *Smith v. Allwright*, 321 U.S. 664 (1944); *Chapman v. King*, 154 F.2d 460 (1946).

10. At the end of the drive, 24,137 blacks were registered, of whom 21,244 lived within city limits. As late as 1945, there were only 3,000 registered black voters in Atlanta. Less than a month before the voter registration drive of 1946 began, an additional 4,000 voters were added to the rolls as a result of interest in a special election (a contest in which African Americans could vote) to replace the congressional representative in the fifth district where most of Atlanta's African Americans resided. C. A. Bacote, "The Negro in Atlanta Politics," *Phylon* 16 (Fourth Quarter 1955): 344–48; Jack Walker, "Negro Voting in Atlanta: 1953–1961," *Phylon* 24 (Winter 1963): 380.

11. Quoted in the *Atlanta Daily World*, July 16, 1946.

12. Transcript of interview of Jacob Henderson, by Duane Stewart, Atlanta, Georgia, June 8, 1989, 16, from the Georgia Government Documentation Project, Special Collections, Pullen Library, Georgia State University, Atlanta, Georgia.

13. Virginia H. Hein, "The Image of 'A City Too Busy to Hate': Atlanta in the 1960s," *Phylon* 33 (Third Quarter 1972): 211. Representative assessments of the importance of the events of 1946, spanning three decades, are Bacote, "The Negro in Atlanta Politics," 342; Alton Hornsby Jr., "The Negro in Atlanta Politics, 1961–1973," *Atlanta Historical Society Bulletin* 21 (Spring 1977): 7–8; Clarence N. Stone, *Regime Politics: Governing Atlanta, 1946–1988* (Lawrence: University Press of Kansas, 1989), 28.

14. "The South's Struggle to Define Itself," *New York Times*, July 21, 1996. For a longer explication of the official history of Atlanta, the place of African Americans in it, and the trajectory of civil rights struggles in Atlanta as emphasizing electoral politics, see Kathryn L. Nasstrom, "Women, the Civil Rights Movement, and the Politics of Historical Memory in Atlanta, 1946–1973" (PhD diss., University of North Carolina at Chapel Hill, 1993), 14–31. White business leaders were often behind-the-scenes supporters of white government officials, and the press in Atlanta was closely tied to both business interests and city government. See Stone, *Regime Politics*, 17, 149, 154, and James Edward Carroll, "Public Images of Atlanta, 1895–1973: Motif, Montage, and Structure" (master's thesis, Georgia State University, 1974), 39. The analysis that follows does not account for conflicts within the black community over political goals and strategies. Differences of opinion on these matters certainly existed, and they were widely reported in the black newspapers and, less often and in less detail, covered in the white dailies. I have restricted my analysis, however, to those elements that became part of the official history.

15. Sharon Mitchell Mullis, "The Public Career of Grace Towns Hamilton: A Citizen Too Busy to Hate" (PhD diss., Emory University, 1976), chap. 2 and 3; Clarence Albert Bacote, *The Story of Atlanta University: A Centennial of Service, 1865–1965* (Atlanta, Ga.: Atlanta University, 1969), 328–30, 353–58.

16. Descriptions of the conduct of the drive include Bacote, "The Negro in Atlanta Politics," 345–48; Mullis, "The Public Career of Grace Towns Hamilton," 119–23; Steven F. Lawson, *Black Ballots: Voting Rights in the South, 1944–1969* (New York: Columbia University Press, 1976), 124–27; Clifford Kuhn, Harlon E. Joye, and E. Bernard West, *Living Atlanta: An Oral History of the City, 1914–1948* (Atlanta and Athens: The Atlanta Historical Society and the University of Georgia Press, 1990), 334–37.

17. *Atlanta Daily World*, May 10, 1946. The paper emphasized the theme of community participation throughout the campaign. See *Atlanta Daily World*, January 10, 20, March 12, April 11, May 7, 10, July 25, 1946. The newspaper had a virtual monopoly on the black news market in Atlanta until 1960. Alton Hornsby Jr., "Georgia," in *The Black Press in the South, 1865–1979*, ed. Henry Lewis Suggs (Westport, Conn.: Greenwood Press, 1983), 127–38.

18. Scrapbook, "Materials Used by Atlanta All-Citizens Registration Committee," Atlanta Urban League Records, Grace Towns Hamilton Papers, Atlanta History Center, Atlanta, Georgia; *Atlanta Daily World*, May 7, 1946.

19. Photographs of the registration drive can be found in the Lane Brothers Collection and Stetson Kennedy Collection, Special Collections, Pullen Library, Georgia State University, Atlanta, Georgia, and the photographic collection of the Atlanta History Center, Atlanta, Georgia. Photographs of registration lines were printed in the *Atlanta Daily World* on April 11, 21, and May 3, 1946. Additional photographs appeared alongside a retrospective assessment of the drive in C. A. Scott, "Did Negroes Elect Talmadge?" *Crisis* 53 (September 1946): 266–67, 283–84. Two photographs were reprinted in Kuhn, Joye, and West, *Living Atlanta*, 335–36.

20. The Georgia Department of Archives and History in Atlanta is the repository for election materials and no voter registration rolls for the 1946 campaign are on file.

21. *Atlanta Daily World*, February 20, March 27, 1946.

22. Both in 1940 and 1950, 82 percent of Atlanta's black teachers were female. Sixteenth Census of the United States, 1940, Population, vol. 3, The Labor Force, Part Two: Reports by States (Washington, D.C.: U.S. Government Printing Office, 1943); 1950 Census of Population, vol. 2, Characteristics of the Population, Part Two (Washington, D.C.: U.S. Government Printing Office, 1952). Annie McPheeters, a longtime librarian in Atlanta and an active member of Atlanta's black political community, informed me of the M.R.S. Club and its constituency. Conversation with author, Atlanta, Georgia, June 8, 1992.

23. Narvie J. Harris, interview with author, Atlanta, Georgia, June 11, 1992, 15, 40. Tapes and transcripts for this interview are available in the Georgia Government Documentation Project, Special Collections, Pullen Library, Georgia State University, Atlanta, Georgia, and the Southern Oral History Program Collection, Manuscripts Department, Southern Historical Collection, University of North Carolina at Chapel Hill. Pagination is taken from the transcript on file in the Southern Oral History Program Collection.

24. Harris, interview, 10–14. On the importance of the connections of teachers and their communities, see Michele Foster, "Constancy, Connectedness, and Constraints in the Lives of African-American Teachers," *NWSA Journal* 3 (Spring 1991): 233–61. For a brief overview of the literature on black teachers and the political content of their work, see Patricia Hill Collins, *Black Feminist Thought: Knowledge, Consciousness, and the Politics of Empowerment* (New York: Routledge, 1990), 150–51. For teaching as one model of leadership, see Payne, "Ella Baker and Models of Social Change," 892–93, 896–97.

25. *Atlanta Daily World*, February 14, 1946. See also *Atlanta Daily World*,

May 15, July 16, 1946. At the time of the registration drive, C. L. Harper, head of the black Georgia Teachers and Education Association, was also the president of the local NAACP. The NAACP bound teachers particularly closely to the registration effort as the organization was carrying forward, at the same time, a suit to equalize salaries among Atlanta's black and white teachers. *Atlanta Daily World*, April 16, 1946.

26. *Atlanta Daily World*, March 10, 1946. In 1940, 67 percent of employed black women in Atlanta were domestic workers; in 1950, the figure was 51 percent. Sixteenth Census of the U.S., 1940, Population, vol. 3, Labor Force, Part Two: Reports by States; 1950 Census of Population, vol. 2, Characteristics of the Population, Part Two.

27. "Seven Years of Progress" [organization brochure], n.d., Ruby Blackburn Papers, Special Collections, Atlanta-Fulton Public Library, Atlanta, Georgia.

28. "Seven Years of Progress"; "Atlanta's TIC Club," *Pittsburgh Courier*, March 6, 1943; "Mrs. Blackburn Pleads for NAACP Members" and "Registration Pleases Atlanta Branch NAACP," undated clippings, Blackburn Papers. Most of the clippings in the Blackburn Papers are undated and lack an indication of the source. It is impossible to be certain that this reference to her leadership in voter registration dates from the drive of 1946. The commendation may date from the World War II years, as both Blackburn and Towns were active in voter registration during the war. However, 1946 is the most likely year, as the commendation came from the chairman of ACRC.

29. *Atlanta Daily World*, March 15, 29, 1946.

30. Quoted in the *Atlanta Daily World*, April 5, 1946. For additional coverage of Bethune's activities, see *Atlanta Daily World*, January 11, 23, 25, February 1, May 23, 1946. On black women's activities at the time of the women's suffrage campaign, see Rosalyn Terborg-Penn, "Discontented Black Feminists: Prelude and Postscript to the Passage of the Nineteenth Amendment," in *Decades of Discontent: The Women's Movement, 1920–1940*, ed. Lois Scharf and Joan M. Jensen (Westport, Conn.: Greenwood Press, 1983), 261–78. For the argument that gender consciousness aided a rising race consciousness, see Evelyn Brooks Higginbotham, *Righteous Discontent: The Women's Movement in the Black Baptist Church, 1880–1920* (Cambridge, Mass.: Harvard University Press, 1993), chap. 2.

31. On the importance of black institutions to the civil rights movement, see Paul Douglas Bolster, "Civil Right Movements in Twentieth-Century Georgia," (PhD diss., University of Georgia, 1972), chap. 1. Historians of black women have outlined the importance of women's networks during segregation. See, for one notable example, Elsa Barkley Brown, "Womanist Consciousness: Maggie Lena Walker and the Independent Order of Saint Luke," *Signs* 14 (Spring 1989): 610–33. In 1952, Eula Mae Jones found that Atlanta men predominated in fraternal

and economic organizations, while women made up the greatest numbers in religious, educational, social, and civic organizations. The NAACP and voters leagues had a fairly equal distribution of the sexes. "Voluntary Associations in the Atlanta Negro Community" (master's thesis, Atlanta University, 1952), 23, 39–40, 52.

32. For the national perspective on the status of women in the Urban League and NAACP during this period, see Paula Giddings, *When and Where I Enter: The Impact of Black Women on Race and Sex in America* (New York: Bantam Books, 1984), 257–58. On Atlanta, see Darlene Rebecca Roth, *Matronage: Patterns of Women's Organizations, Atlanta, Georgia, 1890–1940* (Brooklyn, N.Y.: Carlson, 1994), 59.

33. Bacote, "The Negro in Atlanta Politics," 342–43; Jacqueline Anne Rouse, *Lugenia Burns Hope: Black Southern Reformer* (Athens: University of Georgia Press, 1989), 119–21; Ronald H. Bayor, *Race and the Shaping of Twentieth-Century Atlanta* (Chapel Hill: University of North Carolina Press, 1996), 19.

34. Jacqueline Anne Rouse has the most detailed treatment of the Neighborhood Union in *Lugenia Burns Hope*. See also, Cynthia Neverdon-Morton, *Afro-American Women of the South and the Advancement of the Race, 1895–1925* (Knoxville: University of Tennessee Press, 1989), 145–63; Tera W. Hunter, *To 'Joy My Freedom: Southern Black Women's Lives and Labors After the Civil War* (Cambridge, Mass.: Harvard University Press, 1997), 136–42.

35. On the interconnectedness of politics and social service, see Linda Gordon, "Black and White Visions of Welfare: Women's Welfare Activism, 1890–1945," *Journal of American History* 78 (September 1991): 567, 586.

36. Rouse, *Lugenia Burns Hope*, 118; David Andrew Harmon, *Beneath the Image of the Civil Rights Movement and Race Relations, Atlanta, Georgia, 1946–1981* (New York: Garland, 1996), 58. For an early identification of the pioneering work of the Neighborhood Union and especially its relationship to the Atlanta Urban League, see Louie Davis Shivery, "The Neighborhood Union," *Phylon* 3 (Second Quarter 1942): 149–62.

37. This interpretation of Atlanta fits with Darlene Clark Hine and Christie Anne Farnham's interpretation of the 1930s and 1940s as a time when black women committed themselves to being "race women," with an explicitly political and equal rights agenda, as they worked within single-sex organizations, such as the National Council of Negro Women, and with men in mixed-sex organizations, such as the NAACP. "Black Women's Culture of Resistance and the Right to Vote," in *Women of the American South: A Multicultural Reader*, ed. Christie Anne Farnham (New York: New York University Press, 1997), 215–16.

38. Quoted in Ralph J. Bunche, *The Political Status of the Negro in the Age of FDR*, ed. Dewey W. Grantham (Chicago, Ill.: University of Chicago Press, 1973), 488–89.

39. Quoted in Lorraine Nelson Spritzer and Jean B. Bergmark, *Grace Towns*

Hamilton and the Politics of Southern Change (Athens: University of Georgia Press, 1997), 82.

40. I have found no evidence of an extant list of voter registration workers. My estimation of 10 to 15 percent is based on photographic evidence and occasional short lists of workers in the *Atlanta Daily World*, March 12, 29, April 28, May 2, 4, 1946.

41. This analysis draws on historical and literary theory to explain how the meaning of an event is transformed when it is placed in a narrative structure. See Louis Mink, "Narrative Form as a Cognitive Instrument," in *The Writing of History: Literary Form and Historical Imagination*, ed. Robert H. Canary and Henry Kozocki (Madison: University of Wisconsin Press, 1978), 129–49; Hayden White, "The Question of Narrative in Contemporary Historical Theory," *History and Theory* 23 (1984): 1–33; William Cronon, "A Place for Stories: Nature, History, and Narrative," *Journal of American History* 78 (March 1992): 1347–76; Wallace Martin, *Recent Theories of Narrative* (Ithaca, N.Y.: Cornell University Press, 1986); William H. Sewell Jr., "Introduction: Narratives and Social Identities," and George Steinmetz, "Reflections on the Role of Social Narratives in Working-Class Formation: Narrative Theory in the Social Sciences," *Social Science History* 16 (Fall 1992): 480–88, 489–516. For discussions of the public realm of historical memory and especially official history/memory, see Alessandro Portelli, "The Death of Luigi Trastulli: Memory and the Event," in *The Death of Luigi Trastulli and Other Stories: Form and Meaning in Oral History* (Albany: State University of New York Press, 1991), 1–25; David Thelen, "Memory and American History," *Journal of American History* 75 (March 1989): 1117–29; Geneviève Fabre and Robert O'Meally, *History and Memory in African-American Culture* (New York: Oxford University Press, 1994).

42. Quoted in the *Atlanta Daily World*, July 16, 1946.

43. ANVL letterhead, 1949, Atlanta Urban League Archives, the Atlanta University Center Woodruff Library, Atlanta, Georgia. On the support offered by the *Atlanta Daily World* to ANVL, quite similar to the support it offered ACRC, see Malcolm Suber, "The Internal Black Politics of Atlanta, Georgia, 1944–1969: An Analytic Study of Black Political Leadership and Organization" (master's thesis, Atlanta University, 1975), 71.

44. Report of Executive Secretary, Atlanta Negro Voters League, September 23, 1949, Atlanta Negro Voters League Records, A. T. Walden Papers, Atlanta History Center, Atlanta, Georgia. For a discussion of the evaluation system that assigns prominence to some events over others in narratives, see Steinmetz, "Reflections on the Role of Social Narratives in Working-Class Formation," 498.

45. Notes, Lincoln-Douglass Day Celebration, February 15, 1953, Clarence A. Bacote Papers, the Atlanta University Center Woodruff Library, Atlanta

University, Atlanta, Georgia; Speech, February 18, 1954, Atlanta Negro Voters League Records, Walden Papers.

46. Mass mailing, November 21, 1956, Atlanta Urban League Archives.

47. For a description of historical memory as a mix of the past and present, see Thelen, "Memory and American History," 1117–20. For a definition of collective memory as "shared experiences and perceptions about the past that legitimate action in the present," see George Lipsitz, A Life in the Struggle: Ivory Perry and the Culture of Opposition (Philadelphia, Pa.: Temple University Press, 1988), 228.

48. Bacote, "The Negro in Atlanta Politics," 348–49. In narratives of the past the meaning of earlier events is not identifiable until an impact can be noted. In other words, a cause has no meaning until an effect has been established. Martin, Recent Theories of Narrative, 72–74, 99–100, esp. 74. For a discussion of the consequences of a designation of "first" within a narrative tradition, see Deborah E. McDowell, "In the First Place: Making Frederick Douglass and the Afro-American Narrative Tradition," in Critical Essays on Frederick Douglass, ed. William L. Andrews (Boston, Mass.: G. K. Hall, 1991): 192–214.

49. Jack Walker, "Negro Voting in Atlanta: 1953–1961," Phylon 24 (Winter 1963): 380–81; Pat Watters and Reese Cleghorn, Climbing Jacob's Ladder: The Arrival of Negroes in Southern Politics (New York: Harcourt Brace, 1967), 85; Harry Holloway, The Politics of the Southern Negro (New York: Random House, 1969), 188.

50. See Hayden White's point that "to be historical, an event must be more than a singular occurrence, a unique happening. It receives its definition from its contribution to the development of plot." "The Question of Narrative in Contemporary Historical Theory," 27.

51. On Atlanta, see Jack L. Walker, "The Functions of Disunity: Negro Leadership in a Southern City," Journal of Negro Education 32 (Summer 1963): 227–36, and "Protest and Negotiation: A Case Study of Negro Leadership in Atlanta, Georgia," Midwest Journal of Political Science 7 (May 1963): 99–124; Gerald A. McWorter and Robert L. Crain, "Subcommunity Gladiatorial Competition: Civil Rights Leadership as a Competitive Process," Social Forces 46 (September 1967): 8–21. Other studies of the 1960s that examined the nature of black leadership include Michael Walzer, "The Politics of the New Negro," Dissent 7 (1960): 235–43; James Q. Wilson, Negro Politics: The Search for Leadership (New York: Free Press, 1960); M. Elaine Burgess, Negro Leadership in a Southern City (New Haven, Conn.: College and University Press, in collaboration with the University of North Carolina Press, 1960); Lewis M. Killian, "Leadership in the Desegregation Crisis: An Institutional Analysis," in Intergroup Relations and Leadership, ed. Muzafer Sherif (New York: John Wiley and Sons, 1962), 142–66; Daniel C.

Thompson, *The Negro Leadership Class* (New York: Prentice-Hall, 1963); Everett Carl Ladd Jr., *Negro Political Leadership in the South* (Ithaca, N.Y.: Cornell University Press, 1966); Donald R. Matthews and James W. Prothro, *Negroes and the New Southern Politics* (New York: Harcourt Brace, 1966). In an interesting exception to the neglect of organizing, Wilson discussed "the organizer" as one type of black leader. *Negro Politics*, 269. None of these authors, however, considered the gender dimension of leadership. Some of the studies mentioned or profiled individual women as leaders, but discussion of women as a social group was limited to a general observation that women tended to be leaders much less often than men. See Thompson, *The Negro Leadership Class*, 25; Matthews and Prothro, *Negroes and the New Southern Politics*, 180.

52. A report published in 1967 compiled a table of the frequency with which Atlanta's black leaders appeared in the local press. Martin Luther King Jr. led the list with 157 press reports, Stokely Carmichael followed with 121, and Leroy Johnson with 58. The first and only woman on the list, Grace Hamilton, came in at position number 14; she appeared in the press 18 times. Fred Roberts Crawford, "Civil Aggressions and Urban Disorder: Atlanta, Georgia[,] 1967," (Atlanta, Ga.: Center for Research in Social Change, Emory University, 1967). On the white media's recognition of key black leaders, see Suber, "The Internal Black Politics of Atlanta," 67–68.

53. On the first years of the student movement, see David J. Garrow, ed., *Atlanta, Georgia, 1960–1961: Sit-Ins and Student Activism* (Brooklyn, N.Y.: Carlson, 1989). On the greater visibility of different constituencies within the black community following the student movement, see Francena Edwina Culmer, "Changing Patterns of Leadership in the Black Community of Atlanta, Georgia: 1960–1969" (master's thesis, Atlanta University, 1971).

54. For explicit discussions of the nature of black leadership, see Roger Williams, "The Negro in Atlanta," *Atlanta* 6 (July 1966): 25–30, and the *Atlanta Journal*'s series on "The Two Atlantas," May 12–27, 1968, esp. May 16, 1968. On the tendency of narratives to establish a delimited cast on which attention is focused, see Steinmetz, "Reflections on the Role of Social Narratives in Working-Class Formation," 497–98.

55. "It Can Be Done," July 3, 1969, ABC Television, Civil Rights Documentation Project, Moorland-Spingarn Research Center, Howard University, Washington, D.C.

56. For a similar discussion of the elision of women in the context of a literary tradition, see McDowell, "In the First Place," 197.

57. Organizational list, Atlanta Negro Voters League; March 8, 1951, Atlanta Negro Voters League Executive Committee list, September 1965, Bacote Papers. Diane L. Fowlkes, "Women in Georgia Electoral Politics: 1970–1978," *Social Science Journal* 21 (January 1984): 43–44 and 53 n. 15.

58. Biographical materials, Brayboy Papers.

59. Report on Organizing Activity in Cabbage Town and Vine City, n.d., Information and Research Department Records, Southern Regional Council Papers (Ann Arbor, Mich.: University Microfilms International, 1984). For a fuller discussion of the SNCC Atlanta Project, its relationship to existing community organizations, and media coverage, see Nasstrom, "Women, the Civil Rights Movement, and the Politics of Historical Memory," chap. 4.

60. For coverage of Jackson's election, see *Atlanta Constitution*, October 17, 1973; *Washington Post*, October 17, 1973; *New York Times*, October 17, 1973. For coverage in the national press in the 1970s, see "Atlanta: Black Mecca of the South," *Ebony*, August 1971, 152–57; Fred Powledge, "A New Politics in Atlanta," *New Yorker*, December 31, 1973, 28–40; "Atlanta: Capital of Black-Is-Bountiful," *New York Times Magazine*, April 7, 1974, 28–29, 68, 70, 72, 74, 76, 78; "Black Mayor, White Power Structure," *New Republic*, June 7, 1975, 9–11.

61. Hornsby, "The Negro in Atlanta Politics," 7–8, see also 31. For other scholarly treatments from the 1970s of the importance of 1946, see Hein, "The Image of 'A City Too Busy to Hate,'" 211; Stephan Burman, "The Illusion of Progress: Race and Politics in Atlanta, Georgia," *Ethnic and Racial Studies* 2 (October 1979): 443; Duncan Jamieson, "Maynard Jackson's 1973 Election as Mayor of Atlanta," *Midwest Quarterly* 18 (October 1976): 8. For the importance of endings of narratives as places to evaluate results, see Cronon, "A Place for Stories," 1367.

62. For a fuller discussion of women and the 1973 election season, see Nasstrom, "Women, the Civil Rights Movement, and the Politics of Historical Memory," 330–41.

63. These concluding remarks are inspired by William Cronon's injunction to "tell stories about stories" ("A Place for Stories," 1375), by Deborah McDowell's consideration of the cultural production of literary traditions ("In the First Place," 209–10), and by Gayle Greene's analysis of feminist metafiction and its relationship to "the tradition" (the great works of English literature) in *Changing the Story: Feminist Fiction and the Tradition* (Bloomington and Indianapolis: Indiana University Press, 1991). These thoughts began, however, with the Black Women's Coalition of Atlanta's articulation of the problem of women's leadership, memory, and narrative.

64. "The Legacy of Atlanta's Black Women Pioneers," Program for Awards Dinner, October 28, 1983.

65. Cornel West, "The Crisis of Black Leadership," in *Race Matters* (Boston, Mass.: Beacon Press, 1993), 35–46.

STEVE ESTES

Engendering Movement Memories

Remembering Race and Gender

in the Mississippi Movement

When Stokely Carmichael joked in 1964 that the only position for women in the Student Nonviolent Coordinating Committee (SNCC) was "prone," the women and men gathered around him simply laughed. Or did they? Mary King, Casey Hayden, and other women in SNCC clearly weren't laughing a month or so before when they anonymously penned a position paper, arguing that women were treated as second-class citizens in the movement just as African Americans were in society at large. Nor were these women laughing about sexism when they spoke with historian Sara Evans a decade later about how the "personal politics" of the civil rights struggle inspired them to support the emerging feminist movement. In subsequent interviews and writings, however, King, Hayden, and other activists downplayed the importance of gender tensions in the movement and the seriousness of Carmichael's quip about women in SNCC.[1] To understand why, we must explore the ways that historians and activists have revised movement narratives over the last forty years to provide a usable past that can guide struggles for racial and gender equality.

The first half of this chapter explores the gender dynamics of the movement through sources created during the movement itself, while the second half examines oral history interviews, memoirs, and scholarly sources to show how the narratives of activists and historians have evolved over time. Although movement participation raised both the gender and racial consciousness of participants in the 1960s, most movement-era sources focus on racial consciousness and an understanding of the ways that poverty reinforced the racial hierarchy in America. Remembering the movement in the 1970s, some activists highlighted the gender dynamics of the struggle as part of a narrative of emerging feminist consciousness and solidarity. By the 1980s and 1990s, activists, especially the white women who had been swept up in and empowered by the feminist movement of the 1970s, began to reemphasize racial consciousness in their movement memories and narratives as the struggle for racial equality seemed to falter in an increasingly conservative political era. As the needs of the activists' communities evolved, so did their stories, and this evolution has been reflected in subsequent generations of scholarship.

Many scholars of the civil rights movement are activists as well as academics. Perhaps because of this, we are more comfortable with the symbiotic relationship between the past and the present. There is an implicit assumption in many of our accounts, as in the memoirs of many civil rights veterans, that a deeper understanding of the movement's past will advance race relations and social equality in the present. And yet as much as we have explored the ways that the past can shape the present, civil rights historians have not been as critical in assessing the ways that the present has shaped our understanding of the past. Such an assessment must begin with an examination of movement memories and oral history.

Critics of oral history might argue that interviews magnify the influence of the present on historians' understanding of the past. I believe that we need not see this as a methodological shortcoming, but rather as an opportunity to explore the relationship between past and present that is nowhere more immediate than in the dialogue between historians and historical actors. If oral historians were scientists, we might set up an experiment designed to separate the influence of the present on interviewees' understandings of the past—a fission of memory from historical "reality." Such an experiment would require that historical actors chronicle events as they take place, writing a first draft of history that reflects their immediate reactions to these events and offers a chronology untainted by the passage of time. Then, the oral historian and the historical actors would conduct interviews in five- or ten-year intervals to determine the influence of subsequent events on the interviewees' memories of the past.

Though far from scientific, such an "experiment" has taken place in the oral histories and scholarship on the civil rights movement. Successive generations of historians have interviewed veteran activists, many of whom were fairly young when they participated in the civil rights struggle. Journalists who were covering the movement and college students working with Stanford University's Project South during the summer of 1965 conducted the first generation of interviews with civil rights activists. Subsequent oral history projects on the movement have included individual scholarly investigations by Sara Evans and Clayborne Carson in the 1970s, Charles Payne and Doug McAdam in the 1980s, and many others since the 1990s, including the fine essay about women in the Atlanta movement by Kathryn L. Nasstrom that appears in this volume. There have also been multi-interviewer projects run by Howard University, the Southern Oral History Program, the University of Southern Mississippi, and Duke University. Each generation of historians has asked different questions of these activists, but most of the interviews have touched on the roles of race, gender, and sexuality in the movement. By examining the shifting questions and answers of interviews on these topics, we can explore how events since the 1960s have "engendered" the memories of movement participants and the narratives that they have coauthored with historians.[2]

Questions about gender in the movement are especially pertinent in the scholarship about Mississippi. Segregation, racial prejudice, and state-sponsored violence were so oppressive in the Magnolia State that movement activists who worked there asked the rhetorical question: "Is this America?" The civil rights campaigns in Mississippi were first and foremost struggles for racial equality in a state and region where race had been the primary marker of oppression since the era of slavery. Yet hierarchies of gender and sexuality clearly buttressed the social structure of white supremacy in the Deep South. The architects of racial segregation had long argued that black and white southerners must be separated to protect the purity of white womanhood. In this way, white men used segregation to curtail the freedom of both African Americans and white women, giving themselves the power to govern and traverse both black and white social spaces.[3]

While the racial system in Mississippi strongly affected the gender identities of both blacks and whites, segregation's high walls proved especially confining for black men. For them, any transgression in the white world might lead to lynching for supposed sexual improprieties. When around whites, especially white women, black men had to cloak their sexuality and mask their manhood for fear of trespassing on the race and gender prerogatives of white men. The African American writer Ralph Ellison captured this dilemma in his novel *The Invisible Man*. In the face of racism, the novel's black male protagonist disappears from view altogether, hiding underground until a day that he can re-emerge and confront discrimination. Though black men, like Ellison's protagonist, often performed traditional "manly" roles within the home and the black community, the system of segregation forced them to hide their manhood from the public, white world, rendering them, in a powerful sense, invisible.[4]

When the courageous, unassuming field secretaries for SNCC arrived in Mississippi, they joined experienced local activists in a movement to tear down the walls of segregation and the architecture of white male supremacy. During the early 1960s, SNCC was an integrated, black-led organization. The field secretaries who fanned out through regions such as the Mississippi Delta were primarily young black men and women, idealistic in the belief that nonviolent organizing could move the people against white supremacy. As they worked in the movement, these organizers came face to face not only with violent white supremacy but also with the gender implications of the struggle for racial equality.

The best place to begin digging for firsthand accounts of gender dynamics in the movement is, of course, the archives. The SNCC papers are a virtual treasure trove of documents that chronicle everything from the number of cars and telephones used by the organization to the personal observations of field secretaries. One such personal observation, recorded by Charles McLaurin, reveals some of the gender issues that emerged early in the struggle. A native black Mississippian, McLaurin was inspired by SNCC staffer Bob Moses to join the organization's voter registration drive in the Delta during the summer of 1962. McLaurin began his campaign in Ruleville, Mississippi, a small Delta town where less than 2 percent of eligible African American adults could vote. After some hard work canvassing local neighborhoods, McLaurin convinced several older African American women to join him on the harrowing trip down to the Sunflower County courthouse to try to register. Tall white columns stood like daunting sentinels in front of the courthouse, guarding the franchise from black Mississippians as they had since the end of Reconstruction. As he waited outside for what would surely be a rejection of the women's petition to register to vote, McLaurin had a heartening thought. "The people are the true leaders," he realized. "We need only to move them; to show them. Then watch and learn." In the weeks that followed, McLaurin brought dozens of Ruleville residents—most of them women—down to the courthouse. Among them was a sharecropper named Fannie Lou Hamer, who became one of the most powerful advocates for the rights of women, minorities, and the poor during the 1960s. In McLaurin's later speeches, that first trip still shone brightly on the horizon of his memory. "I will always remember August 22," he said, "as the day I became a man."[5]

Charles McLaurin's reminiscences might seem strange at first. He himself did very little. He did not register to vote. He did not face the white registrar. The women did. Yet McLaurin found his strength that day by helping the women find theirs. He claimed his manhood by helping the women reclaim a bit of their dignity. Coming of age in Mississippi, where respect for black men was all too rare, McLaurin and other SNCC men looked back on their activism as a rite of passage into manhood. The question is *when* did the movement become such a ritual for black men? When did women begin to view their movement experience as a similar rite of passage? What can this tell us about how movement memories have changed over time in response to cultural shifts in the intervening years?[6]

The movement in Mississippi and especially the summer project of 1964 raised broad questions about the gender, racial, and sexual mores of the segregated South and the larger American society. During the summer project, hundreds of young white men and women lived and worked alongside black activists in an attempt to replace segregation with the "beloved community," a society based on equality, democracy, and a love that knew no racial boundaries. As they struggled to obtain an equal education and the right to vote for black Mississippians, these civil rights activists found that segregationists and liberal observers alike fixated on the sexual repercussions of the integrated campaign. For segregationists, it surely must have seemed that the "race mixing" apocalypse had arrived in 1964. The records of white Mississippi authorities that monitored and attempted to undermine the activities of movement activists remain largely untapped by civil rights scholars. Excavating such archival sources exposes the deeper social context in which the movement operated and reveals new evidence concerning gender relations in the movement.

From the very beginning of the summer project, Mississippi authorities sent informants to spy on the young civil rights activists. The governor had set up an investigative bureau known as the Mississippi State Sovereignty Commission in the late 1950s to "defend" the state from outside agitators and native activists. The election of staunch segregationist Ross Barnett to the governor's mansion of the Magnolia State ensured that the Sovereignty Commission would be well funded. By the summer of 1964, the agency had several paid informants in civil rights groups. Though civil rights activists suspected that they were being watched, they had little idea who among their ranks was an informant. With activists from SNCC, the Congress for Racial Equality (CORE), and the National Association for the Advancement of Colored People (NAACP), as well as countless volunteers, the organization that ran the summer project— the Council of Federated Organizations (COFO)—could not be expected to do a background check on everyone who offered to help. As a result, informants observed and participated in many of the movement activities starting with the first orientation meetings for the summer project, held in Oxford, Ohio.[7]

On a mission to gather damning information about the summer project, one such spy wrote secret memos back to the governor of Mississippi, warning of "communist infiltration" and interracial relationships in the ranks of the civil rights activists. "The white girls have been going around with Negro boys, and Negro girls are going with white boys. I have seen these integrated couples going into the dorms together for extended periods of time," one racy exposé revealed. Allegations of such taboo activities reveal more about the obsessions of Mississippi authorities than the reality of everyday life in Oxford. Yet the taboos against interracial relationships haunted the summer project.[8]

When civil rights volunteer Jo Ann Ooiman arrived by train from Oxford, Ohio, in Canton, Mississippi, where her part of the summer project began, the power of such racial and sexual taboos quickly became apparent. A white college student originally from Denver, Colorado, Ooiman had never been to Mississippi, and her introduction began with a barbecue at a local black minister's house. Just as Ooiman and the other volunteers began to dig into the heaping plates of food, police sirens brought the welcome party to a screeching halt. The sheriff hauled the volunteers down to the station, took their mug shots, and then played a taped speech from the district attorney, warning that "the women would be raped by blacks in town and the men would be beaten up." It was a welcome befitting the "closed society."[9]

The frenzied fear of interracial sex, whipped up by the segregationists, contributed to the sexually charged atmosphere of the summer. From the beginning, SNCC organizers warned volunteers to avoid interracial liaisons. Stokely Carmichael, a black SNCC staffer and the project director in the small Mississippi town of Greenwood, admonished white volunteers to be conscious of the history of white men taking sexual advantage of local black women. "As far as white girls with Negro boys," Carmichael said, "of course, none of that on the other side of town." Carmichael opposed all staff dating, feeling that it would only complicate matters during the summer, but he did not prohibit dating altogether. Given the close quarters of communal living arrangements, the stress and strain of daily organizing, and the young age of most movement volunteers and veterans, it is understandable that civil rights workers formed intimate relationships that summer.[10]

Liberated sexuality also represented a logical extension of SNCC's ideals (a truly free society or "beloved community"). The taboos against interracial sex made it that much more enticing. "For black men," historian Sara Evans writes, "sexual access to white women challenged the culture's ultimate symbol of their denied manhood." Writing in the 1970s, Evans based her work both on archival sources and oral history interviews. The interviews and analysis bear the clear imprint of the modern feminist movement. White women staffers and volunteers, who "had experienced a denial of their womanhood in failing to achieve . . . cheerleader standards," told Evans that sexual interest from black men was in many ways empowering. White men and black women also experienced the liberating power of love that summer. Due to the highly politicized nature of interracial sex, however, such relationships could both bring activists together and tear them apart. Activists found that the personal politics of interracial sex could damage the movement. Black women sometimes grew angry when black men dated white women, reinforcing American society's racist standards of beauty. On the other hand, white women may have felt trapped in a catch-22 of being labeled as racist if they declined black men's advances and opportunistic if they accepted. While complications often arose from interracial sex during the movement, these intimate relationships were born out of a faith in love (both platonic and romantic) and a hope that movement ideals were harbingers of a more egalitarian and open society. As one volunteer wrote in his journal at the time, the people in SNCC "already have the 'beloved community' and they rightly see the aim of the movement to be the inclusion of the whole of America into this community. . . . Our aim is indeed miscegenation, more profoundly so than they think."[11]

Though interracial relationships have gained much scholarly attention in the decades since the summer project, they were, in fact, relatively minor distractions from the real work of civil rights activism and organizing that took place during the summer of 1964. Most of the volunteers and veteran activists worked either canvassing door-to-door for voter registration or teaching in the Freedom Schools. The voter registration drive was an attempt to show the federal government (and the national Democratic party) that black Mississippians wanted to vote but were unable to register because of discriminatory laws and racist white registrars. Similarly, the Freedom Schools were set up to show that black children wanted equal access to educational opportunities that were denied them by poorly funded, segregated schools.[12]

According to Doug McAdam, a sociologist who interviewed and surveyed a large number of former volunteers in the early 1980s, gender was an important factor in determining job assignments during the summer. Though SNCC valued Freedom School teaching and voter registration work equally, volunteers had preconceived notions of the work they wanted to do, and some questioned the gender breakdown of work assignments. Speaking to McAdam nearly twenty years after the Mississippi summer project, a female volunteer recalled that she felt "shoved to the side" as a teacher, while male volunteers were "being macho men," facing violence out in the field. One male canvasser admitted to the sociologist that although teaching was important, "it wasn't the same kind of, if you want, macho adventurism that I was into." Based on these volunteer interviews and archived staff rosters, McAdam estimated that women were nearly twice as likely as men to be assigned to teaching, whereas men dominated the ranks of voter registration workers. In response to such assertions, one veteran activist told me in the 1990s that any such restrictions on female canvassing set up at the beginning of the summer had probably gone by the wayside by the end of the project when volunteers simply did whatever jobs needed to be done regardless of race or gender. "Our own ideas are [based on] equality," he said, "and what are we doing if we set up these kinds of rules?" Regardless of their assignments or their gender, all of the volunteers and staff members "put their bodies on the line." Jo Ann Ooiman's assignment in Canton, Mississippi, was teaching at a Freedom School where a bomb had exploded the week before the summer project started. Whether her willingness to take on the teaching assignment was "macho" or not, it was clearly brave.[13]

If volunteers, national civil rights leaders, and other "outside agitators" displayed bravery in journeying to Mississippi to challenge discrimination, what about the men and women from the Deep South who risked their jobs and homes, lives and loved ones to join these idealistic crusaders? "The depth of the involvement [for local folks] . . . nobody understands," Delta native and activist Tommie Jean Lunsford told me. "It's different when you're trying to hide from the police. You can't come to your house. You can't go to your parents' home. You can't visit them. You can't visit your friends, because you're being followed and your name is in the paper." In the late 1980s and early 1990s, scholars finally began to chronicle the courageous involvement of "local people" like Lunsford. Historians Charles Payne and John Dittmer found a very different story of gender relations when they talked with local black men and women. Far from male dominated, the local movement in Mississippi was, according to Payne, a "woman's war." As the black SNCC activist Charlie Cobb explained to an interviewer in the mid-1990s, "I've always thought that women have been the backbone of . . . Mississippi's movement." Corroborating this assessment, Payne's research led him to conclude that local African American women were more politically active, attended mass meetings in larger numbers, and attempted to register to vote more often than Mississippi men during the movement. Though most observers believe that women participated in disproportionately high numbers, few agree on why this was so. Payne offers a variety of explanations, including black women's faith and enthusiasm for the churches that often supported the movement and the possibility that black women may have seemed less threatening to white authorities than black men. [14]

Both of these factors may have facilitated women's participation in the movement, but it may also be instructive to examine the obstacles to men's involvement. Struggling to explain why it seemed so difficult to get local black men to join the movement, members of the mostly white volunteer staff for the summer project were struck by what they perceived as the inability of these men to stand up and fight racism. Segregation has "so smashed and whiplashed" the black community, one volunteer wrote in a letter home, "it makes boys . . . out of men. The men are often so pitifully weak—unable to decide anything." Another wrote of the "absolute castration of the Negro male," who "is trained to be nothing more than a child with his . . . sheepish expression and 'Yessir, yessir' to everything the white man says." Without a deep understanding of the long history of lynching and repression faced by these men or the skillful subterfuge required to survive in the Delta, the volunteers callously criticized the crushing fear that crippled some men's participation in the movement. [15]

Local black women had their own opinions on this issue. Annie Devine, an organizer from Canton, Mississippi, who later ran for Congress, said that she became active in the movement and politics because most men just would not run for office. "Negro men have been pushed around and hounded," she told an interviewer in 1965, so the black man "needs to be reassured that he is a man, and that when he does speak, you know, he'll be looked upon as a man, 'cause right now he's not, and he hasn't been. He's had no control over his woman; he's had no job to take care of her." Fannie Lou Hamer, who became the most eloquent spokesperson for the Mississippi movement after a brutal beating at the hands of local police officers, explained, "If they beat me almost to death in jail, what do you think would happen to my husband? You have to live in Mississippi as a Negro to understand why it's not more men involved than there is."[16]

Despite the obstacles to their participation, many local men rose to the challenge and joined the fight against white supremacy in Mississippi. Highlighting women's activism, civil rights scholars have rightly recognized the integral role that women played as the unsung heroes of the movement. But we must also acknowledge the immense courage of local men who, like local women activists, were often overlooked in contemporary accounts that focused on articulate national leaders and highly educated volunteers. Ridiculed as "outside agitators" by local white supremacists, national civil rights leaders and activists who came into Mississippi during the early 1960s could fly home once campaigns ended. Local men joined the struggle knowing that they would have to deal with the white backlash long after others left.

One such local black hero was C. O. Chinn. Volunteers would have received no welcome at all when they arrived in Canton if not for men like Chinn, who sacrificed everything for the movement. "He was a powerful man," wrote one movement veteran, "known as 'badass C. O. Chinn' to the Negroes and whites alike. All of the Negroes respected him for standing up and being a man. Most of the whites feared him." Within a week of joining the movement in 1963, Chinn lost his business, but he continued to campaign for the right to vote, and his personal loss only made him a more passionate advocate of the civil rights movement. He spoke at mass meetings and organized a local boycott against stores owned by segregationists. Canton police arrested Chinn for trying to organize other local blacks—he was "threatening" them, according to white authorities—making sure that they supported the boycott. But Chinn's real crime was simply movement activism. He was helping SNCC staff prepare for Freedom Summer. At the start of the summer, Chinn was working on the chain gang as a prisoner of the Canton jail. Bone tired at the end of a scorching summer day on the work gang, Chinn would probably have agreed with another local black activist, who observed that in Mississippi, the white man "is our friend, as long as we are 'boys.' But when we act as if we are 'mens,' then we're not his friends."[17]

Working alongside these black activists, white women in the movement found their own voice, and they began to see parallels between racism and sexism. Not long after the summer, two stalwart white movement veterans named Casey Hayden and Mary King coauthored a paper for a SNCC staff meeting late in 1964 on the position of women in the organization and the broader society. "The average white person finds it difficult to understand why the Negro resents being called 'boy,'" the women wrote anonymously, "because the average white person doesn't realize that he assumes he is superior. . . . So too the average SNCC worker finds it difficult to discuss the woman problem because of the assumption of male superiority." Such sentiment had evidently been brewing since the summer project. In July 1964 a spy for Mississippi authorities sent a secret memo to the governor, noting, "The 'strong' females on the permanent office staff have told me earlier of a revolution among females, 'the women's fight for equality with men.' . . . I have watched it gain momentum over the past months. There are many male supporters of this new thing." Though Hayden and King's paper on sexism inspired Carmichael's infamous quip that "the position of women in SNCC is prone," there were clearly men in the organization who encouraged such nascent feminism. Hayden and King's position paper is now seen as an influential document in the history of women's liberation, because it reveals the origins of the modern feminist movement in the struggle for civil rights.[18]

The historians who originally articulated this thesis, Sara Evans chief among them, have come under fire from women and men in the movement as well as other scholars. At a conference on the movement in the late 1980s, Joyce Ladner was one of several black SNCC veterans who were critical of the early feminist scholarship on gender relations in the movement. Ladner believed that Evans's work, in particular, was "total rubbish" and "revisionist to the core." To many of the SNCC veterans, it seemed that Evans had focused too much on gender tension in SNCC and not enough on SNCC's supportive environment that enabled women on staff to voice an emerging feminist consciousness. Ladner felt that this flawed analysis was due, in part, to the fact that Evans "didn't even interview the right people." In the mid-1990s, historian Belinda Robnett picked up this same point, arguing that a focus on interviews with white women and volunteers in SNCC had distorted earlier accounts of gender in the movement. Robnett found that the black women she interviewed had greater opportunities for leadership roles and fewer problems with sexism than white women on the SNCC staff. My own interviews with black women veterans of SNCC in the late 1990s and early 2000s bore this out as well. Thinking back on her time with SNCC in Mississippi, Martha Prescod Norman told me, "I never felt [there was] any position or role or job or task that I was kept from doing on the basis of my sex." In fact, she remembered positive "pressure from the men in SNCC to be brave, to be smart, to be intellectual, to be all of the things that are stereotypically not female." Tommie Jean Lunsford was just a teenager from rural Mississippi when she was swept up into the movement. And she too remembers the empowering and supportive environment that she encountered working alongside women and men of SNCC.[19]

What are we to make of this conflicting testimony? On the one hand, we have a position paper on women in the movement written in the 1960s and interviews with women, most of them white, in the 1970s suggesting that sexism did plague civil rights organizations. On the other hand, we have later interviews with SNCC women, most of them black, who argue that they faced very little sexism. Perhaps, as Belinda Robnett suggests, these contradictions can simply be explained by the race of the interviewees—the different backgrounds and experiences of black and white women. In a black-led organization like SNCC that was struggling for racial equality, it is not surprising that African American women found more opportunities for leadership than white women. Even after the feminist movement raised black women's consciousness of sexism in both civil rights organizations and the larger society, such prejudices may have paled in comparison to the racism that they faced. White women, on the other hand, may have been more likely to remember their feminist epiphanies as having been equally important as their new awareness of racism, especially when being interviewed by Sara Evans, Doug McAdam, or other white scholars who were trying to understand the relationship between the civil rights and feminist movements.[20]

While race is certainly crucial to understanding these conflicting movement memories, I think that there is something else going on here as well. There has been an evolution of the stories and memories of activists in SNCC, including those who authored the position paper in 1964 and those who initially spoke with Evans in the 1970s, about chauvinism and a growing feminist consciousness in the movement. Several of these women now emphasize different facets of their movement experiences. Speaking to Robnett in 1990, Hayden reevaluated her earlier position paper on the movement, saying, "I had a really privileged status. I didn't have any real argument about my place in SNCC." Along with other women who were active in SNCC, she now emphasizes, "the great lifting of sex role expectations and the freedom that ensued" from her movement activism.[21]

Hayden's revisions of her position paper and early interviews speak to the evolutionary nature of memory and historical narrative. Like many movement veterans, Hayden has been interviewed countless times over the years, and these interviews represent a dialogue with the written history and the historical trends of her times. These conversations between the historians and historical actors do not take place in a vacuum; they are shaped by the events of intervening years. Thus, Hayden's early memories and Evans's account of the movement in the wake of women's liberation reflected an emerging feminist consciousness that highlighted and analyzed the role of gender in the movement in ways that might have seemed totally foreign to activists in the 1950s or early 1960s. In subsequent years, Hayden and others revised their stories, perhaps because they were fearful that feminist critiques of civil rights groups from the 1960s and 1970s would contribute to a negative revisionism in historical accounts of the movement.

Recent accounts of the movement have similarly been influenced by new intellectual currents and contemporary events. Scholarly works and interviews of the 1980s and '90s bear the clear imprint of womanist analysis articulated by feminists of color over the last two decades. As movement biographer Cynthia Griggs Fleming emphatically pointed out in her book on the life of SNCC activist Ruby Doris Smith Robinson, "Being an oppressed *black* woman has always been quite different from being an oppressed woman in American society." While womanist scholars discussed the unique confluence of racism and sexism facing women of color, they also theorized about the different support networks and strategies that these women harnessed to overcome oppression. Belinda Robnett's brilliant insights about the importance of black women organizers as "bridge leaders" connecting community activists to the predominantly male national civil rights leadership clearly emerged from this intellectual inquiry. The womanist critique of second-wave feminism's racial blind spot has not simply influenced scholars, however; it has also led white SNCC veterans like Casey Hayden to reevaluate their own experiences in the movement, emphasizing the nurturing and familial relationships in SNCC as well as the strong leadership role of black women whose experience with sexism was different from their own.[22]

At the same time that a womanist critique of early feminist scholarship influenced accounts of black and white women in the movement, the rise of the men's movement and the Million Man March may have also reshaped understandings of movement masculinity. In the 1990s the Promise Keepers and Nation of Islam called for white and black men to accept the responsibility of leadership in their homes and communities, harkening back to very traditional notions of patriarchy and manhood. In particular, black men were called on to protect and provide for women and their families in ways that they had been unable to under the oppressive conditions of slavery or segregation. Though the traditional gender ideologies of these men's movements seemed diametrically opposed to the ideas espoused by womanist scholars, the perceived crisis of masculinity in the 1990s that inspired events like the Million Man March may have also led veteran activists and scholars to reevaluate the role of men in the movement. For instance, Casey Hayden told one interviewer in the early 1990s that the civil rights movement "was really a coming to the fore of Black men—young Black men . . . [because] Black women had always been strong in the local community."[23]

In fact, visions of manhood and men's roles in the movement have evolved in much the same way that women's accounts have, reflecting contemporary gender issues. A quick glance at the story of one oral historian of the movement and a few of his interviews illustrates this point. Robert Wright first traveled to Mississippi with SNCC in the summer of 1963. After graduating from Harvard in 1965, he continued his involvement in the movement and eventually was interviewed and also signed on as an interviewer for the Civil Rights Documentation Project. In his own 1968 oral history interview, Wright tried to explain the complex relationship between nonviolent activism and manhood at a time when many believed that Black Power necessitated taking a violent stance. "What do you feel this does to your manhood," an interviewer asked Wright, "when you sit there and you watch black women beaten and you do nothing?" Recalling a time when violent resistance was not an imperative for manhood, Wright patiently explained that given the repression in Mississippi in 1963 and 1964, nonviolent protest was "a really militant thing to do, to be able to just be a man and not bow down and scratch your head." Tumultuous change in the movement and the wider society had wrought such a transformation in gender identity and racial consciousness by 1968 that it was difficult for many who had not participated in the southern movement to look back on nonviolent activism as a "manly" struggle against racism. The writings of Malcolm X, Eldridge Cleaver, and others had coded such nonviolent resistance as "feminine," contrasting it with the more "masculine" strategy of protecting black women and black communities by any means necessary. By the late 1960s then, militant manhood had come to mean almost exclusively a willingness to support armed self-defense.[24]

Wright's own interviews with movement activists in the late 1960s and early 1970s reveal similar shifts in gender identity and consciousness. In 1970 Wright interviewed Charles Scattergood, a white summer volunteer who worked with Charles McLaurin in Sunflower County and stayed in the Delta until 1965. In hindsight, Scattergood told Wright that tension on the local project was due, in part, to "male chauvinism." When Wright observed that Scattergood seemed "hung up" on chauvinism and women's liberation, the former volunteer explained, "I saw racism spreading all over Mississippi. But I also saw male chauvinism spreading out pretty bad too. . . . I think that women have a definite place in the movement, you know—not just as secretaries either—as leaders. . . . If women stand up, then maybe men won't have to be in this protective bag so much. And that's almost fifty percent of what's happening in Mississippi." From the vantage point of 1970, Scattergood and Wright could wrestle with connections between chauvinism and racism. They understood that white Mississippians had rationalized violence against the movement as a chivalrous duty to "protect" white women from integration and that similar impulses in SNCC ironically may have restricted the role of women at the same time that the organization sought to achieve egalitarian ideals. But this understanding evolved over time, becoming clear long after the summer project ended.[25]

Just as memories of movement gender dynamics have evolved, so too have understandings of the relationship between race and sexuality. The summer volunteer who proudly proclaimed that miscegenation was the ultimate goal of the movement in 1964 was voicing a radical position for both the black and white communities given the taboo against interracial relationships at the time. SNCC veteran Chuck McDew understood this only too well when he married a white woman that same year. Though McDew had endured beatings and extensive jail time for his commitment to racial uplift, his interracial relationship was still suspect in some movement circles. When Malcolm X criticized McDew's marriage, the SNCC field secretary told the Muslim leader, "I've paid some heavy dues . . . [and] nobody else will tell me who I will love." McDew ultimately won Malcolm's blessing, but as black nationalism eclipsed integrationism, interracial relationships in the movement lost their revolutionary character and became vilified as vestiges of an outdated, assimilationist ideology. This was, in part, a response to increasing mainstream acceptance of interracial relationships that grew gradually from the 1970s through the 1990s. By the 1990s movement veterans viewed such mainstream acceptance of interracial relationships with only cautious optimism, understanding earlier than most Americans what historian Renee C. Romano has argued: "The notion that 'love is the answer' serves to mask existing inequalities, not to undo remaining racial hierarchies." Sex and love were clearly important parts of SNCC's beloved community, but they were not the primary objectives of the organization or the movement.[26]

The tensions between the egalitarian ideal in SNCC and the reality of gender relations in 1964 eventually led women (and some men) in the movement to challenge sexism. Feminism, according to historian Belinda Robnett, "did not evolve from the sexist treatment within SNCC," but from the organization's liberating philosophy and open structure that fostered challenges to authority. The structure of the organization, which was founded on principles of participatory democracy, gave both men and women a voice in decisions. In this, SNCC was far more progressive than other movement organizations and most other parts of American society in 1964. Yet SNCC also reflected the larger society's gender bias in work assignments and formal leadership. As Sara Evans originally argued, the women in SNCC experienced both liberation and discrimination. To acknowledge this paradox is not to single out the organization or its male leaders for special criticism; it merely captures the historical reality of 1964. Despite the pervasiveness and intractability of race and gender norms in America during the mid-1960s, the men and women of SNCC attempted to fashion an organization and a movement in which all people could gain personal and political power.[27]

Memories and histories of SNCC activism in Mississippi have evolved in a parallel circuit with one another, reflecting shifts in American society and culture that have taken place in the years since the movement. The SNCC papers and other archival sources reveal some of the gender dynamics that influenced the course of the movement in Mississippi, but for the most part, they focus on the roles of race and poverty in limiting the progress of black Mississippians and civil rights activism. Interviews with activists and histories of the Mississippi movement from the 1970s and early 1980s reflect the influence of the struggles for women's rights and Black Power that emerged from the civil rights movement. It is not surprising then that gender analysis moved to center stage in these accounts, and this was an important innovation in civil rights scholarship, since much of the "master narrative" of the movement had previously downplayed the importance of women's roles. In the early 1990s, a new wave of scholarship focused on local people, who played roles just as important as national leaders. This too revised our understanding of gender in the movement, highlighting the power of local women. Finally, the Million Man March and other consciousness-raising efforts by men in the mid-1990s have led scholars to investigate the role of masculinity in the struggle for civil rights and the influence of the movement on American conceptions of manhood. Movement history, like movement memory, is a dynamic understanding of the past. This is not a progression toward some higher Truth; it is a dialogue between historians and historical actors, between scholarship and activism, between the past and present that keeps us engaged in the struggles for civil rights and social justice today.

Notes

1. In his memoirs, cowritten with Ekwueme Michael Thelwell, Carmichael admitted that he didn't even remember making the joke until Cleve Sellers reminded him about it the next day. Clearly tired of answering questions about a comment that he felt was taken out of context, Carmichael simply acknowledged: "I said it, period." Stokely Carmichael with Ekwueme Michael Thelwell, *Ready for Revolution: The Life and Struggles of Stokely Carmichael (Kwame Ture)* (New York: Scribner, 2003), 431–34.

2. For published collections of oral history interviews from the movement, see Howell Raines, *My Soul Is Rested: The Story of the Civil Rights Movement in the Deep South* (New York: Penguin Books, 1977); Henry Hampton, Steven Fayer, and Sarah Flynn, *Voices of Freedom: An Oral History of the Civil Rights Movement from the 1950s through the 1980s* (New York: Bantam Books, 1990); and Stanford University's *Project South Oral History Collection* (Glen Rock, N.J.: Microfilming Corporation of America, 1975). Archival collections of interviews are scattered across the country, but some of the best collections are the Ralph J. Bunche Oral History Collection at Howard University, the Mississippi Oral History Program at the University of Southern Mississippi, the Southern Oral History Program Collection at the University of North Carolina, and the Behind the Veil Collection at Duke University.

3. "Mississippi: Is This America?" from Clayborne Carson, David J. Garrow, et al., *The Eyes on the Prize Civil Rights Reader* (New York: Penguin Books, 1991), 166. See Lillian Smith, *Killers of the Dream* (1949; repr., New York: W. W. Norton, 1961) for a contemporary southerner's critique of segregation that highlights issues of sex and gender. See also John Dollard, *Caste and Class in a Southern Town* (New York: Harper, 1949), and Neil R. McMillen, *Dark Journey: Black Mississippians in the Age of Jim Crow* (Urbana: University of Illinois Press, 1989), for discussions of segregation in Mississippi. For broader historical analysis of segregation, see Grace Elizabeth Hale, *Making Whiteness: The Culture of Segregation in the South, 1890–1940* (New York: Pantheon Books, 1998), and Glenda Gilmore, *Gender and Jim Crow: Women and the Politics of White Supremacy*

in North Carolina, 1896–1920 (Chapel Hill: University of North Carolina Press, 1996).

4. Ralph Ellison, *The Invisible Man* (New York: Random House, 1952).

5. Voter registration tallies compiled for Mississippi counties in the "Mississippi Handbook for Political Programs," published by Council of Federated Organizations (COFO), 1964. SNCC Papers (on microfilm), Subgroup A, Series XV, Number 123. Hereafter cited as SNCC Papers A-XV-123. McLaurin first described his experiences to the SNCC staff (August 18, 1962–August 31, 1963) in the SNCC Papers A-IV-238. Later recollections come from a speech entitled "To Overcome Fear" (no date) in the SNCC Papers A-XV-207. For another account of this trip to the courthouse, see Tracy Sugarman, *Stranger at the Gates: A Summer in Mississippi* (New York: Hill and Wang, 1966), 211–13.

6. Though there is no date on McLaurin's speech recalling this trip to the courthouse, we can speculate from the language that it was the mid-1960s, after Malcolm X's rhetoric of claiming manhood had gained wide credence within the movement. In recent interviews, this first trip to the courthouse continues to hold a prominent place in Charles McLaurin's memory, though he no longer discusses it specifically as a rite of passage into manhood. McLaurin, interview by author and the students of the Sunflower County Freedom Project, 1999.

7. The main collection of papers from the Mississippi State Sovereignty Commission is held in a searchable computer database at the State Department of Archives and History in Jackson, Mississippi. Many sensitive documents were purged or censored from this central collection before they were released to the public, but additional Sovereignty Commission reports can be found in the personal papers of Mississippi governors from the 1960s. For an analysis of the Sovereignty Commission, see Yasuhiro Katagiri, *The Mississippi State Sovereignty Commission* (Jackson: University of Mississippi Press, 2001).

8. Oxford orientation observations from the Report of Sovereignty Commission Operator number 79 to Governor Johnson, June 26, 1964, Governor Paul Johnson Family Papers, University of Southern Mississippi Special Collections, Box 35, Folder 10.

9. For a detailed written account of this episode see Jo Ann Ooiman Robinson's diary entry for June 29, 1964, in the Robinson Papers, State Historical Society of Wisconsin, Box 2, File 1; Jo Ann Ooiman Robinson, interview by author, 1999; Ron Grele, interview by Karen Duncanwood, Oral History Research Center, Special Collections, Butler Library, Columbia University, 1994, 23–24; and Elizabeth Sutherland, *Letters From Mississippi* (New York: McGraw-Hill, 1965), 37–38.

10. As a psychiatrist for movement participants in the South, Alvin Poussaint was the first to analyze gender and sexual tensions. See Poussaint, "The Stresses

of the White Female Worker in the Civil Rights Movement in the South," *American Journal of Psychiatry* 163, no. 4 (October 1966): 401–7. Carmichael quoted in Sally Belfrage, *Freedom Summer* (1965; repr., Charlottesville: University of Virginia Press, 1990), 42. Carmichael sarcastically dubs the chapter in his memoirs about Freedom Summer "Ten Dollars a Day and All the Sex You Can Handle." In fact, he says that sex was only an issue for the Mississippi police and the white reporters who covered the SNCC after the summer ended. Carmichael and Thelwell, *Ready for Revolution*, 368, 427.

11. Sara Evans, *Personal Politics: The Roots of Women's Liberation in the Civil Rights Movement and the New Left* (New York: Vintage Books, 1979), 79–81, 88. Volunteer's journal quoted in Doug McAdam, *Freedom Summer* (New York: Oxford University Press, 1988), 137. Writing in the 1980s, McAdam argued that the liberated sexuality experienced during Freedom Summer may have been an inchoate expression of the idea of free love that found credence in the counterculture of the late 1960s.

12. For an explanation of the ideas behind the freedom vote and the Freedom Schools, see Clayborne Carson, *In Struggle: SNCC and the Black Awakening of the 1960s* (Cambridge, Mass.: Harvard University Press, 1981).

13. McAdam, *Freedom Summer*, 108–13. Ed King, interview by author, 1999. Carmichael and Thelwell, *Ready for Revolution*, 388. At the beginning of the summer, SNCC organizers did make strategic placement decisions. It appears that they originally kept some volunteers from doing voter registration work in the extremely dangerous counties and restricted white women's roles in the field for fear that their presence would provoke more hostility from local whites, but as the summer progressed, women did work in voter registration even in tough rural counties, and those who worked as teachers also risked violence merely by working in the movement. Jo Ann Ooiman Robinson, interview by author, 1999.

14. Tommie Jean Lunsford, interview by author, 2000; John Dittmer, *Local People: The Struggle for Civil Rights in Mississippi* (Chicago: University of Illinois Press, 1995). For a thorough examination of the question of local women's involvement in Mississippi, see Charles Payne, *I've Got the Light of Freedom: The Organizing Tradition and the Mississippi Freedom Struggle* (Berkeley: University of California Press, 1995), 265–83. See also Vicki L. Crawford et al., eds., *Women in the Civil Rights Movement: Trailblazers and Torchbearers, 1941–1965* (Brooklyn, N.Y.: Carlson, 1990); and Charlie Cobb, interview by John Rachal, University of Southern Mississippi—Mississippi Oral History Program Collection, Volume 668, 1996, 17.

15. Sutherland, *Letters from Mississippi*, 60–61.

16. Interviews with local women are included in Stanford University's Project South Oral History Collection [PSOHC]. See interviews with Annie Devine (Mis-

sissippi Freedom Democratic Party [MFDP] Card 4, Interview #488), 20–21, and Hamer, PSOHC Interview (MFDP Card 16, Interview #491), 17. Perhaps these 1965 interviews with Devine and Hamer reflect the influence of the Moynihan Report, released that summer. The report argued that unemployment, racism, and a lack of male role models hurt minority men. Controversial even at the time of its release, the report has been blasted by scholars and applauded by conservative politicians. For more on this, see Lee Rainwater and William L. Yancey, *The Moynihan Report and the Politics of Controversy* (Cambridge, Mass.: MIT Press, 1967); and Patricia Hill Collins, "A Comparison of Two Works on Black Family Life," *Signs* 14, no. 4 (Summer 1989): 875–84.

17. Chinn's role in the Canton movement discussed by Anne Moody, *Coming of Age in Mississippi* (1968; repr., New York: Bantam Doubleday, 1976), 303–83, and by Jo Ann Ooiman Robinson in her interview by author. Both Chinn and his son withstood jail and beatings for their participation in the movement. See Canton staff lists and incident reports in the CORE papers, SHSW, Box 15, File 2. See also Sovereignty Commission files on Chinn: 9-31-1-41-1-1-1, 2-24-3-42-1-1-1, 2-24-2-11-2-1-1, and 2-112-2-2-1-1-1. State Department of Archives and History in Jackson, Mississippi. Final quote comes from a PSOHC interview of an anonymous black man from Tibbee, Mississippi (MFDP Card 18, Interview #164), 1–2.

18. Original of the SNCC Position Paper housed at the Martin Luther King Jr. Center for Nonviolent Social Change, SNCC Papers, Subgroup A, Series 5 Box 29, File "Staff Position Papers," A-VI-25. Quotation from the Sovereignty Commission spy comes from the Report of Operator #79 (Jackson, Mississippi), July 3, 1964, in Governor Johnson's Papers, University of Southern Mississippi Special Collections, Box 136, Folder 1. Sara Evans analyzed this document in *Personal Politics*, 87. See also Mary Aiken Rothschild, *A Case of Black and White: Northern Volunteers and the Southern Freedom Summers* (Westport, Conn.: Greenwood Press, 1982). Hayden and King would later argue that Carmichael was supportive of their position and that the joke was more an expression of his frustration with interracial sex during Freedom Summer. For more on this see Belinda Robnett, *How Long? How Long?* (New York: Oxford University Press, 1997), 120; and Mary King, *Freedom Song: A Personal Story of the 1960s Civil Rights Movement* (New York: Morrow, 1987), 452.

19. Ladner quoted in Cheryl Greenberg, ed., *A Circle of Trust: Remembering SNCC* (New Brunswick, N.J.: Rutgers University Press, 1998), 144. Robnett, *How Long? How Long?* 9–10, 117–21. See also Cynthia Washington, "We Started from Different Ends of the Spectrum," *Southern Exposure* 4, no. 4:14–15; and King, *Freedom Song*, 459. Martha Prescod Norman and the Reverend Tommie Jean Lunsford, interviews by author, 2000.

20. There were black women, Ella Baker and Septima Clark, in particular, who also acknowledged sexism in the wider movement, especially in the Southern Christian Leadership Conference. For more on this, see Bettye Collier-Thomas and V. P. Franklin, eds., *Sisters in the Struggle: African American Women in the Civil Rights–Black Power Movement* (New York: New York University Press, 2001); and Peter Ling, "Gender and Generation: Manhood at the Southern Christian Leadership Conference," in *Gender in the Civil Rights Movement*, ed. Peter Ling and Sharon Monteith (New York: Garland Publishing, 1999), 101–29.

21. For Hayden's comments, see Robnett, *How Long? How Long?* 119. See also King, *Freedom Song*, 459, 471.

22. Cynthia Griggs Fleming, *Soon We Will Not Cry: The Liberation of Ruby Doris Smith Robinson* (Lanham, Md.: Rowan and Littlefield, 1998), 118. In 2000, Hayden discussed some of these influences when she talked about her SNCC experience in new terms: "I think of it now as womanist, a term I've borrowed from my black women friends." Constance Curry, et al., *Deep in Our Hearts: Nine White Women in the Freedom Movement* (Athens: University of Georgia Press, 2000), 351.

23. The Hayden quote on men in the movement comes from Robnett, *How Long? How Long?* 118. For more on the Million Man March, see Christopher Booker, *"I Will Wear No Chain!": A Social History of African American Males* (Westport, Conn.: Praeger, 2000), 205–7, 220–23; and Haki R. Madhubuti and Maulana Karenga, eds., *Million Man March/Day of Absence: A Commemorative Anthology* (Chicago, Ill.: Third World Press, 1996).

24. Robert Wright, interview by John Button, Howard University Civil Rights Documentation Project, 1968, 22–23. Wright's interviews are an invaluable resource on the movement in Mississippi. See Malcolm X and Alex Haley, *The Autobiography of Malcolm X* (New York: Ballantine Books, 1965), 221, 226–27; Eldridge Cleaver, *Soul on Ice* (New York: Dell, 1968), 152–53, 165–75; and Huey Newton, *Revolutionary Suicide* (New York: Harcourt Brace Jovanovich, 1973), 24–54.

25. Charles Scattergood, interview by Robert Wright, Howard CRDP #576, 1970, 23–24, 54–56.

26. Renee C. Romano, *Race Mixing: Black-White Marriage in Postwar America* (Cambridge, Mass.: Harvard University Press, 2003), 228–29, 246, 291.

27. Robnett, *How Long? How Long?* 119. Evans, *Personal Politics*, 24–25. For a discussion of how the structure of the SNCC facilitated women's participation, see Payne, *I've Got the Light of Freedom*, 268.

PART FOUR

DEPLOYING MEMORY

Whether for strategic political reasons, self-aggrandizement, or a sincere sense of kinship with the movement, many engaged in political struggle since the 1960s have compared their own efforts to those undertaken during the movement. The desire to do so, as R. A. R. Edwards explains in her chapter on the Deaf Rights movement at Gallaudet, is easy to understand. Using civil rights rhetoric allows groups "to tap powerfully into a great wellspring of history, memory, equity, and justice." Using civil rights memory can allow other groups to more easily present themselves in sympathetic terms as citizens who are being denied full political rights by an oppressive system. Yet the three essays in this section raise the question of what complexities are lost in order to make these analogies possible, and what version of the movement other political groups tend to invoke.

Edwards's article on the 1999 Deaf President Now (DPN) strike at Gallaudet University examines the ways in which deaf students deployed civil rights rhetoric and symbols in their fight to force the university to hire a deaf president. Drawing a comparison between their own fight and the civil rights struggle helped deaf students forge a new understanding of themselves as an oppressed group instead of as individuals suffering from medical problems and had some impact on the ways in which the general public thought about disability issues. By highlighting the injustice of public institutions that were inaccessible, disability rights activists helped force passage of the Americans with Disabilities Act (ADA). Edwards argues that civil rights rhetoric offers more to the disability rights movement than the alternative rhetoric of identity politics, which celebrates a distinctive deaf (or disabled) culture. Not only do few hearing or able-bodied people take seriously the argument that a disability can be positive and should be claimed with pride, but some disabled have trouble relating to such an argument themselves. Yet Edwards raises a crucial question of whether a civil rights approach can work if the disadvantage people face is perceived to be curable. The creation of new technologies that can help some deaf people hear has helped reinforce the view that what needs to be fixed is the disabled themselves (through medical advances) rather than a society that favors able-bodied, hearing people. Still, Edwards finds that civil rights rhetoric, even with its limitations, offers the disabled the best hope of convincing others that social and political change is required to enable the disabled to live freely and equally in the United States.

In his chapter, David John Marley also grapples with the question of how effectively a group can transform the public image of itself by drawing on civil rights rhetoric. His essay on the Christian Right since the 1980s demonstrates how Christian Right groups have turned to the language of the civil rights movement in order to describe themselves as an oppressed minority in a world they perceive as increasingly secular. Like blacks forced to the back of the bus, evangelical Christians suffered from religious bigotry, leaders like Pat Robertson claimed. For Ralph Reed of the Christian Coalition and Randall Terry of Operation Rescue, the movement provided not only a model for civil disobedience but a legitimating language for their own battles. Yet the American public did not necessarily see figures like Randall Terry in the same light as Martin Luther King Jr., and many refused to accept the Christian Right's claim to be an oppressed minority akin to blacks. Even so, this chapter makes clear that the historical memory of the civil rights movement has taken on a political life of its own, even appealing to groups who would not have supported the goal of black civil rights in the 1960s.

The section concludes with Sarah Vowell's short humorous piece about the desire so many Americans seem to feel to compare themselves to civil rights icon Rosa Parks. By claiming a kinship with Parks, contemporary Americans seek to transform their own challenge to the status quo—whether that be fighting laws barring lap dancing or standing up to the government's dairy pricing system—into a principled fight for democratic ideals against oppressive institutions. Although the tone of Vowell's essay is light, the phenomenon she points to is real and serious, since these problematic analogies simultaneously hold Rosa Parks up as a national icon while devaluing the actions she actually took in her own fight against oppression.

R. A. R. EDWARDS

Deaf Rights, Civil Rights

The Gallaudet "Deaf President Now" Strike and

Historical Memory of the Civil Rights Movement

For college students across the country, the month of March typically conjures up visions of hedonistic romps on the beaches of Daytona or perhaps Cancun in the annual ritual of spring break. But March 1988 found students at the world's only liberal arts college for the deaf, Gallaudet University, in Washington, D.C., engaged in a very different kind of ritual, one with far deeper historical roots: nonviolent civil disobedience. March 6–13, 1988, was, in the words of strike chronicler Jack Gannon, the week the world heard Gallaudet, as students, faculty, staff, and alumni united in protests that closed the university down in an event that became known as the Deaf President Now (DPN) strike.[1]

The strike was triggered by the selection of a hearing woman with no knowledge of sign language, Elizabeth Zinser, as the seventh president of the university. She was elevated out of a pool of three finalists that included two deaf candidates.[2] Expectations on campus had been high that Gallaudet would finally welcome its first deaf president in its 124-year history. The announcement that Zinser had received the position provoked first anger and then protest on campus.

Participants themselves framed the protest as a civil rights struggle and the mass media covered it from that point of view. As early as March 9, 1988, the *New York Times* described events as follows: "At campus rallies throughout the day . . . protesters repeatedly cited the appointment last weekend as symbolic of the 'oppression' that they contended is often experienced by the nation's deaf people. . . . But (protesters) said their concerns were larger than the appointment of the school's president. The message was that, like the civil rights movement and the women's movement, theirs is a cause for reform."[3] While the reporter still signaled a bit of his own skepticism by referring to the oppression of the deaf in quotation marks, he largely accepted the protesters portrayal of their struggle as being akin to the earlier struggles of African Americans and women. Deaf activists quoted in the article reinforced this view. One Gallaudet student thus declared, "I'm not going to let my deaf rights get hurt. I've waited too long, this is our time," and Gary Olsen, the executive director of the National Association of the Deaf, remarked, "The school educates the deaf to lead, then won't give deaf people a chance to lead. We're tired of oppression and we're going to fight this all the way."[4] The student protesters, as well as their off-campus supporters from across the country, demanded their rights and decried their oppression, which they did not put in quotation marks. Their oppression was real, as was the need to fight to secure deaf rights.

As the week wore on, protesters made the connection between their struggle and earlier civil rights activism still more explicit. In a statement that was widely publicized, from the *New York Times* to *Time* magazine, Gallaudet graduate student Kathy Karcher declared, "It's our Selma. We're going to keep this up until we win."[5] When student protesters and their supporters marched on the Capitol, they did so behind a huge banner that proclaimed, "WE STILL HAVE A DREAM!" And when they arrived, a congressman greeted the crowd warmly with, "If this is your march on Selma, I want to congratulate you on your successful arrival."[6] Political cartoonist Mike Keefe also picked up on this civil rights rhetoric, producing a cartoon picturing a Gallaudet student signing, "We shall overcome."

Using the rhetoric of the civil rights movement allowed the students to tap powerfully into a great wellspring of history, memory, equity, and justice. Portraying their cause as one in which oppression by the hearing world rather than physical disability was the central issue allowed students to make the comparison to the civil rights movement in the first place.

WE   SHALL   OVERCOME.

This 1998 cartoon appeared in the *Denver Post* during the Gallaudet University Deaf President Now (DPN) strike. Depicting a figure signing "We shall overcome," the cartoon demonstrates the close affinity between DPN and the earlier civil rights movement of the 1960s. (Courtesy of Mike Keefe)

Civil rights protesters, from bus boycotts to lunch counter sit-ins, had demanded full citizenship rights for Americans of all colors. The Gallaudet protesters made their cause about claiming their full rights as citizens, too. Theirs was a fight against oppression and prejudice, and the invocation of civil rights rhetoric demonstrated as much. So did press coverage that emphasized the justness of the students' cause more than their hearing loss. News coverage, according to some observers, tended to portray the students as "healthy, bright, articulate, and attractive young people for whom their disability was secondary."[7] Indeed, such a characterization made possible the observation of then presidential candidate Jesse Jackson, who declared, "The problem is not that the students do not hear. The problem is that the hearing world does not listen."[8]

Protesters received unexpected help in making the concerns at stake here apparent even to a formerly inattentive hearing public, one largely unaware of deaf issues. When the chair of the Gallaudet board of trustees, Jane Spilman, was widely reported to have stated, "The deaf are not ready to function in a hearing world," the paternalism at work in the deaf world could not have been made more obvious.[9] Predictably, Gallaudet students and faculty alike responded angrily. Psychology professor Allan Sussmann spoke out against what he called "the plantation mentality" at Gallaudet, a place where most positions of power were in the hands of the hearing.[10] Perhaps in keeping with his description of the situation at Gallaudet, pointed placards went up on campus: "WE DON'T NEED A WET NURSE, MOMMY SPILMAN."[11] A Gallaudet senior, R. G. Gentry, brought together both ends of the rhetoric, the attack on paternalism in deaf institutions and the precedent of previous civil rights movements, in a *Washington Post* editorial: "Many whites were not ready for the *Brown vs. Board of Education* ruling and the wave of desegregation that followed, but blacks were ready. Male-dominated hierarchies were not ready for the consequences of the feminist movement, but women were ready. The hearing-dominated hierarchy of deaf education is not ready for us to assume control, but we are ready."[12]

As strike participants like Gentry and Karcher continued to hammer away at the themes of oppression, civil rights, and justice, more newspaper editorials on the campus uprising followed suit. The *Arkansas Democrat-Gazette* admitted that the strike was "a learning experience for the general public," conceding that most hearing people had been surprised by the students' fervor for a deaf president. "We probably shouldn't have been surprised, but we were. Out of this incident, a better understanding will emerge. And it's hard not to share the students' view that 124 years is long enough to wait for a deaf president at an institution for the deaf."[13] The *Washington Post* responded directly to Spilman's supposed remarks about the deaf being unable to function in a hearing world: "It is akin to suggesting that a black president could not provide leadership at Morehouse College, or a woman at Wellesley, because American society is dominated by white males. . . . [Gallaudet students] want a president who will demonstrate to others how effectively the deaf do 'function in a hearing world.'"[14] And the *New York Times* concluded, "The student protests reverberated with clarity and elemental justice. Deafness, or at least the ability to communicate with the deaf, is not merely an asset, it was a necessary qualification. To impose a president who hadn't even learned the students' language was patronizing, even insulting. Equally offensive was the message that this 124-year-old institution could not produce a leader from the ranks of the deaf."[15] Even Zinser herself, as she finally resigned having never even stepped foot on the embattled campus, portrayed the events in keeping with the prevailing interpretation. She admitted that she was witness "to this extraordinary social movement of deaf people" and based her decision to resign the position of president largely on the "groundswell of concern for the civil rights of deaf persons."[16]

Yet paradoxically, this groundswell of concern for the civil rights of deaf persons hinged on a portrayal in the media of the deafness of the students as secondary to the justness of their cause. Though the protest was, in the end, about deaf rights, the rhetoric focused more on civil rights. At the end of the momentous week, newly installed deaf president Irving King Jordan famously declared that the strike had proven, once and for all, that "deaf people can do anything that hearing people can, except hear."[17] Even here, when the rhetoric was about deaf people asserting their rights, supporters insisted primarily on deaf equality with the hearing, in much the same way that black civil rights protesters had asserted their fundamental equality with whites. These were deaf protesters in search of their civil rights, the same rights that other citizens enjoyed and exercised.

The events of DPN raise interesting questions about the quest for civil rights in American society. How has the civil rights movement been invoked, recalled, and employed in other struggles for rights? Has the invocation of the civil rights movement and its rhetoric been effective in these movements or not? Are the social situations of blacks, women, gays, and the disabled all parallel, so the language of civil rights applies equally to all, or does the rhetoric undergo significant revisions in meaning each time it is appropriated? Are the deaf and the disabled best served by invoking civil rights rhetoric or do we need a new language in these new movements?

Scholars have begun to address some of these questions. In *Deaf President Now! The 1988 Revolution at Gallaudet University*, John Christiansen and Sharon Barnartt frame DPN as a classic civil rights protest. They argue that the students' approach of linking their cause to the great civil rights struggles of the past was a far more effective tactic than that of building a bridge to the then fledgling disability rights movement. As they explain it, people with disabilities were at that time still largely viewed as individuals with medical problems. The students did not want to be seen in that light. Rather, they wanted to present theirs as the struggle of a minority group to secure its rights. Christiansen and Barnartt believe that this public invocation of the civil rights struggles of the past provoked more sympathy for the cause than an appeal on behalf of the disabled would have. And yet, in spite of arguing that the protesters benefited from rejecting the option of portraying their struggle as for disability rights, they nonetheless conclude that DPN paved the way for the Americans with Disabilities Act of 1990. "It seems on the face of it," they write, "that in order for the ADA to be accepted, the frame of civil rights, previously applied to blacks, women, and other groups, had to be extended to persons with disabilities."[18] The key to unraveling the apparent contradiction between their two assertions lies in acknowledging that in order for the civil rights frame to apply to the disabled, the popular understanding of disability itself had to be challenged.

As they explain it, people with disabilities had all too frequently been viewed simply as disparate individuals with various medical problems. Seen through such a lens, the solution for any particular disabled person's problems was medical intervention or physical therapy, not a political movement. In order to make a compelling case for civil rights for the disabled, disability itself would have to be reframed and reconsidered. The disabled would have to see themselves and, equally significantly, be seen, as a people who were denied their rights in social and political settings, not as scattered individuals with personal medical problems.

By the time of DPN, many disabled people were coming to see themselves and their social situation in exactly this light. Mark Johnson, a spokesman for American Disabled for Accessible Public Transportation (ADAPT), remarked on the students' efforts, saying, "It's an example of what we all want—to end paternalism."[19] U.S. *News and World Report* explained to its readers, "More and more, disabled people have come to see their problems as one of civil rights. A recent poll conducted for two disability groups found that 45 percent of disabled Americans identify themselves as members of an oppressed minority. . . . They see prejudice against people with disabilities—whether it's buildings made inaccessible or being turned away at a restaurant—as a bigger obstacle than their physical disabilities." The article concluded that the DPN protesters were very much aware of this new sensibility among the disabled, explaining that, "Gallaudet students were quick to pick up on the parallels to the civil-rights struggles of blacks in the 1960s."[20] The *New York Times* similarly argued that DPN marked the creation of a new civil rights movement. Reporter Tamar Lewis wrote, "The protests at Gallaudet University . . . represent a blossoming of a new civil rights movement, deliberately patterned on the black civil rights actions of the 1960s, according to deaf people and advocates for the handicapped."[21]

The DPN strike, with its very public presence in the streets of Washington, D.C., and in the national news, brought this new civil rights movement with its vision of disabled people as an oppressed minority group to public consciousness, perhaps for the first time.[22] Scholars, activists, and politicians alike have largely agreed that DPN transformed disability into a civil rights issue and fueled the passage of the ADA as a result. Activist Justin Dart, often called the father of the ADA, made the connection. He acknowledged the impact of DPN gratefully, saying, "The long successful struggle by the students and faculty to replace paternalism with empowerment sent a vital message to the nation and [DPN] was a major contribution to the passage of the ADA."[23] Senator Tom Harkin (D-Iowa), one of the major sponsors of the ADA, concurred. Harkin, who was a frequent witness to the discrimination his own deaf brother faced, stated baldly, "This law was pushed along by the students at Gallaudet."[24]

While this progressive argument—civil rights to deaf rights to disability rights—is attractive, is it correct? Given the timing, it would certainly seem that representatives, policy makers, and the mass media had accepted the DPN strike as a civil rights struggle in 1988 and so were similarly willing to see the ADA in the same light two years later. But to truly transform civil rights to deaf rights to disabled rights required more than the willingness of the disabled themselves to embrace this self-understanding. It also required a similar transformation in the thinking of the nondisabled. Just as blacks in the 1960s could not have achieved full citizenship and civil rights legislation if many whites had not come to see their claims as valid and compelling, disability rights activists could not achieve a meaningful disability rights law without a shift in the public thinking about disability. Did the general public undergo this kind of transformation in its thinking about the disabled, coming to see disabled people as an oppressed minority group and the ADA as a much needed and long-overdue piece of civil rights legislation? While the parallels between DPN and the civil rights movement may have drummed up public support for the Gallaudet cause in 1988, did that example cause a major shift in thinking?

Many scholars answer in the affirmative. "The frame of civil rights, which the DPN protesters applied to themselves, was generalized to people with other disabilities," Christiansen and Barnartt conclude.[25] Brenda Jo Brueggemann, in *Lend Me Your Ear: Rhetorical Constructions of Deafness*, likewise argues that DPN "turned deafness and by extension disability as well into an issue of rights rather than a medically certifiable, pathologically correctable thing that happens to *some* people. This is no small revision: for rights concern us *all*."[26] Others likewise believed that an important shift in thinking had taken place. President George Bush viewed the passage of the ADA as one of the most important legislative acts of his presidency. In 1990, the ADA was widely hailed as the last great piece of civil rights legislation in the twentieth century.

But the application of the civil rights argument may have worked only due to the timing of the ADA's passage, with DPN still fresh on legislators' minds. It is not clear that the wider public has accepted the reframing of either deaf or disabled people in the way that academics suggest. At the very least, the evidence is certainly mixed. The Supreme Court, in a string of recent decisions, has chipped away at the protections of the ADA, without much in the way of public outcry following.[27] Over the past decade, the ADA has been painted in some mass media stories as an attempt to carve out special rights for the disabled, not as an attempt to secure basic civil rights.[28] And it is not at all clear that the public at large, beyond the disabled community itself, widely accepts the position that the disabled constitute a minority group.

To begin to answer the question of whether or not such a reframing of disability has occurred, we must look more closely at the rhetorics at play in the public mind. The civil rights rhetoric was soon joined in the public sphere by another, competing, if complementary, rhetoric. The language of civil rights that DPN strikers invoked successfully as they pursued their cause had framed the students' deafness as secondary to the justness of their call for equality. In other words, the students had succeeded in making equal treatment, and not their deafness, the issue. But, unsurprisingly, after the strike's spectacular success, deaf people began to stress their deafness as indeed primary, as lying at the heart of deaf culture. The rhetoric of identity politics, that is, the language of a culturally distinct community seeking recognition as such, emerged on the scene more forcefully after DPN. Katherine Jankowski argues in *Deaf Empowerment: Emergence, Struggle, and Rhetoric* that "the rhetorical trends of the Deaf social movement since the Gallaudet protest indicate this direction."[29] The hearing public therefore had barely begun to address the issue of civil rights for the disabled when it was also asked to confront the idea that deaf people constituted a cultural minority group.

In the years immediately following DPN, deaf people began to assert their cultural identity more readily. This shift from civil rights to identity politics mirrors the shift within the African American community's struggle for rights. A similar progression from civil rights and integration to Black Power and segregation can be noted. Mapping "the rhetorical (shape) of empowerment," Katherine Jankowski draws attention to the way that "the Deaf movement resembles the position taken by Black Power advocates."[30] Very quickly, DPN moved the deaf community from integration to Deaf Power.

Brenda Jo Brueggemann has gone so far as to refer to DPN and its aftermath as the "coming out" of deaf culture.[31] Deaf poets, like Ella Mae Lentz and Clayton Valli, released videotapes of their American Sign Language (ASL) poetry. ASL courses were offered for foreign language credit at various colleges and high schools across the country. Deaf culture received more and more attention in the mass media. Both the *New York Times Magazine* and the *Atlantic Monthly* published major cover stories on deaf culture in the early nineties, introducing more hearing readers to a community most knew little about.[32]

The piece in the *Atlantic Monthly*, Edward Dolnick's "Deafness as Culture," deserves a closer look. Originally appearing in September 1993, it was reprinted in full in one of the premiere magazines of the silent press, *Deaf Life*. In the article, Dolnick acknowledged that "deafness is still seen as a dreadful fate" by many Americans, but explained that deaf people themselves have a very different view of their deafness. "Deafness is not a disability," he wrote. "Instead, many deaf people now proclaim, they are a subculture like any other. They are simply a linguistic minority (speaking American Sign Language) and are no more in need of a cure for their condition than are Haitians or Hispanics."[33]

While the *Atlantic Monthly* chose to publish only a handful of the letters it received in response to the article, *Deaf Life*, with the permission of the *Atlantic Monthly*, published eight pages of them. In this larger sample pool, it is possible to pick out a clear trend: many writers challenged the whole idea that deaf people constitute a minority group with a culture worth preserving. In rejecting the idea that deafness might constitute a culture, many respondents also went on to question the linkage of deaf rights to civil rights. As one letter writer quite bluntly put it, "It is more than a little sad that proponents of Deaf Culture have misappropriated the terminology of the civil rights movement."[34] For this writer, deafness was a medical problem that limited one's options in life. It was thus unreasonable to compare deaf culture to African American culture and to suggest that both groups faced discrimination, which required similar political solutions. Once deafness was defined as an individual medical problem, the civil rights analogy fell apart.

Other letter writers made their skepticism equally clear. Some raised the issue of cochlear implant technology. Cochlear implants are a medical device surgically implanted into the cochlea of a person with hearing loss. A cochlear implant has electrodes that, when placed inside the cochlea, stimulate the auditory nerve directly to create the perception of sound. This is not "sound" as hearing people experience it; it is an electronically induced perception of sound. And those implanted must receive intensive auditory therapy and training in order to learn to interpret the signals their brains receive. Such interpretation is easiest if the implantee has heard before, because she or he will have memories of sound against which to compare the new input, though early implantation in deaf children has produced some promising results and is becoming ever more popular. An implant is thus a very sophisticated kind of hearing aid with tremendous promise to restore awareness of useful auditory input to some people; it is not a bionic ear that provides instant hearing.[35]

Many of the letter writers were enthusiastic about the cochlear implant technology, including one who recommended them for all deaf children upon diagnosis. To explain this position, the writer offered the following observation: "Deaf culture shares many characteristics of the Yiddish culture of pre-war Europe. . . . Both reflect a triumphant expression of will and ingenuity to cope with criminally unfair ghettoization. Both are unsustainable in the absence of the tragic circumstances from which they sprang."[36] Leaving aside the aptness or accuracy of the comparison for the sake of argument, it remains striking that the author apparently assumes that deaf culture is a response, at least in part, to unfair hearing oppression of the deaf. The circumstances in which deaf people have historically found themselves are even admitted to be "criminally unfair." But the author's solution for solving this problem is not the expected one, given the problem's description. A civil rights movement for deaf people is not the proposed solution to the collective problem of hearing oppression that they face. Rather, once more, the problem is transformed into a personal one and the solution advanced is equally personal—acquiring appropriate medical technology. The solution becomes eliminating deafness, not eliminating prejudice.

Other writers displayed a similar ability to recognize that physical deafness may lead to cultural marginalization while still concluding that deafness was a disability that necessitated the intervention of medical science. As one writer admitted, "Insofar as interaction with the 'hearing' segment of society is concerned, the 'disability' of deafness is similar in many ways to the 'disability' of having the wrong skin color." It would seem that the author was on the verge of endorsing the social construction of disability and the civil rights approach to dealing with disability issues that such a model would imply. But this author too immediately pulled back from the logic of the argument by concluding, "There are numerous physical phenomena that a hearing person can sense; as a species, we have evolved hearing ability because it is often useful to sense these things. A person who lacks hearing lacks this ability and, thus, by definition, has a disability. In this context, the politically motivated arguments against cochlear implants are both foolish and cruel. Such implants restore at least part of a physical ability that the implantee would not otherwise have, while subtracting nothing from the individual's physical capabilities."[37]

Again, an argument that began by acknowledging the similarities between deaf Americans and African Americans turned back on itself and undermined its own initial position. Instead of proceeding to recognize deaf people as an oppressed minority group, the author returned to the individual deaf body, now defined as defective and in need of medical intervention. Once again, the problem was not discrimination, but deafness; the solution was not a social movement, but surgery.

Given the fact that Dolnick's piece was sympathetic toward, if not supportive of, both the deaf community and its culture, the way in which readers took issue with the major premises of the article disappointed the *Deaf Life* editorial staff. They had hoped that bringing deaf cultural issues to a mainstream, largely hearing, audience would give readers a chance to get to know this minority group better. They certainly expected that, five years after DPN, there would be grounds to hope for an audience. And perhaps many readers were receptive to the thrust of Dolnick's piece. But letter writers clearly were not; those who took issue with the idea of deafness as a culture worth preserving and deaf people as a minority group akin to other such American minority groups outnumbered those who found the position persuasive. And, more disturbing, even those who seemed to agree that deafness had a cultural component still wanted to eliminate deafness rather than battle hearing prejudice. The reframing that Christiansen and Barnartt and others insist occurred was not much in evidence here.

Though DPN protesters invoked the memory of the civil rights movement effectively during the strike, how successful this linkage proved in the long run remains unclear. Civil rights rhetoric had made hearing oppression the issue. Most Americans had been able to see the injustice of educating deaf people and then denying them opportunities to excel. But that argument persuaded by making the deafness of the students irrelevant to the justness of their cause. Once an increasing number of deaf people wanted to celebrate the culture that had so successfully stood up for itself, hearing Americans were largely baffled. How could deafness be a culture? Fair treatment was one thing; cultural identity was another. Identity politics rhetoric may actually have undermined the civil rights rhetoric in the public sphere.

The emergence of cochlear implants in the nineties clearly changed the terms of the debate about deaf rights. If curing deafness really became possible, most hearing parents of deaf children would choose cochlear implant surgery. They would not see their deaf child, as Christiansen and Barnartt put it, as "healthy, bright, articulate, and attractive," but instead in need of medical care to become healthy, that is, to become hearing. The impact of DPN and its attempt to link deaf rights and civil rights did not linger long in the public mind in part because cochlear implant technology emerged to remedicalize deafness in the public mind once again. Offering civil rights to deaf people would strike most Americans as just and fair. But curing deafness would similarly appear to most hearing Americans to be a good solution, and perhaps a more attractive one. Most hearing people see deafness from a hearing point of view, which means they view it as a great loss. Most hearing parents of deaf children (and 90 percent of deaf children have hearing parents) view their child's deafness as a calamity and fervently wish their child could hear. Identity politics rhetoric is incomprehensible to these parents, who mostly want their child to identify with and fit into hearing culture.

This raises the possibility that a civil rights rhetoric only works politically as long as there is no reasonable possibility of cure. In other words, a hearing parent would agree that his or her deaf child should not face discrimination and oppression in life. We might reasonably predict that the hearing parent would be supportive of efforts to guarantee the civil rights of deaf people. But after cochlear implants exploded onto the scene in the 1990s, hearing parents seemed to face a more attractive option. Only with the emergence of this powerful medical technology could a competing idea emerge, the notion that perhaps the best way to protect the civil rights of deaf people is to transform them into hearing people.

Perhaps as a result, the DPN strike rapidly faded from the nation's collective memory. As quickly as DPN burst onto the national scene, it vanished from national consciousness. Most Americans still recall images from the civil rights movement of the 1960s—the crowd on the Washington Mall, the March on Selma, the young people at lunch counters—and associate those images with acts of courage in a historically significant series of events that transformed the nation. Given the power of such historical memories, the invocation of civil rights phrases like "we shall overcome" and "we still have a dream" during DPN served the cause well in 1988. They also served to build the required momentum to launch the ADA to passage in 1990.

Yet few Americans today remember DPN. They could not name important figures associated with those events. Drawing on the memory of the civil rights movement was an effective rhetorical strategy at the time and made for passionate and positive media coverage, but it did not produce lasting changes in the way that most Americans thought about either deaf or disabled persons. This case of historical amnesia would seem to stem from a certain unwillingness on the part of the hearing, able-bodied public to accept either the identity politics rhetoric heard increasingly after DPN or the accompanying cultural definitions of deafness and disability offered by disabled activists.

The letter writers of the *Atlantic Monthly* are good examples once again. They clearly did not believe that deafness could be experienced as something other than a deprivation. Most of those who wrote in favor of cochlear implants would be surprised to learn that many deaf adults view cochlear implants with disdain at best and hostility at worst, calling them a form of cultural genocide. Deaf activist M. J. Bienvenu attacks those who are "forcing cochlear implants into the skulls of infants. While these people are busy trying desperately to make deaf people into hearing people, those of us who are culturally Deaf hold a very different perspective. Our immediate response is, . . .'Do you want to eliminate people like us from the face of the earth?' "[38] In the 2000 documentary film *Sound and Fury*, a deaf couple decided against implants for their deaf daughter. The father argued that his was a deaf family and they were happy. He feared that cochlear implants were going to create a generation of robots. If the technology ever advanced to the point where it succeeded in completely eliminating deafness, and hence the deaf community, he announced, "My heart would be broken."

But the idea that deaf people value their deafness, and value the deaf community and its culture, is so foreign to most hearing people that they simply do not give it credit. In an online discussion group, one hearing mother of a deaf daughter commented, "My daughter is profoundly deaf. She was implanted five years ago and I am thrilled that she can hear. I do not understand why the so-called 'deaf community' is against anything that improves quality of life. . . . Deafness is not a culture. . . . I also feel it is a terrible injustice for anyone to deny a child the opportunity to have a CI just because they are influenced by a small, and in my opinion, bitter group of persons who are determined to find some sort of 'identity' in deafness."[39] Her bewilderment is clear. She doubts the existence of a deaf community, putting the term in quotation marks, and seemingly denies the possibility that anyone might develop a positive deaf identity. She rejects out of hand the very idea of deaf culture and announces that anyone who finds a cultural identity as a deaf person is simply bitter. This is a parent raising a deaf child and making decisions on her daughter's behalf, exclusively from a hearing point of view. As this mother admits later in the conversation, she has had no contact with the adult deaf community, in part because she does not want her daughter to be part of this "community."[40] If the deaf point of view on deafness cannot find its way even to hearing parents of deaf children, how likely is it to find its way to others without a connection to deafness at all?

Responding in agreement with her, another participant in this online discussion wrote,

> When you are black in a racist society, the challenges you have are external. The problems you encounter are imposed on you by others without merit. If the people around you recognized that being black is not an issue, the problem would cease to exist. When one is deaf, or otherwise impaired, the challenges that person faces are internal. The problems deaf persons face come from what they lack. . . . Now they may be able to still function very well with those limitations, even excel in society. But I can't imagine that a person born with hearing, and that became deaf would opt never to hear music again . . . or other intrinsic aspects of the human experience. . . . But I think the argument

[against cochlear implants] of some people born deaf comes . . . out of misunderstanding. It is a case where some deaf persons doesn't know they are missing [*sic*].[41]

Here the writer attempts to distinguish between the situations of black and deaf Americans and concludes that while blacks face external discrimination unfairly, the problems of the deaf are internal, stemming from their inability to hear rather than hearing prejudice. The rejection of the identity rhetoric, which emphasized the deafness of the participants, led hearing people to reject the civil rights analogy that Gallaudet activists made as well.

This post also questions the social model of disability, which disability rights activists have tried to promote. After all, the author includes not only the deaf in this discussion, but also those "otherwise impaired." The social model of disability posits that disability is more of a social construction than it is a physical fact and that what disabled people need most is not cures or physical therapy but rather social and political change. In this exchange of views on this Web site, however, it becomes clear how much resistance there is to the social model in the public imagination. The more the deaf people in this online conversation tried to assert that their real problems were also external, that, as one respondent put it, the "discrimination and stigma that deaf people face come from such attitudes that people who don't hear and speak are inferior," the more the hearing skeptics simply replied that such remarks come from bitter, misinformed people who just don't know what they are missing.[42]

Through this discussion, there is not much evidence that a reframing of deafness and disability in the public imagination has in fact occurred. Here, in unguarded moments of online exchange, with both hearing and deaf people interacting, the hearing participants never show any signs that they are changing their minds or are even challenged to see things from a different point of view. Instead, they quickly become impatient with or even hostile toward the deaf participants. The more the deaf participants insist there is a deaf culture and that they know more about deafness than the hearing people do, the more the hearing people attack them. Furthermore, the hearing people insist that they know more about deafness than deaf people do because they can hear so they know what deaf people are missing. They reject entirely the idea that deafness seen from a deaf point of view might look very different.

Again, if these hearing people, all voluntarily participating in a conversation about ideas in which they are passionately invested because they have deaf children in their care, are unable to give credit to the arguments coming from the deaf side, how likely is it that the so-called reframing inspired by DPN has sunk deep roots into the public consciousness? It has apparently not even reached hearing parents of deaf children, the hearing people most in need of the empowering, and reassuring, message of DPN, that the deaf can do anything the hearing can do, except hear. The idea that the problem is with the hearing, not the deaf world, has not reached this group. Indeed, it may not have reached as far as we would like to think.

While this analysis has focused most tightly on deaf history and deaf rights, it should be clear that none of this bodes well for the future of the ADA. Continued public support for the ADA also rests on an acceptance of the premise that the law guarantees disabled people their civil rights. But if disabled people, like deaf people, are perceived as facing internal, not external, problems, then their cause cannot long be seen as a battle for civil rights. The public may become more interested in cures, not solutions like curb cuts, the tapered slopes from sidewalks to streets that accommodate wheelchair users.

Much of disability theory, closely allied with disability activism, also rests on the premise that disability can and should be understood primarily as a social construction. The very argument that we should pursue curb cuts, and not cures, depends on the attractiveness of the social model of disability. The case for such things as universal design, ramps, talking ATM machines, and curb cuts also speaks to the underlying assumption that the problems facing wheelchair users, for instance, lie in the external world and its design, not in the body.

Ideally, many disability theorists and activists would like, in the words of Rosemarie Garland Thomson, "to move disability from the realm of medicine into that of political minorities, to recast it from a form of pathology to a form of ethnicity."[43] The theory of disability as ethnicity frames the groundbreaking work of disability theorist Simi Linton. Linton entitled her trailblazing book *Claiming Disability*, a title chosen deliberately to suggest that disability is not a fact of life to be viewed with shame but rather a positive identity that should be claimed with pride.

This move, of course, parallels the emerging focus on cultural identity within the deaf community. But this is precisely why a similar move within the disabled community might be equally problematic. There are millions of Americans with varying degrees of hearing loss. Perhaps one million of those identify themselves as members of deaf culture. While not undermining the argument for the existence of a deaf culture, it points to the fact that not everyone who experiences a hearing loss will choose to identify themselves as culturally deaf. There are multiple ways of experiencing deafness. Those within deaf culture have succeeded in moving deafness "from a form of pathology to a form of ethnicity." Works like *American Deaf Culture*, *Deaf in America: Voices from a Culture*, *Seeing Voices*, and *American Deaf Folklore* ably trace the cultural landscape of this minority group. Works like *When the Mind Hears*, *Forbidden Signs*, and *Signs of Resistance* outline its history.[44] But it remains a minority group within a minority group. And the existence of deaf culture has not succeeded in transforming deafness entirely "from the realm of medicine" into the realm of ethnicity and minority groups. If an active deaf culture, with roots going back in the United States nearly two hundred years, has not made this transformation of the meaning of deafness possible for all deaf people, how likely is it that such a transformation is possible for all disabled people?

Still, the attractiveness of the cultural model holds a powerful grip on the imagination within the deaf and disabled communities. Such ideas have gained traction within the disabled community in recent years. Carol Gill, a quadriplegic psychologist, was among the first to theorize the existence of a disability culture, citing among its values "tolerance for others' differences and highly developed skills at managing multiple problems."[45] Gill offers her vision of ideal future for disabled people:

> Society would accept my experience as "disability culture," which would in turn be accepted as part of "human diversity." There would be respectful curiosity about what I have learned from my differences that I could teach society. In such a world, no one would mind being

called Disabled. Being unable to do something the way most people do it would not be seen as something bad that needs curing. It would be seen as just a difference. . . . In other words, even if I had a difference that might impinge on me in some contexts, I wouldn't be judged *generally* deficient because a recognized feature of Disability culture would be the fact that such limitations can be fodder for innovation and for a rich and valuable human experience.[46]

Of course, once more mirroring the deaf experience, not all disability activists share the vision that a disability culture is a desirable goal for the disability movement. Robert Funk, a prominent proponent of disability integration, believes that for most disabled people, "disability will disappear as an issue" once the disabled are integrated fully into the mainstream society.[47] Having achieved integration, there will no longer be, by Funk's lights anyway, a need for a disability culture, a culture here presumed to be built mostly out of necessity as its members try to find refuge from a hostile ableist culture.

But if the disability movement trades in the language of the civil rights movement for the language of identity politics, it may find itself in the same choppy waters that have threatened to drown the advocates of deaf culture. The more the language of identity politics has been used to frame deafness, the more hearing people have shown they are able to deflect that language and, in turn, have gone further to target even civil rights language as inappropriate for deaf people. The disabled community might be sailing into this same territory.

Both groups might have learned some lessons by studying the shifts in the national treatment of racial issues. Historian Elisabeth Lasch-Quinn advances a strikingly similar argument about the unintended consequences of a move from the language of civil rights to that of identity politics in the nation's conversations about race. She argues, "The civil rights movement reminded Americans of their commitment to true egalitarianism, posited a universal standard of conduct, and placed in the forefront of public interest the quality of democratic civic life."[48] But, she continues, as the 1960s drew to a close, Americans increasingly lost their assurance that racial differences were not important. As the racialist language of the black liberation movement came to dominate much of the country's understanding of race during the 1970s, this new discourse thrived on emphasizing differences, not moving the country beyond them. Lasch-Quinn views this continuing emphasis on irreducible differences as harmful to democratic culture, arguing that "universalism . . . was the genius of the civil rights movement."[49]

It was also the initial genius of the disability rights movement. When ADAPT activists carried signs reading "I Can't Even Get on the Bus" to protest inaccessible public transportation, they were reminding the nation of its historic obligations to justice and equity. Consider too the scene that occurred in March 1990. Disabled activists staged the Wheels of Justice March in support of the ADA. The march culminated on the steps of Capitol Hill. Mike Auberger, ADAPT's national leader, addressed the crowd from his motorized wheelchair. He declared,

> Twenty years ago, I walked up these steps a wholly equal American citizen. Today, I sit here with you as less than second-class citizens who are still legally discriminated against daily. These steps we sit before represent a long history of discrimination and indignities heaped upon disabled Americans. We have faced what these steps have represented. . . . These indignities and injustice must not go on. We will not permit these steps to continue to be a barrier to prevent us from the equality that is rightfully ours. The preamble to the Constitution does not say, "We the able-bodied people." It says, "We the People."

At this point, the crowd began to chant, "Access is our civil right," and some three dozen ADAPT activists hurled themselves out of their wheelchairs in a "crawl-up" of the Capitol Hill steps. Each protestor carried a scroll printed with the opening words of the Declaration of Independence.[50] Pictures of the protest were shown on the national network news, and according to chronicler Joseph Shapiro, the event was characterized exactly as ADAPT had intended, as a protest demonstrating that "disabled people were demanding their civil rights."[51] The civil rights language of egalitarianism and universalism was appealing precisely because that rhetoric still had the power to touch values that Americans were willing to affirm.

Can most Americans, whether disabled or able bodied, be as willing to affirm the statement of Nadina LaSpina, a disabled writer and activist who declares, "I would not trade my disability for anything"?[52] My intent here is not to question the importance of claiming a positive identity and self-image for oneself. It is rather to ask whether this linguistic turn in the public realm, this change in rhetoric from civil rights to identity politics, furthers or hinders the disabled cause in the public sphere. The ADAPT crawl-up was powerful in the public eye in 1990 exactly because people could see the injustice of inaccessibility before them and agree that access is indeed a civil right. It was powerful because the rhetoric of civil rights and street theater tactics of the civil rights movement provided a strong base on which to build a coalition of the disabled and the able bodied, to bring both sides together to support the ADA.

Such coalition building is crucial because it guarantees long-term support for rigorous enforcement of the ADA. Civil rights rhetoric helps the able bodied to understand that the ADA is for them, too, because the disabled are the only minority group any one of us may join at any moment. As disability rights activist Becky Ogle puts it, "The ADA can be viewed as an insurance policy against discrimination that every American in this society should cherish and protect as a matter of enlightened self-interest."[53] Civil rights rhetoric makes this case clear. As Lasch-Quinn would have it, it promotes the kind of radical egalitarianism that a democratic society needs continuously to strive for.

But the language of identity politics raises far different questions in the public sphere. Can the able bodied be equally expected to affirm that disability in itself is a good thing? Can they come to agree with radical disability activists who are opposed to measures to prevent birth defects, arguing that such efforts to prevent disabilities suggest there is something wrong with being disabled?[54] Can they, with an ADAPT activist, affirm that abortion is "this holocaust that is also wiping out our tiny brothers and sisters with disabilities"?[55] Can they agree with British deaf activist Paddy Ladd, who calls cochlear implants "The Final Solution"?[56] Should the formerly able bodied who acquire a disability be expected to think "I would not trade my disability for anything"? Newly disabled people might now indeed be easily persuaded that access, whether to public schools, to public buildings, or to public transportation, is a civil right. But could they as readily be persuaded to believe that disability is an identity they should claim with pride? Do they even have to view disability in this way or, as Robert Funk argues, is it acceptable to view integration as enough? Must they accept, in other words, a disabled identity in order to utilize a civil rights rhetoric? Can they only claim their civil rights on the basis of their identity as a member of an oppressed minority group or are other claims to rights still possible?

It is too soon to know the answers to these questions, as the rhetoric of disability culture is too new on the scene to judge the full extent of its impact. But the example of the deaf community should serve to temper enthusiasm for this approach. The culturally deaf have actively promoted their perspective on deafness for nearly two hundred years in this country. They have done so through the auspices of the deaf press, in publications like *Deaf Life* and the *Silent Worker*, and through deaf organizations, like the National Association of the Deaf. More recently, they have done so in online discussion groups and on Web sites like DeafWorldWeb and DeafNotes. But despite all of these efforts, they have had only limited success in getting hearing people to see deafness from a deaf point of view. They have not even convinced all deaf people to see deafness as an ethnic identity.

But the deaf don't necessarily have to convince hearing people on this score to secure their civil rights. Admittedly, they may have to promote the cultural view of deafness in order to convince hearing people that deafness is not a disease in need of a cure like cochlear implants. But, of course, for every culturally deaf person who is uninterested in implant surgery, there is an adult facing late-onset hearing loss who wants it. Even if there can never be a single deaf position on this question, all deaf people—whatever their degree of hearing loss or their response to it—can agree that they do at least share a common interest in protecting their civil rights. Hearing people may still not widely believe that deafness can be cultural, deaf efforts to show them otherwise aside. But hearing people need not believe that deafness is a culture in order to affirm that discriminating against deaf people on the job is wrong or that failing to provide an interpreter for a deaf defendant in a courtroom is a travesty of justice.

Civil rights arguments based on equity and justice require people to see certain behaviors as wrong; this hearing people can do fairly easily. Able-bodied people can do the same about disability rights in general. But identity politics rhetoric may not offer a language that will attract support from able-bodied people. Even activist Nadina LaSpina admits, "Our most progressive nondisabled friends will support us when we fight for our rights, when we demand access. But they just don't understand what we mean when we say we don't want to be cured because we are 'Disabled and Proud.' "[57] In battles for civil rights of all kinds in a democracy, a minority group needs political support from members of the majority to succeed. The civil rights movement would have failed African Americans if in the end only African Americans had been supportive of the cause. The nation as a whole also had to learn to dream more inclusive dreams. This is equally true as the disabled pursue their rights. Therefore, finding an effective rhetoric is a vital issue for the movement.

Both the civil rights and the identity politics rhetoric have limitations. Identity politics rhetoric raises the risk of fragmentation within the disabled and deaf communities, since not all members of the community either claim a disabled identity or want to. This shift to identity politics rhetoric in some quarters therefore presents a problem for the disability rights movement as a whole, insofar as it makes it that much harder, though not impossible, for the disabled to speak with one voice politically. Civil rights rhetoric, meanwhile, may not be seen to apply if a disability is perceived as fluid and potentially curable. Hearing people have proved quite adept at recognizing the cultural possibilities of deafness while remedicalizing deafness at the same time. It may be that most of the public can only conceptualize civil rights as a concept that applies to those who are perceived as unchangeably, biologically different. Civil rights are important for people of color because they will always be people of color and it not fair to treat people differently because of such fixed difference. But if deaf people can be made to hear, then the solution is perceived to be medical rather than political.

Yet even with this limitation, a civil rights rhetoric offers its own strengths. It is a discourse that all the disparate elements of the disabled community—the blind, the deaf, the diabetic, the cancer survivor, the quadriplegic, the ADHD student—can unite behind. A civil rights rhetoric leaves room for the possibility that some disabled people will think the major obstacle in life is social discrimination, while others continue to experience the disabled body itself as a major obstacle in life. A successful movement for disability rights would seem to need a rhetoric that leaves room for the possibility that at any given moment for any given person perhaps both sides are right.

Finding the most persuasive rhetoric is important to secure the rights of the disabled well into the future. And, as Becky Ogle reminds us, it is important for the temporarily able bodied as well. Since the disabled are the only minority group that anyone of us may join at any moment (and most likely will join, if we live long enough to experience the disabilities that present themselves with advanced age), it is important that activists find a rhetoric that makes the issues at stake in the disability rights struggle clear to all Americans.

Invoking the memory of the civil rights movement and using civil rights rhetoric must be seen as the necessary first step both in securing this support for disability rights and in promoting real social change for both the deaf and the disabled in American society. Civil rights rhetoric has the promise of reminding all Americans of their historic commitment to egalitarianism and justice for all. A fight for civil rights still has the power to move Americans and to force them to rethink their inherited ideas and attitudes. As Nancy Rarus at the National Association of the Deaf commented ten years after DPN, "We still have professional organizations and professional workers such as doctors and lawyers who do not think it is their responsibility to follow the letter of the law, the ADA. I would guess attitude changing is the bottom line."[58] Indeed, attitude changing and consciousness-raising is the bottom line and much of that work as a society remains ahead of us. Only then might a call for a "Deaf President Now!" refer not to a university presidency but rather to the presidency of the United States.

Notes

I would like to thank the editors for their support and their suggestions. I also owe a debt of gratitude to the members of the RUSH (Rochester U.S. Historians) reading group, especially Alison Parker, Joan Saab, Steve Ireland, Victoria

Wolcott, and Lisa Tetrault, for their comments on an early draft. Their thoughtful criticisms opened up avenues of inquiry I had overlooked and taking them into account substantially improved the essay. Finally, Mary Hess offered a valuable suggestion at a critical moment. Any errors of interpretation and argument that remain are my own.

1. Jack Gannon, *The Week the World Heard Gallaudet* (Washington, D.C.: Gallaudet University Press, 1989).

2. While it is a common convention in the field of Deaf Studies to capitalize "Deaf" whenever one refers to Deaf culture and reserve the lower case "deaf" to refer to the audiological condition of deafness, I have chosen here for the sake of clarity to use only the lowercase spelling throughout. There are moments when I am referring to both cultural and physical deafness, and I have chosen to indicate that with adjectives alone, rather than resort to "D/deaf" or "Deaf/deaf."

3. B. Drummond Ayres Jr., "Outsiders Converge on School to Espouse Rights of the Deaf," *New York Times*, March 9, 1988, sec. A, 1.

4. Ibid., sec. A, 1, 14.

5. B. Drummond Ayres Jr., "Many in Faculty Back Protest by Deaf," *New York Times*, March 10, 1988; David Brand, "'This Is the Selma of the Deaf,'" *Time*, March 21, 1988, 64.

6. Representative Steve Gunderson as quoted in John Christiansen and Sharon Barnartt, *Deaf President Now! The 1988 Revolution at Gallaudet University* (Washington, D.C.: Gallaudet University Press, 1995), 153.

7. Ibid., 215.

8. B. Drummond Ayres Jr., "Students Spurn a Compromise at Deaf School," *New York Times*, March 11, 1988, sec. B, 5.

9. The statement was widely reprinted in strike coverage stories. Spilman insisted that she was misquoted, and also cited interpreter error as contributing to the problem. Of course, the fact that she had been chair of a board for a deaf institution for seven years and yet had not ever learned sign language only made her reliance on interpreters another source for outrage on the part of observers.

10. Renee Loth, "New Light Shed on the Deaf at Gallaudet," *Boston Sunday Globe*, March 13, 1988, 10. Supporting Sussman's point, the *Washington Post* reported that, according to the National Commission on Education of the Deaf, while 91 percent of administrators at Howard University were black, only 18 percent of administrators at Gallaudet were deaf. As one official who worked at the commission put it, "What does it say when a university whose purpose for 124 years has been to train deaf people to assume positions of responsibility can't find a deaf person to be its president? It says, 'We have failed so badly at our jobs that we have to hire a hearing person.'" Ed Burke, "Protest Gained Empathy Nationwide," *Washington Post*, March 11, 1988, sec. A, 16.

11. Reported in Oliver Sacks, "The Revolution of the Deaf," *New York Review of Books*, June 2, 1988, 24.

12. R. G. Gentry, "This Time, Our Patience Ran Out," *Washington Post National Weekly Edition*, March 21–27, 1988, 9.

13. *Arkansas Democrat-Gazette*, March 17, 1988, LexisNexis (accessed December 5, 2002).

14. *Washington Post*, March 9, 1988, sec. A, 24.

15. "The Deaf Are Heard," *New York Times*, March 18, 1988, sec. A, 34.

16. As quoted in Jerry Adwell, "Deaf Students Speak Out and the World Listens," *Newsweek*, March 21, 1988, 79; and Brand, " 'This Is the Selma of the Deaf,' " 64.

17. As quoted in Molly Sinclair, "A Man for the Moment," *Washington Post National Weekly Edition*, March 21–27, 1988, 9.

18. Christiansen and Barnartt, 213.

19. As quoted in "A Cry from the Deaf Is Heard in Washington," *U.S. News and World Report*, March 21, 1988, 9.

20. Ibid., 9–10.

21. Tamar Lewis, "Deaf Demand to be Heard on Rights," *New York Times*, March 13, 1988, sec. A, 22.

22. While disabled activists had led earlier protests, including most spectacularly a takeover of the HEW (Health, Education, and Welfare) offices in San Francisco in 1977 for twenty-five days in protest of HEW Secretary Joseph Califano's hesitation to issue regulations to enforce Section 504 of the Rehabilitation Act of 1973, the first piece of civil rights legislation for the disabled, such protests proved to have only limited impact on the national consciousness. As Joseph Shapiro noted of the HEW takeover, "Yet the movement that seemed so promising as the demonstrators left would soon falter. What existed in the San Francisco area simply did not exist elsewhere," namely a true disability rights consciousness. Joseph Shapiro, *No Pity: People with Disabilities Forging a New Civil Rights Movement* (New York: Times Books, 1993), 70.

23. Dart as quoted in Christiansen and Barnartt, *Deaf President Now!* 217.

24. Tom Harkin quoted in Greg Livadas, "Deaf Community Seeking Equal Access," *Democrat and Chronicle*, March 15, 1998, sec. B, 4.

25. Christiansen and Barnartt, *Deaf President Now!* 216.

26. Brenda Jo Brueggemann, *Lend Me Your Ear: Rhetorical Constructions of Deafness* (Washington, D.C.: Gallaudet University Press, 1999), 192.

27. See *University of Alabama at Birmingham Board of Trustees et al. v. Patricia Garrett*, 120 S.Ct. 1669 (2000), which held that the state's employees are not included within the protection of the ADA. *Sutton et al. v. United Air Lines, Inc.*, 119 S.Ct 2139 (1999), *Murphy v. United Parcel Service, Inc.*, 119 S.Ct

2133 (1999), and *Albertsons, Inc. v. Kirkingburg*, 119 S.Ct 2162 (1999). All three Supreme Court cases involved disability and employment issues, and all three held that if an individual has a condition that is easily correctable and/or does not substantially limit a major life activity, then that person is not disabled and does not qualify for the legal protections of the ADA. Disability rights lawyer Chai Feldblum believes that the rulings "create the absurd result of a person being disabled enough to be fired from a job, but not disabled enough to challenge the firing." Quoted in Doris Zames Fleischer and Frieda Zames, *The Disability Rights Movement* (Philadelphia, Pa.: Temple University Press, 2001), 104.

28. See Philip K. Howard, *The Death of Common Sense: How Law Is Suffocating America* (New York: Random House, 1994); Brian Doherty, "Unreasonable Accommodation: The Case against the Americans with Disabilities Act," *Reason*, August/September 1995, 19–26.

29. Katherine A. Jankowski, *Deaf Empowerment: Emergence, Struggle, and Rhetoric* (Washington, D.C.: Gallaudet University Press, 1997), 140.

30. Ibid., 160.

31. See "The Coming Out of Deaf Culture," in Brueggemann, *Lend Me Your Ear*, for a more extensive comparison of deaf and queer cultures.

32. Edward Dolnick, "Deafness as Culture," *Atlantic Monthly*, September 1993, 37–53; Andrew Solomon, "Defiantly Deaf," *New York Times Magazine*, August 28, 1994, 38–45, 62, 65–68.

33. Dolnick, "Deafness as Culture," 37.

34. "Deaf Culture: A Trendy Self-Segregation Movement," *Deaf Life*, December 1993, 30.

35. Michael Chorost's wonderful new memoir, *Rebuilt: How Becoming Part Computer Made Me More Human* (New York: Houghton Mifflin, 2005), tells the author's tale of getting a cochlear implant and how different that experience is from hearing with natural ears.

36. "A Doomed Ghetto Culture," *Deaf Life*, December 1993, 33.

37. "Is Cultural Membership Worth the Handicap?" *Deaf Life*, December 1993, 30, 31.

38. M. J. Bienvenu, "Can Deaf People Survive 'Deafness'"? originally appeared in *Perspectives on Deafness* in 1991. Reprinted in *Deaf World*, ed. Lois Bragg (New York: New York University Press, 2001), 319.

39. Anita Michael Cobbs, "Deafness Is NOT a Cultural Identity," *Gideon's Crossing* message board, January 30, 2001, http://boards.go.com/cgi/a . . . a_ Gideon's_Crossing.

40. Cobbs makes this clear in a later posting where she asks the deaf participants how they deal with social situations where no one knows sign language. A deaf respondent tosses back, "You mean, like virtually every day of my life? . . .

Not to take it out on you, Anita, but there seems to be this myth, particularly perpetuated by the cochlear implant crowd, that deaf people simply can't communicate with the hearing world. This utterly disregards the reality in which we all live in the hearing world." Posted by cochlearimplant, *Gideon's Crossing* message board, January 30, 2001.

41. esprit15d, "Re: Deafness Is NOT a Cultural Identity," on *Gideon's Crossing* message board, January 30, 2001.

42. deafmary, "Re: Deafness Is NOT a Cultural Identity," *Gideon's Crossing* message board, January 30, 2001.

43. Rosemarie Garland Thomson, *Extraordinary Bodies: Figuring Physical Disability in American Culture and Literature* (New York: Columbia University Press, 1997), 6.

44. See for example Sherman Wilcox, ed., *American Deaf Culture: An Anthology* (Silver Spring, Md.: Linstok Press, 1989); Carol Padden and Tom Humphries, *Deaf in America: Voices from a Culture* (Cambridge, Mass.: Harvard University Press, 1988); Oliver Sacks, *Seeing Voices: A Journey into the World of the Deaf* (Berkeley: University of California Press, 1989); Susan Rutherford, *American Deaf Folklore* (Silver Spring, Md.: Linstok Press, 1993); Harlan Lane, *When the Mind Hears: A History of the Deaf* (New York: Random House, 1984); Douglas C. Baynton, *Forbidden Signs: American Culture and the Campaign against Sign Language* (Chicago, Ill.: University of Chicago Press, 1996); Susan Burch, *Signs of Resistance: American Deaf Cultural History, 1900–1942* (New York: New York University Press, 2002).

45. As quoted in Doris Zames Fleischer and Frieda Zames, *The Disability Rights Movement* (Philadelphia, Pa.: Temple University Press, 2001), 204.

46. Carol Gill as quoted in Fleischer and Zames, *The Disability Rights Movement*, 204–5 (emphasis in original).

47. Quoted in Shapiro, *No Pity*, 103.

48. Elisabeth Lasch-Quinn, *Race Experts: How Racial Etiquette, Sensitivity Training, and New Age Therapy Hijacked the Civil Rights Revolution* (New York: W. W. Norton, 2001), xiv.

49. Ibid., 230–31.

50. This story, including the Auberger quote, is recounted in Shapiro, *No Pity*, 132–33.

51. Ibid., 133.

52. As quoted in Fleischer and Zames, *The Disability Rights Movement*, 201.

53. Becky Ogle as quoted in Fleischer and Zames, *The Disability Rights Movement*, 109.

54. See Shapiro, *No Pity*, especially chap. 9.

55. Lillibeth Navarro as quoted in Shapiro, *No Pity*, 278. This is not to sug-

gest that disability activists do not raise important points about the abortion debate. Adrienne Asch has argued most powerfully that as long as society views a disabled life as not worth living, women will feel strongly pressured to abort a disabled fetus, knowing their choice to raise a disabled child will not be widely supported. This in effect undermines their right to choose. I simply think there is a difference between Asch's subtle rhetoric and a statement drawing an analogy with the Holocaust.

56. Paddy Ladd as quoted in Solomon, "Deaf Is Beautiful," 65.

57. Nadina LaSpina, "Disabled Woman: The Forging of a Proud Identity," Keynote address at the Women's Studies Conference at Southern Connecticut State University in New Haven, Connecticut, delivered October 2, 1998.

58. As quoted in Livadas, "Deaf Community Seeking Equal Access," sec. B, 4.

DAVID JOHN MARLEY

Riding in the Back of the Bus

The Christian Right's Adoption of

Civil Rights Movement Rhetoric

If imitation is the sincerest form of flattery, what does it mean when politically conservative groups use the memory of the civil rights movement
to advance their own causes? In the years since the end of the civil rights
movement, many groups, both in the United States and worldwide, have
adapted the rhetoric and the tactics of the movement in their own struggles. In the "Yellow Power," "Red Power" and "Brown Power" movements
of the 1970s, Asian Americans, Native Americans, and Latinos were inspired in part by the success of the black freedom struggle to seek to
change their own status. They drew not only on the lessons of civil rights
struggles but also on a new political context the black movement helped
create, one in which groups found they could organize around their identity and their status as a minority in the United States.

It was not only other racial and ethnic groups that took the lessons of
the movement to heart. The Christian Right also sought to use the movement to its advantage as it struggled for political power and legitimacy
in the 1980s and 1990s. The Christian Right is a generic name given to
a wide array of conservative political organizations that were formed by
evangelical Christians in the early 1970s to combat political liberalism.[1]
These conservatives reached the height of their power in the 1990s when
they declared themselves descendants of King and his movement. This

chapter is concerned with the explicitly partisan Christian Right rather than the broader white evangelical movement. Depicting themselves as an oppressed minority, and comparing their own struggle to those of civil rights icons like Martin Luther King Jr. and Rosa Parks, key leaders of Christian Right organizations sought to draw on popular movement figures and ideas to energize their conservative crusades. When they invoked civil rights memory, Christian leaders such as Pat Robertson, Ralph Reed, and Randall Terry highlighted both the many ways in which civil rights memory can be put to use in contemporary political battles and the growing willingness of the Christian Right to come to terms with the civil rights movement and to seek to appeal to black Christians.

Explicitly partisan evangelical Christian groups emerged in the 1970s and became increasingly powerful on the national stage during Reagan's presidency in the 1980s. Associating themselves with the conservative wing of the Republican party, Christian Right organizations attacked what they saw as the excesses of American society. They lamented the legalization of abortion and decried the rising divorce rate. Arguing for the necessity of bringing Christian belief more openly into the public realm, they have pushed for school prayer, the public display of Christian symbols, and the teaching of abstinence in schools. On economic issues, Christian Right organizations sided with a Republican party that was increasingly critical of the New Deal welfare state and in favor of deregulation and the free market. They, like other Republican groups, opposed affirmative action as reverse discrimination.

By the mid-1970s there were approximately 75 million evangelicals in America, representing about 40 percent of all Americans.[2] *Newsweek* proclaimed 1976 as the year of the evangelical.[3] After years of watching with dismay the social changes of the 1960s, a newly politicized Christian Right was ready to assert itself. Conservatives created groups with names that were meant to project power and leadership. This flood of media attention gave them a sense of optimism, and this became evident in the triumphant rhetoric the groups used. The Christian Voice, a small California-based direct mail group, proudly referred to itself as a group dedicated to making a "Christian majority in a Christian Democracy."[4]

Televangelist Jerry Falwell founded the Moral Majority in 1978 with the goal of bringing religious conservatives into the Republican party and helping to unseat President Jimmy Carter, who, although an evangelical himself, was not politically conservative enough to please Falwell. By 1982, the Moral Majority claimed to have 5 million members and a $5.5 million budget.[5] Christian Right leaders like Falwell promoted the idea that evangelicals were a powerful conservative majority battling a small group of liberal elites; they were Richard Nixon's so-called "silent majority."

When conservative Republican Ronald Reagan was elected in 1980, the Christian Right's claims to be a majority of the country seemed well founded. Journalists associated Reagan with the Christian Right, and soon after the election, Falwell's Moral Majority began advocating for constitutional amendments banning abortion and protecting prayer in school. Yet the Reagan era proved a mixed bag for the Christian Right and its lack of success showed the weakness of its majority rhetoric. Although Ronald Reagan came to office claiming much of the agenda of the Religious Right as his own, the group received next to nothing on its social issues agenda. Paul Weyrich, one of the creators of the Moral Majority, was direct in his analysis of the Reagan era and the Christian Right's response to it. "Most of them [Christian Right leaders] wouldn't admit that they were disappointed. . . . [Reagan] was so nice a guy they really didn't want to come to grips with the fact that he basically didn't do anything for them."[6] Despite its claims of majority status, the Christian Right found it difficult to achieve what it wanted in the political sphere even with a publicly friendly president.

In the early 1990s new leaders of the Christian Right emerged, and they brought new tactics with them. Instead of presenting themselves as a majority battling a small group of liberal elites, Christian Right leaders began to present themselves and their followers as minorities who were persecuted in American legal and political institutions such as schools and local government. In the 1990s, the Christian Right shifted from a strategy of seeking to influence the president as a national lobbying group to instead becoming a grassroots movement fighting for change on the local level, much as the civil rights movement had been.[7] This new version of the Christian Right purposefully copied the words and methods of the civil rights movement. Claiming to be members of an oppressed minority in the United States, newly prominent leaders like Robertson, Reed, and Terry adopted the rhetoric and even some of the tactics of the wing of the civil rights movement represented by Martin Luther King. As a result, by 1994 the Christian Right had become one of the most powerful political forces in modern American history.

The change in tone from evangelical leaders from the late 1970s to the early 1990s was striking. Especially after his 1988 run for the White House, Pat Robertson became the chief spokesperson for the new evangelical-as-minority argument. Robertson had been a fairly consistent proponent of the minority idea, but during the 1970s and early 1980s, when Falwell was promoting the idea that evangelicals were a powerful national majority, there were few who were willing to listen. Robertson gained public recognition as the host of the conservative Christian Broadcasting Network's (CBN) flagship show, *700 Club*. Founded to counter what Robertson viewed as the open hostility of the secular media to conservative Christianity, each edition of the *700 Club* began with a fifteen-minute newscast that provided a conservative Christian perspective on events or stories that they felt the national media had ignored. During the late 1980s, Robertson began to draw analogies between evangelicals and blacks under segregation on the show. Evangelical Christians, like blacks, Robertson said, were being forced to the back of the bus: "That is what is happening now. Christians can go into a tiny, little corner."[8] He took this idea one step further in April 1991 when he claimed that America had been a Christian nation, but "we've come to the point where Christians are being hunted, a persecuted minority in the nation that we founded." He also claimed that secularists were in charge of both the nation and the media, and that evangelicals were in "submission."[9]

The idea that evangelicals were an oppressed minority did not sit well with everyone in the Christian Right. Jay Sekulow, the chief legal counsel of the American Center for Law and Justice (ACLJ), a religious group founded by Robertson to combat the American Civil Liberties Union, downplayed the oppressed minority issue. "We don't have the vaguest clue in this country what persecution is," Sekulow explained in 1997.

"We do have a victim-oriented culture these days and we need to be careful."[10] Moreover, even those Christian Right leaders who publicly presented themselves as members of an oppressed minority could appear on religious television networks such as the Trinity Broadcasting Network (TBN) or CBN and claim to be speaking for both God and the majority will of the people. Leaders like Robertson frequently rallied the faithful with talk of God's will and the power of the ballot on Christian broadcasts, then appeared on secular TV and complained that conservative Christians were a minority. But whether the move from majority rhetoric to minority rhetoric was purely tactical or sincere, the shift was aided by turning to the memory and rhetoric of the civil rights movement.

In many ways, it was logical for the Christian Right to invoke the civil rights movement, especially that led by King. Evangelical theology teaches that Christians are the chosen few (the *Left Behind* series of apocalyptic fiction is a good example). The Christian Right used many of the same philosophical and religious ideas that had empowered the civil rights movement. Both movements employed scripture to defend their causes. King used Amos's hope of seeing "judgment run down like water, and righteousness like a mighty stream," and antiabortion protester Randall Terry used Psalm 82 and its call to rescue "the weak and father-less."[11] Both movements saw their missions as divinely guided, which gave them confidence in the face of adversity. The Southern Christian Leadership Conference and the Christian Right were both led by ministers who talked of God's judgment and the inevitability of freedom for their people. A 1981 letter by Pat Robertson to his critics in the People for the American Way echoed the 1960s. He warned his opponents, "In the words of the old Negro spiritual, 'Your arms are too short to box with God.' The suppression of the voice of God's servant is a terrible thing! God will fight for me against you, and he will win."[12] Leaders of the Christian Right were motivated by their religious ideals and their sense of calling, much as Martin Luther King was.

The Christian Right's invocation of civil rights memory was based on theological similarities and the political reality it faced when it could not get its agenda moved forward by other means. By drawing on movement rhetoric, leaders sought to portray Christians as aggrieved minorities who were fighting for their rights in a society that discriminated against them. For some Christian Right leaders, the civil rights movement provided a model of what a group led by Christians could become. Two major Christian Right groups from the 1990s were particularly explicit in their adoption of civil rights era rhetoric, the Christian Coalition and Operation Rescue. They were also the most successful (and infamous) of the Christian Right groups of their time. Both groups focused their efforts on grassroots mobilization. The Christian Coalition sought to organize evangelicals nationwide to influence local political campaigns, while Operation Rescue mobilized its followers to engage in aggressive protests against abortion. This type of political populism was in direct contrast to the Moral Majority and other 1980s Christian Right groups, which had instead used mass mailings to pressure politicians.[13]

The Christian Coalition rose from the ashes of Pat Robertson's failed campaign for the presidency in 1988. Although he lost the election, Robertson was able to find a use for his new army of politically motivated evangelicals. Unlike earlier Christian Right organizations, the Christian Coalition made no claim to majority status. Its name was chosen to avoid the arrogant-sounding majoritarian words of earlier organizations. It was also meant to echo the name of Martin Luther King's organization, the Southern Christian Leadership Conference (SCLC).[14] The coalition, which began with 20,000 members in 1990, grew to anywhere from 400,000 to 1.6 million members by 1995.[15]

Early in its history, leaders of the Christian Coalition turned to civil rights memory and rhetoric to position their own group. Pat Robertson's 1993 book *The Turning Tide* urged Christians to use the two main weapons that were employed by African Americans in the 1950s and 1960s: civil disobedience and legal action. He called on his readers to participate in religious acts of nonviolent civil disobedience, such as having public school children meet at their school flagpoles to pray. Robertson also wrote at length about the work of his legal organization the ACLJ, which he called God's hammer of justice.[16] At the coalition's yearly "Road to Victory" meetings, pastors, politicians (overwhelmingly Republican), and regular Christian Coalition members heard speeches that were full of civil rights rhetoric, despite the conservative nature of the coalition's political activity. At the 1999 meeting, Representative J. C. Watts, one of a handful of black Republican office holders, defended the role of religion in the modern world. "Martin Luther King Jr. was strong, Jesus was strong," he shouted as the crowded gave him a standing ovation.[17]

Christian Coalition executive director Ralph Reed, who holds a doctorate in history from Emory University, explicitly claimed that the coalition was a descendant of the African American civil rights movement. When Reed first began working for Pat Robertson in the early 1990s, he used majority rhetoric and even military metaphors in his Christian Coalition training sessions. In 1991 Reed was criticized in the media when he used violent imagery to explain his campaign strategy: "I do guerilla warfare. I paint my face and travel at night. You don't know it's over until you're in a body bag."[18] When such quotes were used as evidence of the Christian Right's extremism, Reed changed his tactics. In 1992 he wrote a memo to Christian Coalition staff members, telling them to change their rhetoric, suggesting that if the Christian Coalition was going to be a grassroots movement and not a top-down group like the Moral Majority, it had to adopt a new strategy.[19] By 1996 the *New York Times* reported that Reed's speeches now contained "quotations from liberal icons like the Rev. Dr. Martin Luther King, Jr., and Robert F. Kennedy."[20] Reed did more than just tone down the violent rhetoric; he actively tried to use the memory of Martin Luther King Jr. to strengthen his own movement. In 1995 he introduced a pledge card for Christian Coalition activists to sign by which they promised to "refrain from violence of fist, tongue, or heart."[21] He claimed the card was based on the one that was passed out by King when he led the SCLC. During a speech to the coalition membership in 1995, Reed praised Dr. King and said that his peaceful actions and nonthreatening and inclusive language were a key to his success.[22]

Perhaps more than any other conservative leader, Reed saw the advantage of positioning evangelical Christians as an oppressed minority within American society. In the two books written while he was the head of the Christian Coalition, Reed used the minority idea and claimed the mantle of the civil rights movement. In his 1994 book *Politically Incorrect*, Reed argued that a minority group can appeal for public sympathy, while a majority always runs the risk of looking like a bully. Using chapter titles like "To the Back of the Bus" and "The New Amos and Andy," Reed depicted conservative Christians as the moral equivalent of blacks in the civil rights movement. Both groups were oppressed in politics and popular culture, he argued, although he did not always make it clear that the attacks were by different groups for different reasons. Christians, Reed wrote, were constantly "under attack whenever they enter the public arena."[23] While he did not believe, as Robertson did, that Christians were being systematically persecuted, Reed did claim that conservative Christians had been "viewed as less than full citizens."[24] "To the Back of the Bus" presented a long list of ways in which evangelical Christians had been marginalized by lawmakers and judges. The chapter not only compared evangelicals to blacks, but to women of an earlier era: "Like the separate spheres once assigned to women, religious people are now relegated to their churches and homes where their faith poses no threat to the social order."[25]

Reed's 1996 book, *Active Faith*, contained a chapter entitled "All God's Children," a history lesson on the Social Gospel movement and Martin Luther King's life. For Reed, a key lesson provided by the civil rights movement was that politically successful groups had to build broad coalitions of support. Thus he argued that King's success stemmed from his ability to ally himself with northern Democrats while not alienating liberal Republicans. For compromise-wary evangelicals, Reed argued, the civil rights movement could provide important political lessons.[26] In *Active Faith*, Reed drew back somewhat from his earlier claim that the oppression that the Christian Right faced was similar to that of blacks before the civil rights movement, noting that "there is nothing like a crisp moral equivalence between the civil rights movement of the 1960s and the pro-life, pro-family movement of today."[27] Nevertheless, he still offered a lengthy section of comparisons, suggesting that like the heroic and righteous blacks struggling against the evils of segregation, the Christian Right too was brave and courageous in its struggle against the evils of secularism and religious persecution.

By comparing the modern-day Christian Right to civil rights movement warriors for minority rights, Reed attempted to paint the followers of the Christian Right as oppressed minorities, and he suggested that they, like blacks, were in a heroic struggle against a social evil. Reed, however, may also have had another reason for employing civil rights rhetoric.

Unlike most other members of the Christian Right, Reed understood that many African Americans were socially conservative, and that they might be enticed to join the Christian Coalition if they were convinced that the group was not racist or antiblack. Blacks comprised a significant portion of the *700 Club's* viewership, and Robertson's 1988 campaign had even hoped to attract their votes until Jesse Jackson's campaign derailed that plan.[28]

Reed understood that the modern Christian Right was viewed as an antiminority movement.[29] Since its inception in the early 1970s the Christian Right had been largely comprised of white middle-class Americans, usually under the leadership of southerners. Jerry Falwell had preached sermons in the 1960s against the civil rights movement, and Pat Robertson's father, A. Willis Robertson, had been one of nineteen southern senators to sign the Southern Manifesto, the 1956 document decrying the *Brown v. Board of Education* decision. Most leaders of the Christian Right opposed affirmative action programs and laws or policies that they felt gave preferential treatment to any minority group. While they often couched their attacks on such programs in nonracial terms, Christian Right groups were nevertheless perceived as hostile to minorities and their concerns.[30] Like the Republican party that it was allied with, the Christian Right was perceived as a club for whites.

Throughout his tenure at the Christian Coalition, Reed repeatedly sought to bring more blacks into the fold. In his book *Politically Incorrect*, Reed included an indictment of racism in the evangelical church. He made clear his belief that the "pro-family movement," as Reed called it, should be racially mixed, which would also make it more powerful.[31] In an interview on the *Charlie Rose Show* on PBS, Reed denounced white evangelical hostility toward the freedom struggle of the 1960s. Reed claimed that the racist attitudes of evangelicals "came back to haunt us in our own trek for social justice." He also predicted that America would not accept the Christian Right movement until it "becomes a truly bi-racial or multiracial movement."[32]

On the heels of the Christian Right's enormous success with the Republican takeover of Congress in 1994, Reed attempted to increase the size of the Christian Coalition by actively courting African Americans. In 1997 Reed announced the creation of the Samaritan Project, which sought to reach out to traditionally Democratic African Americans.[33] On May 10, 1997, the Christian Coalition held a "Congress on racial justice and reconciliation" to launch the project. Among the project's goals was obtaining federal funds for low-income area schools and scholarships for disadvantaged youth. The coalition even pledged to raise $10 million to help low-income youth ministries, and to rebuild black churches that had been attacked by arsonists.[34]

While the Samaritan Project had lofty goals, it was viable only as long as Reed was a part of the Christian Coalition. The project was cancelled within months of Reed's departure in September 1997. It had encountered resistance from the beginning, mostly from African American groups that did not trust the coalition's intentions. Despite Reed's efforts to convince Robertson and other Christian Right leaders to include blacks, the vast majority of members of the Christian Coalition remained conservative white Republicans who shared only some of the same socially conservative views with blacks, and little else.[35] It was difficult for a group like the Christian Coalition to attract black members when it claimed the re-election of North Carolina Senator Jesse Helms, a notorious race-baiter, as one of its first political triumphs.

Although the Christian Coalition's use of civil rights rhetoric did not significantly increase the group's appeal among blacks, the success of the Christian Right in the 1990s and through today suggests that its tactic of presenting itself as oppressed and persecuted has yielded some results. Despite black skepticism, Reed's successes laid the groundwork for the multicultural Christian conservatism that re-elected evangelical George W. Bush and his racially diverse cabinet to a second presidential term in 2004.

The one Christian Right group that tried to surpass the Christian Coalition's efforts to sound and act like the civil rights movement was also the one that most often practiced nonviolent resistance: the prolife group Operation Rescue. Randall Terry founded the group in 1987 because he, like many conservative Christians, was angered that abortion continued to be legal. In building his organization, Terry was influenced by books written by Martin Luther King Jr. and King's wife, Coretta Scott King, as well as by the Blackside/PBS documentary on the civil rights movement, *Eyes on the Prize*.[36] From these Terry learned that nonviolent protest could be effective, and he borrowed his tactics directly from the civil rights movement. In their protests, Operation Rescue members blocked the doors of abortion clinics and Planned Parenthood offices while singing the civil rights movement anthem "We Shall Overcome" or old spirituals. They, like civil rights protestors in the 1960s, expected to be arrested. When police arrived, Operation Rescue protestors would go limp and force the police to carry them away to prison, thus seeking to highlight the brutality of police officers who arrested people simply trying to protect the unborn. Hundreds of protesters might be arrested in a single "rescue," as Terry called it. Protesters were asked to read and sign a card that pledged that the participant would "commit to be peaceful and nonviolent in both word and deed."[37] These cards were, like the Christian Coalition's, based on the SCLC's. By the mid 1990s Operation Rescue claimed to be "the largest peaceful civil disobedience movement in American history," accounting "for over 70,000 arrests from 1987 to 1994."[38]

The aggressive tactics of Operation Rescue shocked people on both sides of the abortion issue. Instead of a few people picketing a clinic, hundreds of people participated in a single protest. While Terry claimed his ideas "came directly out of the civil rights activities of Dr. King," Operation Rescue's active blocking of a public building was in many ways the exact opposite of African American college students peacefully sitting-in at a segregated lunch counter.[39] Sit-ins and other civil rights protests sought to win blacks' access to shops, employment, and schools; Operation Rescue instead sought to restrict people's access to abortion clinics.

Yet Randall Terry insisted that Operation Rescue's tactics were akin to those of the civil rights movement of the 1960s and that abortion protestors were the moral equivalents of blacks fighting segregation. When Terry wrote a book in 1998 explaining his organization and its methods, his opening line echoed both Paul the apostle and Martin Luther King Jr.: "I write this book from jail."[40] Terry argued that the civil rights movement provided "the best recent example of changing the course of the nation," and he praised African Americans for their nonviolent bravery and noted that it "helped win the hearts of millions."[41] Randall wrote that he had learned from the movement that peaceful protest was the best way to influence the hearts and minds of the nation. When peaceful, hymn-singing protesters were arrested outside abortion clinics, they became morally sympathetic and received more press coverage. The portrayal of abortion protestors as victims of immoral laws led to the increased participation of evangelical Christians, many of whom had confined their political activity to the polling place, Terry argued.[42]

Selling the protests against abortion as parallel to those against segregation was difficult, of course. For one thing, in most Operation Rescue protests, male protesters targeted young women. It was hard to claim moral superiority when the public target of protest was a scared young woman. The sight on television of men blocking women from entering a building may have looked more like the racist white reaction to school integration than peaceful protesters. Moreover, Operation Rescue never faced a figure like Sheriff Bull Connor, who defied the federal government and attacked African American protesters in the 1960s. Instead of a racist sheriff who helped King gain sympathy from the federal government, Operation Rescue faced local authorities who had been ordered by Washington, D.C., to make arrests. Not only did the federal government not come to Terry's aid as it had eventually done for King (albeit reluctantly), but the Clinton administration targeted the group with a series of laws designed to stop organized crime and the Ku Klux Klan.

Terry and other prolife leaders, however, insisted that abortion protestors were the moral equivalent of civil rights activists. When prochoice advocates called the prolife protesters shrill extremists, or when a former director of a Planned Parenthood clinic echoed 1960s white segregationists with her insistence that antiabortion activists disturbed the peace and were not welcomed by the cities that they protested in, Randall Terry was more than happy to point out the historical parallel.[43] "The majority of Americans were against the tactics of the civil rights workers, the lunch counter sit-ins, etc.," Terry noted. "And yet those street level protests produced political change."[44] Another prolife leader, Randy Alcorn, recalled being released from jail and seeing a quote from King etched into the jail's cornerstone. He urged his readers to remain nonviolent, as King had done, and to keep the faith that they would eventually win. Alcorn wrote that while people have forgotten the names of those "law keepers" who arrested Martin Luther King, he is now honored with a national holiday and his words of rebellion are now seen as truth.[45]

While Operation Rescue tried to claim the moral legitimacy of civil rights protestors and Martin Luther King, most Americans did not view the situation as analogous. Eventually, Terry was sued and forced into bankruptcy. Even more than lawsuits, violence against abortion clinics hurt Operation Rescue. Once bombings of clinics and the murder of doctors who performed abortions began to increase, the movement lost what little popularity it still enjoyed. Some people accused Terry of secretly advocating violence, a charge that was hard to prove, but impossible to refute. Whether Terry supported these violent acts or not, once violence became associated with Operation Rescue, the group lost whatever position of moral leadership that it might have had. Operation Rescue tried to cloak itself in the mantle of the civil rights movement, and in the end it ran into the same problem of being tarred by acts of violence. In his book *Making Peace with the Sixties*, David Burner argues that the violent rhetoric of the Black Panthers and the annual summer riots in large cities were fatal to the civil rights movement.[46] So there was another link, this time an unintentional one, between the Christian Right and the civil rights movement. It was one that Randall Terry would have preferred to have lived without.

What can be learned through an exploration of the modern Christian Right's efforts to wrap itself in the mantle of the civil rights movement? First, the fact that Christian Right leaders decided to use the rhetoric of the civil rights movement legitimized both the tactics and cause of the struggle for racial equality even if that was not their intent. The Christian Right's invocation of the civil rights struggle makes clear that the movement as led by Martin Luther King has been accorded great legitimacy and moral authority in American society. Blacks in the 1960s sought to win the moral high ground in a battle for the hearts and minds of white Americans. The fact that politically conservative Christian evangelicals feel comfortable comparing their own struggle to that of Martin Luther

King and black Americans demonstrates that segregationists lost the fight to portray white supremacy as moral, and even Christian. Without ever saying as much, the Christian Right's use of civil rights rhetoric is founded on the assumption that segregation was wrong and that the black struggle for equality was legitimate.

Moreover, the willingness of the politically conservative, largely white Religious Right to turn to civil rights rhetoric to further its own cause demonstrates that the Christian Right has recognized the importance of coming to terms with a movement that many southern Christians in the 1960s attacked as immoral, wrong, and against God's will. Some, like Ralph Reed, have sought to bring black Christians into their political fold and have made serious efforts to redeem the Christian Right of its reputation of being antiminority and racist. Whether others share Reed's views or not, their praise of Martin Luther King and the civil rights movement makes clear, as David Chappell has argued, that white supremacists failed in their bid in the 1960s to harness white Protestantism to the defense of segregation.[47]

Yet by comparing themselves to blacks in the civil rights struggle, the Christian Right leaders unintentionally downplayed the oppression that blacks faced, while exaggerating the persecution that Christians in the United States supposedly suffer. Only through this kind of misrepresentation could evangelicals suggest that their group was in an analogous position to blacks at the back of a bus or suggest that their enemies, like the American Civil Liberties Union (ACLU), were the equivalent of the Klu Klux Klan. Not being able to pray silently in a public classroom may be seen as oppression, but it cannot compare to not being allowed to vote. Blacks faced an interlocking system of economic, political, judicial, and social discrimination, while evangelicals' concerns, while serious to them, did not result in the kind of total disenfranchisement that blacks contended with.

The issue of who owns history, of who gets to control the metanarrative of their culture or ethnic group, is made even more complicated when the history involved becomes part of American folklore. When King became a national symbol, he became part of the pantheon of heroes who can serve as a model to all Americans. In this context, the evangelical adoption of King as a hero can be understood as part of the Christian Right's hyper-Americanism, where history serves as a tool to promote today's political needs. Whether he would have liked it or not, Martin Luther King Jr. will continue to be used by groups of many different political stripes to promote agendas of which he could never have dreamed.

Notes

1. For an excellent history of the Christian Right, see William Martin, *With God on Our Side* (New York: Broadway Books, 1996).

2. Paul Lopatto, *Religion and the Presidential Election* (New York: Praeger, 1985), 37.

3. *Newsweek*, October 25, 1976.

4. Martin, *With God on Our Side*, 199.

5. Robert Zwier, *Born Again Politics* (Downers Grove, Ill.: InterVarsity Press, 1982), 18.

6. Paul Weyrich, interview by the author, tape recording, Washington, D.C., August 16, 2000.

7. For studies of how the civil rights movement developed, see Charles Payne, *I've Got the Light of Freedom: The Organizing Tradition and the Mississippi Freedom Struggle* (Berkeley: University of California Press, 1995), and John Dittmer, *Local People: The Struggle for Civil Rights in Mississippi* (Urbana: University of Illinois Press, 1994).

8. *700 Club*, Christian Broadcasting Network, September 29, 1993.

9. Ibid., April 1991.

10. Marc Fisher, "Jay Sekulow, Messianic Jew of the Christian Right," *Washington Post*, October 21, 1997.

11. James Morone, *Hellfire Nation: The Politics of Sin in American History* (New Haven, Conn.: Yale University Press, 2003), 417; Randall Terry, *Operation Rescue* (Pittsburgh, Pa.: Whitaker House, 1998), 49.

12. Pat Robertson to People for the American Way, 1981, Archives of the People for the American Way, Washington, D.C.

13. Weyrich, interview.

14. Justin Watson, *The Christian Coalition: Dreams of Restoration, Demands for Recognition* (New York: St. Martin's Griffin, 1999), 136.

15. Duane Oldfield, *The Right and the Righteous* (Lanham, Md.: Rowman and Littlefield, 1996), 211.

16. Pat Robertson, *The Turning Tide: The Fall of Liberalism and the Return of Common Sense* (Dallas, Tex.: Word Publishing, 1993), 125.

17. J. C. Watts, "Road to Victory Speech," Christian Coalition Road to Vic-

tory meeting, Washington, D.C., October 1, 1999. Recording of speech made by author.

18. Martin, *With God on Our Side*, 318.

19. Ibid.

20. Kevin Sack, "A Penitent Christian Coalition Offers Aid to Burned Churches," *New York Times*, June 19, 1996.

21. Watson, *The Christian Coalition*, 79.

22. Ibid.

23. Ralph Reed, *Politically Incorrect: The Emerging Faith Factor in American Politics* (Dallas, Tex.: Word Publishing, 1994), 42.

24. Ibid., 53.

25. Ibid., 42.

26. Ralph Reed, *Active Faith: How Christians Are Changing the Soul of American Politics* (New York: Free Press, 1996), 63.

27. Ibid., 64.

28. Jeffrey Hadden and Anson Shupe, *Televangelism: Power and Politics on God's Frontier* (New York: Henry Holt, 1988), 275; Pat Robertson, interview by the author, tape recording, Virginia Beach, Virginia, May 25, 2000.

29. Watson, *The Christian Coalition*, 68.

30. Kenneth Wald, *Religion and Politics in the United States* (Washington, D.C.: Congressional Quarterly Inc., 1992), 182. Wald has noted that there was a significant gap on these issues between blacks on the one hand and whites of most political types on the other.

31. Reed, *Politically Incorrect*, 241.

32. Martin, *With God on Our Side*, 366.

33. Jonathan Peterson, "Christian Coalition Adds National Budget to Its Agenda," *Los Angeles Times*, October 30, 1995.

34. Watson, *The Christian Coalition*, 69.

35. Wald, *Religion and Politics in the United States*, 188.

36. Martin, *With God on Our Side*, 321.

37. Terry, *Operation Rescue*, 228.

38. John Whitehead, "Barry Manilow Got Saved, Randall Terry Makes a Comeback," http://www.rutherford.org/oldspeak/about/asp (accessed February 10, 2003).

39. Martin, *With God on Our Side*, 323.

40. Terry, *Operation Rescue*, 11.

41. Ibid., 196, 197.

42. Ibid., 25.

43. Michele McKeegan, *Abortion Politics* (New York: Free Press, 1992), 164, 165.

44. Martin, *With God on Our Side*, 323.

45. Randy Alcorn, *Is Rescuing Right? Breaking the Law to Save the Unborn* (Illinois: InterVarsity Press, 1990), 121.

46. David Burner, *Making Peace with the Sixties* (Princeton, N.J.: Princeton University Press, 1996).

47. David Chappell, *A Stone of Hope* (Chapel Hill: University of North Carolina Press, 2003). The author thanks the anonymous reader for his or her comments regarding Chappell's work. I would also like to thank Peter Levy, Leigh Raiford, and Renee C. Romano for their assistance with this chapter.

SARAH VOWELL

Rosa Parks, *C'est Moi*

According to Reuters, on January 20, 2001, in Washington, the special guest at the Florida state inaugural ball was introduced by the country singer Larry Gatlin. He said, "In France it was Joan of Arc; in the Crimea it was Florence Nightingale; in the Deep South there was Rosa Parks; in India there was Mother Teresa; and in Florida there was Katherine Harris."

I leave it to my Indian, Crimean, and French colleagues to determine how the Florida secretary of state is or is not similar to Teresa, Florence, or St. Joan. As for Rosa Parks, Katherine Harris can get in line. Because people around here can't stop comparing themselves to Parks. To wit:

The mayor of Friendship Heights, Maryland, has proposed an outdoor smoking ban because, according to the *Washington Post*, citizens "with asthma or other illnesses 'cannot have full access' to areas where smokers are doing their evil deed. The mayor compares this horrific possibility to Rosa Parks being sent to the back of the bus."

A California dairy farmer protesting the government's milk-pricing system poured milk down a drain in front of TV cameras, claiming that he had to take a stand, "just like Rosa Parks had to take a stand."

A street performer in St. Augustine, Florida, is challenging a city ordinance that bans him from doing his act on the town's historic St. George Street. The performer's lawyer told the *Florida Times-Union*, "Telling these people they can exercise their First Amendment rights somewhere other than on St. George is like telling Rosa Parks that she has to sit in the back of the bus." (Which is, coincidentally, also the argument of another

Florida lawyer, this one representing adult dancers contesting Tampa's ordinance outlawing lap dancing.) I would also like to mention the rocker, marksman, and conservative activist Ted Nugent, who in his autobiography, *God, Guns and Rock 'n' Roll*, refers to himself as "Rosa Parks with a loud guitar." That's so inaccurate. Everyone knows he's more like Mary Matalin with a fancy deer rifle.

Call me picky, but breathing secondhand smoke, being subject to unfair dairy pricing, and not being able to mime (or lap dance), though they are all tragic, tragic injustices, are not quite as bad as the systematic segregation of *public* transportation based on skin color. And while fighting for your right to lap dance and mime and breathe just the regular pollution is a very fine, very American idea, it is not quite as brave as being a middle-aged black woman in Alabama in 1955 telling a white man she's not giving him her seat despite the fact that the law requires her to do so. And, oh, by the way, in the process, she gets arrested, and then sparks the Montgomery bus boycott, which is the seed of the civil rights movement as we know it. The bus boycotters not only introduced a twenty-six-year-old pastor by the name of Martin Luther King Jr. into national public life but, after many months of car pools, walking, and court fights against bus segregation, got the separate but equal doctrine declared illegal once and for all.

It's not just people on the right like Katherine Harris and Ted Nugent who seem especially silly being likened to Parks. I first cringed at this analogy trend at the lefty Ralph Nader's October 2000 campaign rally in Madison Square Garden. Ever sit in a coliseum full of people who think they're heroes? I was surrounded by thousands of well-meaning, well-fed white kids who loved it when the filmmaker Michael Moore told them they should, like Rosa Parks, stand up to power, by which I think he meant vote for Nader so he could qualify for federal matching funds. When Nader himself mentioned abolitionists in Mississippi in 1836 and asked the crowd to "think how lonely it must have been," he was answered, according to my notes, with a "huge, weird cheer." I think I'm a fine enough person—why, the very next morning I was having people over for waffles. But I hope I'm not being falsely modest by pointing out that I'm no Harriet Tubman. And I'm certainly no Rosa Parks. As far as

I'm concerned, about the only person in recent memory who has an unimpeachable right to compare himself to Parks is that Chinese student who stared down those tanks in Tiananmen Square.

I was reminded of those Naderites while watching a rerun of the sitcom *Sports Night* on Comedy Central. Dan, a television sportscaster played by Josh Charles, has been ordered by his network to make an on-air apology to viewers because he said in a magazine interview that he supports the legalization of marijuana. He stands by his opinion and balks at apologizing. His boss, Isaac (Robert Guillaume), agrees but tells him to do it anyway "because it's television and this is how it's done." Dan replies, "Yeah, well, sitting in the back of the bus was how it was done until a forty-two-year-old lady moved up front." A few minutes later Isaac looks Dan in the eye and tells him, "Because I love you I can say this. No rich young white guy has ever gotten anywhere with me comparing himself to Rosa Parks." Finally, the voice of reason, which of course was heard on a canceled network TV series on cable.

Analogies give order to the world—and solidarity. Pointing out how one person is like another is reassuring, less lonely. Maybe those who would compare their personal inconveniences to the epic struggles of history are just looking for company, and who wouldn't want to be in the company of Rosa Parks? On the other hand, perhaps people who compare themselves to Rosa Parks are simply arrogant, pampered nincompoops with delusions of grandeur who couldn't tell the difference between a paper cut and a decapitation.

In defense of Ted Nugent, the street performer, the mayor, the dairy farmer, the lap dancers, the Naderites, and a fictional sportscaster, I will point out that Katherine Harris is the only person on my list of people lamely compared to a civil rights icon who, at the very moment she was being compared to a civil rights icon, was actually being sued for "massive voter disenfranchisement of people of color during the presidential election"—by the NAACP.

Note

Reprinted with the permission of Simon and Schuster Adult Publishing Group from *The Partly Cloudy Patriot* by Sarah Vowell. Copyright 2002 by Sarah Vowell.

SELECTED BIBLIOGRAPHY ON CIVIL RIGHTS

AND HISTORICAL MEMORY

Alderman, Derek H. "A Street Fit for a King: Naming Places and Commemoration in the American South." *Professional Geographer* 52, no. 4 (2000): 672–84.

Armada, Bernard. "Memorial Agon: An Interpretive Tour of the National Civil Rights Museum." *Southern Communication Journal* 63 (1998): 235–43.

Blight, David. *Race and Reunion: The Civil War in American Memory.* Cambridge, Mass.: Harvard University Press, 2001.

Brundage, W. Fitzhugh. *The Southern Past: A Clash of Race and Memory.* Cambridge, Mass.: Harvard University Press, 2005.

Brundage, W. Fitzhugh, ed. *Where These Memories Grow: History, Memory, and Southern Identity.* Raleigh: University of North Carolina Press, 2000.

Carrier, Jim. *A Traveler's Guide to the Civil Rights Movement.* Orlando, Fla.: Harcourt Books, 2004.

Carson, Clayborne. "Martin Luther King, Jr.: Charismatic Leadership in a Mass Struggle." *Journal of American History* 74 (September 1987): 448–54.

Cox, Thomas Hughes. "Reflections on a Place of Revolution and Reconciliation: A Brief History of Kelly Ingram Park and the Birmingham Civil Rights District." Birmingham, Ala.: Birmingham Civil Rights Institute, 1995.

Davis, Townsend. *Weary Feet, Rested Souls: A Guided History of the Civil Rights Movement.* New York: W. W. Norton, 1998.

Daynes, Gary. *Making Villians, Making Heroes: Joseph R. McCarthy, Martin Luther King Jr. and the Politics of American Memory.* New York: Garland, 1997.

Dyson, Michael Eric. *I May Not Get There with You: The True Martin Luther King, Jr.* New York: Free Press, 2000.

———. *Making Malcolm: The Myth and Meaning of Malcolm X.* New York: Oxford University Press, 1995.

Eskew, Glenn. "From Civil War to Civil Rights: Selling Alabama as Heritage Tourism." In *Slavery, Contested Heritage, and Thanatourism,* ed. Graham M. S. Dann and A. V. Seaton, 201–14. New York: The Haworth Hospitality Press, 2001.

Fabre, Geneviève, and O'Meally, Robert, eds. *History and Memory in African-American Culture*. New York: Oxford University Press, 1994.

Foote, Kenneth. *Shadowed Ground: America's Landscapes of Violence and Tragedy*. Austin: University of Texas Press, 1997.

Gillis, John, ed. *Commemorations*. Princeton, N.J.: Princeton University Press, 1994.

Golub, Mark. "History Died for Our Sins: Guilt and Responsibility in Hollywood Redemption Histories." *Journal of American Culture* 21 (Fall 1998): 23–45.

Graham, Alison. *Framing the South: Hollywood, Television, and Race during the Civil Rights Struggle*. Baltimore, Md.: John Hopkins University Press, 2001.

Gray, Herman. "Remembering Civil Rights: Television, Memory and the 1960s." In *The Revolution Wasn't Televised: Sixties Television and Social Conflict*, ed. Lynn Spigel and Michael Curtin. New York: Routledge, 1997.

Griffin, Larry J. " 'Generations and Collective Memory' Revisited: Race, Region, and Memory of Civil Rights." *American Sociological Review* 69, no. 4 (2004): 544–57.

Hall, Jacqueline Dowd. "The Long Civil Rights Movement and the Political Uses of the Past." *Journal of American History* 91, no. 4 (2005): 1233–63.

Harding, Vincent. "Beyond Amnesia: Martin Luther King, Jr., and the Future of America." *Journal of American History* 74 (September 1987): 468–76.

Hendrickson, Paul. *Sons of Mississippi: A Story of Race and Its Legacy*. New York: Knopf, 2003.

Howett, Catherine. "Kelly Ingram Park: A Place of Revolution and Reconciliation." *Landscape Architecture* 83 (March 1993): 34–35.

Kammen, Michael. *Mystic Chords of Memory*. New York: Knopf, 1991.

Lentz, Richard. *Symbols, the News Magazines, and Martin Luther King*. Baton Rouge: Louisiana State University Press, 1990.

Lewis, Earl. "Connecting Memory, Self, and the Power of Place in African American Urban History." *Journal of Urban History* 21 (Summer 1995): 247–71.

Loewen, James W. *Lies across America: What Our Historic Sites Get Wrong*. New York: New Press, 1999.

Madison, Kelly J. "Legitimation Crisis and Containment: The 'Anti-Racist-White-Hero' Film." *Critical Studies in Mass Communication* 16 (1999): 399–416.

Melosh, Barbara. "Historical Memory in Fiction: The Civil Rights Movement in Three Novels." *Radical History Review* 40 (1998): 64–76.

Metress, Christopher, ed. *The Lynching of Emmett Till: A Documentary Narrative*. Charlottesville: University of Virginia Press, 2002.

Morris, Willie. *The Ghosts of Mississippi: Race, Murder, Mississippi, and Hollywood*. New York: Random House, 1998.

Musgrove, George Derek. "Good at the Game of Tricknology: Proposition 209 and the Struggle for the Historical Memory of the Civil Rights Movement." *Souls* 1, no. 3 (Summer 1999): 7–24.

Nossiter, Adam. *Of Long Memory: Mississippi and the Murder of Medgar Evers.* Cambridge, Mass.: De Capo Press, 1994.

Polletta, Francesca. "Legacies and Liabilities of an Insurgent Past: Remembering Martin Luther King, Jr., on the House and Senate Floor." *Social Science History* 22, no. 4 (1998): 479–512.

Reed, Harry A. "Martin Luther King, Jr.: History and Memory, Reflections on Dreams and Silences." *Journal of Negro History* 84, no. 2 (1999): 150–66.

Rhea, Joseph Tilden. *Race Pride and the American Identity.* Cambridge, Mass.: Harvard University Press, 1997.

Ruffins, Fath Davis. "Memory, and History: African American Preservation Efforts, 1820–1990." In *Museums and Communities: The Politics of Public Culture*, ed. Ivan Karp, Christine M. Kreamer, and Steven D. Lavine. Washington, D.C.: Smithsonian Institution Press, 1992.

Sandage, Scott A. "A Marble House Divided: The Lincoln Memorial, the Civil Rights Movement, and the Politics of Memory, 1939–1963." *Journal of American History* 80 (1993): 135–67.

Starnes, Richard D., ed. *Southern Journeys: Tourism, History, and Culture in the Modern South.* Tuscaloosa: University of Alabama Press, 2003.

Stump, Roger W. "Toponymic Commemoration of National Figures: The Cases of Kennedy and King." *Names* 36, no. 3/4 (1988): 203–16.

Torres, Sasha. *Black, White, and in Color: Television and Black Civil Rights.* Princeton, N.J.: Princeton University Press, 2003.

Trouillot, Michel-Rolph. *Silencing the Past: Power and the Production of History.* Boston, Mass.: Beacon Press, 1997.

Tyson, Tim. *Blood Done Sign My Name.* New York: Crown, 2004.

Upton, Dell. "Commemorating the Civil Rights Movement." *Design Book Review* 40 (Fall 1999): 22–33.

Weyeneth, Robert R. "Historic Preservation and the Civil Rights Movement." *CRM Bulletin* 18 (Fall 1995): 6–8.

———. "Historic Preservation and the Civil Rights Movement of the 1950s and 1960s: Identifying, Preserving, and Interpreting the Architecture of Liberation: A Report to Preservation Agencies." Columbia: University of South Carolina, 1995.

Winn, Emmett J. "Challenges and Compromises in Spike Lee's *Malcolm X.*" *Critical Studies in Media Communication* 18 (December 2001): 452–65.

Vollers, Maryanne. *Ghosts of Mississippi: The Murder of Medgar Evers, the Trials of Byron de la Beckwith, and the Haunting of the New South.* Boston, Mass.: Little Brown, 1995.

CONTRIBUTORS

Derek H. Alderman is an associate professor of geography at East Carolina University and coeditor of the peer-reviewed journal *Southeastern Geographer*. His research interests include geographies of public commemoration, the politics of place naming, and cultural struggles in the American South.

Owen J. Dwyer teaches cultural geography at Indiana University's Indianapolis campus. His research on representations of the American civil rights movement has appeared in *Urban Geography*, *Social and Cultural Geography*, and the edited collection *Mapping Tourism*. With Derek H. Alderman, he is currently writing a field guide to interpreting public spaces associated with the movement.

R. A. R. Edwards is an assistant professor of history at the Rochester Institute of Technology. She has written elsewhere on deaf history, including an essay in the anthology *The New Disability History: American Perspectives*. Her article "Sound and Fury, or Much Ado about Nothing: Cochlear Implants in Historical Perspective" appeared in the *Journal of American History* in December 2005.

Glenn Eskew is associate professor of history at Georgia State University. He is the author of the prize-winning book *But for Birmingham: The Local and National Movements in the Civil Rights Struggle* and is currently at work on a study of institutional memory and the civil rights movement.

Steve Estes is assistant professor of history at Sonoma State University and the author of *I Am a Man! Race, Manhood, and the Civil Rights Movement*. He lives in San Francisco, California.

Jennifer Fuller is an assistant professor in the Department of Radio-Television-Film at the University of Texas at Austin. She is working on a manuscript on the rise of civil rights drama in the nineties.

Tim Libretti is professor of English, women's studies, and Mexican and Caribbean studies at Northeastern Illinois University in Chicago. He has published on U.S. working-class and racial and ethnic literatures, Marxism and cultural studies, gay and lesbian literature, race and ethnicity theory, and social justice issues in book chapters and journals such as *Melus*, *Women's Studies Quarterly*, *Amerasia Journal*, and *Modern Fiction Studies*.

David John Marley has a doctorate in American religious history and is an assistant professor of history at Vanguard University in Orange County, California. His research interests include the Christian Right, and he is completing a biography of Pat Robertson.

Edward P. Morgan is professor of political science at Lehigh University, where he teaches courses on 1960s social movements, propaganda and the media, and American politics. He is the author of *The Sixties Experience: Hard Lessons about Modern America* (Temple, 1991), and he is currently writing a book entitled "The Twilight of Democracy: Capitalism, Media Culture, and the Postmodern Sixties."

Kathryn L. Nasstrom is associate professor of history at the University of San Francisco. She is the author of *Everybody's Grandmother and Nobody's Fool: Frances Freeborn Pauley and the Struggle for Social Justice* (Cornell University Press, 2000). Her current project is a book-length study of autobiographies of the civil rights movement.

Leigh Raiford is assistant professor of African American studies at the University of California, Berkeley. Her teaching and research interests include African American social movements, race, gender, and visual culture, racial formations, and black popular culture. She is currently at work on a manuscript entitled "Imprisoned in a Luminous Glare: History, Memory, and the Photography of Twentieth-Century African American Social Movements."

Renee C. Romano is associate professor of history and African American studies at Wesleyan University, where she teaches courses on the civil rights movement and historical memory. She is the author of *Race Mixing: Black-White Marriage in Postwar America* (Harvard, 2003), and she is currently working on a book about the reprosecution of old civil rights cases from the 1950s and 1960s.

Sarah Vowell is an essayist and monologuist who can be heard regularly on National Public Radio's *This American Life*. She is the author of numerous books of essays, including *Take the Cannoli: Stories from the New World*, *The Partly Cloudy Patriot*, and *Assassination Vacation*.

INDEX

Abernathy, Ralph, 11, 35
Adams, Oscar, Jr., 34
affirmative action, xvi
Alabama Christian Movement for
  Human Rights, 31, 35
Alabama Institute of Civil Rights, 37
Alabama Institute of Civil War History,
  37
Alabama Legislative Commission to
  Preserve the Peace, 117
All Citizens Registration Committee
  of Atlanta (ACRC), 258–60,
  263, 265–67, 268–70, 271,
  276
Allen, Louis, 188
America—Black and White, 160
American Center for Law and Justice
  (ACLJ), 349, 351
American Civil Liberties Union
  (ACLU), 349, 359
American Deaf Culture, 334
American Deaf Folklore, 334
American Disabled for Accessible
  Public Transit (ADAPT), 322,
  330–37
American History Workshop, 47–48,
  53, 55
American Indian Movement (AIM),
  198, 200, 209, 346
American Legion, 78, 81, 86
American Sign Language, 325, 326

Americans with Disabilities Act
  (ADA), 313, 323, 324, 333, 336,
  337, 340, 342–43n27
Amnesty International, 18
Amos, Miles, 272
Anthony, Emory, 55
Any Day Now, 136, 176–78, 183, 187
Arrington, Dick, 31–32, 36, 37, 39,
  40–41, 53–54, 62n27, 118; and
  Bond, Ryder, James, 42, 43–44;
  and corruption scandal, 55–58
Asian American movement, 197–200,
  209, 346
Atlanta Daily World, 259–60, 262, 263
Atlanta, Georgia, 274; 1946 voting
  registration drive, 251, 255–67,
  277, 279; 1996 Olympic Games,
  257–58. *See also under* National
  Association for the Advancement
  of Colored People (NAACP)
Atlanta Negro Voters League (ANVL),
  257, 271, 276, 277
Atlanta University (AU), 258–59, 268,
  272
Atlanta Urban League, 258, 267,
  268–70, 276
Auberger, Mike, 336

Bacote, Clarence A., 258, 267, 271,
  281n10
Baker, Ella, 11, 13, 24n13, 183, 188

xiii–xvii passim, 99, 104, 105, 198, 200, 251–52, 255–56, 271, 280; narrative and, 99–100, 251–56 passim, 270, 275, 278–79, 286n41, 291, 303; photography and, 233–35, 236; place and, 5; public, xvi, 98–99, 138–41, 148, 152, 159

Miles College, 32, 40

Milkey and Brown, 42, 55, 63n27

Miller, Aubrey, 29

Miller, Mark Crispin, 160–61

Million Man March, 169, 252, 304, 307–8

Mississippi Burning, xii, 100–101, 185–86, 187, 188, 195n47

Mississippi Freedom Democratic Party, 150, 165n34

Mississippi Freedom Summer, 148, 185, 294–301, 305. *See also* Student Nonviolent Coordination Committee (SNCC)

Mississippi State Sovereignty Commission, 295, 309n7; papers of, 117

Model Cities Program, 158

Monro, John U., 40

Montgomery Bus Boycott, 13, 149, 183

Montgomery Improvement Association, 183

Moore, Amzie, 188

Moore, Michael, 364

Moral Majority, 348, 351

Morehouse College, 320

Morgan, Charles, 122

Morrison, Toni, *Sula*, 200, 207–8

Moses, Robert, 188, 293

Mother Theresa, 69, 363

Mothershed, Thelma, 180

Moynihan Report, 311n16

MP Enterprises, 42, 55, 63n27

Murder in Mississippi, 185

Murray, Richard, 36

Nader, Ralph, 364

Nation of Islam, 304

National Association for the Advancement of Colored People (NAACP), 172, 173, 178, 285n37, 295; Atlanta, Georgia, branch, 258, 260, 266, 267–69, 274, 284n25; Birmingham, Alabama, branch, 124; Montgomery, Alabama, branch, 12; Rosa Parks, member of, xi, xix; sponsor street-naming, 77, 89

National Association of the Deaf, 318, 330, 340

New Black Panther Party, 155, 165n43, 235

New York Times, 101, 104, 122–23, 152, 172, 317–18, 320, 323, 325

Newsweek, 98, 121, 142, 144–45, 149–52 passim, 168–72 passim, 191–92, 347

Newton, Huey P., 194n46, 226–31; Nas photographed as, 242–43

Nixon, E. D., 183

Nora, Pierre, xiii–xiv

Norman, Martha Prescod, 302

Nugent, Ted, 364, 365

Ogle, Becky, 337, 340

Olsen, Gary, 318

Omatsu, Glenn, 197–200

Ooiman, Jo Ann, 11, 183, 296, 298

Operation New Birmingham, 31, 32, 39, 40

Operation Rescue, 314, 351, 355–58

oral history, 33, 290–92, 303, 305; in
    BCRI, 33, 34, 37, 38, 56
OutKast, xvii–xviii

Panther, 154, 155, 156, 159, 165n44,
    244
Parks, Rosa, 11–12, 159, 179, 194n37,
    363–65; discussed in *Barbershop*,
    xi–xii; as icon, xvii–xix, 314–15,
    347; museum, xiii, 11; streets
    named after, 71
Parsons, Frank, 37
Payne, Charles, 292, 299
Peters, Marjorie, 42, 43, 53, 55, 56,
    63n27
Planned Parenthood, 356–57
Poor People's Campaign, 141, 152
Potts, Annie, 177
Powell, Colin, 173
Public Enemy, "Fight the Power,"
    181–83

Rabinowitz, Richard, 47–52, 53, 54
Raines, Howell, 35, 38, 130n43
Randall, Dudley, "Ballad of Birming-
    ham," 106
Rarus, Nancy, 340
Ray, James Earl, 76, 135
Reagan, Ronald, 143, 146, 156, 347,
    348
Reagon, Bernice Johnson, 183
Reed, Adolph, 180
Reed, Ralph, 314, 347, 349, 352–55,
    359
reparations, xvi
Revolutionary People's Constitutional
    Convention, 232
Robertson, Carol, 96, 102; scholarship,
    101. *See also* Sixteenth Street
    Baptist Church

Robertson, Pat, 314, 347, 349–50, 351,
    353, 354, 355
Robinson, Cedric J., 238, 240
Robinson, Jo Ann. *See* Ooiman, Jo
    Ann
Robinson, Johnnie, 104
Robinson, Ruby Doris Smith, 304
Robnett, Belinda, 302, 303, 307
Roseman, Melvin, 33
Rosenberg, Emily, xix, 138

Samstein, Mendy, 148
Sayles, John, 136, 197, 200–204, 206,
    208, 211–18
Scattergood, Charles, 305–6
Schwerner, Michael (Mickey), 98
Seale, Bobby, 155, 226–27
segregation, 49, 173, 304; Jim Crow,
    xi, 17, 145, 153, 191, 205, 267,
    292, 297, 299; urban, 151
Sekulow, Jay, 349
Selma, Alabama: Edmund Pettus
    Bridge, 109; March on, xiii,
    147–49, 150, 158, 182, 318
700 Club, 349, 354
Shames, Stephen, 231
Shapiro, Joseph, 336, 342n22
Sharpton, Al, xii
Sheldon, Andrew, 106
Shores, Arthur, 33
Shuttlesworth, Fred, 14, 56, 96, 123
Simpson, O. J., xi, 136, 145, 160, 168,
    170
Sins of the Father, 107
sit-ins, 159, 164n23, 274, 276, 356
Sixteenth Street Baptist Church,
    Birmingham, Alabama, 48, 51,
    57, 58, 96, 97; bombing of, 3, 51,
    96–131, 178; "four little girls,"
    102–7, 127n14; Martin Luther

380   *Index*